AN ARAMAIC APPROACH TO THE GOSPELS AND ACTS

AN ARAMAIC APPROACH TO THE GOSPELS AND ACTS

BY

MATTHEW BLACK

THIRD EDITION

With an Appendix on The Son of Man
by GEZA VERMES

OXFORD
AT THE CLARENDON PRESS
1967

Oxford University Press, Ely House, London W. 1
GLASGOW NEW YORK TORONTO MELBOURNE WELLINGTON
CAPE TOWN SALISBURY IBADAN NAIROBI LUSAKA ADDIS ABABA
BOMBAY CALCUTTA MADRAS KARACHI LAHORE DACCA
KUALA LUMPUR HONG KONG TOKYO

FIRST EDITION 1946
SECOND EDITION 1954
THIRD EDITION 1967

REPRINTED LITHOGRAPHICALLY IN GREAT BRITAIN
AT THE UNIVERSITY PRESS, OXFORD
BY VIVIAN RIDLER
PRINTER TO THE UNIVERSITY

PREFACE TO THIRD EDITION

SINCE the second edition of this book appeared in 1954, two major discoveries in the field of Aramaic studies—the Qumrân texts and the Neofiti Targum—have been made available to scholars. These, along with some important publications on the subject, have made this third edition necessary. The book has been completely revised and reset and the supplementary notes of the second edition have been incorporated in the text: a new chapter has been added to take account of the implications of the new discoveries for previous views about the language of Jesus. Those parts of the book dealing with Acts have been revised and supplemented in the light of Dr. Max Wilcox's important book on the Semitisms of Acts.

An Appendix by Dr. Geza Vermes, Reader in Jewish Studies at Oxford, has been added containing fresh evidence for the use of the expression 'son of man' in Palestinian Aramaic.

I am grateful to my secretary, Miss Mary C. Blackwood, who typed and prepared the manuscript for the printer, and who, with the help of my daughter Elizabeth, has also kindly assisted me in the preparation of the indexes.

MATTHEW BLACK

St. Mary's College
University of St. Andrews
January 1966

CONTENTS

PART I. THE APPROACH

PART II. SYNTAX, GRAMMAR, AND VOCABULARY

PART IV. TRANSLATION OF ARAMAIC

PART I
THE APPROACH
CHAPTER I
PREVIOUS WORK ON THE ARAMAIC OF THE GOSPELS AND ACTS

IN his *Worte Jesu*, the most elaborate study of the Aramaic of the Gospels hitherto undertaken, Gustaf Dalman includes a review of work prior to and contemporary with his own;[1] his account may be supplemented by Arnold Meyer's *Jesu Muttersprache*, in which Meyer also undertook to interpret and explain the Gospels from Aramaic originals.[2]

Among earlier scholars the two most outstanding names are those of Wellhausen and Nestle. In his *Einleitung in die drei ersten Evangelien*,[3] the former presented a certain amount of linguistic evidence which led him to think that an Aramaic document had been used by the author of the common source of Matthew and Luke known as Q, and possibly also by Mark. Similar views were held by Nestle,[4] and, among others, by Blass, who believed that Acts i–xii was originally composed in Aramaic by Mark, and that Luke was using a translation of this work.[5]

The criticism which applies to this earlier work generally, and which was made by Dalman,[6] is that it is defective on the linguistic side: Wellhausen, for instance, made no attempt to illustrate his observations of Aramaic construction or usage from the available sources of Palestinian Aramaic literature.

[1] 2nd edit., Leipzig, 1930; English translation, Edinburgh, 1902. For his account of earlier work, see pp. 45–57. For a historical survey of work on the problem of Aramaic sources in Acts, see M. Wilcox, *The Semitisms of Acts* (Oxford, 1965), pp. 1 ff.

[2] Leipzig, 1896; cf. pp. 72–140. An historical sketch of early ecclesiastical interest in the subject is given, pp. 7–35.

[3] 1st edit., Berlin, 1905; 2nd edit., 1911.

[4] *Philologica Sacra* (Berlin, 1896).

[5] *Philology of the Gospels* (London, 1898), p. 193 f.

[6] Op, cit., p. 50.

In spite of this serious defect, however, much of the work of these earlier scholars is of permanent value. Not every Aramaism requires to be fully 'documented'; an Aramaic idiom may be so well known that illustrations of it are superfluous. And in other cases examples from the literature are not difficult to produce. In at least two instances of this kind from the work of Wellhausen and Nestle, Dalman did less than justice to the evidence, and the alternative explanations which he offers are much less satisfactory than those which he rejects.

Wellhausen's brilliant conjecture that the Synoptic variants *καθάρισον* (Mt. xxiii. 26) and *δότε ἐλεημοσύνην* (Lk. xi. 41) go back to *dakkau* and *zakkau* respectively, and that in Luke the former, 'cleanse', has been wrongly read as the latter, 'give alms', has survived criticism.[1] The objection raised by Dalman, though with obvious hesitation, to the possibility of a confusion between the two verbs is unreal; and his alternative explanation that Luke is a kind of exposition of Matthew's Greek, the 'cleansing' of the vessels consisting of the distribution of their contents as alms, is forced.

It may be that *δότε ἐλεημοσύνην* in Luke is less a mistranslation than a wrong but deliberate interpretation of the Aramaic, made all the more easy, if, as Wellhausen maintained, the two verbs were originally identical in orthography. But the genesis of Luke's reading is quite certainly to be found in a wrong understanding of Aramaic *dakko,* 'cleanse' (*dakkau* is a Syriac form).

To Nestle's explanation that Luke's 'cities' in his form of Matthew's parable of the Talents (Lk. xix. 17 f.) has arisen as a result of a misunderstanding of ככרין 'talents' (כרכין being 'cities'), Dalman objected that *karᵉkha* is not the usual word for 'city' in Palestinian Aramaic.[2] There is, it is true, a more general word corresponding to *πόλις*, namely, *mᵉdhinta*; but both for

[1] *Einl.*[2], p. 27; cf. Dalman, op. cit., pp. 50 and 71. Both verbs are fully attested for Jewish Palestinian Aramaic in these senses, *zakki*, 'to give alms', by Dalman himself from the Palestinian Talmud (p. 71, *Worte Jesu*).

[2] *Worte Jesu*, p. 53. The suggestion was first made by Nestle in the *Theologische Literaturzeitung* for 1895, No. 22; it is repeated in his *Philologica Sacra*, p. 22, and endorsed by Meyer, op. cit., p. 137.

larger and smaller 'cities', and especially for the fortified towns of Palestine, for which πόλις is employed in both LXX and New Testament, *karᵉkha* is the usual word; in the Pseudo-Jonathan Targum of Num. xxiv. 19, *karᵉkha* is used of Rome.

An observation of Nestle in his *Philologica Sacra*,[1] unnoticed by Dalman, is worth recalling. Nestle cited from a privately circulated essay of Field (of the Hexapla) on the 'First Recorded Utterance of Jesus Christ' the latter's claim that ἐν τοῖς τοῦ πατρός μου in Lk. ii. 49 mistranslated Hebrew *beth 'abhi*; this 'original Hebrew' of Luke should have been rendered ἐν τῇ οἰκίᾳ τοῦ πατρός μου: the LXX's rendering of *beth* occasionally by the neuter plural of the definite article, e.g. Gen. xli. 51, Esther v. 10, vi. 12, vii. 9, Job xviii. 19, was adduced in support of the conjecture, and Irenaeus's version of Jn. xiv. 2, ἐν τοῖς τοῦ πατρός μου,[2] for the Greek text of John, ἐν τῇ οἰκίᾳ τοῦ πατρός μου, was cited as a case of the opposite mistranslation.[3]

What Field claimed for Hebrew holds also for Aramaic: Aramaic *beth 'abba* is ambiguous and may be rendered in either way; F. C. Burkitt actually renders the Old Syriac translation of ἐν τοῖς τοῦ πατρός μου in Lk. ii. 49, namely, *beth 'abh*(*i*), by 'at my Father's House';[4] this is a legitimate rendering of the Syriac, if it were not a translation of Lk. ii. 49; Burkitt's wrong translation, however, illustrates the ambiguity in Aramaic.

Since Wellhausen and Nestle, and partly contemporaneous with their work, the studies of Dalman represent the most important contribution which has been made to the subject.[5] Dalman rejected all theories of written Aramaic sources as unproven, and believed that it was in the Words of Jesus only that we had the right to assume an ultimate Aramaic original. Whether he was justified in so confining the range of his study

[1] P. 49.

[2] Edit. Harvey, ii, p. 428.

[3] For the use of ἐν τοῖς in the Papyri in the sense of 'in the house of', Moulton, *Prol.*, p. 103.

[4] *Evangelion da-Mepharreshe*, i, in loc.

[5] *Worte Jesu* and *Jesus-Jeschua* (Leipzig, 1922); *Grammatik des jüdisch-palästinischen Aramäisch* (1st edit., Leipzig, 1894; 2nd edit., 1905; reprinted, Darmstadt, 1964); *Aramäische Dialektproben* (Leipzig, 1927); *Aramäisch-neuhebräisches Handwörterbuch* (2nd edit., Frankfurt, 1922).

remains to be considered. In his investigation of the Words of Jesus the exegetical interest is foremost: Dalman is less concerned to consider or estimate the extent of Aramaic influence on the language of the Gospels; he selected a number of the main conceptions, such as 'the kingdom of God', 'the World', 'the Father in Heaven', and sought to elucidate them in the light of their Jewish antecedents and parallels. The Words of Jesus which are discussed under these headings are themselves considered in their Jewish Aramaic form and context. The branch of Palestinian Aramaic to which Dalman attached most importance for his reconstruction of the Words of Jesus was the Aramaic of the Jewish Targums to the Pentateuch and the Prophets.[1]

Since Dalman, C. C. Torrey and C. F. Burney are the best known names; each attempted to prove the existence of Aramaic originals, the latter to the Fourth Gospel;[2] Burney, in a subsequent work, undertook a study of the poetry of Jesus.[3] Torrey goes so far as to claim in his first larger work that Aramaic originals lie behind all four Gospels,[4] and, on the basis of this

[1] *Infra*, p. 15 f.

[2] *The Aramaic Origin of the Fourth Gospel* (Oxford, 1922).

[3] *The Poetry of Our Lord* (Oxford, 1925).

[4] *The Four Gospels: A New Translation* (Harpers, 1933); he makes an exception of Lk. i–ii (Hebrew), Old Testament quotations (Hebrew), and Jn. xxi (Greek). An earlier work is his *Composition and Date of Acts* (Cambridge, Mass., 1916).

In addition to the main works cited, C. C. Torrey has written a number of articles on the subject, e.g. in *Studies in the History of Religions, Presented to C. H. Toy* (New York, 1912), pp. 269–317; *Harvard Theological Review*, xvi (1923), pp. 305–44. The work of Burney and Torrey gave a fresh impetus to the study of the subject in America; see, e.g., articles in *Princeton Theological Review*, vol. xxvi, *Journal of Biblical Literature*, vols. xlix, li, and liii, *Journal of Near Eastern Studies*, vol. i. Torrey's most recent article is 'Julius Wellhausen's Approach to the Aramaic Gospels' in *Zeitschrift der deutschen morgenländischen Gesellschaft*, Band CI. (N.F. xxvi, 1951), pp. 125–37. Aramaic influence on John was rejected *in toto* by E. C. Colwell, *The Greek of the Fourth Gospel* (Chicago, 1931). A most useful discussion and summary of conclusions for St. Mark will be found in the chapter on 'The Semitic Background of the Gospel' in Dr. Vincent Taylor's *The Gospel according to St. Mark* (London, 1952). Among more recent continental work, reference should be made to the commentaries of A. Schlatter (who is more concerned, however, with rabbinical and Hebrew parallels), and to P. Joüon's 'L'Évangile de Notre-Seigneur Jésus-Christ, traduction et commentaire du texte

view and of numerous conjectural reconstructions of Aramaic, has produced a new translation. He bases his conclusions mainly on examples of mistranslation of Aramaic originals. Most of his examples of mistranslation, however, and several of Burney's, are open to grave objection. Torrey's attempt at a new translation of the Gospels before any adequate presentation of the philological evidence was premature. His second larger study,[1] in which the evidence of language is presented more fully, would have been of greater value had it been undertaken for the Aramaic scholar, and not for 'popular' reading by those who are unacquainted with Aramaic or have no more than a slight working knowledge; the evidence is often over-simplified and incomplete.

Burney's main approach was in this respect the right one, even if he failed to prove his theory of an Aramaic original for the whole of John; he investigated the grammar and syntax of the Gospel in the light of our knowledge of the Aramaic language.

Both Burney and Torrey approach the study of the Aramaic of Jesus on the same linguistic assumptions as Dalman, that the Aramaic of the Targums of Onkelos and the Prophets is the best representative of the Aramaic of Jesus.

Two important articles have recently appeared from the pen of the late A. J. Wensinck of Leyden.[2] The second of these,

original grec, compte tenu du substrat sémitique' (*Verbum Salutis*, v, Paris, G. Beauchesne, éditeur, Rue de Rennes 117, 1930). This latter work contains the results of a number of detailed studies with special reference to Aramaic in *Recherches de science religieuse*, vols. xvii and xviii, 'Quelques aramaïsmes sous-jacents au grec des Évangiles' and 'Notes philologiques sur les Évangiles'. Some extremely valuable observations have been made by J. Jeremias in his *Abendmahlsworte Jesu* (3rd edit., Göttingen, 1960), *Die Gleichnisse Jesu* (6th edit., Zürich, 1962), and in two articles in the *Zeitschrift für die neutestamentliche Wissenschaft*, xxxiv (1935), xxxix (1940). Consult also, among earlier works, A. Schlatter, *Sprache und Heimat des vierten Evangelisten* (Gütersloh, 1902). See further *infra*, p. 19 n.

[1] *Our Translated Gospels* (Hodder Stoughton).

[2] 'The Semitisms of Codex Bezae and their Relation to the non-Western Text of the Gospel of Saint Luke', in the *Bulletin of the Bezan Club*, xii (Leyden, 1937); the earlier article was 'Un Groupe d'Aramaismes dans le Texte Grec des Évangiles' (*Mededeelingen der koninklijke Akademie van Wetenschappen, Afdeeling Letterkunde*, Deel 81, Serie A, No. 5).

'The Semitisms of Codex Bezae', represents, in the principles of its approach to the Aramaic of the Gospels, as well as in some of its results, the most important advance in the subject in recent years. Wensinck no longer shared Dalman's view of the importance of Targumic Aramaic; and he extended his investigations to the text of Codex Bezae. Most other Aramaic scholars, in particular Torrey and Burney, have based their investigations either on the text of Westcott and Hort or on that of Tischendorf.

Three main criticisms may be made of this earlier work of Dalman, Torrey, and Burney, and of the studies of their predecessors and contemporaries such as J. T. Marshall[1] or Arnold Meyer. They apply to a less extent to the pioneer work of Wellhausen or Nestle.

(1) While Dalman's criticism of the inadequacy of the linguistic approach of Wellhausen and Nestle is fully justified, the large claims he makes (accepted without criticism by succeeding workers in the field) for Targumic Aramaic as the primary authority for the language of Jesus cannot now be justified. This criticism, together with suggestions for a fresh approach to the language of Jesus, is developed in the following chapter.

(2) Hitherto most Aramaic scholars of the Gospels have confined themselves almost exclusively to the investigation of Aramaisms in one text only, that of Westcott and Hort or that of Tischendorf. The unexamined assumption of this textual approach to the subject is that no other text has the same claim to the confidence of scholars as the best single representative of the Apostolic autographs. Wensinck, alone among modern scholars, but following the tradition of Wellhausen, Nestle, and Blass, included in his investigations the text of Codex Bezae, and was able to claim, as a result of his comparison of the Bezan text with non-Western texts of Luke, not only that there was much more evidence of Aramaic influence in Bezan Luke, but also that the isolation and establishment of Aramaisms in that text contributed substantially to the solution of the great textual problem. For if Aramaic influence is more extensive in one text

[1] In the *Expositor*, Ser. IV, ii, iii, iv, vi, viii.

rather than another, the presumption is that the 'Aramaized' text stands nearer to the kind of Greek which the Apostles wrote. Other great texts had passed through the process of διόρθωσις; their more polished Greek is the work of later editors.

Has the Bezan text any claims to represent a more primitive type of text than that of the Vatican and Sinaitic Codices? If it has, then Wensinck's approach is justified, and the Bezan authority, as the best representative of the 'Western' text, should certainly be included in any investigation of the Aramaic of Jesus and the Gospels, including Luke–Acts. Moreover, in view of such a textual approach, the study of the Aramaic of the Gospels will not concern itself solely with estimating the extent of Aramaic influence, or with questions of source-criticism; it may also contribute to the textual criticism of the Greek Gospels. This textual approach is also discussed more fully in Chapter II.

(3) The third criticism of earlier work, especially the more recent studies of Torrey and Burney, may be conveniently considered in the present chapter. Both Torrey and Burney attach much importance to conjectural mistranslations of Aramaic as proof of source. Mistranslation of an original is, it is true, the best proof of translation;[1] but it is doubtful if it can ever have scientific value as evidence except in cases where we possess not only the translation but also the original work. Even then demonstrative proof is not always possible: not all Syriac scholars accept Burkitt's view that the Acts of Thomas was an original Syriac work and the Greek a translation, though we possess both Syriac and Greek and Burkitt based his hypothesis largely on alleged misrenderings of the Syriac by the Greek text.[2] What is not always possible in the most favourable of circumstances becomes difficult in the extreme when there is no original with which to compare the 'translation'.

When a strong case can be made out for the mistranslation of original Aramaic in the Gospels or Acts, such evidence must be stated fully. But there are two demands which we can justifiably

[1] Cf. Burney, *Aramaic Origin*, p. 101.

[2] Cf. *Evangelion da-Mepharreshe*, ii, p. 101; *J.T.S.* i, p. 280 f., ii, p. 429, iii, p. 94.

make of all such conjectural evidence or proof: the mistranslation must at least be credible; and the conjectured Aramaic must be possible.

Both offences, incredible 'mistranslations' and impossible Aramaic, are among the worst features of recent work in the Aramaic of the Gospels. Nearly two generations after J. T. Marshall's elaborate failure to prove on internal evidence of 'mistranslation' the existence of 'an Aramaic Gospel', and the considered verdict on such work given by the great Oxford Semitist S. R. Driver, the same kind of mistakes continue to be made. All dialects of the language are ransacked for an expression or usage, however rare and unusual, to explain a difficulty. There are even cases where Aramaic words which do not exist, or are not at any rate found in the lexica or literature, have been invented; and such false coin continues to be circulated by the non-specialist.

S. R. Driver's judgement of Marshall's work deserves to be quoted in full:

'In composition in a foreign language, it is better, surely, to be cautious than to be bold, to be even (it may be) too scrupulous in the choice of expressions than to be not scrupulous enough; and I cannot understand how Prof. Marshall could have postulated for his original Aramaic Gospel, words of which there could be the slightest doubt that they were properly and correctly used, and that they really and unquestionably bore the meanings which he attributes to them. But again and again we find him making use of words to which some *doubt* attaches: they are not the ordinary and natural words that would be expected; sometimes they are words that do not exist at all; at other times they are either very rare words, the precise meaning of which is not readily determinable, or they are words which do not really express the idea required.'[1]

The following are examples from recent work of mistranslations which are either incredible or linguistically unsound, or both.

In Mk. vii. 3, C. C. Torrey has suggested that an original Aramaic 'the Jews do not eat *at all* (לגמר, *ligmar*) without washing their hands' has been misrendered 'the Jews do not eat

[1] *Expositor*, Ser. IV, viii, p. 428.

without washing their hands πυγμῇ, *with the fist* (לגמד, *ligmodh*)'.[1] But לגמד (= πυγμῇ) can only be pointed and read as Hebrew *l^egomedh*; the alleged Aramaic word *gumda*, 'fist',[2] and from which *ligmodh*, πυγμῇ, is formed, occurs in none of the lexica. Moreover, Hebrew *gomedh* never means 'fist'; *gomedh*, Aramaic *garmidha*, as likewise πυγμή when their equivalent, mean 'cubit', 'ell', the length of the arm from elbow to finger-tip.

The most likely explanation of the unusual πυγμῇ νίπτεσθαι is that given by John Lightfoot, who cited parallels from the Talmud on the ritual hand-washing before meals which is not to go *beyond the wrist*.[3] Hand-washings were graded according to the degree of ritual pollution. When a strict ritualist came from the market-place, the greater pollution demanded a 'plunging' of the hand to the wrist in special water not less than forty seahs in quantity and contained in a special basin. The 'dipping' of the hand or the pouring of water on the hands for lesser degrees of ritual uncleanness did not require such elaborate precautions or preparations. The Talmudic phrases are 'to plunge to the wrist (*ṭ^ebhal ʿadh happereq*)' and 'to dip or lustrate to the wrist (*n^eṭal* or *m^eshi ʿadh happereq*)'. Mark's βαπτίζεσθαι in verse 4 corresponds to the first phrase, where the reference may be to the first type of ritual washing; πυγμῇ νίπτεσθαι may correspond to the second phrase. We may thus take the Marcan expression as equivalent to the Talmudic phrase and meaning 'to wash the hands in ritual washing'.[4]

In Mk. xiv. 3 (cf. Mt. xxvi. 6), Σίμωνος τοῦ λεπροῦ is said by Torrey to contain a mistranslation of גרבא, *garabha*, 'a jar-merchant'; the same consonants had been misread as *garba*, λεπρός.[5] The noun *garba* is the usual one for 'leper', and there is another word with the same consonants found in the Targum and meaning 'a wine-skin'. But no noun *garabha* meaning 'a jar-merchant' appears in any of the lexica.[6]

[1] *The Four Gospels*, in loc., and *Our Translated Gospels*, p. 93.

[2] *The Four Gospels*, in loc.

[3] In his *Horae Hebraicae*, in loc.

[4] Cf. further Turner, 'Marcan Usage', *J.T.S.* xxix (1928), p. 278.

[5] *The Four Gospels*, in loc., and *Our Translated Gospels*, p. 96.

[6] Mt. xxvi. 6 (D) has λεπρωσοῦ; the Aramaic equivalent adjective is *garban*, a word which might easily be confused with (Talmudic) *gardan* (Targumic *gardai*), 'a weaver'.

Torrey's restoration of the Aramaic of Acts ii. 47 has been accepted by a number of scholars; in the *Beginnings of Christianity* J. de Zwaan speaks of this 'splendid observation of Torrey',[1] and Foakes-Jackson agreed that 'an Aramaic original is at the back of this and other strange expressions'.[2]

Torrey rejects the ordinary LXX meaning of ἐπὶ τὸ αὐτό, 'together' (Hebrew *yaḥdau*), and suggests that Luke's Greek phrase misrenders Aramaic *laḥda*; the adverb is found in the Palestinian Syriac version of Jn. xvii. 23 and in the Syriac versions of Jn. xi. 52. In Judean dialects of Aramaic it means 'greatly' (σφόδρα), and is the Targum equivalent of *m^e'odh*: a compound of *l^e*, 'to' and *ḥadh*, 'one', *l'aḥda* had been mistranslated ἐπὶ τὸ αὐτό. The following was the correct translation: 'And the Lord added *greatly* day by day to the saved.'

But, as Howard has pointed out,[3] if Luke is translating Aramaic, then he gives the correct rendering of *laḥda*, namely, σφόδρα, in Acts vi. 7. A still more serious objection is the assumed equation of ἐπὶ τὸ αὐτό with *laḥda*; the evidence of the Syriac versions is irrelevant; *laḥda* is there equivalent to a quite different phrase, εἰς ἕν. The Aramaic adverb *laḥda* could never be represented in Greek by ἐπὶ τὸ αὐτό; the Aramaic for Luke's Greek adverbial phrase is *kaḥda*.[4]

In Jn. i. 5, Burney takes up the earlier suggestion of C. J. Ball

[1] See *Composition and Date of Acts*, p. 10 f., and *Beginnings of Christianity*, I, ii, p. 55, iv, p. 30.

[2] *Harvard Theological Review*, x, p. 358.

[3] Moulton, *Gramm.*, ii, p. 473.

[4] This adverb means both 'together' and 'at the same time', e.g. Isa. lxv. 25, Hebrew *k^e'eḥadh* (LXX ἅμα), Dan. ii. 35, Aramaic *kaḥda* (LXX ἅμα). This latter meaning would suit Acts ii. 47 (D): 'And the Lord was adding those who were being saved *at the same time* in the ecclesia'; the adverb refers back to verse 46—they continued in prayer in the temple, and were breaking bread from house to house, and *at the same time*, the Lord was adding those who were being saved in the ecclesia. Fresh light is shed on the peculiar Lucan expression προστιθέναι ἐπὶ τὸ αὐτό by an exact parallel in the *Manual of Discipline* (ed. M. Burrows, 1951), Plate V, line 7, בהאספם ליחד, where the phrase means 'to join the congregation'. The relevant Qumrân evidence has now been fully examined by M. Wilcox, op. cit., pp. 93 ff. This is the fullest treatment available of this idiomatic Lucan expression and the Qumrân usage seems conclusive for the sense, 'to be united to the (Christian) fellowship' at Acts ii. 47.

that κατέλαβεν is a mistranslation of *'aqbel*, 'darkened', which had been misread as *qabbel*, 'received'.[1] A similar mistranslation is suspected in Jn. xii. 35, ἵνα μὴ σκοτία ὑμᾶς καταλάβῃ. But whatever meaning is to be given to κατέλαβεν here, it is not simply 'received', and cannot therefore be equated with *qabbel*. It may be possible that an original Aramaic read *la qabbleh qabhla*, 'the darkness did not receive it', a characteristic Aramaic word-play. It is this idea which we find in verse 11. But we have still to account for κατέλαβεν as a rendering of *qabbel*. Is it perhaps Greek interpretation, the choice of the Greek verb being suggested by its idiomatic use for darkness or night 'overtaking' a person? We may compare xii. 35 or Diodorus, 20. 86, τῆς νυκτὸς καταλαβούσης.

One of Burney's most valuable observations of this kind is that μονογενὴς Θεός in Jn. i. 18 mistranslates *yᵉḥidh 'ᵉlaha*, 'the only-begotten of God'.[2] It has an attractive simplicity, is free from philological difficulties, and the Greek reading is unusual. Equally remarkable, however, would be the ignorance of the translator who made the blunder, unless we look on his 'version' as a deliberate theological interpretation of the Aramaic.

Similar objections, mainly philological, may be made to most of the examples of 'mistranslation' of original Aramaic which have been adduced by Torrey and Burney.[3] Nevertheless, it would be unfair to overlook a number of valuable suggestions, credible and sound in their proposed Aramaic, of both these scholars. Some of these are quite certainly the best and probably the right explanations of the difficulty in the Greek. And it is only in such instances, where a case both credible and philologically sound can be made out for mistranslation, that this precarious method of approach is justifiable. 'The fascinating pursuit of Aramaic originals may lead to a good percentage of successful guesses; but they are mere guesses still, except when a decided failure in the Greek can be cleared up by an Aramaic

[1] *Aramaic Origin*, p. 29 f.

[2] Ibid., p. 40. Professor G. D. Kilpatrick draws my attention to the reading (ὁ) μονογενής alone (without υἱός or θεός), and adds that some think this is original.

[3] Cf. G. R. Driver in *Jewish Guardian*, Jan. 1923.

which explains the error, and this acts as corroboration.'[1]

Several of Burney's and Torrey's more convincing examples of mistranslation are considered in later chapters; especially valuable are the former scholar's examples of the mistranslated Aramaic particle *d^e^*. The following two examples from the work of Torrey merit the description 'brilliant', and deserve to rank with Wellhausen's observation on Mt. xxiii. 26 (Lk. xi. 41).

In Lk. i. 39 he suggests that *εἰς πόλιν 'Ιούδα* mistranslated either Hebrew *'el m^e^dhinath y^e^hudhah* or Aramaic *liy^e^hudh m^e^dhinta*, i.e. 'into the province, country of Judea', *εἰς τὴν χώραν τῆς 'Ιουδαίας*; Semitic *m^e^dhina* may be either 'province' or 'city'.[2] The objection that *m^e^dhina* cannot be shown to have the meaning 'city' when Luke wrote is without foundation so far as general Aramaic, uninfluenced by any local usage, is concerned. But there is reason to think that *m^e^dhina* was specially and locally employed in Palestine for 'the Province', i.e. Palestine itself.[3] The definite form *m^e^dhinta* meant 'city', and the two forms and uses are as a rule distinguished. An Aramaic *l^e^wath m^e^dhinath y^e^hudha*[4] might be translated either *εἰς πόλιν 'Ιούδα* or *εἰς τὴν χώραν τῆς 'Ιουδαίας*. A translator who was not a Palestinian Jew may not have been acquainted with the special Jewish Palestinian use of the word, and have rendered by the familiar 'city'.[5]

In Lk. xi. 48 = Mt. xxiii. 31 it is surely remarkable that the parallel in Matthew to Luke's 'ye are building' should be 'ye

[1] Moulton, *Gramm.* ii, p. 16.

[2] In *Harvard Theological Review*, xvii, pp. 83–89; cf. *Our Translated Gospels*, p. 82 f.

[3] Maimonides knew the whole of Palestine as 'the Province' (Levy, *Chaldäisches Wörterbuch*, ii, p. 10).

[4] Where does Torrey's 'stereotyped' *y^e^hudh m^e^dhinta* occur? (cf. *Harvard Theological Review*, xvii, p. 87).

[5] May the Greek *πόλις* not even have taken on something of the wider meaning of *m^e^dhina* = Province, *Gouvernement*, especially in Aramaic/Syriac-speaking areas? (See further, Wilcox, pp. 5 ff., 42 ff.)

At Mk. vi. 21 the Harclean Syriac has the interesting marginal variant for *τῆς Γαλιλαίας*, ܕܡܕܝܢܬܐ i.e. *τῆς πόλεως*.) There is no mention made of any 'city' in the context and 'district', 'province' by itself seems bare: perhaps the text read by Sy^h^ was *τῆς Γαλιλαίας πόλεως* (גליליא מדינתא), the 'Province of Galilee'.

are children (of)'; an Aramaic אתון בנין אתון could be rendered in either way.[1] Moreover, Luke's 'and ye are building' is obviously anti-climax as compared with the clear point made by Matthew. An intentional word-play in the employment of two such similar sounding words may well have been original in the Aramaic of this saying from Q.[2]

Wilcox recalls two examples of alleged mistranslation in Acts ii. 47 and iii. 14, both of which possess a high degree of plausibility.[3] The first is the Bezan variant *κόσμον* for *λαόν*, possibly arising from the confusion of עלמא and עמא in the original Aramaic (the confusion is also possible in Hebrew). Alternatively we may prefer to detect the influence on D of a Syriac version, where ܥܡܐ and ܥܠܡܐ have been similarly confused. Neither explanation can be more than plausible, for it is also possible to explain an alteration of *λαόν* to *κόσμον* as the work of a scribe seeking to magnify the impression made by these early converts on the 'whole world'.

The second instance is the Bezan *ἐβαρύνατε* (d *aggravastis*) for *ἠρνήσασθε* at Acts iii. 14: here the original in Aramaic (or Hebrew) of *ἠρνήσασθε* (undoubtedly the 'true' text) can only have been כפרתון or כַּדֵּבְתּוּן. It has been suggested that the variant *ἐβαρύνατε* has arisen by confusing the roots כפר and כבר or (so Torrey) כדב and כבד. Wilcox tends to favour Torrey's explanation, but suggests reading אכבדתון, Aphel, (= *ἐβαρύνατε*) instead of Torrey's כבדתון, which it is by no means certain could mean *ἐβαρύνατε*. The same doubt, however, attaches to the Aphel which (like its Syriac equivalent) means 'to irritate' rather than 'to oppress' (*βαρύνειν*). Nevertheless, some such explanation of this curious variant does seem plausible, for it is difficult to imagine a scribe arriving at *ἐβαρύνατε* in any other way. Another suggestion is that from an original כדבתון (or כפרתון) a translator gave *ἐβαρύνατε* in addition to *ἠρνήσασθε* by way of an alternative *pesher* on the original, perhaps understanding the Aramaic word in a Hebrew sense; or he

[1] *Our Translated Gospels*, p. 103 f.

[2] For another instance of this word-play, see *infra*, p. 145.

[3] Op. cit., pp. 1 ff. and pp. 140 ff.

may have found a variant which had arisen by corruption, e.g. כבדתון, and understood it in the sense of 'oppressed'.

This line of evidence, mistranslation of Aramaic, while it can have a secondary value only as necessarily conjectural, cannot therefore be ignored altogether. But it must be pursued with the greatest caution.

The fulfilment of a third condition is desirable. The strongest argument in favour of a mistranslation is its inherent probability in its Aramaic context. Possible mistranslations should be studied, not as isolated phenomena, but, so far as that is possible, in their setting in the Aramaic saying or passage. The advice of S. R. Driver is again worth quoting in full: '. . . in order to judge of it [the translation and mistranslation of Aramaic] properly, we ought to have not single isolated phrases, but entire verses, or at least entire *sentences*, retranslated into Aramaic, and the origin of the variants in the parallel texts, examined and accounted for, one by one.' [1]

[1] *Expositor*, Ser. IV, viii, p. 430 f.

CHAPTER II

THE LINGUISTIC AND TEXTUAL APPROACH

The Linguistic Approach

ARAMAIC was one of the great languages of the civilized East. It flourished mainly from the sixth to the third centuries B.C., during the period when oriental empires ruled the civilized world, when it was the international medium of governmental, cultural, and commercial intercourse from the Euphrates to the Nile, even in countries where there was no indigenous Semitic culture. It became the language of the Jews, when exactly is not known, but probably during and after the Exile.

With the rise of the Empire of Alexander the Aramaic language was superseded throughout the civilized world by the Koine, but Greek never wholly displaced Aramaic among the Jews of Palestine or Babylon, or among peoples with a Semitic culture in Syria and Mesopotamia, where Greek was cultivated, but Aramaic, in one of its main branches, Syriac, was still the chief spoken and written language of the people. Even as far west as Syrian Antioch, Syriac in the first century flourished along with Greek, and was as firmly established there as Jewish Aramaic was in Palestine.[1]

Four languages were to be found in first-century Palestine: Greek was the speech of the educated 'hellenized' classes and the medium of cultural and commercial intercourse between Jew and foreigner; Latin was the language of the army of occupation and, to judge from Latin borrowings in Aramaic, appears also to some extent to have served the purposes of commerce, as it no doubt also did of Roman law; Hebrew, the sacred tongue of the Jewish Scriptures, continued to provide the lettered Jew with an important means of literary expression and was cultivated as a spoken tongue in the learned coteries of the Rabbis; Aramaic was the language of the people of the land and, together with Hebrew, provided the chief literary

[1] Nöldeke speaks of 'the semi-Greek' Antioch (*Syriac Grammar*, p. xxxii).

medium of the Palestinian Jew of the first century; Josephus wrote his *Jewish War* in Aramaic and later translated it into Greek.[1]

If Jesus was a Galilean Rabbi, it is not unlikely that He made use of Hebrew as well as Aramaic, especially, as T. W. Manson has suggested, in His formal disputations with the Pharisees.[2] M. H. Segal has gone so far as to claim that 'Mishnaic' Hebrew, the kind of Hebrew we find in the Mishnah, was actually a spoken vernacular in Judea in the time of Christ.[3] In the Palestinian Talmud Aramaic and Hebrew are found together, sometimes in the form of a kind of *Mischsprache*; sentences half Hebrew, half Aramaic, are familiar to the reader of the Talmud, and this artificial language, rabbinical in origin, may well have been in use before as after the Fall of Jerusalem.[4]

The Gospels were written in a predominantly hellenistic environment, and they were written in Greek. But Greek was not the native language of their central Figure, nor of the earliest apostles, if it was not unfamiliar to them. Jesus must have conversed in the Galilean dialect of Aramaic, and His teaching was probably almost entirely in Aramaic. At the basis of the Greek Gospels, therefore, there must lie a Palestinian Aramaic tradition, at any rate of the sayings and teaching of Jesus, and this tradition must at one time have been translated from Aramaic into Greek. Some have thought that the Evangelists themselves were the translators of these Aramaic sources of the Gospels; they certainly must have utilized, if they did not themselves translate, early translation sources. The 'Aramaic problem' of the Gospels is to determine, by internal evidence,

[1] Preface, § 1; cf. *Antiquities*, xii. 2. Dalman's important study of the three main languages of first-century Palestine, 'Die drei Sprachen', in his *Jesus-Jeschua*, should be consulted. These languages were, for the Jew, Aramaic, Hebrew, and Greek, the first and the last in everyday use, especially in the cities. The results of Dalman's study for the general question of the language of Jesus may be regarded as firmly established: Jesus may have spoken Greek, but He certainly did speak and teach in Aramaic.

[2] *Teaching of Jesus*, p. 46 f.

[3] *Mishnaic Hebrew Grammar*, p. 17.

[4] Cf. Merx, *Die vier kanonischen Evangelien, Lukas*, p. 418, where an example of this *Mischsprache* may be conveniently studied.

to what extent the Greek Gospels are written in or embody 'translation Greek' or how much Aramaic influence can be detected in them.

The Aramaic study of the Gospels has been mainly concerned with this problem. But Aramaic, other than Jewish Palestinian, may have influenced the Evangelists' work and the early transmission of the Gospels in Greek. Syriac was widely spoken and written, especially in Antioch, the first great Christian centre, and there is a respectable tradition that St. Luke was a native of that city.[1] If the third Evangelist was a 'Syrian of Antioch', he was probably bilingual, with Syriac as his second language. Moreover, Palestinian Jewish Aramaic was a dialect little known outside of Palestine: much of the Palestinian Aramaic Gospel tradition may have passed through the more familiar medium of Syriac before it was finally written down in Greek. The influence of Syriac, therefore, as well as of Jewish Palestinian Aramaic, may have contributed to the shaping of the Gospel Greek.

A Palestinian Aramaic approach to the Gospels has more formidable obstacles to overcome than a study of Syriac influence. In the case of the latter, there is no dearth of Syriac literature, most of it, it is true, later than the first century, but possessing a large enough scope and sufficient unity and linguistic integrity to make the grammatical, syntactical, and lexicographical problems comparatively simple. It is, moreover, a well-cultivated field of study. Palestinian Aramaic, on the other hand, presents us with a major problem.

The literary remains of the Western dialect of Aramaic comprise the Aramaic of the Jewish colony of Elephantine (*c.* 500–400 B.C.),[2] the Aramaic portions of Ezra (*c.* 500–450 B.C.) and Daniel (*c.* 200 B.C.), the Aramaic of the Jewish Targums or paraphrases of the Pentateuch, Prophets, and Hagiographa, the Aramaic portions of the Palestinian Talmud and Midrashim, Samaritan Aramaic (a Pentateuch Targum, a liturgy, &c.), and

[1] Eusebius, *H.E.* iii. 4, and Jerome, *de vir. illustr.*

[2] E. Sachau, *Aramäische Papyrus und Ostraka aus Elephantine* (Leipzig, 1911), and A. E. Cowley, *Aramaic Papyri of the Fifth Century* (Oxford, 1923).

Christian Palestinian Syriac, consisting mainly of versions of parts of the Old and New Testaments. The latter are all much later than the second century A.D.: we possess no Aramaic writing of any extent belonging to the first century;[1] Josephus's *Jewish War* in its original Aramaic has disappeared along with practically all contemporary Aramaic literature. Aramaic sources from a date after the second century B.C. and before the second century A.D. are known to lie behind some of the Apocalyptic and Pseudepigraphic writings of the Jews, but they no longer exist except in translation. We are dependent, therefore, for our ideas of first-century Palestinian Aramaic on sources earlier than the second century B.C. and not all Palestinian, or later than the second century A.D., and mostly translations of Greek or Hebrew.[2]

In the almost complete absence of literary Aramaic writings contemporary with the Gospels, the question of the best use of the actual sources of knowledge available becomes important. Where, in extant West Aramaic literature, are we most likely to find the language most nearly representative of the Aramaic of first-century Palestine?

Several answers have been given to this question. In all of them the value of the older Aramaic so far as it goes is recognized. The chief matter of debate has come to be the comparative value of the later sources, which are so much more extensive than the older literature. Friedrich Schulthess found in Christian Palestinian Syriac the Aramaic dialect most closely akin to the Aramaic of the Gospels,[3] and in this he had the support of two Cambridge scholars, Agnes Smith Lewis and Margaret Dunlop Gibson.[4] Their view was rejected by Dalman, who found in the Aramaic of the canonical Jewish Targums to the Pentateuch

[1] Cf. *infra*, p. 39 f. For an admirable discussion of this problem, see Millar Burrows, 'Translation of the Gospels', in *Journal of Biblical Literature*, liii (1934), pp. 16 ff.

[2] For an authoritative account of Aramaic dialects and their literature, see F. Rosenthal's *Die Aramaistische Forschung* (Brill, Leiden, 1939).

[3] *Das Problem der Sprache Jesu* (1917); cf. p. 30 f.

[4] *Codex Climaci Rescriptus* (Cambridge, 1909), p. xvi.

and the Prophets the best representative of early Palestinian Aramaic.[1]

Dalman distinguishes two dialects or forms of Jewish Palestinian Aramaic, the first represented by Old Testament Aramaic and the Aramaic of the Targums to the Pentateuch and the Prophets, the second by the popular Aramaic anecdotes of the Palestinian Talmud, together with parts of the Palestinian commentary on the Old Testament in the older haggadic Midrashim. The first he describes as 'Judean', and detects in it the literary type of Palestinian Aramaic which came from Jerusalem as cultural centre and was employed in first-century Palestine as universal 'Schriftsprache'. The relevant portions of the Palestinian Talmud and Midrashim dated to a period when the centre of Jewish learning had been removed from Jerusalem to lower Galilee and were consequently composed in the Galilean dialect of Palestinian Aramaic.

As the literary Aramaic of Judea as well as the dialect of his native Galilee may well have been used by Jesus, Dalman takes account of both 'Judean' and 'Galilean' dialects in his reconstruction of the Words of Jesus. For his two dialects his literary sources are mainly Targumic and Talmudic Aramaic respectively. But they are not both of equal value or importance. It is the Aramaic of the Targums of Onkelos to the Pentateuch and Jonathan to the Prophets in which Dalman finds the nearest representative of first-century Aramaic. Galilean Aramaic, and the Aramaic of the lesser known Targums, the Pseudo-Jonathan Targum (Jerusalem Targum I) and the Fragment Targum (Jerusalem Targums II and III) to the Pentateuch, and the Targums to the Hagiographa, are all given a secondary place; Palestinian Syriac and Samaritan Aramaic are of still less importance.

[1] *Worte Jesu*, p. 72. In meeting a contemporary criticism that he was thereby making a rabbinical *Schulsprache* the model for a living language, Dalman conceded, in his second edition of the *Worte Jesu* (p. 371), a much greater importance to the Galilaean Aramaic portions of the Talmud and Midrashim than to Targumic Aramaic. Cf. J. Jeremias, 'Die aramäische Vorgeschichte unserer Evangelien', in *Theol. Literaturzeitung*, 1949, Nr. 9, p. 528, and my note on 'The Aramaic Spoken by Christ and Lk. 14. 5' in *J.T.S.* i (1949), p. 60.

There are two main objections to this high valuation of the Aramaic of Onkelos and Jonathan for the language of Jesus. In the first place, it renders the Hebrew so literally in many places that it becomes 'hebraized' Aramaic. The name 'Onkelos' is itself a hebraization of the Greek name 'Aquila'.[1] And Onkelos is in fact the 'Aquila' of the Aramaic versions, even if the abuse of Aramaic is not so flagrant as Aquila's distortion of Greek idiom. Secondly, it is well known that the Onkelos and Jonathan Targums were for a time in Babylon, and traces of Babylonian Aramaic influence have been left on their language.[2]

Dalman was well aware of these difficulties. Account had to be taken of 'Hebraisms' and the deflexion of Aramaic idiom by Hebrew usage.[3] Nevertheless, when this had been done, the Aramaic, especially in the free paraphrase where the Hebrew is not closely followed, was still our most reliable guide to the early 'Judean' dialect. The extent of Babylonian influence Dalman did not estimate as large; this East Aramaic element in the language of the Targums does not substantially affect their essential Palestinian character.

Recent Aramaic discoveries have given greater force to this second objection and shown that Dalman has over-estimated the value of Targumic Aramaic for the Aramaic of the Gospel period, while his judgement of the worth of the language of the lesser known Targums and of Palestinian Syriac and Samaritan Aramaic has been practically reversed, in the case of the last two in favour of the estimate of Schulthess, with perhaps some slight modification.

In the same year as the appearance of the second edition of the *Worte Jesu*, fragments of a new Palestinian Pentateuch Targum were published.[4] The new manuscripts formed part of

[1] *Worte Jesu*, p. 66.

[2] Cf. Nöldeke, *Die semitischen Sprachen* (1887), p. 32.

[3] *Worte Jesu*, p. 66.

[4] Paul Kahle, *Masoreten des Westens*, ii (Stuttgart, 1930). In *The Cairo Geniza* (London, 1947; 2nd edit., 1962), Kahle has further developed the view first stated in his *Masoreten des Westens*, ii, of the importance of this new material for the language of Jesus. See especially pp. 129 ff. (2nd edit., pp. 200 ff.).

the valuable find of Semitic documents made in the now famous Genizah or lumber-room of a synagogue in Old Cairo. They consist of five substantial fragments of a Palestinian Pentateuch Targum, not Onkelos, and differing widely in both text and language from that Targum. The manuscript fragments have been dated to a period roughly from A.D. 700 to 900.

The Samaritan Pentateuch Targum provides the only parallel to the type of Targum text we find in the new manuscripts. The new Targum is often a free paraphrase with haggadic additions and occasionally presupposes an underlying Hebrew consonantal text differing from our Massoretic Text. Two of the fragments (D and E) contain a Targum of the same passage from Genesis (D, Gen. xxxviii. 16–26; E, Gen. xxxviii. 16–xxxix. 10), and a comparison of the two texts shows that variants are substantial. Variants of any consequence in the Onkelos Targum are practically unknown. In the new Palestinian Pentateuch Targum we have to do with a type of Jewish Targum which has never, like the text of Onkelos, been finally edited and brought into conformity with the Massoretic Text, but which has itself been freely altered at different stages in its transmission.

The Palestinian Pentateuch Targum fragments are evidence, that is to say, for a stage in the development of the Targum corresponding to the period in the history of the Hebrew text before its standardization as the official Massoretic Text, or to the history of the Qoran text when the recensions in use in Basra, Kufah, Homs, and Damascus all differed in various degrees from one another. Onkelos corresponds to the standard text of the Qoran prepared in the Caliphate of Othman. That such a Targum as the new fragments contain ever circulated in Palestine when Onkelos was the official authoritative standard there is quite impossible: but we know that it was used in Palestine till as late as the tenth century; the inference is unavoidable that Onkelos as we know it was completely unknown in Palestine as late as the tenth century A.D.[1]

[1] Cf. *Masoreten des Westens*, ii, p. 12*.

The Babylonian phase in the history of the Targum of Onkelos is obscure; all that appears to be certain is that the name Onkelos was first given to the Targum in the Babylonian Talmud and that the Babylonian Schools highly esteemed this Targum.[1] In the light of the knowledge obtained by the discovery and valuation of the new Targum that Onkelos cannot have been known or officially used in Palestine as late as the tenth century, the presumption is that the Onkelos Targum was introduced into Palestine from Babylonia in the ninth or tenth centuries at the earliest and became the official canonical Targum; and that the newly discovered fragments were collected and condemned to oblivion in the Genizah after this event.

The bearing of this discovery on our estimate of the value of Onkelos for first-century Palestinian Aramaic is evident and of great importance: 'In the Onkelos Targum we have to do with an official . . . Targum . . . which was composed in a language which was never actually so spoken, and which had to take account of the condition that it must be intelligible in Palestine as well as Babylon. For this neither the actual Palestinian nor the Babylonian dialect could be employed.'[2] The Onkelos Targum, that is to say, and the Prophetic Targum which is modelled on it, were largely composed in the artificial Aramaic of the Jewish Schools. It is a purely scholarly product, even if its ultimate basis was a Palestinian Aramaic Targum. It can therefore be regarded as a secondary authority only for the language of Jesus.

The language of the Palestinian Pentateuch Targum is, on the other hand, first-century Aramaic. Not only does the large number of borrowings in it from Greek point to a period for its composition when Palestinian Aramaic was spoken in a hellenistic environment, but parts of its text can be dated with certainty to the first Christian century or even earlier (the comparatively late date of the manuscripts has nothing to do with

[1] Cf. P. Kahle. *Masoreten des Ostens* (Leipzig, 1913), p. 203.

[2] *Masoreten des Westens*, ii, p. 11*; cf. p. 12*. Cf. *The Cairo Geniza*, pp. 122 ff. (2nd edit., pp. 191 ff.).

the date of the translation). The Targum fragment A of Exod. xxi, xxii is a rendering and paraphrase made not later than the first century A.D.; it contains halachic material which, when compared with the regulations of the Mishnah, must be pronounced pre-Mishnaic, and may even be pre-Christian. Moreover, it was such an ancient Palestinian Aramaic Pentateuch Targum which formed the basis of the Peshiṭta Pentateuch.[1] The date of the latter is not known, but it is certainly not later than the second century A.D. and is probably earlier.

The closest affinities in language of this Targum are with Samaritan Aramaic and Christian Palestinian Syriac.[2] The literary remains of both these Palestinian dialects are comparatively late, but their propinquity in language to that of the Palestinian Pentateuch Targum establishes their value as certainly greater than that of Onkelos or Jonathan.

In one of the instances where we find a transcription of an Aramaic word in the Gospels, the pronunciation of the word as preserved in the Gospel transcription agrees with the pronunciation in the new Targum, against that of the Onkelos Targum.[3] The Gospel ῥαββουνί, ῥαββουνεί (Mk. x. 51; Jn. xx. 16)

[1] See P. Kahle, op. cit., p. 3* f.; cf. C. Peters, 'Peschitta und Targumim des Pentateuchs', in *Museon*, tom. xlviii.

[2] Cf. P. Kahle, op. cit., p. 11*.

[3] Cf. *The Cairo Geniza*, p. 129. Jeremias (op. cit., p. 528) draws attention to the use of *barnash(a)* in the Geniza fragments: 'In einem bedeutsamen Aufsatz: "The Background of the Term 'Son of Man'" (*Expository Times*, lix, 1948, s. 283–8) hat ... John Bowman darauf hingewiesen, daß in den neuen Fragmenten, "in Gn. 4, 14 Bar-Nash is used for 'anyone' while in Gn. 9, 5–6 Bar-Nasha (thrice) and Bar-Nash (twice) alike translate Ha-Adam man" (s. 286). Auch dieser weite Gebrauch von "Menschensohn" entspricht dem Sprachgebrauch der Evangelien, in denen das Wort z. B. Mk. 2, 28 die Bedeutung "der Mensch" (im generischen Sinn) haben dürfte; Dalman's (auf dem Targum Onkelos fußende, von ihm selbst aber später erheblich modifizierte) These, daß בַּר נָשָׁא nicht der palästinischen Umgangsprache angehört habe, ja in der älteren jüdisch-aramäischen Literatur vollständig unerhört sei, ist denach definitiv ad acta zu legen.' An example of *barnasha* for 'man' (generic) in the free Aramaic of the Palestinian Pentateuch Targum, to which Professor T. Jansma of Leiden has drawn my attention, occurs in the Ginsburger fragments at Gen. xlix. 22; for *barnash*, 'anyone', cf. *Bereshith Rabbah*, section 7, Beginning (ed. J. Theodor, Berlin, 1927). On Mk. ii. 28, see further T. W. Manson, *Conjectanea Neotestamentica*, xi (Lund, 1947), and my article on 'The Son of Man in the Teaching of Jesus', *Expository Times*, lx, pp. 34 ff. and *infra* pp. 106 ff. and Appendix E, p. 310 f.

occurs several times in the new Targum fragments; thus in D, Gen. xliv. 18, it is found twice fully vocalized as רַבּוֹנִי; in other instances the vocalization of the word is not complete (D, Gen. xliv. 5; A, Exod. xxi. 4, 5, 8). Dalman gives two instances of the word, the first רִבּוֹנִי, so vocalized, Onkelos Gen. xxxiii. 11, the second רִבּוֹנַנָא, Onkelos Gen. xxiii. 6, both in the sense, which the word has in all the Palestinian Pentateuch Targum occurrences, of a human lord.[1] In Jewish literature generally the word is usually reserved for the Divine Lord.[2] Its use in the Palestinian Pentateuch Targum shows that it cannot have been uncommon in earlier Palestinian Aramaic for a human lord. The pronunciation of the noun in Onkelos contrasts with the correct Palestinian pronunciation of the new Targum, agreeing with the Gospel transcription.

The Pseudo-Jonathan Targum, the Fragment Targum, and the Targum to the Hagiographa have been generally regarded as much later productions than Onkelos, and their language consequently of less importance for the Aramaic of an earlier period; Dalman did not ignore them altogether, but did not rate their evidence very highly. It is of much greater value than he thought: the basis of the so-called Jerusalem Targums is in fact Onkelos, but into them has been gathered some of the earlier halachic material of the Palestinian Pentateuch Targum.[3] This Aramaic, when Onkelos has been subtracted, is evidence for the same kind of Palestinian Aramaic as is contained in the fragments of the Palestinian Targum from the Genizah.

The Targum to the Hagiographa never achieved any position of influence or authority in the Synagogue; its redaction has consequently been less rigorous than in the case of Onkelos, and its Aramaic is thus more idiomatic as its rendering of the Hebrew is freer and more paraphrastic. It is also an ancient Aramaic composition. It has long been known that in the Book of Proverbs there existed an almost literal identity, of language as well as of text, between the Jewish Targum and the Peshiṭta.

[1] *Worte Jesu*, p. 266; cf. *Jesus-Jeschua*, p. 12.
[2] *Worte Jesu*, p. 267.
[3] Cf. *Masoreten des Westens*, ii. p. 9* and *infra*, p. 41 f.

The explanation of this usually offered is that given by Strack: 'Der Targum zu den Sprüchen ist eine jüdische Bearbeitung des Peschittha-Textes;'[1] such a view is as unconvincing as the circumstances implied, the indebtedness of the Synagogue to the Christian Church for its Targum is without parallel in the history of the relations of Judaism and Christianity. No conclusion as to the relation of the two texts can be possible without an investigation and comparison of them, but it may be that the exact opposite took place: the Syrian Church took over its version of Proverbs from the Jewish Synagogue, as it did in the case of the Pentateuch.[2] In that event, the origins of the Targum to the Hagiographa must be earlier than the Peshitta.

The Aramaic portions of the Palestinian Talmud and Midrashim, written in the dialect of Galilee, represent one of our most valuable sources for the language of Jesus. It is true that it belongs to a period fourth to sixth century, and that between then and the first century changes were bound to have taken place in the spoken and written language, but they can hardly have been far-reaching. The Aramaic of the Palestinian Talmud is especially valuable for the language of Jesus, not only because of its identity with the Galilean dialect spoken by Him, but, perhaps even more important, because it is not a translation Aramaic but original Aramaic composition and written in the simple, unliterary style of the popular anecdote. A number of these Aramaic anecdotes have been published by Dalman,[3] but a great many more remain unexamined from this point of view in the vast text of the Talmud.[4]

The two remaining sources of knowledge for the Aramaic of Palestine are the literature of Aramaic-speaking Christians in Palestine and that of the Samaritans. It has already been seen

[1] *Einleitung in das alte Testament* (Munich, 1898), p. 187.

[2] Dr. Jeremias has kindly drawn my attention to an article by R. Abramowsky, 'Eine spät-syrische Übersetzung des Buches Ruth' (*Abh. der Herder-Gesellschaft und des Herder-Instituts zu Riga*, vi. 3 (1938), pp. 7 ff.), where it is claimed that, so far as Ruth is concerned, Peshiṭta and Targum are quite independent of each other.

[3] In his *Aramäische Dialektproben*.

[4] I have had available the edition of Krotoschin, 1866.

that both these sources possess a greater value than Dalman believed. The remains of Palestinian Syriac are nearly all translations from the Greek, and for that reason their language, like that of all translation literature, must be used with caution and checked wherever possible with other sources. The Palestinian Syriac version of the Scriptures probably dates, in its origins, to a period before the fifth century, and may be even earlier. Friedrich Schulthess is responsible for a grammar and a lexicon of the language.[1]

A literary connexion with Judaism has recently been claimed for the Palestinian Syriac, and, if this could be established, would bring back its origin to a still earlier date. The view is that of Dr. Anton Baumstark, editor of the *Oriens Christianus*, who holds that the Palestinian Syriac version of the Pentateuch was not, as is generally assumed, an Aramaic version made *de novo* from the LXX, but that its ultimate basis, in text and language, was a Jewish Palestinian Pentateuch Targum, of the type of the Genizah Targum, which the early Church in Palestine took over from the Synagogue, and which has been progressively edited to conform with the LXX.[2] The evidence for this view consists of a number of singular readings in the Palestinian Syriac Pentateuch which agree with the Jewish Targum only, and which certainly must derive ultimately from that source. There is, however, an alternative and much more probable explanation of this 'Targumic' element in the Palestinian Syriac Pentateuch: it may have come from the Targum by way of the Peshitta, where the direct influence of the Targum is unmistakable, and which has, in turn, deeply influenced the Palestinian Syriac version. The fact that the 'variants' noted by Baumstark as common to the Palestinian Syriac Pentateuch and the Targum do not occur in our Peshiṭta does not mean that they were absent from the form of the Syriac Old Testa-

[1] *Grammatik des christlich-palästinischen Aramäisch* (Tübingen, 1924) and *Lexicon Syropalaestinum* (Berlin, 1903). For the origins of the Malkite Church which used the Palestinian Syriac version, see Burkitt, 'Christian Palestinian Literature', *J.T.S.* ii, p. 174 f.

[2] 'Das Problem des christlich-palästinensischen Pentateuchtextes', *Oriens Christianus*, IIIte Serie, x, pp. 201–24.

ment used by the Palestinian Syriac translators or influencing their version. What we most probably have in such 'Targum' readings is that *rara avis* a pre-Rabbulan Peshiṭta variant.[1] Whichever view is taken of the source of this element in the Palestinian Syriac Pentateuch, it does not diminish our respect for its antiquity.

Except for the Samaritan Pentateuch Targum, the literature of the Samaritans is not earlier than the fifth century A.D. But its value as a source of knowledge of Palestinian Aramaic is considerable. Like the Aramaic portions of the Talmud of Palestine it is original Aramaic composition, and not a translation literature; but unlike the popular Aramaic stories in the Talmud, it is a literary Aramaic, containing poetry as well as prose. Schulthess regarded the language of the Samaritan Pentateuch Targum as a primary source for the language of Jesus; even more valuable are these literary works contained in the so-called Samaritan Liturgies.[2] The chief obstacle to the use of Samaritan Aramaic as a source lies in the present backward state of Samaritan studies together with the extreme difficulty of the texts. No lexicon of the language has so far been compiled; all that we possess for the Liturgy is the very slight glossary of Cowley at the end of his edition; the small grammar of Petermann is no longer adequate. The translation of the Liturgy done by Heidenheim is very inaccurate and will require to be done over again.[3] A number of poems were published by Gesenius,[4] and various studies have appeared, of which one of the most valuable is a translation of twelve hymns of the Samaritan poet Marqa (fourth century A.D.).[5] Otherwise, the

[1] See further 'A Christian Palestinian Syriac Horologion', in *Studia Semitica et Orientalia*, ii (Glasgow, 1945), p. 336 and *infra*, p. 297.

[2] A. E. Cowley, *Samaritan Liturgy* (Oxford, 1909).

[3] M. Heidenheim, *Die Samaritanische Liturgie* (Bibliotheca Samaritana, Leipzig, 1885).

[4] W. Gesenius, *Carmina Samaritana* (Leipzig, 1824).

[5] P. Kahle, 'Die zwölf Marqa-Hymnen aus dem "Defter" ', *Oriens Christianus*, IIIte Serie, vii, pp. 77–106. Other recent Samaritan studies are D. Rettig, *Memar Marqa* (Bonn Oriental Studies, viii, 1934), L. Goldberg, *Das samaritanische Pentateuchtargum* (Bonn Oriental Studies, xi, 1935), John Macdonald, *The Theology of the Samaritans* (S.C.M., London, 1964).

study of Samaritan is as good as a virgin field, the cultivation of which would greatly enrich our knowledge of Palestinian Aramaic.

From this brief survey of the kind of material at the disposal of the scholar for the investigation of the Aramaic of Jesus and the Gospels, it will be seen that perhaps the greater part of the preliminary work in extending our knowledge of the Aramaic dialects of Palestine has still to be done; and it might appear that the task of determining the Aramaic word or construction used by Jesus or in the source of the Gospel writers might be at once too complicated, and any result too precarious in its foundations to have scientific value. To such difficulties on the Aramaic side are to be added the obstacles in the Greek Gospels themselves, for the Gospel writers did not only translate Aramaic, they also wrote Greek.

The outlook is, however, not so unpromising as it may appear on a first impression. It is not necessary to be acquainted with the minutiae of the Palestinian dialects of Aramaic to be in a position to recognize a Semitism or Aramaism or to decide on the possible Aramaic words or construction used by Jesus; and there is sufficient evidence of translation Greek in the Gospels which our present knowledge of Aramaic is well able to confirm and illustrate. Provided the actual difficulties are not minimized and precautions taken against the rash use of doubtful sources, the task is not unrewarding, if the results are unspectacular.

The Textual Approach

It has not seemed necessary to the majority of Aramaic scholars of the New Testament to extend their investigations beyond the 'neutral' or 'true' text of Westcott and Hort to include the variants of the Bezan Codex. The reason for this neglect is to be sought in the general assumptions of the textual criticism of the Greek New Testament which have held the field, especially in English scholarship, since the work of Westcott and Hort. The most faithful representative of the original Apostolic text is to be found in the 'neutral' text of WH's theory, a text based on the combined authority of the two great fourth-century Uncials, Codex Vaticanus and Codex Sinaiticus.

The text of the Bezan authority, Codex Cantabrigiensis, the chief representative of the so-called 'Western' family or group of families, was regarded as a type of text lying for the most part outside the main stream of the 'true' textual tradition; in general, in spite of the early attestation of some of its remarkable variants by second-century Fathers and by its chief allies, the Old Latin and Syriac versions, it was a later, free and paraphrastic text, which had suffered so much from ignorant ill-usage that little confidence could be placed in it. In view of such a textual theory, it seemed gratuitous to look for Aramaisms in any text other than that of WH.

But Biblical Criticism has come to revise its estimate of both Western and non-Western texts of the Gospels in the light of fresh discoveries. The question whether the texts of the Vatican and Sinaitic Codices can still be regarded as the two best single representatives of the primitive Apostolic text may still be open, but they can no longer claim to be the sole representatives of the primitive Greek text of the Gospels. The identification of the so-called 'Caesarean' text, combining features of the Bא text and of the families called 'Western', and the discovery of such a text in the Chester Beatty Papyri from Egypt, in a manuscript which can be assigned to the third century, have led to certain important modifications in textual theory. In the General Introduction to his edition of these papyri their editor, Sir Frederic Kenyon, writes (the italics are mine):

> 'It (this new type of text from a MS. of the third century) points perhaps decisively, to the conclusion that *the Vatican MS. does not represent a text of original purity dominant in Egypt throughout the second and third centuries . . . and that the Vatican text represents the result, not of continuous unaltered tradition, but of skilled scholarship, working on the best available authorities.* It may still be, in result, the best single representative of the original text; that problem remains open as before: but the claim made for it of an almost exclusive predominance and primitive purity is shaken.'[1]

[1] *The Chester Beatty Papyri* (London, 1933), p. 16.

On the Bezan text Kenyon writes:

'Some of these [variant readings in D] may well be superior to some which eventually found a place in the Vatican recension; . . . all readings which can be shown to be of an early date must be considered on their merits, without being absolutely overborne by the weight of the Vatican MS.'[1]

Westcott and Hort's views of the primitive Greek text of the Gospels did not exercise so great an influence on continental scholarship as they did on that of England and America. This recent statement of Kenyon's confirms the critical judgement of scholars such as, most notably, Julius Wellhausen. Unlike Westcott and Hort, who stood at the one extreme in their valuation of D and Lagarde at the other (the latter would have made Codex Bezae the basis of a critical edition of the Gospels and Acts),[2] Wellhausen recognized the claims of both texts, Bא and D, to be representative of the primitive text, wherever either had preserved unrevised and uncorrected the textual tradition of the earliest period.[3] Each text was the result of an independent recension or of different recensions of earlier texts: each could therefore supplement the other; D's text had frequently escaped revision where the text of Bא had not, and vice versa. But the claims of the Bezan text to represent, and not infrequently, the primitive Apostolic text, in its purity, or more correctly in its impurity, were in every way as respectable as those of Bא.

Next to the Chester Beatty discoveries, the work of A. C. Clark has done most to establish the claims of Codex Bezae to represent the primitive text. Attempts had been made by various scholars to account for the longer and more circumstantial text of D as a deliberate expansion of the 'true' text, and to study the methods of the 'paraphrast'.[4] An entirely

[1] *The Chester Beatty Papyri* (London, 1933), p. 16.

[2] '. . . facile patet . . . totius editionis meae quasi fundamentum futurum esse hunc codicem Cantabrigiensem.' (*Gesammelte Abhandlungen*, p. 98, quoted in Nestle, *Textual Criticism of the Greek Testament* (London, 1901), p. 224.)

[3] *Einl.*[1], p. 9.

[4] Cf. J. H. Ropes, *Beginnings of Christianity*, Part I, iii, p. ccxxi.

opposite estimate of the longer text of D has been proposed by Clark, who found in the Bezan Uncial, not only a text which is the better representative on the whole of the primitive text of both Gospels and Acts, but a fuller and more circumstantial text of which the Vatican recension represents a shorter edition and a deliberate scholarly abridgement.[1]

Clark's thesis has been more successfully maintained for the Bezan text of Acts than for the Gospels, and it is perhaps significant that, in a recent consideration of it, Sir Frederic Kenyon, so far as the evidence for Acts is concerned, does not seem to be prepared to give any clear or final verdict: it is when the evidence for the Gospels is considered that the balance is felt to tilt against D in favour of the Vatican authority, and that Clark's view of the relations of the two texts is held to be untenable.[2]

It is in this latter connexion that the textual results of Wensinck's study of the Aramaisms in Western and non-Western texts of Luke are important. The Bezan Codex 'represents the Aramaic background of the Gospel tradition as utilized by St. Luke more faithfully than the non-Western manuscripts do. . . . D and the non-Western group represent two different stages of the influence of Aramaic tradition in the transmission of the Lucan writings. D seems, from this point of view, to have a claim for precedence.'[3] The results of Wensinck's inquiry for Luke's Gospel appear to run parallel to Blass's two-edition theory for Acts: Luke's first primitive 'Aramaized' text, found predominantly in D, was later corrected by him and issued in a form such as we find in non-Western tradition. Whether this theory of two drafts of the Gospel made by Luke himself is the true explanation of the phenomena, the fact that D stands nearer the underlying Aramaic tradition is of the greatest importance; in Luke it is the more primitive type of text.

[1] *The Primitive Text of the Gospels* (Oxford, 1914) and *The Acts of the Apostles* (Oxford, 1933).

[2] 'The Western Text in the Gospels and Acts', in the *Proceedings of the British Academy*, vol. xxiv.

[3] *Semitisms*, p. 47.

In view therefore of the orientation which the Chester Beatty Papyri have obliged in textual theory, and the importance of Clark's hypothesis, together with Wensinck's investigations in Luke, it is no longer possible to approach the study of the Gospels and Acts, from whatever point of view, on the assumptions of the Westcott and Hort hypothesis, with its almost total rejection of the evidence of D.[1]

Yet this is what has been done, not only in recent as in former work on the Aramaic of the Gospels (Blass, Wellhausen, and Nestle excepted), but in the field of New Testament Criticism generally: the critical apparatus to St. Matthew's Gospel, prepared by S. C. E. Legg (for the Committee for the new Oxford edition of the Greek New Testament), still assumes the undisputed primacy of the Bℵ text.[2] In the Aramaic approach, the textual problem is not even considered by Burney or Torrey, if reference is occasionally made to the 'Western' text. The basic text quoted by Dalman is that of Bℵ, and that of D is cited usually in brackets as a secondary authority.

This still prevailing view in textual scholarship not only explains the neglect of Codex Bezae in the Aramaic approach to the Gospels, but it can also account for the failure to recognize what has for long been known to be a special feature of the text of D, namely, its Semitisms, as in any way relevant to the problem of Aramaic sources behind the Gospels or Acts. Many of these Semitisms of D have been attributed to Aramaic influence, only they are described as 'Syriacisms', the result of the reaction of the Syriac allies of D on the Greek text; D is a 'syriacized' Greek text.

The hypothesis of Syriac influence on Codex Bezae was worked out in detail by F. H. Chase, who, assuming the Westcott and Hort view of D, regarded it as a 'syriacized' descendant

[1] Wilcox, pp. 12 ff., adopts the same textual approach to the problems of the Semitisms in Acts.

[2] The statement that the new critical apparatus to the new Clarendon Press New Testament 'still assumes the undisputed primacy of the Bℵ text' requires to be modified. Professor Kilpatrick points out that the choice of the WH text was a matter of convenience; it was the intention of the Committee to leave the standing of the text entirely open.

of the 'true' text: it was a type of Greek text current in a Syrian or Syro-Greek environment, such as Syrian Antioch, which had been assimilated in language and idiom as well as in text to an Old Syriac Gospel.[1]

Within the evidence which he adduces for his theory, Chase makes no distinction between textual affinity and linguistic influence. In the case of the former, there is no need to assume 'assimilation' to a Syriac version or Gospel to account for common variants in D and the Old Syriac; such variants prove nothing more than the employment by the Syriac translator of a 'Western' type of Greek text similar to that used by the Old Latin. But neither does evidence of a Syriac idiom or construction in D necessarily mean that its source was a Syriac version or Gospel, even where the same construction or idiom is found in the corresponding place in the version. The Syriacism may be centuries earlier; it may in fact come from the pen of the Evangelist himself. The fact that it is not found in non-Western manuscripts need not imply that the more respectable Greek, where the Syriacism is not present, was the work of the Evangelist; on the contrary, the Evangelist may himself have been guilty of the solecism, and the Syriac construction have been removed by later editors in the interests of a more polished Greek.

Moreover—and this is the crux of the matter—many of the alleged 'Syriacisms' in D may not have been the result of Syriac influence at all. They may be Aramaisms and come from the Aramaic sources and background of the Gospels. Syriac and West Aramaic can be clearly distinguished as different dialects of Aramaic, but they have also so much in common (the language is, after all, Aramaic) that what may be explained in Greek texts, where dialectical distinctions of Aramaic cannot always be detected, as a Syriacism may in fact prove to be an Aramaism.

If the text of Codex Bezae has equal claims with WH to be investigated for Aramaisms, without any presuppositions being

[1] *The Syro-Latin Text of the Gospels* (London, 1895) and *The Old Syriac Element in the Text of Codex Bezae* (London, 1893).

entertained about the best single manuscript source for the earliest text, its Aramaisms must likewise be first approached impartially and without any prejudice as to their source, whether Syriac or Jewish Palestinian.

If it is not always possible to distinguish the source of an Aramaism, Syriac or Jewish, it is even more difficult at times to decide the source of a Semitism, which may be explained as either a Hebraism or an Aramaism; Wensinck, for instance, has recently challenged what has been hitherto regarded as one of the best established cases of Hebraism, Luke's *καὶ ἐγένετο*, claiming that it may also be Aramaic.[1] Obviously it is impossible to exclude the evidence of such Semitisms in an Aramaic approach to the Gospels: their source in the majority of ambiguous cases will be Aramaic rather than Hebrew, if the preponderating Semitic influence in the Gospels is found to be Aramaic. The only Semitisms, therefore, which are excluded from consideration in this study are those which have been shown to be genuine and characteristic Hebraisms.

[1] *Semitisms*, p. 38. Wensinck noted that the 'Hebraism' is found in the free Aramaic of the Palestinian Pentateuch Targum at Gen. iv. 16 (G, F), xv. 11 (F), Lev. i. 1 (F): cf. *infra* Appendix C, p. 299. It seems more likely, however, that this is a 'Hebraism' in Aramaic rather than a genuine Aramaic idiom. Cf. Gen. xxix. 10, xxx. 25 in all Targums, following the Hebrew, and Nöldeke, *Syriac Grammar*, § 338 C.

CHAPTER III

RECENT DISCOVERIES AND DEVELOPMENTS IN PALESTINIAN ARAMAIC

SINCE the conclusions were reached which are set out in the foregoing chapters, there have been a number of new Aramaic discoveries, most notably at Qumrân, which are of great importance for the study of first-century Palestinian Aramaic. There have also been some significant developments in the study of the history of the Targums, which bear directly on the problem of first-century Aramaic. And this problem too has been further discussed in other connexions by several scholars.

Apart from the immensely important new finds at Qumrân and the publication of other Aramaic texts, none of this new material necessitates any far-reaching modification in the views presented in Chapter II. The Qumrân Aramaic texts are naturally first-class evidence for the language of Jesus, since they are certainly mostly pre-Christian documents and possess a literary and linguistic value not less than that of the old *Reichsaramäisch*, with which they have their closest affinities.[1] Any new discoveries or developments in the *Überlieferungsgeschichte* of the Targums require at the most some modification or supplementation of the conclusions of Chapter II. These modifications however, are so slight that I have left this chapter as it stands, supplementing it only by this new chapter on the subject of the linguistic approach.

The New Discoveries

The most significant new discovery in recent years in the field of Palestinian Aramaic is Codex Neofiti I to which attention was first drawn by Professor Alejandros Díez Macho of

[1] See further *infra*, pp. 39 ff.

Barcelona in *Estudios Bíblicos*, xv (1956), pp. 446–7.[1] Dr. Díez Macho wrote:

'I am happy to be able to say that a copy of the Jerusalem or Palestinian Targum of the whole Pentateuch has been identified. This Targum used to be called the Fragment Targum, for until now we only knew it in fragment form as contained in Cod. 110 of the National Library in Paris (published Ginsburger, Berlin, 1899), cod. 440 of the Vatican collection, or in some other manuscripts, as well as the fragments represented in the Rabbinical Bibles. Some new fragments have been published by Paul Kahle in his '*Masoreten des Westens*' and by myself in *Sefarad*, xv (1955). Another two fragments of the Palestinian Ṭargum which I came upon in New York will appear in the memorial publication in honour of Renée Bloch. The fragments published by Kahle and those published by myself seem to have their source in the 'Geniza' of Cairo. Such fragments of the 'Geniza' are valuable because their language is largely free of the distortion of the Targumic or Eastern (Oriental) Aramaic such as is found in all the MSS. of Aramaic from Palestine which were copied by European scribes, themselves ignorant of Aramaic. Unfortunately such old fragments of the Palestinian Targum from Eastern sources are very scarce. And yet the fragments of such a Targum gathered together in European MSS. preserve to some slight extent the said Aramaic paraphrase.

From this it will be seen how important it is that this summer I successfully identified in the Targumic School at Barcelona a complete copy of the Palestinian Targum of the Pentateuch. Thanks to the good offices of Father Juan Arias we have managed to obtain from the Vatican library a microfilm of 'Cod. Neofiti I'. It was enlarged and handed over to my collaborator and colleague J. G. Larraya for study; he was able immediately to identify it as an excellent copy of the whole Jerusalem Targum. This splendid MS. contains 450 folios. From now on we shall not be able to speak of the Fragment Targum. Sr. Larraya has sent a brief description of the MS. to Paris to be published for the memorial to Renée Bloch. Just now I only wish to stress the importance of the entire discovery and that the text of 'Cod. Neof. I' represents a critical examination and revision of the Palestinian Targum, distinct from that of MS. 110 of Paris and akin to that of MS. 1440 of the Vatican. The marginal comments of the new MS. show a large number of variant

[1] See further M. Black, 'The Recovery of the Language of Jesus' in *N.T.S.* iii, pp. 305 ff.

readings many of them in rabbinical script, some of them coinciding with those on the texts of MS. 110 of Paris or 440 of the Vatican but others are not to be found in these sources. A quick glance at the Aramaic of 'Cod. Neof. I' has shown us that in quite a few cases it is more purely Palestinian than the Aramaic of MS. 110 of Paris, although its purity of Palestinian [form] is not so complete as in the MS. Bereshith Rabba Vat. 30.

The identification of the complete Palestinian Targum signifies an important step in our knowledge of the vocabulary and grammar of Palestinian Aramaic, Galilean Aramaic, the language spoken by our Lord.'

I have been in correspondence with Dr. Díez Macho and have also been able to obtain a microfilm of this important codex.[1]

Díez Macho wrote to me on 18 March 1957:

'As for the MS. Neofiti I, I think, too, that it is an important MS. for the knowledge of Palestinian Aramaic. It contains the complete text of the Palestinian Targum with a critical apparatus of continuous variant readings written on the margins. The 450 folios are in excellent state of preservation and not a single verse is missing. Only the marginal notes in some pages are difficult to read (they are not only in cursive script but also written with poor ink). I am dealing now with the facsimile edition of this MS. In the next issue of *Sefarad* will appear a short note, similar to that which has already appeared in *Estudios Bíblicos*, and a facsimile of one page. Another facsimile probably will appear in *Estudios Bíblicos*, next issue. The Aramaic of Neofiti I is of the same kind as that of the Palestinian Targum of *Masoreten des Westens*, ii. But the recensions do not entirely agree. The MS. has been copied in Rome, probably in the fifteenth century, by an Italian Jew.'

An examination of two sample passages, Gen. xiii. 16–xv. 1 and Exod. xxxiii. 3–xxxiv. 6 (four double columns), shows clearly that we have to do with a Targum differing widely from Onkelos, agreeing in a number of readings with the Pseudo-Jonathan Targum and with the Fragment Targum where extant for these verses and against the Onkelos text. For instance, the King of *Bela* (מלך בלע) at Gen. xiv. 2 is rendered 'the king of the city

[1] Through the good offices of the late Professor Paul Kahle formerly of Bonn; Dr. Díez Macho was a pupil of Dr. Kahle.

which swallowed up (בלע) its inhabitants' as in P–J *contra* Onkelos.

Even more instructive are the passages Gen. iv. 4–16, xxxviii. 13–28, Exod. xxi. 1–8, 18–xxii. 26, since here the Geniza Targum is, for the most part, extant. If there ever could have been any doubt, it is now finally dispelled: agreement with the Geniza Targum against Onkelos is now substantial and, in some verses, 100 per cent.; I have counted an average of two to three variant readings per verse.

In sending me these specimens for examination Dr. Kahle wrote (on 20 March 1957):

'Ich habe mir das wesentliche von Gen. 4, 38, und Ex. 21, 22 abgeschrieben.... Es ist tatsächlich so, dass wir hier im wesentlichen ein vollständiges palästinisches Targum vor uns haben, das abgesehen von dem sachlichen Interesse, das natürlich sehr gross ist, für die aramäische Sprache Palästinas von ganz grosser Bedeutung ist. Es bestätigt sich, dass das palästinische Targum in verschiedener Form im Umlauf gewesen ist, wie das ja auch bei dem samaritanischen Targum der Fall ist. Sehr interessant aber ist, dass Exod. 22, 4 und 5 sehr gut zu dem von mir veröffentlichten Texten stimmt. Natürlich sind im einzeln diese Verschiedenheiten vorhanden und der Text in Gen. 28 ist hier viel ausführlicher als in den beiden von mir veröffentlichten Fassungen. Aber die Verwandtschaft ist ganz deutlich.'

Dr. Kahle was able to add: 'Die Handschrift hat den Titel: Jerusalemer Pentateuch Targum (תרג חומש ירושלמי), und ist im wesentlichen gut geschrieben. Die zahlreichen Randnotizen . . . lassen sich gut lesen.'

An illustration of the character and antiquity of this new Targum occurs in the *halakha* of Exod. xxii. 5, 6.[1] According to the Mishnah these two verses refer to the damage done to a neighbour's field, (*a*) by a straying ox (damage to field or vineyard, verse 4), and (*b*) by fire spreading to a neighbour's field, &c. The Hebrew of verse 4, however, is ambiguous, and can be taken to mean that fire (not a beast) had strayed or spread into a neighbour's field. This is how the Geniza Targum

[1] Cf. Kahle, *The Cairo Geniza*[1], pp. 122 ff.

understood the words, and thus both verses refer to damage wrought by fire. The Neofiti MS. agrees with the Geniza Targum, and, if anything, is even more explicit.[1]

On this *halakha* Dr. Kahle writes (ibid.): '. . . this interpretation is in clear contrast to all the official Jewish authorities and can be understood in an old Jewish text only on the assumption that it goes back to very ancient times, before the oral law codified in the Mishnah had any validity. That such a translation is preserved in an old scroll of the Palestinian Targum is certainly of importance. It shows that written Targums must have existed in very ancient times.'

All interested in this important discovery look forward to the publication of Professor Díez Macho's edition, the publication of which, it is hoped, will not be much longer delayed;[2] and he is to be congratulated on a first-class discovery, second only to the Qumrân Aramaic scrolls, to a consideration of which I now turn.

In comparison with the extensive Hebrew discoveries, only a small number of Aramaic texts have so far come to light at Qumrân. They consist, for the most part, of small fragments, miscellaneous 'bits and pieces', sometimes containing no more than one word or even just a single letter,[3] and only occasionally extending to several lines of text, as, for instance, in the fragments from 'apocryphal works' (from the Book of Enoch, or the Testaments of the Twelve Patriarchs).[4] Where, in one case, a longer text has existed, it has been preserved in so dilapidated a condition as to be at times barely legible.[5] In view of this

[1] The Geniza Targum renders יבער by יבקר, a word normally used in the Targums in the sense 'to search out', and in this connexion 'to let (a field) lie fallow'; to render 'burn over' is to give the word the meaning of the Hebrew original. In Neofiti, on the other hand, Heb. יבער is rendered by יוקד ('If a man *sets* a field or orchard *alight* . . .').

[2] For a recent discussion, see R. L. Déaut, 'La Nuit pascale', *Analecta Biblica*, 22 (Rome, 1963), pp. 32 ff. A sample of the projected edition has now appeared: *Biblia Polyglotta Matritensia*, Series iv, *Targum Palaestinense in Pentateuchum* (Deuteronomium Caput I), Matriti, MDCCCCLXV.

[3] See Barthélemy, Milik, & others, *Discoveries in the Judaean Desert* I, *Qumran Cave I* (Oxford, 1955), pp. 97, 147.

[4] Ibid., pp. 84, 87.

[5] Cf. M. Baillet, 'Fragments araméens de Qumran 2. Description de la Jérusalem nouvelle', in *Revue Biblique* (April 1955), pp. 222 ff.

situation, the discovery at Qumrân of an entire scroll of twenty-two columns, with approximately thirty-five lines to each column,[1] makes a welcome and significant addition to the Qumrân library, and, in particular, to its sadly decimated Aramaic contents.

The new Aramaic document is a kind of *midrash* on Gen. xii and xiv.[2] The date is not absolutely certain, but, if we accept the general conclusions of the archaeologists, the scroll itself must have been written before A.D. 70. Affinities with the apocrypha and the pseudepigrapha (especially the Book of Jubilees) support this early dating. Before a sufficient number of characteristic Aramaic idioms of a particular period can be adduced to identify the period of the scroll by linguistic criteria, we shall have to await publication of the whole text.[3] The published folios, however, already yield one important philological fact: the scroll makes use of the Aramaic temporal conjunction אדין, בדין (e.g., col. xxii, lines 2, 18, 20), found no less than twenty-six times in Daniel alone, but *never* in Targumic Aramaic. In several other cases we meet with non-Targumic usage, e.g., חלתא (col. xxii, line 4) in the sense of a 'valley'; Targ. חללא means a 'cavern'; Syriac ܚܠܬܐ, the 'sheath' of a sword. The verb אתחלם (line 5) in the meaning 'grow strong' is attested in Syriac, but not in Targumic Aramaic. Linguistically the scroll would seem, therefore, to belong to the age of the 'old Aramaic'. Both from a linguistic and literary point of view, it is an invaluable witness to the Aramaic language and literature of the time of Christ.

Some parts of the text have a considerable literary merit,

[1] *A Genesis Apocryphon, A Scroll from the Wilderness of Judaea*, Description and Contents of the Scroll, Facsimiles, Transcription and Translation of Columns II, xix–xxii, by Nahman Avigad and Yigael Yadin (Jerusalem, 1956).

[2] Earlier I was inclined to regard the so-called 'Apocryphon' as a 'Targum' ('Recovery of the Language of Jesus', pp. 309 ff., *The Scrolls and Christian Origins*, pp. 193 ff.): in fact, it is much more of the character of a *midrash* than a targum.

[3] The 'apocryphon' has been made the subject of an extensive linguistic study by E. Y. Kutscher of Jerusalem: 'The Language of the Genesis Apocryphon', in *Scripta Hierosolomitana*, iv (Jerusalem, 1957), pp. 1–35.

e.g., the description of Sarah's beauty at col. xx and the Parable of the Palm and the Cedar at col. xix. The second (in Avigad and Yadin's English version) reads:

And I, Abram, dreamed a dream . . .
and lo! I saw in my dream one cedar tree
and one palm
. . . And men came and sought to cut down
and uproot the cedar and to leave the palm
by itself.
And the palm cried out and said, 'Cut not
down the cedar . . .'
And for the sake of the palm the cedar was saved.

(The cedar is Abraham, the palm Sarah, through whose offer of herself Abraham was saved in Egypt.) These are probably the closest literary parallels we possess in Aramaic to the original (poetic) parables and poems of Jesus.

The Aramaic Targums and the Language of Jesus

Since the publication of Kahle's views in *Masoreten des Ostens* and *Masoreten des Westens*, ii, and subsequently in his Schweich lectures, on the history and relationships of the Targums, a new edition of the Aramaic Targums has appeared,[1] and other important studies have been published. Sperber's magnificent work has resulted in an edition of Onkelos and Jonathan which must remain a model of its kind: Sperber did not, however, concern himself with questions of the history and development of the Targum tradition. The same is true of other scholars, like Díez Macho, who edited fragments of the Targum to the Prophets,[2] and in 1956 announced the discovery of the new Targum to the Pentateuch, Codex Neofiti.[3] The question of the *Überlieferungsgeschichte* of the Aramaic Targum has been raised recently by E. Y. Kutscher, and Kahle's view challenged.[4] Kutscher's arguments, however, which will be considered later,

[1] Alexander Sperber, *The Bible in Aramaic*: i. *The Pentateuch according to Targum Onkelos*; ii. *The Former Prophets according to Targum Jonathan*; iii. *The Latter Prophets according to Targum Jonathan* (Brill, Leiden, 1959–62).

[2] See *infra*, p. 45. [3] See *supra*, p. 35. [4] See *infra*, pp. 45 ff.

were anticipated by the work of a younger scholar, Dr. Gerard J. Kuiper, now Associate Professor of New Testament at the Theological Seminary, Johnson C. Smith University, Charlotte, North Carolina. Dr. Kuiper undertook, under my supervision, an investigation into the relationship between the different strands of the Targum tradition, and in particular the question of the relationship of the Pseudo-Jonathan Targum and Targum Onkelos.[1] The results, which it is hoped will be published soon, have proved surprisingly interesting: Onkelos, while admittedly showing traces of Babylonian influence, appears nevertheless to have been an authoritative redaction of the same kind of Palestinian Targum tradition as is preserved, still in its fluid state, in the Fragment Targum, the Geniza Fragments, Pseudo-Jonathan, and Targum Neofiti I.

We need not, therefore, be so sceptical about the value of Dalman's *Aramaic Grammar* as Kahle was: at the same time, it must be admitted with Kahle that the more idiomatic and freer Aramaic of the pre-Onkelos Palestinian Targum tradition, uninfluenced by the Babylonian dialect or the need to translate the Hebrew word by word, is a much better source of knowledge for the Aramaic of the New Testament period.

Work on the problem of the connexions and interrelations of the different strands in the Palestinian Targum tradition is still in progress, and must inevitably be delayed until the (long-awaited) publication of the *editio princeps* of Neofiti I, promised by Professor Díez Macho of Barcelona as part of the great modern Spanish Polyglot project.[2] Nothing so far, however, has led anyone to cast serious doubts on Kahle's view that what we have in the extant Palestinian Targum is a free, developing tradition with very substantial differences between the different manuscripts: indeed, this has, if anything, been confirmed by the text of the Neofiti manuscript, which seems to

[1] Gerard J. Kuiper, *The Pseudo-Jonathan Targum and its Relationship to Targum Onkelos*, Ph.D. thesis, St. Andrews, 1962. Dr. Kuiper spent some time in Oxford, where he had the privilege of consulting Dr. Kahle.

[2] Cf. Kahle, *The Cairo Geniza*², pp. 201 ff. The *Bibliotheca Vaticana* is also proposing to bring out a facsimile edition. (Kahle, ibid.)

represent an entirely different and independent translation from anything we know of in the Geniza fragments or the Fragment Targum. The importance of this work cannot be over-emphasized, since it forms an essential preparation for an edition (or editions) of the Palestinian Targum (or Targums), without which the study of their vocabulary, grammar, syntax, &c., is premature. Professor Kahle himself was convinced of the need for a new edition of his Geniza fragments, and entrusted this task several years ago to his pupil Pater Georg Schelbert.[1] My own pupil, Dr. Malcolm C. Doubles of Lebanon, Virginia, worked, under the joint supervision of myself and Dr. Kahle, on the problem of the Ginsburger edition of the Fragment Targum: that edition did much less than justice to the Vatican manuscript of these fragments, and the full text of this is now available in Doubles's work.[2] There is still an enormous amount of preparatory work to be done, but some rough pattern of relationships appears to be emerging. As Kuiper's work seems to point to Onkelos as an official redaction of one Palestinian tradition, so the close connexion of the Paris, Nürnberg, Leipzig, and Vatican manuscripts of the Fragment Targum seem to point to a likewise official rabbinical redaction undertaken in the Middle Ages, with the purpose of preserving something (in addition to the official Onkelos) from the previous Palestinian Pentateuch Targumic tradition. Neofiti I is still a vast open question, and its marginalia, some of which can be traced in the Fragment Targum, may further enrich our knowledge of the Palestinian Pentateuch Targum.[3]

So far as the language of the Targums was concerned, Kahle was firmly convinced that Dalman was wrong in taking Onkelos and the related Targum to the Prophets as his main authorities for first-century Palestinian Aramaic, the so-called 'Jerusalem'

[1] See *The Cairo Geniza*[2], p. 201.

[2] *The Fragment Targum: A Critical Examination of the Editio Princeps, Das Fragmententhargum, by Moses Ginsburger, in the Light of Recent Discoveries*, Ph.D. thesis, St. Andrews, 1962.

[3] One of my pupils, Miss Shirley Lund of Boston, is at present engaged on a study of the Neofiti text of Deuteronomy.

Targums having been relegated to a secondary position:[1] the latter, together with such close relatives as Samaritan Aramaic and Christian Palestinian Syriac, seemed to Kahle to be much closer to the original language of Jesus and the best post-Christian sources for the reconstruction of the Aramaic of the *verba Christi*. This he sought to demonstrate by his now well-known discovery that *ribboni* (my Lord) in Onkelos was pronounced *rabbouni* in the Geniza fragment targum, exactly as at John xx. 16 (cf. Mark x. 51).[2] In view of this, Kahle held that a study of the grammar, syntax, and vocabulary of his Geniza fragments, and indeed of the whole of the Palestinian Targum tradition, so far as it was extant, was the next urgent task in Aramaic studies. This view was shared—and to a large extent reached independently through the study of *Masoreten des Westens*, ii—by the late Professor A. J. Wensinck, who carried his work to the point of preparing, on the basis of existing editions of the Palestinian Pentateuch Targum, a lexicon of these texts to supplement Levy's *Chaldäisches Lexicon* (or the smaller lexica of Jastrow and Dalman).[3]

No one will deny the urgency or the need for grammatical and lexicographical studies in those particular areas if we are to extend our knowledge of the Aramaic language, and particularly of the language as it was spoken and written in the New Testament period. The situation, however, has changed in some important respects since the publication of *Masoreten des Westens* (or *The Cairo Geniza*). There are the new Qumrân Aramaic texts to study, for the most part exhibiting a language closer to the old *Reichsaramäisch*, but also in their literary form and character, no less than in language, exhibiting a literature which serves as a much closer prototype of the Aramaic portions and especially the original Aramaic poetry of the Gospels. There is also the inestimably valuable text (450 folios) of Neofiti, which will also have to be scrutinized by the philologist, once

[1] *Aramäische Grammatik*[2] (Leipzig, 1905; reprinted, Darmstadt, 1964), pp. 30 ff., *supra*, pp. 18 ff.

[2] See *The Cairo Geniza*[2], p. 204, and *supra*, pp. 23 ff.

[3] This material was very kindly lent by Mrs. Wensinck to Professor Kahle and myself for a period (see *infra*, p. 296, n. 2).

an edition is available. In fact, it is this last difficulty, applying to all the Palestinian Pentateuch Targums, which makes grammatical investigation or lexicographical studies at present difficult, if not impossible. Our first and most urgent needs are for editions of the Palestinian Pentateuch Targum (or Targums) similar to Dr. Sperber's splendid edition of Onkelos and Jonathan, which must also, however, not be overlooked in any full study of early Palestinian Aramaic.

It was characteristic of Kahle that he lost no opportunity of presenting positions with which he had once identified himself in the light of the latest developments in his field. Thus, just shortly before the second edition of his *Cairo Geniza* was published he wrote a long article in *Z.N.T.W.* entitled 'Das palästinische Pentateuchtargum und das zur Zeit Jesu gesprochene Aramäisch'[1] in which he took cognizance of the new Qumrân discoveries, in particular of the so-called Genesis Apocryphon (or Genesis Midrash, as he himself preferred to describe it). The article (which forms most of Chapter III of *The Cairo Geniza*[2]) brought *inter alia* an up-to-date report on work on the Targums and the scrolls by W. H. Brownlee,[2] Naftali Wieder,[3] Díez Macho,[4] &c. In the course of the article Dr. Kahle had occasion to criticize some of the methods of Professor E. Y. Kutscher of Jerusalem in his dating and localizing of the Genesis Midrash, and this criticism drew a lively rejoinder from Dr. Kutscher in which he not only replied to the points of Kahle's criticism but called in question Kahle's general position on the relation of the Palestinian Pentateuch Targum to Targum Onkelos, and on its value linguistically as a primary source for the language of Jesus.[5] Kutscher's reply called forth in turn an equally lively riposte from Kahle.[6]

1 *Z.N.T.W.*, Band 49, Heft 1/2 (1958), pp. 115 ff.

2 'The Dead Sea Habakkuk Midrash and the Targum of Jonathan', Duke University, 1953. Cf. *Journal of Jewish Studies*, viii, pp. 169–86.

3 'The Habakkuk Scroll and the Targum', *J.J.St.*, iv (1953), pp. 14–18.

4 'Un nuevo Targum a los Profitas', *Estudios Bíblicos*, xv (1956). Cf. also *Sefarad*, xvi (1956). Cf. also G. Vermes, *Scripture and Tradition in Judaism: Haggadic Studies* (Leiden, 1961).

5 'Das zur Zeit Jesu gesprochene Aramäisch', in *Z.N.T.W.*, Band 51, Heft 1/2 (1960), pp. 46–54.

6 Op. cit., p. 55.

The controversy centred mainly on the exception Kahle had taken to Kutscher's methods of determining the date of the Genesis midrash: he accepted Kutscher's conclusions that this text, composed in a literary Aramaic (of the type we find in Daniel, Ezra, &c.), was Palestinian, belonging to the first century B.C. or earlier. Kutscher's attempt to show that the language of the Palestinian Pentateuch Targum was not one of our best representatives of the spoken language of the time of Christ was unconvincing. It is true, the view that Onkelos is a purely Babylonian composition is doubtful,[1] but the fact that it may have had its origin in Palestine does not mean that its language is, therefore, a pure spoken Aramaic of the time of Jesus: it is, in fact, as Kahle held, an artificially literal translation of the Hebrew, composed in its present and final redaction in a form of 'literary' Aramaic which is neither pure Palestinian nor pure Babylonian dialect.

In one point Kutscher challenged Kahle's claim that the Palestinian Pentateuch Targum alone knew the New Testament word *rabboni* (ῥαββουνί, Mark x. 51, John xx. 16).[2] Kutscher is, of course, right in maintaining that the word does appear in rabbinical texts, and this Kahle never sought to deny: it was the pronunciation of the word in the Palestinian Pentateuch Targum as *rabbo(u)ni* in contrast to the rabbinical *ribboni* which was unique and adduced as proof by Kahle that it was this Palestinian Targum tradition which correctly preserved the accents of the living speech and dialect of Palestinian Aramaic. To prove that this was not so, Kutscher adduced one instance from one Mishnah codex where the pronunciation *rabbouni* is preserved, evidently as a 'Verbesserung': but all that this, in fact, proves is that at least one scribe knew of this particular pronunciation and objected to the probably artificial (Babylonian?) pronunciation *ribboni*. The instance from the Mishnah confirms rather than refutes Kahle's argument: it is a reminiscence of how the word was actually pronounced in Palestinian spoken Aramaic.

[1] Cf. *supra*, p. 42, and see especially Kutscher, op. cit., p. 48, n. 11.

[2] Kutscher, op. cit., p. 53.

The problem of the original language (or languages) of Jesus has been reopened more than once in recent years. A. W. Argyle and others have sponsored the claims of the Koine as a 'second language' of Jesus.[1] The Qumrân discoveries have also shed fresh light on the problem: M. Wilcox writes (italics mine): 'With regard to the matter of language, we ought to note that the discovery of the Dead Sea Scrolls has now placed at our disposal information of a highly interesting and relevant nature. . . . The non-Biblical texts show us a *free, living language*, and attest the fact that in New Testament times, and for some considerable time previously, Hebrew was not confined to Rabbinical circles by any means, but appeared *as a normal vehicle of expression.*'[2]

It would seem from this description of Hebrew in the time of Christ as a 'free, living language' and 'a normal vehicle of expression' that Dr. Wilcox intends us to understand that Hebrew was in fact a spoken Palestinian language in New Testament times, and not merely a medium of literary expression only or a learned language confined to rabbinical circles (as well, of course, as being the sacred tongue of the Hebrew Scriptures). If this is a correct estimate of the Qumrân evidence, where Hebrew certainly vastly predominates over Aramaic, then it may be held to confirm the view identified with the name of Professor Segal that Hebrew was actually a spoken vernacular in Judaea in the time of Christ.[3]

This view—or a closely similar one—has been argued in recent years by Professor H. Birkeland of Oslo, who set out, in a learned article,[4] to challenge the usual view that Aramaic was the regular spoken language of first-century Palestine, and, therefore, the language of Jesus; according to Dr. Birkeland, Hebrew not Aramaic was the regular and normal language of the Jews in first-century Palestine, and certainly so, so far as the masses of the Jewish people were concerned; it was only

[2] *The Semitisms of Acts*, p. 14. [3] See *supra*, p. 16.

[4] 'The Language of Jesus', in *Avhandlinger utgitt av Det Norske Videnskaps-Akademi i Oslo*, II. Hist.-filos. Klasse, 1954, No. 1.

the educated upper classes who spoke (or used) Aramaic and only the learned who were familiar with both languages.[1] The Aramaic Targums were intended for the benefit, not of the masses of the people who could understand the Hebrew Scriptures without an Aramaic paraphrase, but for the upper classes who understood Aramaic only.[2]

This extreme position has found little if any support among competent authorities: the evidence of the Aramaic *ipsissima verba* of Jesus in the Gospels is impossible to explain if Aramaic was not his normal spoken language. Moreover, it is absurd to suggest that the Hebrew Scriptures were paraphrased for the benefit of the 'upper classes': these Scriptures were provided with a Targum for the benefit of the Aramaic-speaking masses who could no longer understand Hebrew. The use of the term 'Hebrew' to refer to Aramaic is readily explicable, since it described the peculiar dialect of Aramaic which had grown up in Palestine since the days of Nehemiah and which was distinctively Jewish (with a distinctive Hebrew script associated with it, and a large proportion of borrowings from classical Hebrew). It is these differences to which the letter of Aristeas is referring and not to two different languages, Hebrew and Aramaic (Syriac).[3]

While this extreme position must be rejected, there is nevertheless a case, certainly for a wider *literary* use of Hebrew in New Testament times. This much is certain from the Qumrân discoveries. It is also possible, however (as Professor Segal argues) that Hebrew did continue as a spoken tongue: it seems unlikely, however, that this was outside the circles of the learned or the educated, i.e., in learned Pharisaic, priestly, or Essene

[1] Op. cit., p. 39. [2] Ibid.

[3] Cf. Birkeland, op. cit., p. 14. See also R. H. Charles, *Apocrypha and Pseudepigrapha of the Old Testament*, ii, p. 95. The passage reads: 'They (the Hebrew Scriptures) need to be translated', answered Demetrius, 'for in the country of the Jews they use a peculiar alphabet, and speak a peculiar dialect. They are supposed to use the Syriac tongue, but this is not the case; their language is quite different.' The reference is to the peculiar dialect of Aramaic spoken by the Jews, a dialect of West Aramaic; quite different from Syriac, the dialect of East Aramaic which was in regular use as the standard Aramaic language.

circles. We must nevertheless allow possibly more than has been done before for the use of Hebrew in addition to (or instead of) Aramaic by Jesus Himself, especially on solemn festive occasions; there is a high degree of probability that Jesus began his career as a Galilaean rabbi who would be well versed in the Scriptures, and able to compose (or converse) as freely in Hebrew as in Aramaic.

ADDITIONAL NOTE

Since this chapter was written other important Targumic studies have appeared or been noted, e.g., P. Grelot, *Semitica* ix (1959), pp. 59–88; Díez Macho, 'The Recently Discovered Palestinian Targum: Its Antiquity and Relationship with the other Targums', Supplements to *Vetus Testamentum* vii (1959), pp. 222–45; also articles in *Sefarad* xv (1955), xvii (1957), xx (1960); *Oriens Antiquus* ii (1963), *Nouvelles Chrétiennes d'Israel* xiii, 2 (1962); S. Lund, 'The Neofiti Marginalia to Deuteronomy'.

Miss Lund has conclusively identified one of the sources of the marginalia in Neofiti as belonging to the Fragment Targum, and akin to the Nürnberg and Vatican texts. These results are appearing in the forthcoming Memorial Volume to the late Professor Paul Kahle (as *Beiheft* to *Z.A.W.*, 1967); M. McNamara, 'Targumic Studies', *Catholic Biblical Quarterly* xxviii, 1 (1966); P. Wernberg Møller, on the date of Neofiti I, in *Vetus Testamentum* xii, p. 462.

PART II

SYNTAX, GRAMMAR, AND VOCABULARY

CHAPTER IV

STYLE AND STRUCTURE OF THE SENTENCE

Order of Words

A Semitism to which Wellhausen attached much importance was the position of the verb in the sentence or clause.[1] In all the Semitic languages the verb tends to be set first, except where the order is inverted for emphasis or in certain subordinate clauses. A number of arguments have been advanced to show that the order of words in the Gospels is not noticeably un-Greek,[2] but when all due allowance has been made for them, the predominance of the initial position of the verb remains unusual. The judgement of an eminent Hellenist, E. Norden, is: 'Placing the verb first is, next to parallelism of clauses—the two are very often combined—the surest Semitism of the New Testament, especially in those instances in which this position comes in a series of clauses.'[3] Norden instances the second half of the Magnificat, and compares the distinctive position of the imperatives in the Lord's Prayer with the style of Jewish prayers, as in Isa. xxxvii. 17–20, Sir. xxxvi. 1–17.[4]

A. J. Wensinck claims that the Bezan text of Luke contains a large number of instances of Semitic word-order (not only the initial position of the verb), where non-Western manuscripts have a more idiomatic Greek order.[5] The chief difficulty, however, is to be certain of what is not idiomatic Greek order. The most that Wensinck succeeds in showing is that D has an order that agrees with the Semitic order and differs from that of non-

[1] *Einl.*[2], p. 10 f. See also Wilcox, pp. 112 ff.

[2] Such as those of Lagrange, *S. Marc*, p. lxxxviii, and Thumb, in the section on *Wortstellung* in Brugmann's *Griechische Grammatik*, 4th edit., p. 658 f.

[3] *Agnostos Theos*, pp. 257, 365.

[4] Cf. Moulton, *Gramm.* ii, p. 417.

[5] *Semitisms*, p. 24 f.

Western manuscripts. Thus in Lk. i. 14,[1] WH read καὶ ἔσται χαρά σοι, D καὶ ἔσται σοι χαρά: the first order is un-Semitic and the order of D agrees with the Aramaic order, but there is nothing to suggest that it is not legitimately Greek as well as correct Semitic word-order. The result of Wensinck's observations is negative: the order of words in D is not un-Semitic, as it frequently is in WH, but it is likewise not un-Greek.

It is the proportion in the Gospels as compared with other Greek writings of the initial position of the verb mainly, and not any individual case of word-order, which is unusual and un-Greek: '. . . the predominance of initial position (of the verb) in Luke and John is remarkable.'[2]

No doubt a large number of the instances of the verb in the initial position come from translation Greek sources, but no inference as to translation of Aramaic sources can be made from this Gospel Semitism. The main reason, I would suggest, is, not that we do not have here a genuine and important Semitism, nor that, to prove translation, more evidence of irregular Greek word-order would be required, but the difficulty of determining what order is un-Greek. It is only because the verb comes so frequently first that the Greek style, not the Greek word-order, becomes such that no native Greek writer, uninfluenced by Semitic sources or a Semitic language, would have written it.

Casus Pendens and Hyperbaton

Casus pendens is not specially a Semitism. It is used with effect in classical Greek, and parallels to instances in the Gospels have been cited from the papyri and elsewhere.[3] But the construction is much more frequent in Hebrew or Aramaic than in the Koine. Especially characteristic of Hebrew and Aramaic is the resumption of the subject or object by the personal pronoun; Burney illustrates from Dan. ii. 37, 38, iii. 22, iv. 17–19, Ezra v. 14.[4] A typical example occurs in the Elephantine

[1] *Semitisms*, p. 25.

[2] Moulton, op. cit. ii, p. 418.

[3] Cf. ibid., p. 425.

[4] *Aramaic Origin*, p. 64 f.

Papyri, 28, 15, 'My sons—*they* shall pay thee this money'; for an instance from the Palestinian Talmud we may compare *Kil'aim*, ix. 4, f. 32*b*, line 47.

Burney rests his case for the Aramaic origin of the Johannine *casus pendens* on the over-use of the construction in the Fourth Gospel, as compared especially with the Synoptics.[1] He found 27 instances in the former (another example from a saying of Jesus occurs in x. 25) and 21 in the latter; in Matthew 11, in Mark 4, and in Luke 6. This is certainly a remarkable proportion for John alone (it is not, however, as Burney calculates, six times that of Luke). In a number of John's instances Lagrange believed that there was an emphasis intended which accorded with classical usage, but he recognized the resumptive pronoun after πᾶς as a Semitic locution.[2]

Burney accounted for the frequency of the construction in John as due to translation of an Aramaic original. Lagrange thought that we had to do less with translation Greek than with a Semitic locution which would come naturally to those accustomed to this vigorous Semitic idiom.[2] The distribution of the construction in John is interesting, and may be held to support the translation Greek hypothesis: in 22 cases out of 28 we have to do with examples from the sayings and speeches of Jesus; two of the six exceptions are from the Prologue (i. 12, 18), two from sayings of the Baptist, one in the Prologue (i. 33, iii. 32), one from a conversation of the disciples of John (iii. 26), and the sixth is spoken by the man healed at the pool of Bethesda (v. 11). All examples are from direct speech.

The distribution of the construction is even more significant in the Synoptics and Acts. In the Fourth Gospel the sayings and speeches of Jesus make up the larger part of the book. But in the Synoptics, narrative outweighs dialogue, yet there too the same high proportion of examples of this construction occurs in the Words of Jesus. It is true that a vigorous idiom of this kind is more natural in direct speech than in narrative, but the almost total absence of the idiom outside of direct speech in

[1] *Aramaic Origin*, p. 64 f.

[2] *S. Jean*, p. cxi. For examples in Aramaic, Ezra vii. 24, 26.

the Gospels and Acts cannot be due entirely to this fact. In the following survey of the distribution of *casus pendens* in the Gospels and Acts, examples which are found in Old Testament quotations are not included. Examples from sayings of Jesus are in italics.

Matthew: v. *40* (D); vi. *4* (D); x. *11* (D), xii. *32, 36*; xiii. *20, 22, 23, 38*; xv. *11*; xix. *28*; xxiv. *13*; xxv. *29*; xxvi. *23*.
Mark: i. 34 (D); vi. 16 (Herod); vii. *20*; xiii. *11*.
Luke: i. 36 (direct speech); viii. *14, 15*; xii. *10, 48*; xiii. *4*; xxi. *6*; xxiii. *50–1*.
Acts: ii. 22–23 (Peter); iii. 6 (Peter); iv. 10 (Peter); vii. 35, 40 (Stephen); x. 36, 37 (Peter); xiii. 32 (Paul); xvii. 23, 24 (Paul).

The construction appears most frequently in the Bezan Uncial (all the above examples occur in D). In this respect D has preserved the primitive text more faithfully than Bא; a typical instance is Mt. vi. 4, καὶ ὁ πατήρ σου ὁ βλέπων ἐν τῷ κρυπτῷ, αὐτὸς ἀποδώσει σοι.

An extension of this hyperbaton consists of the displacement of the subject or object of a subordinate clause to become subject or object of another clause, usually the main clause of the sentence, thus giving special emphasis to it. An example from Aramaic occurs in *Midrash Echa*, i. 51, 'I am not going until I see that Menahem how he is faring.'[1] Wellhausen noted the following instances of this hyperbaton in the Gospels: Mt. x. 25; Mk. vii. 2, xi. 32, xii. 34; Lk. ix. 31, xxiv. 7.[2] Mk. vii. 2 reads καὶ ἰδόντες τινὰς τῶν μαθητῶν αὐτοῦ ὅτι κοιναῖς χερσίν ἐσθίουσιν, '... and having seen that some of his disciples ate with defiled hands'; Lk. xxiv. 7 is, λέγων τὸν υἱὸν τοῦ ἀνθρώπου ὅτι δεῖ παραδοθῆναι. Wellhausen gives Lk. iv. 3 (D), εἰπὲ οἱ λίθοι οὗτοι ἵνα γένωνται ἄρτοι, but no such reading appears to exist.

This idiom can account for the difficult and confused construction of Mk. viii. 24, βλέπω τοὺς ἀνθρώπους ὅτι ὡς δένδρα ὁρῶ περιπατοῦντας. The only legitimate rendering of the Greek as

[1] See Dalman, *Aramäische Dialektproben*, p. 15.

[2] *Einl.*², p. 12. Lk. ix. 31 is an important example containing also a mistranslated Aramaic *dᵉ*; it is discussed in this connexion, *infra*, p. 75 f.

it stands is that of the R.V.: 'I see men; for I see them as trees walking'. . . . Codex Bezae, with a number of other authorities, reads *βλέπω τοὺς ἀνθρώπους ὡς δένδρα περιπατοῦντας*, which gives, in a straightforward text, the kind of answer we would expect. But the more difficult text of Bא is probably original, and has led to correction in D. W. C. Allen sought to explain the *ὅτι* as a mistranslated Aramaic *de* which should have been represented by the relative *οὕς*, 'I see men *whom* I see as trees walking', the accusative participle *περιπατοῦντας* having then an accusative relative in its own clause with which to agree.[1] But 'I see men whom I see as trees walking' is still an unusually complicated way of saying, 'I see men like trees walking', which seems clearly what was intended.

This simple statement would be expressed idiomatically in Aramaic, with emphatic hyperbaton, 'I see men that like trees they are walking'.[2] A translator who failed to recognize the idiom appears to have taken the participial present '(are) walking'[3] as a true participle and made it agree with the accusative 'men'—*βλέπω τοὺς ἀνθρώπους ὅτι ὡς δένδρα περιπατοῦντας*. An additional verb in the subordinate clause would be necessary in Greek to make sense.

Mk. vii. 4 contains an example of an emphasizing hyperbaton along with a characteristic Semitic use of the preposition *ἀπό* (= *min*), namely, in a partitive sense:[4] *ἀπ' ἀγορᾶς* means '(anything) from the market-place'; 'And (anything) from the market-place, unless they sprinkle, they do not eat'. The Arabic Diatessaron has so understood the words (xx. 20), 'They used not to eat what is sold from the market, except they washed it.' The Arabic does not, of course, imply any variant text, but the Semitic idiom has been recognized and correctly rendered.[5]

Another possible instance of this partitive construction but with *ἐκ* instead of *ἀπό* is the difficult omission of the article at 1 Cor. ix. 13 *οἱ τὰ ἱερὰ ἐργαζόμενοι [τὰ] ἐκ τοῦ ἱεροῦ ἐσθίουσιν*.

[1] In the *Expository Times*, xiii, p. 330.

[2] In Aramaic, *ḥame 'ana bene 'enasha dehekh 'illanin mehallekhin.*

[3] See *infra*, p. 130.

[4] See *Ges.-Kautzsch*, p. 382, note 2.

[5] Cf. Burkitt, *Evangelion da-Mepharreshe*, ii, p. 281.

The article is omitted by 𝔭[46] A C K pl d 𝕾. Zuntz[1] favours the omission and writes 'In 1 Cor. ix. 13, however, the omission of τά before ἐκ τοῦ ἱεροῦ is correct on internal grounds. Paul does not here refer (like Mk. ii. 26, par.) to the fact that the priests may eat "the things in the temple": he stresses their right to live by their priestly office (ἐσθίειν ἐκ τοῦ ἱεροῦ, parallel with ἐκ τοῦ εὐαγγελίου ζῆν in ver. 14; cf. Heb. xiii. 10). The added article (in ℵ B D * F G 181 1739 vg. Aug. sah. boh.) perverts the meaning. The Byzantine text has not got it. It is infinitely improbable that considerations like those just indicated could have induced the Byzantines to delete the article. Here again their agreement with 𝔭[46] A C (and perhaps some versions) can show how they could inherit a genuine tradition which the Old Uncials missed.' It seems to me doubtful, however, if we can equate ἐσθίειν ἐκ τοῦ ἱεροῦ with ἐκ τοῦ εὐαγγελίου ζῆν: the alternative explanation of a partitive construction seems preferable.

The general conclusion to which the evidence of *casus pendens* and related hyperbata points is that, while such constructions cannot be described as specially Semitic, though in much more frequent use in Aramaic than in Greek, their preponderance in the sayings of Jesus supports the view that a translation Greek tradition is to be found there. No Greek writer would have included in one part only of his work what is, compared with instances in the surrounding narrative, a very high proportion of examples, unless he was reproducing an Aramaic tradition. Outside of the sayings, hyperbata are most frequent in dialogue and direct speech, and in Mark's Gospel. In Acts, *casus pendens* appears to be confined to speeches, and for the most part those of Peter and Stephen in the early chapters.

The Distribution of Asyndeton in the Gospels and Acts

Asyndeton is, on the whole, contrary to the spirit of the Greek language. Most Greek sentences are linked by a connecting

[1] *The Text of the Epistles*, p. 51.

particle, and, where asyndeton is found, it is generally employed with rhetorical effect, especially in admonition.

The high proportion of sentences in connected narrative and speeches set down ἀσυνδέτως is one of the striking features of the style of the Fourth Gospel.[1] Occasionally this preponderance of asyndeton gives weight and solemnity to the discourse and appears to be nothing more than a feature of the author's style. But in the majority of cases there does not appear to be any rhetorical justification for the construction.

Asyndeton is highly characteristic of Aramaic, and C. F. Burney attributed the excessive use of the construction in John to the influence of an Aramaic original, illustrating from Biblical Aramaic.[2] In the long Aramaic passage in the Palestinian Talmud, *Kil'aim*, ix. 4, f. 32*b*, lines 38–48, there is one connecting particle only (line 40). Especially prominent in this passage, and frequent in the Aramaic portions of the Palestinian Talmud generally, is the asyndeton opening *'amar* (participle) and *'am^{e}rin*, 'he says, was saying', 'they say, were saying'; e.g. *'amar*, f. 32*b*, lines 38, 39 (bis), 41, 44 (bis), 45, 46, 47; *'am^{e}rin*, f. 32*b*, line 71, and earlier at lines 11, 17, 23. It is one of the most characteristic of Aramaic asyndeton openings; it is not found, however, in Biblical Aramaic, which prefers the formula ענה ואמר, 'speaks up and says' or 'spoke up and said', and Burney illustrates from Syriac.[3]

The frequent use of asyndeton in John is best explained as the result of Aramaic influence. But it is not necessary to seek the source of the Johannine asyndeton in an Aramaic original. The construction is one which would tend to predominate in Jewish or Syrian Greek. Unfortunately our materials for comparison are limited: most Jewish Greek of the period which may be compared with the Gospels is translation from Hebrew or Aramaic. The asyndeton construction is notably absent from Josephus, whose native language was Aramaic, but who shows considerable skill in his employment of Greek connecting particles. In the *Shepherd of Hermas*, however, which, if it is not

[1] Cf. E. A. Abbott, *Johannine Grammar*, p. 69 f.

[2] *Aramaic Origin*, p. 49 f.

[3] Op. cit., p. 55.

Jewish Greek, was not uninfluenced by Semitic idiom,[1] there are parallels to the Johannine over-use of asyndeton, especially in speeches and in those formulae of narrated dialogue where so many of John's instances are found. Examples from *Hermas*[2] are: *Vis.* i. 1. 6 (λέγω αὐτῇ), 7 (ἀποκριθεὶς αὐτῇ λέγω), 8, 9; iii. 10. 2, 9 (ἀποκριθεῖσά μοι λέγει, ἀποκριθεὶς αὐτῷ λέγω, ἀποκριθείς μοι λέγει), 10; iii. 10. 8, 11. 4*c*, 12. 2, 13. 4*b*; iv. 1. 2, 6, 9, 2. 2, 3 (ἀποκριθεῖσά μοι λέγει), 4 (bis); *Mand.* iv. 3. 2 (λέγει μοι), &c. The construction is more frequent in the Fourth Gospel than in *Hermas*. Noteworthy is the occurrence in the latter of the same asyndeton formulae in narration as in John, all of them Aramaic in origin.[3]

The Aramaic asyndeton λέγει, λέγουσι, occurs in all four Gospels, and Burney has discussed fully its incidence in John. He gives in addition 16 instances of asyndeton λέγει in Matthew; there are 4 more in the Bezan text, xiii. 52, xvii. 26, xxii. 20, xxvii. 23, and one in the Vatican Codex, xix. 21, where WH, which Burney is following, adopts the reading of אD, ἔφη. Burney gives 10 examples of asyndeton λέγουσι for Matthew; the following additional examples are found: xiii. 28*b* (D), xxii. 21. Mark has no instance of λέγει, and one only of λέγουσι (viii. 19), but he has several examples of asyndeton ἔφη, ix. 38, x. 29, xii. 24. Asyndeton ἔφη appears most frequently in Matthew: iv. 7, xix. 21 (B λέγει), xxi. 27, xxii. 37 (D), xxv. 21, 23, xxvi. 34, xxvii. 65 (D ἔφη δέ). The Bא text of Luke has two instances of λέγει, xvi. 7 (D ὁ δὲ λέγει), xix. 22 (D ὁ δὲ εἶπεν), but none of λέγουσι.

In the Synoptics asyndeton generally does not occur so frequently as in the Fourth Gospel. Blass drew attention to it in the passage Mt. v. 3–17 from the Sermon on the Mount, 'not only where there is no connection of thought, but also in spite

[1] Zahn maintained that the writer had been educated among Jews; see his *Hirt des Hermas*, pp. 77 f., 487 f., 496 f.; cf. *Hermae Pastor* (*Patrum Apostolicorum Opera*, iii, edit. Gebhardt and Harnack), p. lxxii.

[2] Edit. Gebhardt and Harnack.

[3] Cf. Burney, op. cit., p. 54. For the Aramaic origin of ἀποκριθεὶς λέγει, see Wellhausen *Einl.*[1], p. 16.

of such connection'.[1] Hawkins noted that it occurred more frequently in Mark than in Matthew and Luke,[2] and Lagrange pointed out that it preponderated in the sayings of Jesus in Mark: '... l'asyndeton se trouve surtout dans le langage parlé, et très spécialement dans le langage de Jésus'.[3]

The following survey of the distribution of the asyndeton construction in the Gospels and Acts is based on a study of the text of both WH and of Codex Bezae. Examples in italics are sayings of Jesus. The instances given are not exhaustive of the construction in the sayings, where the more important examples only are shown, but care has been taken, so far as possible, not to omit examples outside of the sayings. No account has been taken of natural Greek asyndeta, e.g. in commands or admonitions, at the opening of a continuous passage or speech or where a sentence begins with a demonstrative, or of asyndeta where there is no connexion between sentences, as, for instance, in the unconnected apophthegms of Jesus (e.g. Mk. ii. 21; but cf. Mt. ix. 16). The construction is more frequent in Mark, which is taken first.

Mark: x. *25* (Lk. xviii. 25, γάρ; cf. Mt. xix. 24), 27 (D δέ = Mt. xix. 26, Lk. xviii. 27), 28 (D καί), 29 (D δέ = Lk. xviii. 29); xii. *9* (D οὖν = Mt. xxi. 40, Lk. xx. 15*b*), 20 (D οὖν = Lk. xx. 29; cf. Mt. xxii. 25, δέ), 23 (D οὖν = Mt. xxii. 28, Lk. xx. 33), 24 (D δέ = Mt. xxii. 29), *27* (Lk. xx. 38, δέ), 29 (D δέ = Mt. xxii. 37, Lk. x. 26), 31 (D δέ = Mt. xxii. 39 in D), 32 (D καί), *36* (D καί; Lk. xx. 42, γάρ), *37* (Mt. xxii. 45, Lk. xx. 44, οὖν); xiii. *6* (D γάρ = Mt. xxiv. 5, Lk. xxi. 8), *7b* (D γάρ = Mt. xxiv. 6*b*, Lk. xxi. 9*b*), *8b* (Mt. xxiv. 7, καί; Lk. xxi. 11, τε, καί, καί), *8c* (Mt. xxiv. 8, δέ), *9b* (Mt. x. 17, γάρ), *15* (D καί), *17* (D = Lk. xxi. 23; WH δέ); xiv. *3b* (D καί), *6c* (Mt. xxvi. 10, γάρ), *8*, 19 (D δέ; Mt. xxvi. 22, καί).

Other examples: iii. *35* (D γάρ = Mt. xii. 50); iv. *28* (D ὅτι); v. *39b* (cf. Mt. ix. 24, Lk. viii. 52); vi. 26 (D), viii. 29*b* (D δέ = Mt. xvi. 16, Lk. ix. 20); ix. 24 (D καί); x. *9* (D), 41 (D); xi. 14 (D); xiii. *34* (Mt. xxv. 14, γάρ); xvi. 6*bc*.

[1] *Grammar*, p. 278.

[2] *Horae Synopticae*, p. 109.

[3] *S. Marc*, p. lxvii.

Matthew:[1] xix. 18, 20, 21, 22 (D); xxv. *14* (D), *21*, *22* (D δέ), *23*.
Other examples: vi. *14* (D); xii. *42* (= Lk. xi. 31); xxii. *25* (D; ex Mk. xii. 20).

Luke: i. 51–4 (Magnificat); vi. *42* (D ἤ), *43* (D), *44* (D), *45*, *47*, *48*, *49b* (D); xi. *8*, *21*, *23*, *24* (D δέ), *26* (D); xvii. *29* (D), *30*, *33*, *34*; xviii. *11*, *12*, *14*.
Other examples: iv. *25* (D); vii. *28* (D δέ); x. *22*, *31* (D); xi. *31* (= Mt. xii. 42); xii. *37*, *51*; xiv. *27* (D καί), *34* (D); xv. *7* (D δέ); xvi. *10*, *13* (bis); xx. *12* (D), *16* (= Mk. xii. 9), *29* (D; cf. Mk. xii. 20); xxi. *19*; xxii. *68* (D).

Acts: iii. 13, 25, 26 (Peter); iv. 14 (D), 15 (D), 17 (D); vii. 2*b*, 15 (D), 44, 52 (Stephen); x. 36 (D γάρ), 37 (Peter); xvii. 24, 26 (D) (Paul); xx. 29, 33, 34, 35 (Paul).
Other examples: i. 7; ii. 5 (D); v. 30 (Peter); vi. 2 (D); vii. 60 (D); viii. 2 (D), 21 (Peter); xi. 12*b* (D), xiii. 19 (Paul); xviii. 7 (D); xix. 2 (D), 19 (D); xxiv. 23; xxv. 10*b* (Paul); xxvi. 8 (Paul).

In the Matthaean parable of the Tares (xiii), to select one typical example in illustration from the Bezan text, no less than three asyndeta are found in verses 28 and 29: ὁ δὲ ἔφη αὐτοῖς, ἐχθρὸς ἄνθρωπος τοῦτο ἐποίησεν. λέγουσιν αὐτῷ οἱ δοῦλοι, Θέλεις ἀπελθόντες συλλέξωμεν αὐτά; λέγει αὐτοῖς οὔ· (Bℵ, οἱ **δὲ** δοῦλοι αὐτῷ λέγουσι, Θέλεις **οὖν** ἀπελθόντες συλλέξωμεν αὐτά; ὁ **δὲ** φησίν οὔ). The best manuscript authorities have no connecting particle after ἄφετε in verse 30, but such an asyndeton is not unnatural with commands in Greek. Verse 28*b* has the Aramaic order (verb first), λέγουσιν αὐτῷ οἱ δοῦλοι. In verse 30, Epiphanius read δέσμας δέσμας (D, δέσμας; WH, εἰς δέσμας), an Aramaic distributive.[2]

Individual cases may be defended as Greek; the asyndeton in Paul's speech at Miletus (Acts xx. 17 f.), where there is no possibility of Semitic sources (though Semitic influence is not thereby excluded), is rhetorically effective. But when all allowances have been made for Greek uses of the construction, there remains in both the Gospels and Acts a very substantial number of non-Greek asyndeta.

[1] With the exception of those instances at xix. 18, 20, 21 and at xxv. 21, 23, Matthew's λέγει, λέγουσι, ἔφη are not included.

[2] See *infra*, p. 124.

A comparison of the instances in Mark with the parallels in Matthew and Luke shows that 'the smoother and more connected forms of the sentences in Matthew and Luke were altered from the more rough and crude forms in Mark'.[1] In view of the preponderance of asyndeton in Aramaic, it seems likely that, as in John, the explanation of the 'rough and crude' Marcan asyndeton is either that Mark wrote Jewish Greek as deeply influenced in this respect as the Greek of the *Shepherd of Hermas*, or else that he is translating Aramaic sources or employing such translations. It is probable that he did both: where Mark is reporting the Words of Jesus, not as single isolated sayings but in a group of collected sayings, he is most probably incorporating in his Gospel the translation Greek of a sayings-tradition: Mk. xiii. 6–9, where asyndeton occurs no less than 4 times in 7 connected sentences, is an instance of translation Greek.

Asyndeton in Matthew and Luke, with the exception of Matthew's λέγει, λέγουσι, ἔφη in narrative, occurs almost exclusively in the sayings and parables of Jesus. With the exception of the two examples in the Magnificat (which is generally believed to have been modelled on a Semitic poem or to be a rendering of a Semitic original), it is not without significance that three of the four longer passages from Luke, containing a number of asyndeta together, come from Q (in chapters vi, xi, xvii); the fourth (chapter xviii) is in a parable from Luke's special source. All the Lucan cases (the Magnificat excepted) are in sayings of Jesus. To appreciate the significance of this result, it must again be borne in mind that in the Synoptics narrative greatly outweighs the reported sayings and parables of Jesus; the largest proportion of the latter is contained in Q, which in Matthew is about one-sixth of the whole Gospel and in Luke is even less.[2]

That asyndeton should so preponderate in the Words of Jesus and be virtually absent in the longer narrative portions of the Synoptics, except in Mark's Gospel and in certain Jewish Greek formulae chiefly in Matthew, points to the conclusion that a sayings-tradition, cast in translation Greek and reflecting faith-

[1] Hawkins, op. cit., p. 109.

[2] Hawkins, op. cit., p. 89.

fully the Aramaic construction, has been utilized by the Evangelists. The examples outside of the Words of Jesus do not necessarily imply Aramaic sources: they are no more numerous than are to be found in the *Shepherd of Hermas* and for the most part of the same type. Their greater frequency in Mark, however, as compared with the other two Synoptic Gospels, may point to translation of an Aramaic narrative tradition about Jesus.

In the Fourth Gospel, where the construction has been examined by Burney, it again predominates in the sayings and speeches of Jesus, which form, however, the greater part of the work. A modification of Burney's hypothesis may be the best explanation of the excessive use of asyndeton in John: John may not be as a whole a translation of an Aramaic original, but, in the sayings and speeches of Jesus, as in the Synoptics, may contain translations of an Aramaic tradition, edited and rewritten by the author of the Gospel in Greek.

Except in Mark, the construction is most frequent in the Bezan text. The latter in Mark has, in this respect, been harmonized with Matthew and Luke, the 'rough and crude' asyndeton construction being removed by the insertion of the connecting particles in the parallels in the first and third Gospels.

The Paratactic Construction

Parataxis is much more frequent in Aramaic than it is in Greek. In less literary Greek and in the papyri the construction is not uncommon, and this alone has been regarded as a sufficient justification for its frequency in the Gospels.[1] In the first edition of his *Einleitung* Wellhausen attributed the over-use of simple parataxis in the Gospels to the influence of Aramaic:[2] but in the second edition it is stated, 'the predominance of parataxis, not only in the sayings of Jesus, but also in the Marcan narrative, is, in general, no sure sign of Semitic conception'.[3] This agrees in the main with the verdict of Deissmann and Moulton;

[1] Deissmann, *Light from the Ancient East*, p. 129 f.

[2] p. 20.

[3] p. 13.

the latter states more positively, '. . . in itself the phenomenon proves nothing more than would a string of "ands" in an English rustic's story—elementary culture, and not the hampering presence of a foreign idiom that is being perpetually translated into its most literal equivalent'.[1] C. F. Burney took a different view, especially with regard to the excessive use of the construction in the Fourth Gospel; he argued against Deissmann and Moulton that unliterary works or business documents and letters from Egyptian papyri are not *in pari materia* with St. John's Gospel,[2] and he assigned Johannine parataxis, along with the related asyndeton construction, to the influence of an Aramaic original.

So far as the Fourth Gospel is concerned, the perpetually recurring paratactic *καί* is certainly an overstraining of Greek literary usage. Milligan thought it 'impossible to deny that the use of *καί* in the LXX for the Heb. ְו influenced the Johannine usage'.[3] Lagrange, who was very cautious in questions of Aramaic influence in the Gospels, was of the opinion that, in view of the slight trace of LXX influence in John, the source of the Johannine paratactic *καί* was Aramaic.[4]

A detailed study of the relative frequency of *καί* and *δέ* co-ordinating independent clauses has been undertaken by R. A. Martin for the Book of Acts: 'Syntactical Evidence of Aramaic Sources in Acts i–xv' in *New Testament Studies*, xi, pp. 38–59. On the basis of this and similar evidence for Luke–Acts, Mr. Martin has concluded (p. 59):

'It is apparent from the above study that the style of Luke–Acts is not consistent with respect to the use of *καί* and *δέ*; the use of prepositions; and the separation of the article from its substantive. Further, in some of the subsections of Acts i–xv and Luke i and ii the usage, on the one hand, is strikingly parallel to that of the translation Greek of the Old Testament, and, on the other, differs significantly from the other subsections of Acts i–xv, Luke i and ii, the subsections of Acts xvi–xxviii and of original Greek writings such as Plutarch, Polybius, Epictetus, Josephus and the papyri.

[1] *Prol.*, p. 12.
[2] *Aramaic Origin*, p. 6.
[3] *Vocabulary of the Greek New Testament*, s.v. *καί*.
[4] *S. Jean*, p. cvi.

The most natural explanation for this phenomenon is that Semitic sources can be detected as lying behind those subsections of Luke i and ii and Acts i–xv which have the greatest preponderance of translation Greek frequencies for these three syntactical phenomena.'

In the Synoptics the paratactic construction is most characteristic of Mark, who, as Wellhausen observed, has one instance only (v. 25–7) of a longer Greek period with subordinating aorist participles;[1] a typical example of Marcan parataxis is x. 33–4. A survey of the occurrences of the subordinating aorist participle in the sayings of Jesus in the source Q gives for Matthew roughly one instance to the page of WH, for Luke about 2. The proportion for John given by Burney was one to a page of WH, whereas in Matthew there were 5, in Mark about the same, and in Luke roughly 4. Account has, however, to be taken of the style and character of the sayings of Jesus in Q; in Lk. xxi, for instance, the prophetic utterance attributed to our Lord falls naturally into short graphic sentences.

Significant is the greater frequency of the hypotactic participle in the parables. In such brief narrative stories the Greek aorist participle describing events anterior to the action of the main verb is regular; its absence here would be a fair test of translation Greek. But in this respect the parables, on the whole, are written in idiomatic Greek; the 'translation' has certainly not been a literal one; in Lk. xv. 11–32, for example, the longer parable of the Prodigal Son, the subordinating aorist participle occurs no less than 11 times in 21 verses, and in the parable of the Unmerciful Steward in Mt. xviii. 23–35 it is found 11 times in 13 verses. In contrast with this, however, is the Marcan parable of the Sower (iv. 3–9 = Mt. xiii. 3*b*–9, Lk. viii. 5–8), where there is not one instance of a hypotactic aorist participle. Luke has three (verses 6, 7, 8), and the one certain example in Matthew (verse 6) is a genitive absolute which replaces a 'when' clause, so characteristic of Aramaic subordination. Here in Mark we may speak with confidence of a literal translation Greek version of a parable of Jesus. Mt. vii. 24–7, the parable of the House built on a Rock, has likewise the predominating

[1] *Einl.*[2], p. 13.

paratactic construction, but it is most effective in Greek.

The absence of the hypotactic aorist participle, not only in the parables but in the Gospels generally, does provide a fairly reliable criterion of unidiomatic or of simple, unliterary Greek, or of translation Greek. The only Gospel where it is consistently absent is that of Mark; elsewhere we find it used idiomatically and frequently, and in the parable narratives, the best test case for the sayings of Jesus, it is only in Mark that there is any evidence of unidiomatic and probably translation Greek. This does not mean, of course, that the parables are not translations of Aramaic; it does mean that they are not literal renderings but something more of the nature of literary reproductions of the Aramaic story.

In observing that the predominance of parataxis in the Gospels is in general no sure sign of Semitic conception, Wellhausen recognized that in certain special kinds of parataxis purely Semitic constructions were recognizable. The examples of paratactic imperatives without any connecting particle adduced in this connexion in the first edition of the *Einleitung*[1] are omitted in the second edition without comment. Such imperatives are certainly more common in Hebrew or Aramaic than in Greek, with such exceptions as the classical use of *ἄγε*, *ἴθι* with a second imperative, with which may be compared the use of *ὕπαγε* in the Gospels.[2] It is doubtful, however, if Mk. ii. 11, *ἔγειρε ἆρον* (cf. Mt. ix. 6, *ἐγερθεὶς ἆρον*), iv. 39, *σιώπα πεφίμωσο*, Mt. xxviii. 19 (D), *πορεύεσθε νῦν μαθητεύσατε*, Lk. xix. 5 (D), *σπεῦσον κατάβηθι*, can be described as un-Greek, though more literary Greek would prefer the subordinating aorist participle or join with *καί*; the parallel in Mt. ix. 6 (א) to Mk. ii. 11 has, significantly, the participial construction. The use of paratactic imperatives where the second is a prohibition is certainly attested in the papyri, e.g. *ὁρᾶτε μὴ ὀλιγοψυχῆσθε*,[3] with which should be compared Mt. ix. 30, *ὁρᾶτε μηδεὶς γινωσκέτω*, xxiv. 6, *ὁρᾶτε μὴ θροεῖσθε*. At the same time, the use of the characteristic Semitic auxiliaries, *ἔγειρε*, *πορεύεσθε*,[4] in Mk. ii. 11 and Mt. xxviii.

[1] p. 20.
[2] e.g. Mt. v. 24, viii. 4, xviii. 15; Mk. vi. 38; Jn. ix. 7.
[3] Wilcken, *Archiv*, vi. 204, 10.
[4] See *infra*, p. 125.

19 (D), must be taken into account, and all the above instances are from sayings of Jesus.

Paratactic imperatives are not uncommon in Greek when they are connected by simple *καί*. The more literary construction, however, puts the first verb in the participle, subordinated to the second imperative. Two such imperatives joined by *καί* alternate in the manuscripts with the hypotactic participle: they occur more frequently in D than in WH; examples are, Mt. xxii. 13, xxiv. 31; Lk. v. 14, 24, xv. 23, xxii. 32; Acts xiv. 10. Lk. viii. 39 is paratactic in WH, hypotactic in D.

The most characteristic kind of Aramaic parataxis occurs when two indicatives are set down side by side without any connecting particle, a construction limited in Greek to rhetorical statements or to explanatory clauses following *τοῦτο*.[1] Lk. xvii. 28, *ἤσθιον, ἔπινον, ἠγόραζον, ἐπώλουν, ἐφύτευον*, belongs to the rhetorical type, though it probably also reflects the underlying Aramaic parataxis; the parallel in Mt. xxiv. 38 connects the verbs with *καί*. One instance only of this construction has hitherto been claimed in the Gospels where there is a violation of Greek usage, Mk. ii. 7, *τί οὗτος οὕτω λαλεῖ βλασφημεῖ;* (without stop). 'Two Aramaic participles have been understood as presents, whereas the second should have been left as a participle.'[2] This explanation by Wellhausen of the idiom is so condensed as to be misleading. It appears to imply that the second Aramaic participle was a true participle, 'What is this man thus saying, blaspheming', whereas, in this paratactic construction, it must have been, not a participle at all, but a participial present indicative,[3] 'What is this man thus saying, is blaspheming?'[4] It ought to have been represented in Greek by a participle

[1] Cf. Blass, *Grammar*, § 79, 4. Examples of the construction are common in Aramaic; thus, Dan. iii. 27, Elephantine Papyri, 1, 8. 9, and in the Palestinian Talmud, *Kil'aim*, ix. 4, f. 32*b*, line 32.

[2] *Einl.*[2], p. 14.

[3] See *infra*, p. 130.

[4] In Aramaic, *ma hadhen* (*gabhra*) *k^edhen m^emallel m^egaddeph*. This kind of parataxis is especially idiomatic where, as here, the two verbs supplement each other to form a single idea; cf. Nöldeke, *Syriac Grammar*, p. 274. Nöldeke illustrates from the Peshiṭta rendering of Lk. xiii. 7, *ἔρχομαι ζητῶν*, 'I am coming, I am seeking', and from Judges iv. 20, 'And if any man doth come, doth enquire of thee'.

(cf. Lk. xxii. 65), instead of being rendered by the literal Greek equivalent of the Aramaic idiom, a second present indicative.

On this claim of Aramaic influence by Wellhausen Moulton writes: 'Whether this is the most probable Aramaic original we need not enquire: it is enough to reply that no Greek reader could possibly suspect any other sense than that which the R.V. represents, and that Luke's paraphrase is no warrant for making Mark guilty of a wildly impossible Greek combination, with no second offence to create a presumption against him.'[1] This is the strongest argument for rejecting the explanation, but if there had indeed been Aramaic behind the words, it could never have been understood as the R.V. punctuates and renders, 'What doth this man thus speak? He blasphemes.': two such indicatives would naturally be taken as in emphatic parataxis, which we should render, 'What is this man thus blasphemously saying?' It is true, however, that such Greek is 'wildly impossible' as Greek. But would it have been unintelligible to a Palestinian Jew or to the first Jewish-Greek readers of Mark? Moreover, if we are prepared to accept the authority of the Bezan Uncial, a 'second offence' occurs in Mk. xiv. 56, *πολλοὶ γὰρ ἐψευδομαρτύρουν ἔλεγον κατ' αὐτοῦ*. The omission of *καί* may, of course, be accidental, for it is present in the Latin column, *et dicebant*, but the occurrence of such a combination again in Mark may be held to support the authenticity of the Bezan text.

The temporal and consecutive uses of *καί* in parataxis in the Gospels have been variously claimed as Hebraic or Aramaic. Wellhausen again retracts, in the second edition of his *Einleitung*, his earlier views of the Semitic origin of the temporal *καί*, as, e.g. in Mk. xv. 25.[2] The usage is recognized as a Greek one. Thumb pointed out that *καί* in place of hypotaxis occurs in modern Greek and is to be found in Aristotle.[3] The consequential *καί*, e.g. Mt. vi. 4, has also been defended as at least vernacular Greek.[4] None of these considerations need, however,

[1] *Gramm.*[3] ii, p. 16; cf. i, p. 231.

[2] p. 13.

[3] *Hellenismus*, p. 129.

[4] Radermacher, *Neutestamentliche Grammatik*, p. 223.

exclude altogether the possibility of the influence of the Semitic temporal and consequential 'and'.[1]

Simple parataxis with *καί* is much more frequent in Codex Bezae than in WH. Whether the construction is to be traced to Semitic influence or not, its textual distribution must affect our estimate of the comparative antiquity of the rival texts. The less literary paratactic construction seems more likely to be characteristic of the more primitive type of text.

A different interpretation and explanation of the Bezan parataxis with *καί* is given by Lagrange, who attributed the greater frequency of the construction in D to Latin influence from the opposite column of the bilingual manuscript.[2] The hypotaxis of the 'true text' had been altered to parataxis so as to bring the Greek text of D into conformity with the parataxis of *d*, which represented nothing more than a Latin translation of the Greek hypotactic construction.

It is not necessary to deny latinization in D altogether to reject this explanation; a brief consideration of it will show it to be untenable. In a number of instances D's paratactic construction is to be found in non-Western manuscripts also, in the Greek Fathers, and in ancient versions other than the Old Latin. Examples where non-Western manuscripts have the construction along with D and where WH has hypotaxis are: Mt. v. 13, xvii. 7; Mk. xii. 21; Acts xiii. 12, xix. 21. If the construction in D is to be explained as a Latinism, how are we to

[1] Temporal and consequential 'and' are found in both Hebrew and Aramaic, but are much more common in the former. One special form of the usage, the redundant 'and' introducing the apodosis of a conditional sentence, is almost unknown in Aramaic. An example occurs in the Elephantine Papyrus 10. 19, 'Even should they go to law, (and) they would not be vindicated (*wᵉla yiṣdᵉqun*)'. The usage is not found in classical Syriac but occurs, curiously enough, in the Old Syriac Gospels (see Burkitt, *Evangelion da-Mepharreshe*, ii, p. 69 f. and p. 74).

[2] *S. Marc*, p. lix f. The case for the 'latinization' of D in this construction has again been argued by E. Haenchen (*Die Apostelgeschichte*, Göttingen, 1956, pp. 49 ff.). It seems to me unlikely that the Latin column exercised so extensive an influence on the Greek text as Haenchen here assumes. The literary process which is going on in these Greek texts is that of *diorthosis*, the progressive improvement of the style, in particular of the simple paratactic style, to a more idiomatic hypotactic style.

account for it in non-Western texts? How are we to explain a case where D has parataxis, *d*, with WH, hypotaxis, as e.g. Mk. vi. 45, or account for those instances where it is D that has the hypotactic construction and WH the parataxis, e.g. Mk. ii. 15, v. 28?

In D, *καί* occasionally introduces a finite verb after a participle, e.g. Mt. xxvi. 14, *τότε πορευθεὶς . . . καὶ εἶπεν*, Lk. ix. 6, *ἐξερχόμενοι . . . καὶ ἤρχοντο*. Wellhausen explained this curious *καί* as a survival in an imperfectly revised text of a full paratactic construction.[1] Lagrange again accounted for the construction by the theory that *καί* had been inserted in D to make the number of words in the Greek line correspond with the number in the line of the Latin column opposite. But we do not always find such exact numerical correspondence (cf. Mk. ii. 1, v. 27, vi. 48, xiv. 1); and, in any case, there is exact numerical correspondence between D and almost every line of *d*; the bilingual scribe intended the Greek and Latin lines to correspond.

Lagrange's 'latinization' is not a successful explanation, either of the full paratactic construction with *καί* in D or of this curious *καί* after a participle and before a verb. It is noteworthy that the latter occurs most frequently in Mark, the texts of which were the least carefully revised in the Gospels,[2] and this supports Wellhausen's explanation. But his alternative suggestion that the participle is in such cases the equivalent of a full indicative merits equal consideration.[3]

In addition to the examples of the full parataxis with *καί* in D already noted, the following occur:

Matthew: iv. 3; ix. 28, 29; xix. 3; xx. 30; xxvi. 66; xxvii. 49, 58. In xvii. 2 WH has parataxis, D hypotaxis.

Mark: ii. 12, 16; iv. 31, 36 (= *Θ*); vi. 45 (= *Θ*); vii. 6; viii. 10, 26; x. 16, 22; xii. 20 (= *Θ*); xiv. 4 (= *Θ*), 22, 57; xvi. 4 (= *Θ*). In the following examples D has hypotaxis, WH parataxis: i. 37; ii. 15; iv. 38; vi. 7, 13, 22, 34; vii. 28; viii. 25, 33; xi. 4; xiv. 13; xv. 24.

[1] *Einl.*[1], p. 21; cf. 2nd edit., p. 14 (note 1).

[2] In several cases a scribe has deleted the *καί*, e.g. Mk. v. 27, vii. 25, xiv. 1.

[3] *Einl.*[2], p. 14; cf. *infra*, p. 130.

Luke: ii. 42; v. 19; viii. 28; ix. 39; xxii. 51; xxiii. 35, 36; xxiv. 5. In the following examples D has hypotaxis, WH parataxis: v. 6; vi. 8; viii. 27; x. 31; xii. 45.

Acts: vi. 15; xv. 7; xvi. 30. In xiv. 3; xv. 4, D has hypotaxis, WH parataxis.

The following are additional examples in D of the construction with *καί* after a participle:

Mark: xi. 2; xiv. 63; xv. 46; xvi. 11.

Acts: iv. 3; v. 21; vii. 4; viii. 2; x. 27; xii. 16; xiii. 7; xiv. 6, 14; xx. 10.

These examples are not exhaustive, but they are sufficient in number to illustrate the preponderance of the less literary construction in the Bezan Uncial.

Three important points emerge generally from this study of parataxis in the Gospels and Acts:

1. Considerable importance must be attached to the observation that, in the parables, where we have the best examples in the Words of Jesus of continuous narrative, parataxis, except in Mark, is the exception, the idiomatic Greek hypotactic construction almost the rule. We have not always literal translations of Aramaic therefore in the Words of Jesus as they have been transmitted by the Evangelists, but, in this respect at any rate, literary compositions.

2. The high proportion, nevertheless, of instances of parataxis in the Gospels and Acts cannot be set down as unliterary Greek only; Aramaic influence must have been a contributory factor.

3. The less literary paratactic construction, regular in Aramaic, preponderates in the Bezan text. It cannot be explained away as a 'Latinism', but must be recognized as a feature of the more primitive type of text. The unliterary paratactic construction is, however, by no means confined to D; in not a few instances it occurs in WH where D has hypotaxis. No single manuscript has a complete monopoly of the construction.

CHAPTER V

THE ARAMAIC SUBORDINATE CLAUSE

The ד Clause

THE translation and mistranslation of the ambiguous Aramaic particle *d*ᵉ is one of the best known of Gospel Aramaisms. Burney has given an account of the meaning of the particle:[1] it is a relative, the sign of the genitive, and a conjunction; it may be equivalent to ὅτι, 'because', or ὅτι *recitativum*, or ἵνα; it may also have the force of ὅτε or ὥστε, the latter use not noted by Burney. In view of so wide an ambiguity, the particle was almost bound to give rise to misunderstanding or to different interpretations in any rendering into Greek.

An examination of the instances which have been adduced for the mistranslation of this ambiguous Aramaic particle in the Gospels leads to the observation of three classes: (1) there are a few instances where, along with one translation of the *d*ᵉ, there is an alternative translation or interpretation in the form of a Synoptic variant; (2) in a number of other examples an alternative rendering or interpretation of the underlying Aramaic exists in the form of a textual variant, either in Greek manuscripts or in one or more of the ancient versions; (3) the third class consists of the remainder of examples which have neither Synoptic not textual attestation for the alternative rendering which consideration of the Aramaic *d*ᵉ suggests. Examples are discussed under the usual headings, the first two classes, to which naturally more weight is to be attached, being given first.

1. *Relative d*ᵉ *rendered by* ὅτι

(i) *With Synoptic Variants*

Burney pointed out that an ambiguous Aramaic *d*ᵉ could account for the Synoptic variants ὅτι βλέπουσιν and οἱ βλέποντες in Mt. xiii. *16* and Lk. x. *23* respectively.[2] The Lucan version

[1] *Aramaic Origin*, p. 70. [2] *Poetry of our Lord*, p. 145 (note).

gives the more natural and probably original meaning of the saying in Aramaic. But Matthew need not be regarded as 'mistranslation'. It may represent a deliberate interpretation of the Aramaic designed to emphasize that it was *because* the disciples' eyes were open to see, as contrasted with the blindness of the crowds, that they merited the Lord's blessing.

In Mk. ix. 38 (dialogue) a clause *ὃς οὐκ ἀκολουθεῖ ἡμῖν* (*μεθ' ἡμῶν*), omitted by Bא, is inserted by D (after *δαιμόνια*) along with A and a few other Uncials of the Byzantine text; the relative has also the support of the Old Latin. The Bא text has the clause in the form *ὅτι οὐκ ἠκολούθει ἡμῖν*, which differs only slightly from the parallel in Lk. ix. 49, *ὅτι οὐκ ἀκολουθεῖ μεθ' ἡμῶν*. The Synoptic variants, the Marcan relative and the Lucan conjunction, go back to the same Aramaic, *d^e^la 'athe bathrenan*. Not only is the *d^e^* ambiguous and capable of being rendered by either relative or conjunction, but the tense of the Aramaic verb may be represented by either a present or an imperfect. The observation supports the authenticity of the relative clause in Mark, and indeed it is difficult to account for that clause unless it is Marcan. It may be the true Marcan clause, representing the Greek rendering of the Aramaic of Mark's source; the clause in the Bא text of Mark may be a harmonization with Luke, this form of the clause being Luke's received translation of the ambiguous Aramaic. There is, however, no reason why both clauses should not be Marcan, and Luke's clause derive from no other source than a Greek Mark.[1]

(ii) *With Textual Variants*

Moulton accepted Wellhausen's explanation of Mk. iv. 41 (dialogue), *τίς ἄρα οὗτός ἐστιν, ὅτι καὶ ὁ ἄνεμος καὶ ἡ θάλασσα ὑπακούει αὐτῷ;* (cf. Mt. viii. 27; Lk. viii. 25).[2] Wellhausen had suggested that *ὅτι* had been employed as a translation of *d^e^* to

[1] Mark may have found the two renderings of the Aramaic in existence in Greek and set them down side by side in his 'conflate text'. A parallel would be Mk. v. 23, *ἵνα σωθῇ καὶ ζήσῃ*, a combination impossible in Aramaic, for both Greek verbs go back to Aramaic *ḥ^a^ya*; a less satisfactory explanation would be to account for *καὶ ζήσῃ* as a harmonization with Mt. ix. 18, *καὶ ζήσεται*.

[2] Cf. *Gramm.* ii, p. 436.

avoid an un-Greek ᾧ . . . αὐτῷ.[1] Both scholars failed to note the important variant reading of the Old Latin (*ff*[2], *i*, *q*), '*cui* et ventus et mare obaudiunt'. The Old Latin assumes a Greek variant ᾧ without αὐτῷ, unless we are to believe that the Latin translator is himself here correcting and altering.

While an underlying Aramaic *dᵉ* clause is clearly the explanation of Mark's Greek and the Old Latin variant, the former is again not necessarily to be regarded as a mistranslation and the latter the correct rendering. It is true that the Old Latin gives the more natural sense of the Aramaic. But the Marcan Greek is a possible, if artificial and forced, interpretation of the clause; the translator may have been influenced by the desire to give a Greek equivalent of every word he found in his Aramaic.

Mt. vi. 5, καὶ ὅταν προσεύχησθε, οὐκ ἔσεσθε ὡς οἱ ὑποκριταί· ὅτι φιλοῦσιν, is given in the Vulgate as 'non eritis sicut hypocritae *qui* amant . . .' The Arabic Tatian also reads a relative, but no importance can be attached to it, for it may be no more than the translator's interpretation of the ambiguous Syriac *dᵉ* in the Peshiṭta. But it is worthy of note that a Semitic translator, confronted with *dᵉ* in this connexion, does not hesitate to render it as a relative. Both renderings are defensible.

The text of Jn. v. 39 in WH reads, ἐραυνᾶτε τὰς γραφάς, ὅτι ὑμεῖς δοκεῖτε ἐν αὐταῖς ζωὴν αἰώνιον ἔχειν· καὶ ἐκεῖναί εἰσιν αἱ μαρτυροῦσαι περὶ ἐμοῦ. One Old Latin manuscript, *b*, has a double rendering of the verse: its main clause agrees with the Greek (ἐραυνᾶτε, *scrutate*, is an imperative), but there are two versions of the subordinate clause: (1) *quoniam putatis vos in ipsis vitam aeternam habere*, a literal equivalent of the Greek; (2) the second form is *in quibus putatis vos vitam habere*. The clause in this form alone appears in several other Old Latin texts (*a*, *e*, *ff*[2], *q*) and in both forms in the Armenian version.[2]

[1] *Einl.*[1], p. 22; 2nd edit., p. 15.

[2] The Curetonian Syriac has a similar clause. For further evidence, see T. W. Manson, *Journal of Egyptian Archaeology*, xxiii, pp. 130–2; H. I. Bell, 'Search the Scriptures', in *Z.N.T.W.* xxxvii (1938), p. 12; and, for the complete textual evidence conveniently put together, L. Vaganay, *Rev. des sciences religieuses*, 1937, p. 56; Vaganay noted that the relative is read by the Arabic Tatian, the Liège Diatessaron, and in quotations of Irenaeus, Tertullian, and Cyprian.

The two clauses may be traced to the same Aramaic with an ambiguous *d^e^*, *dis^e^bhirin 'attun b^e^hon.*[1] The case is exactly parallel to that discussed above for Mk. iv. 41. In this instance, however, there is Greek as well as Latin attestation for a relative. The papyrus fragment of an unknown Gospel, edited by Bell and Skeat,[2] contains, by a fortunate chance, this verse of John, and in the following form:

εραυ
(νατε τ)ας γραφας· εν αις υμεις δο
(κειτε) ζ̣ωην εχειν εκειναι ε̣ι̣(σ)ι̣ν̣
(αι μαρτ)υρουσαι περι εμου.

The omission of *καί* before *ἐκεῖναι* has the support of Cyprian and Irenaeus; such asyndeton, as has been seen, is characteristic of the sayings of Jesus: we may render, 'Search the Scriptures in which ye think ye have life. Those are the (Scriptures) bearing witness of me . . .'

The relation of the new papyrus fragments to our canonical Gospels is by no means certain. But if this verse, as has seemed most likely to scholars, is dependent on John, then we have preserved here a genuine Greek variant text. It is also possible, however, that this fragmentary saying from an 'unknown Gospel' is independent of the Fourth Gospel, coming from some extra-canonical sayings-source. The variant reading may in that case have been completely unknown to the writer of St. John's Gospel; this particular saying may have reached him in its mistranslated form only, or in the one translation or interpretation of the Aramaic preserved by him. The existence now of the saying in another translated form, explicable in its relation to the Johannine saying from a common Aramaic, is important evidence for an Aramaic source or tradition behind the sayings of Jesus in the Fourth Gospel.

The following examples are all from the Fourth Gospel. In

[1] The verb is ambiguous in Aramaic; it may mean *sperare* as well as *putare* (cf. *infra*, p. 247), The original may have been, 'Search the Scriptures *by which ye hope to have eternal life*'.

[2] *Fragments of an Unknown Gospel and Other Early Christian Papyri* (London, 1935).

Jn. viii. 45, ἐγὼ δὲ ὅτι τὴν ἀλήθειαν λέγω, there is Latin support for a relative in two manuscripts of the Vulgate, 'ego autem *qui* veritatem dico'. The relative gives a much better contrast to the 'father of lies' in the previous verse: 'But as for me *who* speak the truth . . .' In verse 53 of the same chapter, μὴ σὺ μείζων εἶ τοῦ πατρὸς ἡμῶν Ἀβραάμ, ὅστις ἀπέθανεν, a Greek variant ὅτι is found in D. In Jn. ix. 17 (dialogue), τί σὺ λέγεις περὶ αὐτοῦ, ὅτι ἠνέῳξέν σου τοὺς ὀφθαλμούς, the best attested Latin reading is '*qui* aperuit': 'What sayest thou of him *who* hath opened thine eyes?'

Two instances occur in the speeches of Peter and Stephen in Acts: Acts i. 17, τοῖς συλλαβοῦσιν Ἰησοῦν, ὅτι κατηριθμημένος ἦν ἐν ἡμῖν, is in the Latin column of the Bezan Uncial, 'hiis qui adpraehenderunt Jesum *qui* adnumeratus erat inter nos'. In Acts vii. 39, ᾧ οὐκ ἠθέλησαν ὑπήκοοι γενέσθαι, D reads ὅτι οὐκ ἠθέλησαν. Joüon gives a further example, Mt. v. 45, *Quelques Aramaïsmes*, p. 211 (note 1). He compares also Jn. viii. 53, xiv. 16 (*L'Évangile*, ad Mt. v. 45).

On the first instance, Acts i. 17, Wilcox is inclined to argue that, since the reading of a relative is confined to Latin versions, the *qui* for *quia* is an inner Latin corruption.[1] This seems to me to overlook the fact that the context of this clause is overwhelmingly in favour of a relative. The fact that a relative ὅς is not attested in Greek manuscript tradition is not a convincing argument for its non-existence: at Acts vii. 39 (Wilcox's next example) the variants, relative and conjunction, are found in Greek manuscripts.[2]

Wilcox has argued for an Aramaic ד clause of purpose underlying Acts xiii. 28*b* (D) ἵνα εἰς ἀναίρεσιν, viz. דלקטלא, 'in order to put to death', the infinitive being translated as a noun. The conjecture is a plausible and defensible one: the only objection which may be made is that this Aramaic infinitive of purpose seems to be very rare: it has not so far been attested in Targumic Aramaic. The more regular and natural Aramaic original

[1] Cf. Wilcox, op. cit., pp. 115 ff.
[2] Wilcox, loc. cit.

here would be בדיל לקטליה 'in order to put him to death', and this was perhaps the text translated by D.[1]

(iii) *Without Synoptic or Textual Attestation*

The most convincing of the remaining examples is Jn. i. 16, *ὅτι ἐκ τοῦ πληρώματος αὐτοῦ ἡμεῖς πάντες ἐλάβομεν*, which Burney would render, 'Full of grace and truth was He of Whose fullness we have all received';[2] in an original Aramaic the *d^e* in this clause would be most naturally understood as a relative.

Burney cited Jn. i. 4 as an example of the opposite kind of mistranslation, the Aramaic conjunctive *d^e* rendered by a relative; Burney's Aramaic for *ὃ γέγονεν ἐν αὐτῷ ζωὴ ἦν* is *dah^awa beh ḥayyin*, '*Because* in Him was life'. There is, however, no equivalent here of the Greek *ἦν*. To represent it in Aramaic by a second *h^awa*, as we are bound to do, unless some good reason can be given for its presence in the Greek and absence in the Aramaic, gives an Aramaic which can only be rendered, '*That which* was in Him was life'. Schaeder accounted for the *ἦν* as an addition made by the Greek translator of the Aramaic once the initial mistake had been made of taking the *d^e* conjunction as a relative.[3] The explanation fails to convince, though it is less drastic than the proposal of Bultmann to remove *ὃ γέγονεν* as a gloss.[4] The Greek writer or translator of the Prologue clearly means 'That which was in Him was life'. But the original Aramaic may nevertheless have been 'Because in Him was (*h^awa*) life': *γέγονεν* and *ἦν* look very like alternative renderings of the Aramaic verb, combined, by the Greek writer, in an entirely new and individual interpretation.

A much more convincing example of this kind of mistranslation was observed by Wellhausen in Lk. ix. 31, *ἔλεγον τὴν ἔξοδον αὐτοῦ ἣν ἤμελλεν πληροῦν ἐν Ἰερουσαλήμ*. Wellhausen maintained that the correct rendering of the Aramaic should have been *ὅτι*.[5] Even with *ὅτι*, however, the construction of the sentence is an

[1] For the construction, see Dalman, *Aram. Grammar*², p. 237 (Exod. i. 11, Onk.).

[2] *Aramaic Origin*, p. 39.

[3] In *Studien zum antiken Synkretismus* (Berlin, 1926), iii, p. 312.

[4] *Gunkel-Festschrift*, ii, p. 4 (note 2).

[5] *Einl.*², p. 12.

unusually clumsy one in Greek and certainly not normal. Wellhausen's observation might have commended itself more widely had he underlined more the emphatic hyperbaton,[1] the accusative after the main verb being in reality the object of the verb in the subordinate clause, removed to its present position solely for the sake of emphasis: 'They were saying that he was about to accomplish his departure (demise) in Jerusalem.'

2. *Relative dᵉ rendered by ἵνα*

The frequent use (and misuse) of ἵνα in the Gospels, especially in the Gospel of St. John, has been attributed by Burney to the influence of Aramaic. The extension of the use of ἵνα in the Koine, even to the extent of usurping ὥστε, goes a long way to explaining Johannine usage, but the excessive use of ἵνα in John is unparalleled; for statistics, reference may be made to Burney.[2]

In the instances which have hitherto been given where ἵνα is alleged to mistranslate a relative, I have so far not encountered a single case where some confirmation of the mistranslation might be got from a Synoptic variant. One is given by Burney. The explanation of the parallels in Mk. iv. 22, ἐὰν μὴ ἵνα φανερωθῇ, and Mt. x. 26, ὃ οὐκ ἀποκαλυφθήσεται (Lk. viii. 17, ὃ οὐ φανερὸν γενήσεται), as the result of the translation of an ambiguous *dᵉ* was first made by Wellhausen[3] and worked out in detail by Burney.[4] The latter explained Mark's ἐὰν μὴ ἵνα φανερωθῇ as a mistranslation of Aramaic *'illahen dᵉ'ithgᵉli*, not 'except in order that it may be revealed', but 'except that which shall be revealed', and this is then said to be the same in meaning as 'which shall not be revealed'. For 'except that which shall be revealed', we would require an Aramaic verb in the imperfect, *'illahen dᵉyithgᵉle*; no justification can be given for Burney's perfect tense. But a much more serious blunder is his assumed equation of 'except that which shall be revealed' with 'which shall not be revealed'; the words are no more the same in meaning in Aramaic than they are in English; *'illahen*

[1] *Supra*, p. 53.

[2] *Aramaic Origin*, p. 69.

[3] *Einl.*², p. 15.

[4] Op. cit., p. 76.

d^e^yithg^e^le can mean only 'except that which shall be revealed' or 'except in order that it may be revealed', the Marcan text. To make 'except that which shall be revealed' original contributes nothing to our understanding of Mark, and it in no way accounts for the Synoptic parallels.

Both Matthew and Luke assume the same Aramaic, *d^e^la yithg^e^le*, 'which shall not be revealed'. This meaning commends itself as the simpler and as the necessary and natural one in the context. The Marcan reading in Aramaic might be explained as having arisen by an error out of *d^e^la yithg^e^le*. It is much more probable, however, that Mark gives here a Greek version of the saying, the work not of a translator at this point but of a Greek writer. We can only guess at how he arrived at his curious expression.

Mk. iv. *12*

(For a discussion of this alleged mistranslation of relative *d^e^* by *ἵνα*, see below, p. 212. f.)

Burney found most cases where *ἵνα* mistranslated a relative in the Fourth Gospel. Examples he gives are: i. 8; v. 7; vi. 30, 50; ix. 36; xiv. *16*.[1] The last instance only is a saying of Jesus, and this is the only case where there is textual support for the alternative rendering of the Aramaic: the Greek text is *καὶ ἄλλον παράκλητον δώσει ὑμῖν ἵνα ᾖ μεθ' ὑμῶν εἰς τὸν αἰῶνα*; two Old Latin manuscripts (*m*, *q*) read, 'et alium paracletum dabit vobis *qui* maneat vobiscum et sit in aeternum'. The importance of this observation (it occurs in a saying of Jesus from one of the longer Johannine speeches) need not be stressed. As elsewhere, we have here a piece of valuable evidence for an Aramaic tradition behind a Johannine saying of Jesus.

In Jn. i. 8, apart from the lack of any textual support, there are linguistic objections to Burney's conjecture. Burney would have rendered 'He was not the light, but *one who* (*ἵνα*, *d^e^*) was to bear witness of the light'. It is doubtful if *d^e^* in the sense of 'one who' could stand alone in this emphatic position without being reinforced by the indefinite *man* as antecedent.

[1] *Aramaic Origin*, p. 75 f.

In the other instances it is not always clear that the *d*ᵉ would really have been relative and not telic even in the Aramaic. The ἵνα in most of these cases is employed in a common Koine use; in v. 7 it is used much as we use 'to', 'I do not have anyone *to* put me into the water'. In Jn. vi. 30 the purpose clause is important: it is not 'What sign doest thou which we may see', as Burney suggests, but 'What sign doest thou in order that we may see'; the emphasis is on the last word; proof by sight was the purpose of the sign.

3. *Temporal d*ᵉ *rendered by* ἵνα *or* ὅτι

Strictly speaking, *d*ᵉ is not a temporal conjunction, but, as a relative or relating particle after such antecedents as 'time', 'day', 'hour', or adverbs of time, it becomes the equivalent of 'when'. The conjunction *d*ᵉ standing alone without any such antecedent and meaning 'when' is a much rarer use. An example is to be found in *Vayyikra Rabba*, 10:[1] 'Antoninus went up to the house of our Rabbi. He found him when he was sitting (*d*ᵉ*yathebh*) with his disciples before him.'

Five out of the six examples which Burney gives for John where he regards ἵνα or ὅτι as mistranslating a temporal *d*ᵉ have nouns or adverbs of time preceding them; thus Jn. xvi. 2, ἔρχεται ὥρα ἵνα πᾶς ὁ ἀποκτείνας ὑμᾶς δόξῃ λατρείαν προσφέρειν τῷ Θεῷ, 'the hour[2] cometh *when* every one that slayeth you will think that he doeth God a service'. 'That in all these cases ἵνα simply stands by mistranslation for ὅτε, and that no mystic final sense is to be traced in the usage such as is postulated by Westcott, is proved by the use of the normal phrase ἔρχεται ὥρα ὅτε in $4^{21.23}$, 5^{25}, 16^{25}, and ἔρχεται ὥρα ἐν ᾗ in 5^{28}.'[3] In Jn. ix. 8 and xii. 41 Burney claims that ὅτι mistranslated temporal *d*ᵉ.

In none of the above instances is there any textual variant to support the suggestion, though this can scarcely be taken as conclusive against it. Jn. xvi. 2 is quoted by Eusebius[4] in

[1] Given in Dalman's *Aramäische Dialektproben*, p. 34.

[2] Definite; cf. *infra*, pp. 93 ff.

[3] *Aramaic Origin*, p. 78.

[4] *H.E.* v. 1.

the form, 'the time will come in which (ἐλεύσεται καιρὸς ἐν ᾧ) everyone that slayeth you will think that he doeth God a service', but the quotation appears to be free. In Jn. ix. 8 the ὅτι clause may be construed after the verb θεωρεῖν, 'Those who were seeing formerly that he was a beggar', though Burney's explanation may be preferable.[1] In Jn. xii. 41, ταῦτα εἶπεν 'Ησαίας ὅτι εἶδεν τὴν δόξαν αὐτοῦ, there is no temporal antecedent.[2] The reading ὅτι is the best attested, but the variant ὅτε, found in D and a number of other ancient authorities, is not to be left out of all consideration. But the ὅτι is the more difficult reading, and the Bezan variant is probably a correction. The difficulty about mistranslation is that it seems incredible that any translator could have been guilty of such an error. A more satisfactory alternative may be to regard the ὅτι as a deliberate theological interpretation of the ambiguous Aramaic particle.

Four of Burney's six examples come from sayings of Jesus, and are typical cases where, with its temporal antecedent, *d*[e] means 'when', and where, elsewhere, as Burney emphasizes, ὅτε is found. So that the hypothesis of mistranslation must be seriously entertained. But a possibly loose temporal use of ἵνα or ὅτι, like English 'that', especially after a temporal antecedent, may be the right explanation of the Johannine usage, without any appeal to Aramaic: 'The hour is come *that* the son of Man should be glorified' (xii. 23). Here in English there is no mystic telic force, but a simple extension, after a temporal antecedent, of normal usage. May the same not apply to the use of ἵνα?

4. *The Indeclinable and Ambiguous d*[e]

There is one Synoptic variant where the parallels are capable of explanation in the light of the indeclinable and ambiguous Aramaic particle. It occurs in the passages Mk. xiv. 68 (cf. Mt. xxvi. 70; Lk. xxii. 57, 60) and Mk. xiv. 71 (= Mt. xxvi. 74; Lk. xxii. 60). Torrey suggested that Mark's οὔτε οἶδα οὔτε ἐπίσταμαι

[1] Cf. Moulton, *Gramm.* ii, p. 469.

[2] John is here drawing on the Targum to the Prophets, which adds the words, 'For the Glory of the Shechinah of the King of the Ages, the Lord of Hosts, hath mine eye seen'.

σὺ τί λέγεις was a mistranslation of an Aramaic which should have been rendered, 'I neither know nor am I acquainted *with him of whom you speak*':[1] the last clause reads, in Torrey's Aramaic, *di 'amar 'ant*, where the *di* is ambiguous;[2] Mark has rendered it by a neuter. In the Lucan parallel, Peter replies, *οὐκ οἶδα αὐτόν*.

Such a sense suits context and circumstances much more appropriately than the Marcan reading; it is a curious statement for Peter to make, that he did not know nor understand what the serving-maid said. Were there not indications to the contrary elsewhere, one might suspect an attempt to whitewash Peter. Mark is certainly interpreting his tradition, and here wrongly.

Burney has noticed a number of relatives in John (vi. *37, 39*; x. *29*; xvii. *2, 11, 12, 24*) where he suggests that the indeclinable d^e has given rise to anomalies in the Greek.[3] In xvii. *24* it is clear that the neuter relative refers to persons; it is later completed in the sentence by the masculine, *πατήρ, ὃ δέδωκάς μοι, θέλω ἵνα ὅπου εἰμὶ ἐγὼ κἀκεῖνοι ὦσιν μετ' ἐμοῦ*. There is much to be said for the hypothesis of the influence of the indeclinable d^e here, reflected in the Greek neuter, but are we justified in describing it as an 'unintelligent rendering'? The *casus pendens* gives emphasis to the Johannine neuter phrase, and the employment of the neuter is not ineffective as a generalization—Thy gift to me—explained more fully in the sequel.

Mistranslation seems more evident in x. *29*, which Burney would read (with the less well authenticated text), *ὁ πατήρ μου, ὃς (ὃ) δέδωκέν μοι, μείζων(ον) πάντων ἐστίν*. The 'mistranslation' would have been more convincing had there been an object to

[1] *Our Translated Gospels*, p. 16 f. I have given my own translation of the verbs.

[2] In this Aramaic *di* has the sense of 'that which', 'he who', and corresponds to *τί*. A more exact equivalent of the Greek would be *man 'amar 'a(n)t*, 'what thou sayest' or 'whom thou meanest'. The two uses of the Aramaic *ḥ^{a}kham* (*ἐπίσταμαι*), 'to understand' and 'to know', of a person, are well known; cf. Targum, Eccles. vii. 23, and in the Palestinian Talmud, *Terum*. xi. 7, f. 48*b* (second last line). The verb is generally followed by l^e (to) introducing the direct object. (Cf. *infra*, p. 115.)

[3] *Aramaic Origin*, pp. 101–3.

δέδωκεν; 'My Father, Who hath given (them) to me is greater than all'; it is doubtful whether we are justified in simply supplying an object.

5. *Consecutive dᵉ rendered by ἵνα*

In view of the establishment of the 'ecbatic' ἵνα in the Koine,[1] it may appear entirely unnecessary to appeal to Aramaic. But the latter may well have been a contributory factor in the extension of the use of ἵνα even to the extent of taking the place of ὥστε.

Cases in question in the Gospels all come from dialogue: Mk. vi. 2 (D), xi. 28; Lk. i. 43; Jn. ix. 2. Mk. vi. 2 reads in D: 'And what is the wisdom given to this man, so that (ἵνα) even such miracles are done (γίνωνται) by his hand.' It is always possible, of course, to defend the final sense of the ἵνα, but in all of the above cases a final use goes against the natural meaning required by the context.

The Circumstantial Clause

One of the commonest of Semitic subordinate clauses, characteristic of both Hebrew and Aramaic, is the so-called Circumstantial Clause, by which circumstances are described which are attendant on and necessary to the understanding of the action of the main verb, but subordinate to it. It is introduced in both Hebrew and Aramaic by Waw followed by a noun or pronoun and verb, in that order. Its translation may vary with the requirements of the context, but it is usually best rendered by 'now', 'while', 'when'. An example in Aramaic is *Midrash Echa*, i. 4, 'Now he was aware (*wᵉhu' hᵃwa yadhaʿ*) of the name of that man, (so) he came and sat by the gate'; id. i. 31, '. . . Ben Batiah walked in front of him, with his garments rent' (*umanoi bᵉziʿin*).[2]

Wellhausen cited Mk. i. 19 as an example of the clause, καὶ προβὰς ὀλίγον εἶδεν Ἰάκωβον . . . καὶ Ἰωάννην . . . καὶ αὐτοὺς ἐν τῷ πλοίῳ καταρτίζοντας τὰ δίκτυα, 'And advancing a little, he

[1] Moulton, *Prol.*, p. 206.

[2] For further examples from Biblical Greek, see *infra*, p. 88.

saw James . . . and John . . . *while they were mending their nets in the boat.*'[1] Wellhausen comments, 'Actually *καὶ αὐτοὶ . . . καταρτίζοντες* should have been written.' This certainly would have been the exact and literal Greek equivalent of the Aramaic clause, but the result would not have been Greek. As the text stands, the accusative *αὐτούς* construed after *εἶδεν* brings the clause within the grammatical structure of the Greek sentence. While it seems probable that the Marcan construction does reflect a circumstantial clause—to assume the influence of such a clause not only results in a better understanding of the Greek, but it also explains the clumsy Greek construction—it is also important to note that Mark is not translating Aramaic literally into a translation Greek equivalent, inadmissible as Greek; he is also writing Greek, though the result still reveals the influence of the Aramaic.

A similar instance is Lk. xiii. 28, *ἐκεῖ ἔσται ὁ κλαυθμὸς καὶ ὁ βρυγμὸς τῶν ὀδόντων, ὅταν ὄψησθε Ἀβραὰμ . . . καὶ πάντας τοὺς προφήτας ἐν τῇ βασιλείᾳ τοῦ Θεοῦ, ὑμᾶς δὲ ἐκβαλλομένους ἔξω.* As Greek, we must render, 'There shall be weeping and gnashing of teeth,[2] when ye see Abraham . . . and all the prophets in the kingdom of God, and (when ye see) yourselves being cast out . . .' In Aramaic, however, the last clause is clearly circumstantial, 'There shall be weeping and gnashing of teeth when ye see Abraham . . . and all the prophets in the kingdom of God, *while ye are cast out . . .*'

In Mk. vi. 45 (D), *ἠνάγκασεν τοὺς μαθητὰς αὐτοῦ . . . προάγειν αὐτὸν . . . πρὸς Βησσαϊδάν, αὐτὸς δὲ ἀπολύει τὸν ὄχλον,* the last clause can only be rendered in Greek, 'and he himself was dismissing the crowd'—an instance of simple parataxis.[3] In Aramaic the clause would be circumstantial, 'while he was dismissing the crowd'. The clumsy Greek parataxis of D is replaced in the Bא text by *ἕως αὐτὸς ἀπολύει τὸν ὄχλον.* The latter may well be a correction made by a scholarly editor who recognized in the

[1] *Einl.*[1], p. 19; cf. *Ev. Marci,* in loc.

[2] For the expression, cf. in the Palestinian Talmud, *Kil'aim,* ix. 4, f. 32*c*, 13 lines from foot. Wensinck adds *Kethub.* xii. 3, 35[r]*b*, lines 32, 33, 38.

[3] Cf. *supra*, p. 65.

primitive text in D a circumstantial clause, for which he gives the idiomatic Greek equivalent.

Luke is specially fond of sentences beginning with *καὶ αὐτός*, where we may suspect that this unfamiliar and unusual Greek construction is again 'translation Greek', rendering a circumstantial clause. It is especially noteworthy that most examples occur in the WH text of Luke; D has generally the idiomatic Greek participle or genitive absolute construction. The substitution in D of the idiomatic Greek equivalent is the best proof that Luke's *καὶ αὐτός* construction was felt by the Greek editor of D responsible for the alterations to be unidiomatic as Greek. Examples are: Lk. v. 1, *καὶ αὐτὸς ἦν ἑστὼς* (D, *ἑστῶτος αὐτοῦ*) *παρὰ τὴν λίμνην*; v. 17, *καὶ αὐτὸς ἦν διδάσκων* (D, *αὐτοῦ διδάσκοντος*); vii. 12, *καὶ αὐτὴ ἦν χήρα* (D, *χήρα οὖσα*); xvii. 16, *καὶ αὐτὸς ἦν Σαμαρείτης* (D, *ἦν δὲ Σαμαρείτης*); xix. 2, *καὶ αὐτὸς ἦν ἀρχιτελώνης καὶ αὐτὸς πλούσιος* (D, *οὗτος ἦν ἀρχιτελώνης πλούσιος*). If, as seems highly probable, we have here traces of the Aramaic circumstantial clause, then in this respect WH preserves the more primitive 'Aramaized' text.

There are two possible instances of the construction in Acts: Acts xv. 32: *Ἰούδας τε καὶ Σιλᾶς, καὶ αὐτοὶ προφῆται ὄντες, διὰ λόγου πολλοῦ παρεκάλεσαν τοὺς ἀδελφούς* . . . 'Judas and Silas, *inasmuch as they were prophets*, said much to encourage the brethren.' At Acts x. 6 three minuscules (68, 137, 614) read *καὶ αὐτός ἐστιν ξενιζόμενος πρὸς Σίμωνά τινα* for the usual *οὗτος ξενίζεται παρά τινι Σίμωνι*; Chrys. and Theophyl. (teste Tisch.) also support this variant form of text. It is certainly the more difficult reading, and it seems more likely that the usual text here is the correction, since it is difficult to imagine *οὗτος* being deliberately changed by any scribe to *καὶ αὐτός*.

Additional Note on Heb. xi. 11 and the Circumstantial Clause in Hebrews*

The *crux interpretum* of Hebrews xi. 11 has been well characterized and defined by Professor Jean Héring as follows (italics

*This note appeared originally as a contribution to the *Festschrift* for E. Haenchen, *Apophoreta* (Berlin, 1964).

mine) : 'Une croix des exégètes franchement trop lourde à porter se présente dans ce verset. Il y est brusquement question de Sarah qui disparaît à la suite pour laisser de nouveau la place à Abraham seul. *Mais ce qui est bien plus curieux et même inconcevable, c'est qu'on lui attribue, grâce à sa foi, un acte spécifiquement masculin, à savoir καταβολὴ σπέρματος (emissio seminis).*'[1]

So far as Hellenistic (and Classical) usage is concerned καταβολὴ σπέρματος can only refer to the sexual function of the male (the verb is καταβάλλειν or καταβάλλεσθαι) : the function of the female in conception is expressed by the term ὑποδοχή (ὑποδέχεσθαι).[2] In consequence, the early Greek commentators are forced to explain καταβολή as if it could bear the sense of ὑποδοχή, e.g., Chrysostom comments τί ἐστιν ⟨εἰς καταβολὴν σπέρματος⟩; εἰς τὸ κατασχεῖν, εἰς ὑποδοχὴν δύναμιν ἔλαβεν ἡ νενεκρωμένη ἡ στεῖρα,[3] and Oecumenius (cited by Bleek), ἐνεδυναμώθη εἰς τὸ ὑποδέξασθαι . . . σπέρμα. Stephanus, who felt the difficulty of the Greek usage, has the ingenious solution: *vim ad jaciendum sive emittendum semen accepit nam καταβολή interpretari conceptionem violentum esse videtur.*[4] Nevertheless *conceptio* is the noun which makes its appearance in the Latin Versions: *virtutem in conceptionem seminis accepit.*[5] These can only be described as unsuccessful attempts to force on the word καταβολή a sense which it could never bear, simply because the

[1] *Commentaire du Nouveau Testament* XII, *L'Épître aux Hébreux* (Paris, 1954), p. 106.

[2] Numerous examples in Wetstein; thus, Philo, *De ebrietate* 211. Cf. F. Field, *Notes on the Translation of the New Testament* (Cambridge, 1899), p. 232, who cites from Wetstein, Galen, *De Semine* 1, τὸ τοῦ ἄρρενος σπέρμα τὸ καταβαλλόμενον εἰς τὰς μήτρας τοῦ θήλεως, and Lucian, *Amor.* 19 (quoted by L. Bos) τοῖς μὲν γὰρ ἄρρεσιν ἰδίας καταβολὰς σπερμάτων χαρισαμένη (ἡ τῶν ὅλων φύσις). For a full documentation cf. also F. Bleek, *Der Brief an die Hebräer* (Berlin, 1840), pp. 763 ff.

[3] Ed. *Opera Omnia* (Paris, 1873), p. 34.

[4] *Thesaurus*, s.v. καταβολή.

[5] Theophylact's ingenious suggestion that the *emissio spermatos* could strictly also (according to experts) be attributed to the female is 'nichts als ein verfehlter Versuch das richtige Verständnis des Wortlauts mit der unrichtigen Beziehung auf Sara zu verbinden'. (E. Riggenbach, *Der Brief an die Hebräer*, Zahn, *Kommentar* (Leipzig, 1913), p. 358 n. Cf. also Lactantius, *De opif. dei*, xii, 6, and H. J. Cadbury in *The Expositor*, 1924, pp. 430–9.)

context appears to require no other meaning than εἰς ὑποδοχὴν σπέρματος: but if this had been intended the author would surely have written εἰς ὑποδοχήν and not εἰς καταβολήν.

The variant readings ἔτεκεν and εἰς τὸ τεκνῶσαι, &c., which a number of late manuscripts add after ἔλαβεν and ἡλικίας respectively, are obviously *Schlimmbesserungen*, making explicit this interpretation of εἰς καταβολὴν σπέρματος.[1]

This same type of forced interpretation survives into modern commentators. Theophylact's incursion into gynaecology is paralleled by the observation, repeated in several modern commentaries, that the medical ideas of some Jewish rabbis attributed a relatively active role to the female in conception:[2] this solution was rightly characterized by H. J. Holstein as *ein Fündlein der Exegeten.*[3] If such inventions are to be firmly set aside, so too are modern attempts to foist a passive meaning on the noun καταβολή: thus Spicq supports his contention that εἰς καταβολὴν σπέρματος is the equivalent of εἰς σύλληψιν καταβεβλημένου σπέρματος (*in conceptionem jacti seminis*) by the Papyrus usage of καταβολή as a banking term for payment, receipt (Moulton–Milligan, p. 324*b*): 'ce terme, ayant une acception fondamentale de rétribution et de correspondance, pouvait s'employer en gynécologie de la participation réciproque des conjoints à la génération.' This *tour de force* of ingenuity is matched by the proposal to interpret καταβολή passively like καταβολαῖος from the sense the latter word has in the Papyri of 'storehouse'. (M.M. loc. cit.)[4]

The fact remains that εἰς καταβολὴν σπέρματος must be understood in an active sense, and in all normal Greek usage can only refer to the active function of the male in generation.

A more respectable exegetical tradition interprets καταβολή in the sense of 'establishing' and σπέρμα = 'posterity', and renders 'she received power to establish a posterity'. Both are

[1] Cf. Zuntz, *The Text of the Epistles*, p. 170.

[2] Héring, loc. cit., '*Talmud Nidda* 31*a* (Goldschmidt xii. 442) parle uniquement de la part de la femme dans la formation de l'enfant'.

[3] Cited by Héring, loc. cit.

[4] See R. V. G. Tasker, *N.T.S.*, i, p. 183. See also T. Hewitt, *The Epistle to the Hebrews* (Tyndale Commentary), p. 175.

well-attested meanings for these terms and occur in Hebrews itself, e.g., ii. 16, xi. 18 (σπέρμα), iv. 3, ix. 20 (καταβολή). More than one serious objection, however, can be brought against such a general sense: the whole context (as well as the similar tradition at Romans iv. 19), and particularly the following words παρὰ καιρὸν ἡλικίας and νενεκρωμένου, point unmistakably to an understanding of the miracle of Isaac's birth as his generation (or conception) *against nature*.

Two further solutions have been given for this notorious *crux*. The first was that favoured by Westcott and Hort, namely to read αὐτῇ Σάρρᾳ as a *dativus commodi*, thus leaving Abraham as the subject of both verses; alternatively it is proposed to read a dative and understand in the sense of 'along with'.[1] Zuntz considered it a disservice to the memory of Westcott and Hort to recall this suggestion, and he is probably right: such a construction is both clumsy and unnatural. The second alternative (favoured by Zuntz, following Windisch and Field) is to remove altogether the words καὶ αὐτὴ Σάρρα as a gloss 'condemned by a welter of converging objections'.[2] This is, no doubt, as Windisch remarks,[3] the simplest solution, and there is certainly evidence of other additions (cf. above, ἔτεκεν, εἰς τὸ τεκνῶσαι). Field pointed out (loc. cit.) that 'if we suppose καὶ αὐτὴ Σάρρα to be an interpretation from the margin, the 11th and 12th verses will be continued to Abraham without interruption, and leave nothing to be desired'. Of all the solutions hitherto offered this 'super-interpolation' theory (so Zuntz, loc. cit.) has the greatest merit: but it may still be felt (as Tasker put it)[4] that it is 'too drastic a cutting of the knot'.

There is little doubt, as we have seen, that we have in this verse a 'growing text'. The difficulty, however, is to decide at what point the 'growth' begins. I would suggest that the original text had καὶ αὐτὴ Σάρρα στεῖρα [οὖσα]: the οὖσα is less firmly attested than the στεῖρα. Zuntz regards the latter as having arisen by a dittograph of Σάρρα, even with the supporting

[1] Cf. Moffatt, I.C.C., *Hebrews*, p. 171.

[2] Zuntz, op. cit., p. 16 n. 4.

[3] *Handbuch zum NT*, p. 93.

[4] Op. cit., l.c.

testimony of 𝔓[46] and 1739 for the reading. It may also, however, be an omission due to its similarity to *Σάρρα*. If we assume *καὶ αὐτὴ Σάρρα στεῖρα* [*οὖσα*] as original, then the clause is explicable as a Biblical Greek Circumstantial Clause and the verse translated 'By faith, *even although Sarah was barren*, he (Abraham) received strength for procreation, even though he was past the age'. To take the clause in this way leaves nothing to be desired: the subject throughout these verses 8–13 is Abraham: yet Sarah's condition too is mentioned but in a subordinate role; the words *καὶ παρὰ καιρὸν ἡλικίας* also refer to Abraham not to Sarah; and no difficulties are then raised about her faith or lack of faith,[1] since it is the faith of Abraham and not that of Sarah which is the whole point of the passage.

The only question that remains to be considered is whether we can reasonably claim that the clause *καὶ αὐτὴ Σάρρα στεῖρα* [*οὖσα*] is a genuine instance of a circumstantial clause in this passage. Was the *auctor ad Hebraeos* capable of writing such 'hebraized' Greek? What traces are there of such clauses in the New Testament? Since the claims made above for the presence of this Semitic construction in the New Testament, Dr. Klaus Beyer's important pioneering book on *Semitische Syntax im Neuen Testament*[2] has appeared and thrown fresh light on the *Zustandsatz* in the New Testament, as on other peculiarities of New Testament syntax.

The so-called *Zustandsatz* or circumstantial clause is usually introduced by simple Waw followed as a rule by noun or pronoun; its normal equivalent is a clause introduced by 'while', 'though', 'since', &c. In Greek its idiomatic equivalent is a subordinate clause with *ὡς*, *ὅτε*, &c., or a genitive absolute construction, e.g., 1 Sam. ix. 11, *αὐτῶν ἀναβαινόντων . . . εὑρίσκουσιν*: here the idiomatic Hebrew circumstantial clause is rendered by an equivalent idiomatic Greek type of clause.

[1] Zuntz (op. cit., p. 16) finds Sarah less suited than most to serve as a model for unfailing trust. The difficulty that Sarah laughed the idea of a succession at her (and Abraham's) age to scorn has been felt acutely since the exegesis of the early Fathers, and again commentaries excel themselves in ingenuity in explaining how Sarah's manifest unbelief and lack of faith could be regarded as exemplary of her faith and trust.

[2] Göttingen, 1961.

The Greek renderings of the LXX are not always so idiomatic, however, and more often than not Hebrew idiom is reproduced quite literally, resulting in 'translation Greek', where the words are Greek but the vocabulary, grammar and syntax may be Hebrew. It is true, the LXX can generally be understood and construed as Greek first; the Hebrew idiom may be obscured by the Greek construction. This is particularly so in the case of the circumstantial clause, which is often reproduced in Greek, not as a subordinate clause but as a main clause; and in some cases the translation turns the main clause into a subordinate one.[1] An example is: 1 Sam. vii. 10: *καὶ ἦν Σαμουὴλ ἀναφέρων τὴν ὁλοκαύτωσιν, καὶ ἀλλόφυλοι προσῆγον εἰς πόλεμον ἐπὶ Ἰσραήλ.* In the Hebrew the first clause is subordinate to the second: 'While Samuel was bringing the burnt-offering, the Philistines invaded Israel.' In other cases, however, the literal Hebrew construction is reproduced. Judges xix. 22: *αὐτοὶ δ' ἀγαθύνοντες καρδίαν αὐτῶν, καὶ ἰδοὺ ἄνδρες τῆς πόλεως . . . ἐκύκλωσαν τὴν οἰκίαν. . . .* II Kgdms. xx. 8: *καὶ αὐτοὶ παρὰ τῷ λίθῳ τῷ μεγάλῳ τῷ ἐν Γαβαών, καὶ Ἀμεσσαεὶ ἦλθεν ἔμπροσθεν αὐτῶν. . . .* 2 Sam. iii. 6: *καὶ Ἀβεννὴρ ἦν κρατῶν τοῦ οἴκου Σαοὺλ κ.τ.λ.* The idiom with *καὶ αὐτός* is particularly predominant in Luke,[2] possibly through LXX influence, but it is also found elsewhere in the New Testament.

The circumstantial clause is not unknown to the writer of Hebrews; and this is not surprising for one so deeply versed in the Old Testament. The *καὶ αὐτός* construction appears at i. 5, where the LXX is quoted and where the subordinate clause has been turned into a main clause: *καὶ αὐτὸς ἔσται μοι εἰς υἱόν*: iii. 10 is also a LXX quotation, where the *αὐτοὶ δέ* represents a circumstantial clause in the original. At xi. 39, 𝔓[46] and 1739 omit *οὗτοι* and the reading is accepted by Zuntz,[3] who describes its insertion after *καί* as 'intolerable': 'v. 39 means "and although they had all won their record because of their faith, etc." Full stop before the clause ruins the context.'[4] The clause with *καὶ*

[1] Dan. viii. 2. Cf. Beyer, op. cit., p. 45, n. 1.

[2] See *supra* p. 83, and Beyer, op. cit., p. 44.

[3] Op. cit., p. 34.

[4] Loc. cit., n. (3).

πάντες is, in fact, a typical Hebraic circumstantial clause. At xiii. 21 some of our oldest and weightiest manuscript authorities read an apparently intrusive *αὐτο(ω)*, *αὐτος* (1912), after *τὸ θέλημα αὐτοῦ* and the 'addition' has been explained as a very ancient dittograph.[1] It is, however, a reading which has Old Latin support, e.g., *d, ipso faciente*: the error may have been one of haplography, and the original reading *αὐτός*. The Old Latin by rendering by an ablative absolute has understood the idiom: it may be claimed as a circumstantial clause, 'He working in you', 'While He works in you', &c.

These examples show that the construction was by no means an unfamiliar one to the writer of Hebrews (a further scrutiny of his style might produce other instances); and they make the assumption of such a clause at xi. 11 a reasonable one.

If we explain Heb. xi. 11, *καὶ αὐτὴ Σάρρα στεῖρα* [*οὖσα*], in this way as a Semitism, it may perhaps be better to include the participle as part of the original text: but this is not strictly essential. It is possible that the *αὐτὴ Σάρρα* may also be a Semitism—'and she, Sarah'—cf. Mt. iii. 4, *αὐτὸς δὲ ὁ Ἰωάννης*. These points, however, are of minor importance: the main issue is the nature of the *καὶ αὐτός* clause, gloss or original: if it is original, then the assumption of a Semitism and its explanation as a circumstantial clause removes the main difficulty in this puzzling *crux interpretum*.

The Temporal Clause

Temporal *ὡς* occurs, according to Sir John Hawkins's figures, no less than 48 times in St. Luke's writings (19 times in the Gospel and 29 times in Acts), 16 times in John, and 4 times only in the remainder of the New Testament. One instance is recorded for Mark, but two other examples are found, the second in the Bezan text, iv. 27, vi. 26. There are no instances of the temporal *ὡς* in Matthew.

When idiosyncrasies of style have been allowed for, it is surely remarkable that Luke and John should make such a comparatively frequent use of this conjunction, practically unknown in

1 Cf. Zuntz, op. cit., p. 62.

the rest of the New Testament, and that even the shortest Gospel, Mark, should have the same number of instances (3) as are to be found in the whole of St. Paul's writings; outside of Paul, temporal ὡς does not occur at all in the remaining books.

The Aramaic temporal conjunction *kadh* (a compound originally of *k*[e], 'as', and *di*) is of frequent occurrence in Aramaic narrative. Can we infer that the unidiomatic frequency of temporal ὡς, especially in Luke's writings, is to be traced to the use of ὡς as a standing translation equivalent for *kadh*? At any rate the suggestion offers a reason for the Lucan peculiarity. Matthew prefers ὅτε, as does also Mark; Mt. ix. 25; xiii. 26, 48; xxi. 34; Mk. i. 32, 37 (D); iii. 21 (D); iv. 10; ix. 25 (D); xv. 20. It will be noted that examples of temporal ὅτε are more frequent in the Bezan text of Mark; WH has a more idiomatic Greek participial construction.

Conditional or Concessive Imperative

The use of the Imperative as the equivalent of a concessive clause is familiar in most languages, e.g., *divide et impera*, granted you divide, the consequence will be that you will rule; Gen. xlii. 18, 'This do, and live', i.e., and the consequence will be that you will continue to live. The Imperatival clause in such uses is the equivalent of the protasis of a conditional sentence. Blass–Debrunner give as an example of this concessive imperative Jn. ii. 19, λύσατε τὸν ναὸν τοῦτον (= ἐὰν καὶ λύσητε) καὶ ἐν τρισὶν ἡμέραις ἐγερῶ αὐτόν. As Bultmann (*Komm.* in loc.) remarks, however, we ought rather to explain the imperative here as an ironical Prophetic Imperative in the style of Amos iv. 4 or Is. viii. 9:

Come to Bethel, and transgress;
to Gilgal, and multiply transgression;
bring your sacrifices every morning,
your tithes every three days. (Amos iv. 4)

Be broken, you peoples, and be dismayed;
give ear, all you far countries;
gird yourselves and be dismayed;
gird yourselves and be dismayed. [R.S.V.] (Is. viii. 9)

The thoroughly Semitic character of the construction here is fully confirmed by the use of *καί* in the Apodosis with the force of *Waw* consecutive.

Since the usage cannot be declared un-Greek, the Greek concessive imperative may be all that is required to explain Mk. xi. 22: *Ἔχετε πίστιν Θεοῦ, Ἀμὴν λέγω ὑμῖν ὅτι ὃς ἂν εἴπῃ τῷ ὄρει τούτῳ κ.τ.λ.* The *ἔχετε* clause, however, has not been recognized, at any rate by the English versions or most commentaries, as having this force of a concessive imperative in the protasis. The variant readings in D, *Θ*, &c., are obviously harmonizing variants from Lk. xvii. 6 or Mt. xxi. 21, but these Synoptic variants clearly indicate that this is how we are to understand the clause, viz., 'Granted you possess faith in God, truly I tell you that whosoever says, &c.'

General Results

The more general results of this study of the Aramaic subordinate clause may be summarized:

1. Aramaic *d*[e] has undoubtedly given rise to difficulties when it came to be rendered into Greek, and there may be several genuine instances of mistranslation. But in most cases we appear to be dealing less with mistranslation than with deliberate (and legitimate) interpretations of the Aramaic, which can be defended in the sense they have in the context and connexion in which the words have been set by the Evangelists. Such interpretations do not always give the most natural meaning of the underlying Aramaic, and to this extent they may perhaps be described as misinterpretations. But they are not simply errors of translation. They are deliberate Greek renderings of a meaning possible in the original. The Greek Gospels in this respect are not just literal renderings of Aramaic originals, but to some considerable extent original Greek compositions incorporating interpretations of Aramaic sources.

2. The distribution of the evidence for the translation and mistranslation of Aramaic *d*[e] is again decisive for the existence of an Aramaic sayings-tradition behind the Words of Jesus, not excluding the sayings in the Fourth Gospel: thus, Mt. vi. 5,

xiii. *16*; Mk. iv. *12*; Jn. v. *39*, viii. *45*, xiv. *16*. But a considerable proportion of examples occur outside the sayings of Jesus, and almost exclusively in dialogue: thus, Mk. iv. 41, ix. 38 (cf. v. 23), xiv. 68; Jn. viii. 53, ix. 17; Acts i. 17, vii. 39. This evidence is not perhaps extensive enough to allow of any definite conclusion, but it clearly suggests that, besides a written or oral tradition of the sayings of Jesus, the Evangelists, and especially Mark, may have possessed an Aramaic tradition of the dialogue and speeches of Jesus' many interlocutors. The evidence in Acts, though slight, speaks for itself.

3. The traces of the influence of the Aramaic circumstantial clause may be claimed as evidence that the Gospels are translations of Aramaic. The fact remains, however, that, while the Greek is clumsy and unidiomatic, it is neither ungrammatical nor altogether impossible as Greek. The best explanation may be that we have here to do with genuine examples of translation of Aramaic sources; the circumstantial clause in the saying of Jesus in Lk. xiii. 28 almost certainly reflects such a clause in the Aramaic saying. But the proof elsewhere is not irrefragible, for the Gospel writers may be thinking in a Semitic language and converting the construction into its nearest Greek equivalent. It is very unlikely that an exact literal translation of an Aramaic circumstantial clause in Mk. i. 19, καὶ αὐτοὶ . . . καταρτίζοντες, ever existed in Greek. If we had such a construction in the Gospels, it would be possible to claim literal translation of Aramaic; but what we do have is a Greek sentence, not an Aramaic one.

4. The textual variants from an ambiguous Aramaic *d*[e] occurred mostly in D and the Old Latin or the Vulgate. The evidence of Luke's circumstantial clause, however, where the Aramaism predominates in WH, warns, as did the evidence of asyndeton for the Bezan text of Mark, against any hasty judgement as to the priority of the claims of any one Uncial authority to represent more fully the primitive text.

CHAPTER VI

ARAMAIC INFLUENCE ON GRAMMAR AND VOCABULARY

The Definite Article

THE hitherto recognized Semitisms in the use of the definite article in the New Testament are: (*a*) the omission of the article before a following genitive, through the influence of the Semitic *status constructus*, e.g. Mt. xii. 42, *βασίλισσα Νότου*, '*the* queen of the South',[1] and (*b*) the insertion of the article in accordance with the Semitic idiom by which a noun is made definite 'to denote a single person or thing (primarily one which is as yet unknown, and therefore not capable of being defined) as being present to the mind under given circumstances',[2] e.g. Mt. x. 29 (D), *τοῦ ἀσσαρίου*, 'for *a* farthing'.[3]

(*a*) The first construction is more Hebraic than Aramaic, for the construct has largely fallen into abeyance in all Aramaic dialects; except in a number of stereotyped expressions, its place has been taken by the genitival construction with *d^{e}*. (*b*) While the second idiom is common in Hebrew (and in the LXX), it is doubtful if it is Aramaic. There certainly was no special form by which it could be recognized, for the *status emphaticus*, by which the definite article was originally expressed, had lost its significance in first-century Aramaic and was used for definite and indefinite nouns alike.[4]

[1] *Einl.*[1], p. 26; Moulton, *Prol.*, p. 236 (note on p. 81).

[2] Ges.-Kautzsch, *Gramm.*, p. 407 f. [3] *Einl.*[1], l.c.; 2nd edit., p. 19; Moulton, l.c.

[4] See, however, Jeremias's statements (in *Theol. Literaturzeitung*, 1949, Nr. 9, p. 530) on the view that the disuse of the *status emphaticus* has influenced New Testament usage: 'Auch ich habe diese Erklärung früher vertreten, habe mich aber bei näherer Prüfung überzeugen müssen, daß man viel vorsichtiger formulieren muß. Die Setzung des Artikels trotz indefinitiver Bedeutung findet sich schon im A. T. unter anderem öfter bei Vergleichen und in Bildreden. Dem entspricht auch der Tatbestand in den Evangelien, nur daß das Phänomen darüber hinaus Terrain zu erobern beginnt. Es ist aber im I. Jahrhundert keineswegs bereits so weit, daß der status emphaticus schon völlig seine determinierende Bedeutung verloren hätte.' Is this use of the article in the Old Testament to be set down to the influence of the Hebrew idiom discussed above? Jn. iii. 10 may perhaps be so explained, and rendered, 'Art thou a teacher, &c.'. Cf. further, *Die Gleichnisse Jesu*[6], p. 7 (note 2).

The disappearance of this formal distinction between definite and indefinite nouns in Aramaic may have been a further cause of anomalous insertions and omissions of the Greek article in the Gospels.[1] Since the same form could be employed for both definite and indefinite, a translator from Aramaic into Greek may on occasion have rendered a noun as indefinite which was, in its context, definite, and vice versa; or Aramaic usage in this respect may have even led to an obscuring, in everyday speech, of the distinction between definite and indefinite.

This suggestion was made by A. J. Wensinck, who cited instances from the Bezan text of Luke where the article has been inserted or omitted wrongly but is correctly present or absent in the WH text.[2] Two of his examples (vii. 10, ix. 61) are cases of anarthrous nouns after a preposition, an omission of the article sanctioned by Koine usage.[3] Two others (xi. 2, 19) are of nouns followed by a personal pronoun in the genitive: in Hebrew and Aramaic pronouns are affixed to nouns and the noun is definite in virtue of the affix; the article is similarly omitted in the Gospels when a noun is followed by a possessive pronoun in the genitive in accordance with this Semitic usage.[4] Lk. xiv. 9 and xi. 44 are relevant examples: in the first, *ἔσχατον τόπον*, it is to *the* last place that the presumptuous guest is to be degraded. In the second, WH read *τὰ μνημεῖα τὰ ἄδηλα*, where the noun is properly indefinite, as in D.

Examples of an anomalous omission of the article are rare in the WH text. Mk. ii. 21 (and parallels) is one: the A.V., with more regard to the natural meaning of the words than to strict grammar, renders, '. . . and *the* rent (*σχίσμα*) is made worse'. But the words can only be translated, as Swete insists,[5] '. . . and *a* worse rent is the result', or, as the R.V. renders, '. . . and *a* worse rent is made'. In support of the A.V. it may be urged

[1] Moulton (*Prol.*, p. 81) states that the New Testament is 'remarkably correct' in its use of the definite article as compared with the papyri. While this is true of the Vatican text, in D, 'the Greek article is perpetually left out, where no native would have dispensed with it' (Scrivener, *Codex Bezae Cantabrigiensis*, p. xlviii).

[2] *Semitisms*, p. 11 f.

[3] Cf. Moulton, *Prol.*, p. 81 f.

[4] *Einl.*[1], p. 26.

[5] *The Gospel according to St. Mark*, in loc.

that in the Greek rendering of the Aramaic a *status emphaticus* has been wrongly understood as indefinite. The noun may have been, however, anarthrous in Aramaic, in the *status absolutus*, and yet have been definite: the saying is a poetic one, and in Semitic poetry anarthrous nouns may be definite. We are justified in rendering, '. . . and the rent is made worse'.

Examples where the article is anomalously inserted are more frequent in the WH text: Mt. v. 15, ὑπὸ τὸν μόδιον, 'under *a* measure', ἐπὶ τὴν λυχνίαν, 'upon *a* lamp-stand', xii. 24, 27, τὰ δαιμόνια, 'demons', xv. 29, εἰς τὸ ὄρος, 'to *a* mountain'; Mk. vi. 55, ἐπὶ τοῖς κραβάττοις, 'on beds' (D omits τοῖς).

A long list of unusual omissions and insertions of the definite article in the Bezan text of the Synoptic Gospels is given by von Soden.[1] Many of the omissions occur before proper names. The latter are *ipso facto* definite in Aramaic and are generally given in the *status absolutus*. D, in this respect, reflects the Semitic idiom, whereas WH has the correct Greek honorific article, and especially before the name Jesus; numerous examples appear in von Soden.

A large proportion of von Soden's omissions occur before nouns followed by a genitive, Semitism (*a*) above. Other omissions and insertions are before parts of speech other than nouns; some are in Old Testament quotations; and not all are accurately reported. A typical example of anomalous omission is Mk. vi. 35, ἔρημός ἐστι τόπος, '*the* place is deserted'; an insertion is Mt. xii. 12, πόσῳ οὖν διαφέρει ἄνθρωπος τοῦ προβάτου, 'How much then is a man better than *a* sheep'. The following examples occur; most come from sayings of Jesus.

Omissions: Mt. xii. *35*, ὁ ante ἀγαθός: xix. *17*, τοῦ a. ἀγαθοῦ.
Mk. vii. *6*, τῶν a. ὑποκριτῶν: ix. 15, ὁ a. ὄχλος: xiv. *62*, τῆς a. δυνάμεως.
Lk. vi. *45*, τὸ a. ἀγαθόν: xiv. *21*, τούς a. πτωχούς.

Insertions: Mt. xviii. *19*, τοῦ a. πράγματος.
Mk. ii. *7*, τάς a. ἁμαρτίας: xii. *1*, τοῖς a. γεωργοῖς.
Lk. vii. *32*, τοῖς a. παιδίοις: τῇ a. ἀγορᾷ; x. *19*, τῶν a. ὄφεων: τῶν a. σκορπίων.

[1] *Schriften des neuen Testaments*, I. ii, p. 1309.

The Pronoun

1. *Redundant Pronouns*

Semitic languages make use of a pleonastic or redundant pronoun, where in English an article is all that is required to express the meaning. Thus Mk. xiv. 25, ἕως τῆς ἡμέρας ἐκείνης, 'until the day'. For the idiom in Aramaic and Syriac, see Jeremias, *Abendmahlsworte Jesu*[2], 1949, p. 94 (note 1); cf. further *Die Gleichnisse Jesu*[2], p. 25 (note 8).

2. *The Proleptic Pronoun*

The employment of a personal pronoun in the nominative or the oblique cases to anticipate, for the sake of emphasis, a following noun, is a well-known Aramaic idiom. Some examples, in illustration, are given by Burney.[1] If the existence of the construction can be established for the New Testament, then we have a pure Aramaism, giving clear indication of linguistic influence, and, since the usage is not only clumsy but indefensible in Greek, possible evidence of literal translation of sources.

Not all examples which have been claimed for the construction in the Gospels are equally convincing. To explain the variant of D in Lk. xxii. 48, ὁ δὲ Ἰησοῦς εἶπεν, for Ἰησοῦς δὲ εἶπεν, as reflecting an Aramaic proleptic pronoun in the nominative, is entirely unnecessary:[2] the words in D do not mean, 'And He, Jesus, said', but simply, 'And Jesus said'; we have to do, not with a 'proleptic pronoun', but with the insertion of the Greek honorific article, omitted in WH, which in this case is more Semitic than the Bezan text.[3]

True examples of the proleptic pronoun in the nominative were pointed out by Wellhausen in Mt. iii. 4, αὐτὸς δὲ ὁ Ἰωάννης, and Mk. vi. 17, αὐτὸς γὰρ ὁ Ἡρώδης;[4] to them may be added Mk. xii. 36, 37, αὐτὸς Δαυείδ.

[1] *Aramaic Origin*, p. 85 f.

[2] Wensinck, *Semitisms*, p. 19.

[3] *Supra*, p. 95.

[4] *Einl.*[1], p. 27; cf. Moulton, *Prol.*, p. 91, *Gramm.* ii, p. 431. For examples of the construction in Aramaic, see Burney, l.c.

In several other cases a scribal error and not an Aramaic idiom may best account for the impossible Greek: thus Acts iii. 2 (D), παρ' αὐτῶν εἰσπορευομένων, is probably no more than a mistake for παρὰ τῶν εἰσπορευομένων: in Lk. xxiv. 10 (D), πρὸς αὐτοὺς ἀποστόλους (claimed as proleptic pronoun by Wensinck),[1] the first syllable of the apparent pronoun may come from the following ταῦτα. Similarly, in Lk. iv. 43 (D), (δεῖ με καὶ εἰς τὰς ἄλλας πολεῖς) εὐαγγελίσασθαι αὐτὴν βασιλείαν τοῦ Θεοῦ, the αυ may have arisen through a dittograph of the last two letters of the verb; in this case, however, the appearance of a construction such as εὐαγγελίζεσθαι εἰς makes one pause; it is an Aramaic construction,[2] and occurs here in a saying of Jesus.

In other more striking cases the pronoun is found along with the definite article in combinations of letters where scribal carelessness may not be so readily assumed. One such is the reading of AC in Mk. vi. 22, αὐτῆς τῆς Ἡρῳδιάδος.[3] The less difficult αὐτοῦ, weightily supported, makes out that the girl bore her mother's name and was Herod's daughter. But we know that her name was Salome, and that she was the grand-niece, not the daughter, of Herod Antipas.[4] The masculine αὐτοῦ appears to be a correction of the more difficult αὐτῆς. We may wish to press the pronoun; it was the daughter of Herodias herself who danced like a common courtesan. But the solecism occurs again in the text of D in verse 18 (four verses earlier), αὐτὴν γυναῖκα τοῦ ἀδελφοῦ σου, and in its other rare occurrences appears most frequently in Mark (see below).

Two explanations may be given of Lk. x. 7, ἐν αὐτῇ δὲ τῇ οἰκίᾳ. It may be a literal rendering of the Aramaic proleptic pronoun, 'in it (namely) the house'; in the context of this saying of Jesus, such an emphatic proleptic pronoun is idiomatic and natural; to reproduce the required emphasis in translation we should require to use the demonstrative adjective, '. . . in *that* house remain . . .' The assumption of a 'semi-demonstrative'

[1] l.c.

[2] e.g. Jer. Targ., Gen. xxi. 7, '. . . who announced to (*b^e sar l^e*) my lord'; cf. Sy^s in Lk. iv. 43.

[3] Cf. Wellhausen, *Einl.*[1], p. 27; 2nd edit., p. 19.

[4] Justin., *Dial.* 49.

use of *αὐτός* for Hellenistic Greek, such as the pronoun has in Modern Greek, to explain the difficult *αὐτῇ* is unwarranted by Koine usage; some other examples than those given by Moulton[1] would require to be adduced; *ὁ αὐτὸς Ὧρος* from a papyrus is 'the same Horus', and may be understood as 'the aforesaid Horus', but it is not *ille* Horus. The pronoun may, however, be explained as a misrendering of an Aramaic demonstrative; personal and demonstrative pronouns in Aramaic are liable to be confused in texts and manuscripts (there is nothing to suggest that they were ever confused in speech).[2] The first explanation is the more probable: Luke is reproducing unedited a translation Greek version of the saying of Jesus from his source; in this case he is drawing on Q.

This Aramaism may shed light on three passages in the Gospels. In the parallels, Mk. viii. 38, *ἐν τῇ δόξῃ τοῦ πατρὸς αὐτοῦ*, Lk. ix. 26, *ἐν τῇ δόξῃ αὐτοῦ καὶ τοῦ πατρός*, the difference in Aramaic is slight. The Marcan form would read literally, 'in his glory (namely that) of his Father', where the first pronoun is proleptic and looks forward to the Father; the second is the usual possessive pronoun referring back to the Son of Man. But a translator, either because the idiom was unfamiliar or (more probably) for an obvious dogmatic reason, made the proleptic pronoun refer to the Son of Man and expanded the Marcan saying by way of interpretation into 'in his glory and (in the glory of) his Father'.

A similar example of the same kind of interpretation of an Aramaic proleptic pronoun can account for an unexpected *αὐτοῦ* in the quotation of Isa. xl. 3, occurring in the same form (from Mark) in all the Synoptics (Mk. i. 3; Mt. iii. 3; Lk. iii. 4), *εὐθείας ποιεῖτε τὰς τρίβους αὐτοῦ*: the LXX reads *τὰς τρίβους τοῦ Θεοῦ ἡμῶν*, and no Old Testament authority attests a variant *αὐτοῦ*. The 'variant' is really an alteration or adaptation of the Old Testament quotation to suit the Marcan interpretation of it:

[1] *Prol.*, p. 91.

[2] I have noted examples of the confusion in Jer. Targ. i, Num. xxiv. 19, and in the Krotoschin edition of the Pal. Talmud in *Kiddush*. i. 7, f. 61*a*, 12 lines from foot of col., *Ma'aser Sheni*, iv. 9, f. 55*b*, line 51, and *Ta'anith*, i. 4, f. 64*b*, line 51.

the Lord is Jesus, announced as Christ, the Son of God, and it is *His* paths that John the Forerunner summons men to make straight. We need not, however, assume that Mark simply leaves out τοῦ Θεοῦ ἡμῶν and inserts his own αὐτοῦ to suit his special purpose; the pronoun may already have been present in the Aramaic quotation, 'his paths (namely those) of our God';[1] Mark is interpreting the Aramaic to suit his argument. There is evidence elsewhere that Mark draws on Aramaic Old Testament sources;[2] and the Jews never altered the words of Scripture, though they did not shrink from interpreting or adapting them, sometimes in the most fantastic ways, to a theological argument.

The third example of a possible survival of a proleptic pronoun occurs in Jn. viii. 44, where the difficulty is the αὐτοῦ: it has been taken along with ὁ πατήρ, its natural Greek connexion, '. . . for his father also is a liar' (so the early Fathers); some explain ψεύστης as antecedent and render, '. . . for he is a liar and the father of him (the liar)'; the A.V. gives the most reasonable sense by referring the pronoun back to τὸ ψεῦδος, '. . . for he is a liar and the father of it (the lie)'. However we try to account for it, there is a decided failure in the Greek. The only satisfactory version is that of the Arabic Tatian, which contains an idiomatic proleptic pronoun, '. . . for he is a liar and the father of it (namely of) the lie'.[3] The Arabic reading is not that of the Peshiṭta, and where the Arabic differs from the latter it occasionally preserves a reading of Tatian;[4] we may have here a genuine *varia lectio*, perhaps the primitive text, and may be justified in translating, '. . . for he is a liar and *the father of lies*'.

Wilcox has drawn attention to two other possible examples of this unidiomatic pronoun at Acts vi. 7 (D), ὑπήκουον αὐτῇ πίστει, and xi. 27 (Bℵ), ἐν αὐταῖς δὲ ταῖς ἡμέραις (other MSS. ἐν ταύταις δὲ ταῖς ἡμέραις).[5] The distribution of the construction in the Gospels and Acts is instructive. With the exception of Mk. vi. 22,

[1] Sy^c in Mt. iii. 3 has the LXX reading with the Aramaic idiom, 'his paths (namely those) of our God'.

[2] *Infra*, p. 214 f.

[3] In MSS. B and E of Marmardji's edition; see Appendix B.

[4] See Appendix B.

[5] Op. cit., pp. 128 ff.

Acts vi. 7, xi. 27, and two doubtful cases which Burney found in Jn. ix. 13, 18,[1] it is confined to four sayings of Jesus and elsewhere to dialogue or direct speech. It appears almost exclusively in the Bezan text.

Mt. xii. *45* (D); Mk. v. *15* (D), *16* (D), vi. 18 (D) (direct speech), 22 (AC); Lk. iv. *43* (D), x. *7*; Acts vii. 52 (D) (Stephen).

Lk. i. 36, *αὐτῇ τῇ καλουμένῃ στείρᾳ* (direct speech), may also be claimed.[2]

The best explanation of this linguistic oddity in the Gospels and Acts is that it is a genuine Aramaism, evidence for a very primitive kind of translation or Semitic Greek. It would not, of course, be understood by Greek readers who were not Jews or Greek-speaking Syrians; they would have no alternative but to make the best they could of the construction. Many other examples were probably removed from the primitive text; the examples that have survived are the few that have escaped correction. Those in the sayings of Jesus may owe their survival to the religious conservatism that preserves unaltered a fixed tradition.

3. *The Relative Pronoun*

Burney has shown that the characteristic Semitic construction of a relative completed by a personal pronoun at the end of its clause is found in the Fourth Gospel.[3] The construction occurs in the LXX and elsewhere in the New Testament; Moulton noted six examples from the Apocalypse, Rev. iii. 8; vii. 2, 9; xiii. 8, 12; xx. 8.[4] Parallels to the construction have been cited from the papyri.[4] In the LXX, it 'undoubtedly owes its frequency to the Hebrew original',[5] but Isa. i. 21, where it is not in the Hebrew, shows that it does not only occur where the LXX is slavishly translating the Hebrew idiom.

The construction may be possible in Greek, but it is not native to it, as it is in Hebrew and Aramaic. Its distribution in the

[1] *Aramaic Origin*, p. 85.

[2] A further example of the Aramaism in a temporal conjunction is discussed *infra*, p. 108.

[3] *Aramaic Origin*, p. 84 f.

[4] *Gramm.* ii, p. 435.

[5] Thackeray, *Grammar of the LXX*, p. 46.

Gospels gives clear proof of its Semitic origin (as does its appearance in the Apocalypse). Of some twelve instances which have been claimed, Jn. ix. 36 is a doubtful case; it involves the assumption of an Aramaic relative mistranslated by ἵνα. In the remaining ten, six come from sayings of Jesus, and one only is not from dialogue or direct speech; it comes significantly from Mark (vii. 25). Lk. xii. *43* (D) does not appear to have been noted before: *μακάριος ὁ δοῦλος ἐκεῖνος, ὃν ἐλθὼν ὁ κύριος αὐτοῦ εὑρήσει αὐτὸν ποιοῦντα οὕτως.* At Acts x. 38 Wilcox argues for the reading of D *ὃν ἔχρισεν αὐτὸν ὁ Θεός* as the original, because the most 'Semitic' reading. If it is original, then it reflects this idiom of the resumptive pronoun following a preceding relative. In this case, however, the alternative possibility must be borne in mind that the 'Semitism' may reflect the influence of a Syriac version at this point; the idiom does occur in the Peshiṭta for this verse (ܕܐܠܗܐ ܡܫܚܗ). The construction again predominates in the text of D.

Mt. iii. 12 (= Lk. iii. 17) (Baptist), x. *11* (D), xviii. *20* (D); Mk. i. 7 (Baptist), vii. 25; Lk. viii. *12* (D), xii. *43* (D); Jn. i. 27 (Baptist), 33 (Baptist), ix. 36 (dialogue), xiii. *26*, xviii. *9*; Acts x. 38.

4. *The Reflexive Pronoun and the Ethic Dative*

The absence of reflexive pronouns proper in the Semitic languages is, according to Wellhausen, the cause of the comparative rarity of reflexives in the Gospels.[1] Semitic influence, here as elsewhere, has no doubt contributed, but other purely Greek influences were also at work: the difference between reflexive and non-reflexive pronominal forms tends to disappear altogether in the papyri, and not only do the simple personal pronouns come to be used as reflexives, but even the rare reflexive forms as personal pronouns.[2] The comparative rarity, therefore, of distinctive reflexive forms in the Gospels need not be attributed solely, if at all, to Semitic influence.

[1] *Einl.*[1], p. 30; 2nd edit., p. 23. The manuscript tradition varies as to the third person reflexive, ἑαυτοῦ or αὐτοῦ, and Wellhausen believed that the latter (without *spiritus asper*) represented the primitive text (l.c.).

[2] See E. Mayser, *Gramm. der griech. Papyri*, i, p. 304, 4, and ii, p. 67, *2b*.

The use of the noun ψυχή as a reflexive is, on the other hand, a pure Semitism: the difference between Mk. viii. 36 and Lk. ix. 25 is that between a literal and a more literary version. Mt. vi. 25, μὴ μεριμνᾶτε τῇ ψυχῇ, may contain a reflexive 'for yourselves', but the meaning 'life' ought perhaps to be pressed.

The place of reflexives in the Semitic languages is largely taken by the *dativus ethicus*, a very common construction in Aramaic. It is not unknown in Greek, where it is usually classed as an extension of the *dativus commodi* or *incommodi*,[1] but it is rare as compared with Aramaic usage, where it is a means of stressing the action of the subject and corresponds more to the Greek Middle than to the *dativus commodi*. The following examples will illustrate: *Eleph. Pap.* 41. 6, 'I *went me* (*'ᵃzaliṯh li*) home'; Palestinian Talmud, *Kil'aim*, ix. 4, f. 32*b*, line 25 f., 'As soon as he had thus heard, he *betook himself up* (*sᵉlaq leh*) to the roof'; *Terumoth*, viii. 5, f. 45*c*, line 60, '. . . he ate, slumbered, and *fell him asleep* (*dᵉmakh leh*)'.

The clearest cases in the Gospels occur where a pronoun in the dative follows the verb: Mt. xxiii. 31, μαρτυρεῖτε ἑαυτοῖς, Jn. xix. 17, βαστάζων ἑαυτῷ τὸν σταυρόν, are usually explained as cases of *dativus incommodi*, but they may also be claimed as ethic datives. Two less familiar instances, difficult to defend as Greek, are found in the Bezan text: Torrey noted Mt. xxiii. 9, μὴ καλέσητε ὑμῖν;[2] the second is Mk. vii. 4, ἃ παρέλαβον αὐτοῖς τηρεῖν, '. . . which they received *them* to keep'.

The best proof of the un-Greek character of the construction in several other examples is to be found in the difficult expedients to make it intelligible as Greek. In Lk. xxiv. 12, ἀπῆλθε πρὸς ἑαυτὸν θαυμάζων, the prepositional phrase is usually connected with the participle, '. . . he went away, wondering in himself'. But that it is really to be taken with ἀπῆλθε is clear from the Johannine parallel, xx. 10, where we read ἀπῆλθον οὖν πάλιν πρὸς αὐτοὺς οἱ μαθηταί.[3] The R.V. renders the latter, '. . . departed

[1] Cf. A. T. Robertson, *Grammar of the Greek New Testament*, p. 538 f.

[2] *Our Translated Gospels*, p. 76.

[3] Cf. further Josephus, *Antiq.* viii. iv. 6, and A. Schlatter, *Der Evangelist Johannes*, p. 357, W. Howard, *London Quarterly and Holborn Review*, Apr. 1947.

unto their home', no doubt a defensible rendering. The expression ἀπελθεῖν πρὸς αὐτόν corresponds to Aramaic *'ᵃzal leh*, as in the example from the Elephantine Papyrus above, 'took him off', 'went him away'.[1]

In Mk. x. 26 (D), λέγοντες πρὸς ἑαυτούς (= Lk. xxii. 65 (D), εἰς ἑαυτούς), we have a phrase which occurs in all texts of Jn. xii. 19, εἶπον πρὸς ἑαυτούς. Both passages may be understood as the A.V. renders, 'saying among themselves', 'The Pharisees . . . said among themselves', though such a translation puts a decided strain on the Greek preposition. Understood as *dativus ethicus* the phrase is simple, emphatic, and effective, 'were *them* saying' or 'did *them* say'. The reading of WH in Mk. x. 26 = Lk. xxii. 65, εἰς αὐτόν, presents no difficulties, and that is probably the reason for it; it represents a correction of the more difficult reading of D.

A difficult construction is found in Lk. vii. 30, ἠθέτησαν εἰς ἑαυτούς, which, as it stands, raises as serious a problem of exegesis as it does of philology.[2] As ethic dative the words mean, 'did *them* annul the counsel of God'; the idiomatic Aramaic construction gives a most effective emphasis to the action of the Pharisees and lawyers in withholding themselves from the baptism of John.

A further example with πρός is Mk. xiv. 4, ἦσαν δέ τινες ἀγανακτοῦντες πρὸς ἑαυτούς, which gives the apparent sense, 'some were vexed with themselves'; 'among themselves', the only possible meaning that can be given to the Greek, again strains the preposition. On the other hand, 'some were *indeed* vexed' gives excellent sense.

Lk. xviii. 11 may be another instance, if we can agree to take πρὸς ἑαυτόν immediately after σταθείς (with the Textus Receptus); the Aramaic ethic dative follows the verb it is designed to emphasize. The words then mean, 'The Pharisee, taking his stand, prayed . . .'[3] But our better manuscript authorities take the phrase with προσηύχετο, which also gives a good sense; the

[1] Cf. Meyer, *Jesu Muttersprache*, p. 124, and Torrey, op. cit., l.c.

[2] Cf. Wellhausen, *Evangelium Lukae*, in loc., and Torrey, op. cit., p. 79.

[3] Cf. Torrey, op. cit., p. 79.

Pharisee prayed 'in himself'. Wilcox cites two additional examples from Acts: Acts xiv. 2 (D) *οἱ δὲ ἀρχισυνάγωγοι . . . καὶ οἱ ἄρχοντες . . . ἐπήγαγον αὐτοῖς διωγμὸν κατὰ τῶν δικαίων κ.τ.λ.* '. . . the chiefs of the synagogues . . . and the rulers . . . stirred *them* up persecution, &c.' Acts xv. 2 (D) has *οἱ δὲ ἐληλυθότες ἀπὸ Ἱερουσαλὴμ παρήγγειλαν αὐτοῖς τῷ Παύλῳ καὶ Βαρνάβᾳ.* As Wilcox has pointed out, the pronoun may be explained as *proleptic*, but it may also represent this *dativus ethicus*: as Greek it certainly is not easily explained.[1] Two further examples may be Acts i. 26, *ἔδωκαν . . αὐτοῖς* (D* *αὐτῶν*) and the reading of 𝔭45 at Acts viii. 17: *τότε ἐπετίθουν αὐτοῖς τὰς χεῖρας ἐπ' αὐτούς.*

The distribution of the construction is as follows: out of sixteen possible examples, four occur in sayings of Jesus, three are from Mark, and three from John, of which xx. 10 may be claimed with confidence in view of the failure in the Greek. Lk. xxiv. 12 has a Johannine parallel in xx. 10; both may go back to the same piece of Aramaic tradition. The construction is most frequent in D.

Mt. xxiii. *9* (D), *31*; Mk. vii. 4 (D), x. 26 (D), xiv. 4; Lk. vii. *30*, xviii. *11*, xxii. 65 (= Mk. x. 26), xxiv. 12 (= Jn. xx. 10); Jn. xii. 19, xix. 17, xx. 10; Acts i. 26, viii. 17, x. 2, xiv. 2.

5. *Indefinite Pronouns*

As Howard has pointed out,[2] Wellhausen claimed a Semitic origin for three substitutes for *τις*, (*a*) *εἷς*, (*b*) *ἄνθρωπος*, (*c*) an indefinite plural expressed by *ἀπό* or *ἐκ* with following Gen. (Semitic *min*).[3]

(*a*) *Εἷς* for *τις*. The use of *εἷς* in this way in Hellenistic Greek, and especially in the Papyri,[4] has led to the denial of Semitic influence. Blass–Debrunner remark, however, that 'für das NT war auch das hebr. *'äḥad* und das aram. *ḥad* Vorbild'.[5]

Examples of Aramaic *ḥadh* given by Dalman are of pronominal adjectives only, e.g. *ḥadh barnash*, 'a certain man'.[6] An

[1] Cf. Ropes, *Beginnings of Christianity*, I. iii. 139*b*.

[2] *Gramm.* ii, pp. 432 ff.

[3] *Einl.*[1], p. 27; 2nd edit., p. 20.

[4] Howard, l.c.

[5] *Gramm.*, § 247.

[6] *Gramm.*[2], p. 121.

example of *ḥadh* as indefinite pronoun is cited by Wensinck from *Ned.* x. 10, f. 42ʳ*b*, line 16, '. . . he was concerned about a certain one (*ḥadh*) . . .'. Especially idiomatic in Hebrew and Aramaic is a usage of this pronoun with a following genitive or partitive *min* where the compound expression means nothing more than 'a certain so-and-so'; e.g. in Dalman's *Aram. Dialektproben*, p. 36, line 2, 'a certain water-carrier' (*ḥadh mashqai dᵉmayyim*, lit. a certain one of the providers of water); in Hebrew, Gen. xxxvii. 20, 'into one of the pits' (*lᵉ'aḥath habboroth*), i.e. 'into a certain pit', or simply, 'into a pit'; no mention has previously been made of 'pits', and none is required for this idiom; LXX εἰς ἕνα τῶν λάκκων. Other examples, Gen. xxi. 15, Lev. xiv. 30, Dan. vii. 16, 1 Macc. iv. 38, ὡς ἐν ἑνὶ τῶν ὀρέων, 'as on a hill'.

Instances of εἷς as indefinite pronoun in the New Testament fall into two classes: (i) where εἷς is a pronominal adjective; and (ii) where it is a full pronoun, generally followed by this genitive construction or partitive ἐκ.

(i) *Mk.*: xii. *42* (cf. Lk. xxi. *2*).

Mt.: viii. 19 (cf. Lk. ix. 57); ix. 18 (cf. Mk. v. 22[1]); xii. *11* (cf. Lk. xiv. 5); xviii. *24*; xxi. 19 (cf. Mk. xi. 13 א); xxvi. 69 (cf. Mk. xiv. 66).

Jn.: xx. 7.

Acts: xii. 10.[2]

Rev.: viii. 13; ix. 13; xviii. 21; xix. 17.

(ii) *Mk.* v. 22, 'a certain ruler of the synagogue'[3] (cf. Mt. ix. 18); vi. 15 (viii. 28),[4] ix. 17; xii. 28; xiii. 1; xiv. 10,[5] 20, 43, 66 (cf. Mt. xxvi. 69, Lk. xxii. 56).

Mt.: xxii. 35 (cf. Mk. xii. 28, Lk. x. 25); xxvii. 48 (cf. Mk. xv. 36 T.R.).

Lk.: v. 3, 12, 17 (= viii. 22, xx. 1, ἐν μιᾷ τῶν ἡμερῶν, 'on a certain day', Moffatt, 'one day'); xiii. 10; xv. *15*; xvii. 15; xxii. 50 (nonn. mss. om. τις); xxiv. 18.

[1] Cf. Hawkins in *Hor. Syn.*², p. 30.

[2] Cf. Torrey, *Composition and Date of Acts*, p. 7.

[3] Cf. Hawkins, op. cit., p. 20.

[4] Cf. Joüon, *L'Évangile*, in loc., who compares 1 Kings xix. 2, Obad. 11 'like any of the prophets', i.e. a prophet like any (true) prophet.

[5] Is the article here to be explained as on p. 93? Cf. Gen. xlii. 32; LXX; Moulton, *Prol.*, p. 97.

Jn.: vi. 8 (xii. 4, xiii. 23); vi. *70*; xii. 2; xviii. 22(?), 26; xix. 34; xx. 24.

Acts: xi. 28.

Rev.: v. 5 (vii. 13); xvii. 1 (xxi. 9).

(*b*) Ἄνθρωπος = τις. Wellhausen drew attention to the use of an indefinite ἄνθρωπος 'zur stärkeren Hervorhebung der Indetermination' in Matthew (e.g. xiii. 28 ἐχθρὸς ἄνθρωπος) and added 'vergeblich sucht man zu leugnen daß hier ἄνθρωπος etwas anderes sei als das aramäische *nâsch*, welches im Status absolutus für quidam gebraucht und den Hauptwörtern vor- oder nachgesetzt wird.'[1] The usage is not, however, confined to the first Gospel (or to Aramaic); and ἄνθρωπος (like Heb. *'ish*, Aram. *barnash*) appears alone = τις without any following substantive.[2]

The idiom in the Gospels must therefore be strictly described as a Semitism, though its origin in most cases is almost certainly Aramaic.

The use of ἀνήρ in this way with a following noun is relatively infrequent in Mark and Matthew (Mk. vi. 20; Mt. vii. *24, 26*, xii. 41) but very common in Luke–Acts, where I have noted some forty instances (consult Moulton–Geden, s.v. ἀνήρ). Is St. Luke writing 'Septuagintal Greek'?

[1] *Einl.*[2], p. 20; 1st edit., p. 27.

[2] By far the commonest Heb. usage is with prefixed *'ish* (cf. Thackeray, *Gramm.*, p. 45, Howard, *Gramm.*, ii, p. 433); the LXX as a rule renders by ἀνήρ (Gen. xlvi. 34), but sometimes by ἄνθρωπος (Gen. xli. 33, ἄνθρωπον φρόνιμον). In addition to *'ish*, both *'adham* and *'enosh* are employed (Gen. xvi. 12, Jer. xx. 10). A similar situation is found in Aram. (*g^{e}bhar*, *'^{e}nash* (*barnash*)): Wensinck has noted Gen. xxxvi. 39 (F), *gabhra saradha*, 'a netmaker', Gen. iv. 2 (P–J), *Kil'aim*, ix. 4. f. 32^r*a*, line 2, *Midrash Koheleth*, f. 43^r, line 8, and Lev. xxii. 6 (P–J), *barnash kohen*, verse 11, *barnash nuchra'ah*, 'a stranger'; for *'^{e}nash*, see Targ., Job xxxi. 35, Jer. xv. 10. For ἄνθρωπος alone = τις, see Blass–Debrunner, *Gramm.*, § 301, p. 136. Examples in Aram. are frequent: *Kil'aim*, ix. 4, f. 32^r*a*, line 40, '. . . and he went out but did not find *anyone* (*barnash*)'. Wensinck gives examples from *Ned.*, v. 4, f. 39^r*b*, line 28, *Sota*, v. 2, f. 20^r*b*, line 25 (*'^{e}nash*), and with a negative *Erub.* vii. 11, f. 24^v*b*, line 22, *la ba'e barnash*', 'no one wishes'. He also noted a similar usage in the plural, citing Onk. Gen. iv. 26, '. . . in his days *men began* (*ḥalu b^{e}ne '^{e}nasha*: MT *ḥuḥal* pass.) to pray &c.' Occasionally the indefinite *barnash* may be used to refer to the speaker and becomes equivalent to the 1st person, e.g. *Bereshith rabba*, section 7, beginning; see my article in *Expository Times*, lx, p. 34 and Appendix E. Cf. Dalman, *Gramm.*[2], p. 122.

Examples are:

(i) With following substantive or adjective.

Mk.: xiii. 34.

Mt.: ix. 32 (D); xi. *19* (= Lk. vii. *34*); xiii. *28*, *45* (D); *52* (= xx. *1*, xxi. *33*) xviii. *23* (= xxii. *2*); xxv. *24* (= Lk. xix. *21*, *22*); xxvii. 32, 57.

Lk.: (in addition to Q passages noted under Mt.) ii. 15 (D), xiv. 2 (D).

Jn. ix. 1, 16.

Acts iv. 9 (Peter), 13; xvi. 37 (Paul); xxi. 39 (Paul); xxii. 25 (Paul).

James v. 17.

(ii) Ἄνθρωπος simple = τις.

Mk.: i. 23 (= Lk. iv. 33); iii. 1 (= Mt. xii. 10, Lk. vi. 6); iv. *26*; v. 2 (Lk. viii. 27, ἀνήρ τις); vii. *11* (cf. Mt. xv. *5*); vii. *15* (ter) (= Mt. xv. 11), *18*, *20* (= Mt. xv. *18*); *23* (= Mt. xv. 20); viii *36* (= Mt. xvi. *26*, Lk. ix. *25*), *37* (= Mt. xvi. *26*); x. *7* (= Gen. ii. 24, Mt. xix. *5*), *9* (= Mt. xix. *6*); xi. *2*(?); xii. *1* (Lk. xx. *9*; cf. Mt. xxi. *33*); xiv. *13* (= Lk. xxii. *10*).

Mt.: viii. 9 (= Lk. vii. 8 dial.); ix. 9; xi. *8* (= Lk. vii. *25*); xii. *43* (= Lk. xi. *24*); xiii. 31 (= Lk. xiii. 19); xiii. 44 (multi τις); xvii. 14 (cf. Mk. ix. 17, Lk. ix. 38); xxi. *28* (multi τις); xxii. *11*.

Lk.: ii. 25; v. 18 (cf. Mk. ii. 3, Mt. ix. 2); vi. *48*, *49* (cf. Mt. vii. 24, 26); xiv. *16* (nonn. om. τις).

Jn.: i. 6; iii. 1, 4 (dial.), 27; iv. 29 (dial.); v. 5 (D, dial.), 7 (dial.); 34, 41(?); vii. *22*, *23*; 46 (dial.), 51 (dial.); viii. *40*.

Acts: iv. 17 (nonn. ἀνθρώπῳ, dial.); x. 28 (Peter).

Examples in plural: Mk. viii. 27 (= Mt. xvi. 13, cf. Lk. ix. 18); Mt. viii. 27; Lk. vi. 22; Jn. iii. 19; vi. 14.

Other examples in N.T.: 1 Cor. iv. 1; vii. 26; xi. 28(= *'ish*, each one?); 2 Cor. xii. 2 (referring to speaker?), 4; Gal. i. 12; ii. 6, 16; vi. 1, 7.

In the Gospels most examples come from sayings of Jesus, and the idiom is found most frequently in Mark and Q.

(*c*) The use of partitive ἀπό or ἐκ is not confined to the plural of an indefinite 'some', and examples are more frequent in the New Testament than Howard's survey shows.[1] The construction is again paralleled in the Koine, but its source in the New Testament is almost certainly Semitic.

[1] Cf. E. F. F. Bishop in *Expository Times*, lxi. 7, p. 219.

It is not always possible to be certain that such a usage is present, where alternative explanations of the preposition may be given. The following are among the more certain cases:

(i) *Partitive ἀπό.*

Mk. v. 35 (cf. Lk. viii. 49); vi. 43; vii. 4 (? cf. *supra*, p. 54);[1] xii. 2 (cf. Lk. xx. 10, Mt. xxi. 34).
Jn.: vii. 17 (? ἀπ' ἐμαυτοῦ λαλῶ); xxi. 10.
Acts: ii. 17, 18 (OT).

(ii) *Partitive ἐκ.*

Mt.: xxiii. *34* (Lk. xxi. *16*); xxv. 8.
Jn.: i. 16(?); iv. 30(?); vii. 40; xvi. 14, 15, 17.
2nd Jn. 4.
Rev. ii. 10; xi. 9.

εἷς . . . εἷς (ἕτερος)

The use of εἷς . . . εἷς (ἕτερος) appears to be a recognized New Testament Semitism. Blass–Debrunner, § 247 and Howard, *Gramm.* ii, p. 438, citing 2 Sam. xiv. 6; Wensinck illustrates from Bikk. iii. 3, f. 65^{v}*a*, line 41.

Examples are:

Mk.: ix. 5 (Mt. xvii. 4, Lk. ix. 33) (dial.); x. 37 (Mt. xx. 21, dial.); xv. 27 (Mt. xxvii. 38; cf. Lk. xxiii. 33).
Mt.: vi. *24* (Lk. xvi. *13*); xxiv. *40, 41* (Lk. xvii. *34, 35*).
Lk.: vii. *41*; xviii. *10*.
Jn.: xx. 12.
Acts: xxiii. 6.
1 Cor. iv. 6.
Gal. iv. 22.
1 Thess. v. 11 (cf. Blass–Debrunner, l.c.).

Temporal and Inferential Conjunction and Adverb

1. *Luke's (ἐν) αὐτῇ τῇ ὥρᾳ*

Wellhausen, noting the Synoptic variants, Lk. xii. 12, ἐν αὐτῇ τῇ ὥρᾳ, Mk. xiii. 11 (= Mt. x. 19), ἐν ἐκείνῃ τῇ ὥρᾳ, remarked that αὐτός and ἐκεῖνος appear to be used without distinction.'[1] There is no trace of such a confusion in the Koine, and no reason to believe that personal and demonstrative pronouns were confused in Aramaic, except in texts and manuscripts.[2] But in the light of this and other instances in Luke, the view that αὐτός

[1] *Einl.*[1], p. 30; 2nd edit., p. 23.

[2] *Supra*, pp. 97 ff.

means at times little more than 'that' has come to be widely held.[1] Howard observed that the variants in Lk. xii. 12 and parallels 'can hardly be accounted for by fidelity to an Aramaic original', since we find the same phrase, αὐτῇ τῇ ὥρᾳ, occurring where there is no question of Semitic sources, in Acts xvi. 18, xxii. 13. The expression, he concluded, is a 'Lucan peculiarity' or mannerism. He has nothing to say about the philological problem of Luke's αὐτός.[2]

The phrase (ἐν) αὐτῇ τῇ ὥρᾳ occurs nine times in Luke–Acts: Lk. ii. 38, vii. 21 (D; Bℵ, ἐν ἐκείνῃ τῇ ὥρᾳ), x. 21, xii. 12, xiii. 31, xx. 19, xxiv. 33; Acts xvi. 18, xxii. 13. It is clearly a Lucan peculiarity, but it is not a coinage of the author of Luke–Acts. It is the translation equivalent of two closely related Aramaic temporal conjunctions. There are several conjunctions in Aramaic formed from the word for 'hour' or 'moment', the primary meaning of the word: the first is בה־שעתא 'in it (namely) the moment', and corresponds exactly to Luke's ἐν αὐτῇ τῇ ὥρᾳ; in Aramaic the pronoun is proleptic. The conjunction means 'at the same time', 'immediately', 'forthwith', passing into 'then', 'thereupon', and is common to all dialects of Aramaic; Burkitt has made a study of its incidence in the Old Syriac Gospels, where it renders the Marcan εὐθύς.[3] The meaning 'immediately', 'forthwith', is found in the older Aramaic in Dan. iii. 6, 15, iv. 30, v. 5; thus iii. 6, 'And whoso falleth not down and worshippeth shall *forthwith* be cast into the midst of a burning fiery furnace'. Both LXX and Theodotion render iii. 6 by αὐτῇ τῇ ὥρᾳ; Theodotion has the same equivalent at iii. 15 and iv. 30, and both have it again at v. 5, this time in the full form ἐν αὐτῇ τῇ ὥρᾳ. The meaning 'then', 'thereupon' is found in a passage occurring in the free paraphrase of the Palestinian Pentateuch Targum to Gen. xxxiv. 9 (C), '*Then* it was announced that Rebecca his mother was dead'. The two meanings pass

[1] Cf. Moulton, *Prol.*, p. 91.

[2] Moulton, *Gramm.* ii, p. 432.

[3] *Evangelion da-Mepharreshe*, ii, p. 85 f. The Aramaic expression may in fact be the word which lies behind Mark's εὐθύς, εὐθέως; none of the other Aramaic words which have been proposed can be satisfactorily equated with εὐθύς; see Burkitt, op. cit., p. 89; Lagrange, *S. Marc*, p. xcii; E. A. Abbott, *Johannine Grammar*, p. 20; Dalman, *Worte Jesu*, p. 22 f.

readily into one another and are not always clearly distinguishable. The meaning 'then', 'thereupon' is shared by this first form of the conjunction with a second, בההיא שעתא 'at that moment', 'at that time', and so again 'then', 'thereupon': we find it used, in the same sense as the first, in the Palestinian Pentateuch Targum to Gen. xxxviii. 25 (E), '*Then* YHWH beckoned to the Angel Michael and said . . .'; it occurs also in the Jerusalem Targum of Exod. xxiii. 5, and in the Palestinian Talmud, *Kil'aim*, ix. 4, f. 32*b*, line 58, *Sheqal.* v. 1, f. 48*d*, line 1, and in the same sense but without the preposition, ההיא שעתא, *Kil'aim*, ix. 4, f. 32*c*, line 39. A third expression in the Talmud is מן ההיא שעתא 'from that hour', e.g. *Kil'aim*, ix. 4, f. 32*b*, line 58, *Shabb.* vi, f. 8*d*, line 1. The frequency with which the conjunction is repeated in the passage from *Kil'aim* will be noted.

If we examine the Lucan expression in its various contexts in the light of these Aramaic temporal conjunctions, we find that it covers all of them with the exception of the last, 'from that hour': it can mean 'immediately', 'forthwith', or 'then', 'thereupon', and 'at that time'.[1] In the following group of examples the sense of 'immediately' is fully borne out by the context.

(1) In Lk. vii. 21 Jesus' response to the disciples of John who came inquiring if He was the Coming One, was *forthwith* to proceed to heal many of their diseases, thus giving His credentials in immediate act; the reading of D, ἐν αὐτῇ τῇ ὥρᾳ, is, in that case, preferable to that of WH, ἐν ἐκείνῃ τῇ ὥρᾳ, '*Forthwith* he proceeded to heal (ἐθεράπευεν) many . . .'; the sense of an immediate response in act is lost by WH's 'at that time'; the imperfect in D is suitably appropriate to the conjunction (WH ἐθεράπευσεν). The meaning 'forthwith' is also

[1] ἐν αὐτῇ τῇ ὥρᾳ. See further J. Jeremias in *Z.N.T.W.* Band 42 (1949), pp. 214–17. Some account must also be taken of the use of the Greek temporal adverb αὐθωρεί(ί), e.g. Plut. 2. 512 E, Dan. iii. 15 (LXX).

That the expression ἀπὸ τῆς ὥρας ἐκείνης (Mt. ix. 22, xv. 28, xvii. 18, Jn. xix. 27; cf. Mt. viii. 13) is an Aramaism is recognized by Joüon, who gives it the sense *au moment même* ('Notes philologiques', *Recherches de science religieuse*, xviii (1928), p. 345). The expression is especially rabbinical; this may account for its frequency in Matthew.

suitable in xx. 19: the scribes and chief priests *forthwith* (an immediate consequence of the terrible words just spoken by Jesus) sought to lay hand on Him. In Acts xvi. 18, the evil spirit *immediately* left the possessed man on Paul's word of command; and in Acts xxii. 13, as soon as the devout Ananias said 'Brother Saul, receive thy sight', *forthwith* Paul saw.

(2) In the second group the sense of 'immediately' may occasionally be present, but is not obvious from the context. In Lk. ii. 38 Anna the prophetess came 'at that time' or 'at that moment' and gave thanks to the Lord. We may render x. 21, '*Thereupon* Jesus rejoiced in spirit'. In xii. 12, 'at that time', the meaning given by the Marcan parallel, is what was clearly intended; Luke's expression, however, as the equivalent of the first form of the Aramaic conjunction and meaning 'then', is equally possible. In both xiii. 31 and xxiv. 33 the meaning is that of 'then', or 'at that time': '*Then* or *at that time* there came certain of the Pharisees'; 'They *then* rose up and returned to Jerusalem.'

The temporal conjunction (ἐν) αὐτῇ τῇ ὥρᾳ is, therefore, a Lucan Aramaism. It may be due to Syriac influence, or it may have come from the LXX version of Daniel, but its ultimate source is Aramaic. The fact that Luke appears to use it indiscriminately for two Aramaic conjunctions cannot be the basis for any inference as to the demonstrative use of αὐτός: the two Aramaic conjunctions are closely connected in meaning, and Luke's expression, which can only mean in Greek 'in the very hour' (and was no doubt so understood by Greek readers), is made to do service for both.

The hypothesis of translation of source would give the most satisfactory account of the Lucan usage—it is translation Greek. And even in this case, that hypothesis cannot be excluded. In Acts the conjunction occurs in the account of a healing miracle of Paul and in Paul's own account of his conversion. If these were not transmitted originally in Aramaic, they would certainly be in Semitic Greek, and it may have been Semitic Greek accounts of the two stories on which Luke is dependent. Of the seven occurrences in the Gospels, three are in Luke's special material, ii. 38, xiii. 31, xxiv. 33, two come from Q, vii. 21, x. 21 (where Matthew has the more literary and correct ἐν ἐκείνῳ τῷ καιρῷ), and the two remaining instances are in passages where Luke supplements Mark's account, xii. 12 (Mk. xiii. 11), xx. 19 (Mk. xii. 12) (Proto-Luke?).

2. *The Conjunction* πάλιν

Wellhausen noted the very frequent use which Mark makes of πάλιν (there are 26 instances against Matthew's 6 and Luke's 2), and saw in its use a reflection of the Aramaic temporal and inferential conjunction *tubh*, 'then', 'further', 'thereupon'.[1]

Against this it has been urged that in many of the Marcan examples, 'the meaning is really iterative, and when the meaning is inferential, it is unnecessary to go back to Aramaic'.[2] One clear example where πάλιν cannot be iterative, xv. 13, οἱ δὲ πάλιν ἔκραξαν, the first outcry of the mob, provides a test case for the Marcan usage. It is an inferential conjunction, 'They thereupon shouted . . .' Moffatt, who denied Aramaic influence here (and has been followed in this by Moulton and Milligan), contended that πάλιν had already the force of an inferential conjunction in the Koine: he cited the Oxyrhynchus Papyrus xiv. 1676, 20, ἀλλὰ καὶ λυποῦμαι πάλιν ὅτι ἐκτός μου εἶ, which he renders, '*Still* I am sorry you are not beside me';[3] Grenfell and Hunt translate, 'But *yet* I am grieved that you are away from me.' Clearly πάλιν is a conjunction here, but it is not inferential and it is not parallel to Mk. xv. 13. A much better parallel from classical usage is the meaning which the adverb has in Aristophanes' *Acharnians*, 342, and Sophocles' *Electra*, 371, 'on the other hand', 'in turn', and this meaning suits Mk. xv. 13, 'But they, on the other hand, shouted . . .' But it is inferior in the Marcan context to the inferential *tubh*:[4] 'And Pilate answered and said again unto them, What will ye then that I shall do

[1] *Einl.*[1], p. 28; 2nd edit., p. 21. [2] Howard in Moulton, *Gramm.* ii, p. 446.

[3] In the *Expositor*, viii. 20, p. 140 f.

[4] For the Aramaic word see Dalman, *Gramm.*[2], p. 209. I have nothing to add on the Marcan πολλά, full references on which will be found in Howard's article in Moulton, *Gramm.* ii, p. 446.

unto him whom ye call the King of the Jews? And they, thereupon, shouted, Crucify him.'

3. *Luke's* ἀπὸ μιᾶς (xiv. *18*)

Wellhausen attached importance to his observation that ἀπὸ μιᾶς was a literal rendering of an Aramaic adverb *min ḥ^a^dha, mĕḥda*, meaning 'at once', 'immediately'.[1] A similar expression has appeared in the Greek Enoch, ἐπὶ μιᾶς, meaning 'at once', and has been traced to Aramaic *kaḥda* or Hebrew *k^e^'eḥadh.*[2] The phrase really corresponds to Hebrew *b^e^'eḥadh,* and it is a good example of translation Greek. No manuscript authority, however, attests an ἐπὶ μιᾶς for Luke.

Targumic Aramaic employs *kaḥda* for 'at once', but *min ḥ^a^dha, mĕḥda,* appears in Palestinian Syriac too frequently to be dismissed as a borrowing from Syriac (where the adverb is common): in Jn. xiii. 32 it renders εὐθύς; in Acts xvi. 26, παραχρῆμα, and in Rom. vi. 10, 1 Cor. xv. 6, Heb. ix. 12, ἐφάπαξ. The adverb, however, does not occur in Jewish Palestinian Aramaic, and this has led R. H. Connolly to claim ἀπὸ μιᾶς in Lk. xiv. 18 as a 'Syriacism'.[3]

Moulton's objection that, while Mark might have been capable of such translation Greek, Luke could never have written it,[4] ignores the fact that Luke as well as Mark is dependent on sources; besides, Luke can write or leave unaltered ἐν αὐτῇ τῇ ὥρᾳ.

4. *The Conjunction* ἀλλά = εἰ μή

The possibility of an underlying Aramaism in the extension of the use of adversative ἀλλά in the sense of εἰ μή was first mooted by Wellhausen.[5] Moulton replied in the German edition of his *Prolegomena,*[6] comparing the use of ἀλλά at Soph. *O.T.* 1331, adding 'Of course I have nothing against the recognition of an Aramaic idiom as the reason for the choice of a similar Greek usage to render an Aramaic locution'.[7] Before him

[1] *Einl.*[2], p. 26.
[2] J. Jeremias in *Z.N.T.W.* xxxviii (1939), p. 118.
[3] *J.T.S.* xxxvii, p. 378.
[4] *Gramm.* ii, p. 29.
[5] *Einl.*[1], p. 24.
[6] Heidelberg, 1911; p. 269, n. 1.
[7] Cf. Moulton–Howard, *Grammar*, p. 468.

Winer had spoken very decisively against such a meaning for *ἀλλά*.[1] That there are parallels to this use in Greek literature is not denied,[2] but they seem to be decidedly rare, and it is doubtful if it can be regarded as a vernacular usage.[3] The most striking case in the Gospels is at Mk. iv. 22 where *ἐὰν μή* and *ἀλλά*, both in the sense of 'except', occur in parallel clauses in a reported saying of Jesus; the simplest explanation is that we have to do with a piece of translation Greek reflecting Aramaic idiom, and this may also apply to other instances of the usage.

Wellhausen's explanation of the Aramaic usage has been generally accepted: he regarded the Aramaic אֶלָּא as combining exceptive and adversative meanings. An alternative view is found in Levy who regarded Aramaic אלא = *ἀλλά* as a borrowing (and transcription) of the Greek word,[4] and this seems the more probable explanation. Levy cited the Fragment Targum to Gen. xxii. 14 (the same אלא is found in Targum Neofiti) and Berach 5*a*.

What appears to have happened in the Gospels is that a translation from Aramaic, confronted with אלא, which could be *either ἀλλά or* אֶלָּא = *εἰ μή*, mistranslated אֶלָּא = *εἰ μή* by *ἀλλά* (and vice versa).

The most certain examples of the usage occur in Mark and this supports the Aramaic explanation. Examples are Mk. ix. 8 (Mt. xvii. 8, *εἰ μή sine var.*), Mk. x. 40 (= Mt. xx. 23).

The opposite, the use of *εἰ μή* for simple adversative *ἀλλά*, may be put down to the same cause, though here again the usage is not unparalleled in Greek writing. Examples are: Mt. xii. 4, Lk. iv. *26*; Gal. ii. 16 and Rev. xxi. 27 are similar cases.[5]

The Preposition[6]

A characteristic feature of Semitic usage is the repetition of a preposition before every noun of a series which it governs; the

1 Eng. edit. *A Treatise on the Grammar of New Testament Greek* (Edinburgh. 1802), p. 566.

2 Moulton–Howard, l.c.

3 Moulton, *Prol.* p. 242.

4 *Chald. Wörterbuch*, s.v.

5 Moulton–Howard, l.c.

6 G. Wilcox, op. cit., pp. 132 ff.

construction is intolerable in literary Greek. Semitic repetition occurs in the WH text in Mt. xiii. 57; Mk. iii. 7, 8, vi. 56, xi. 1; Lk. viii. 34; Acts xiv. 21. The construction is much more frequent in D, which shares all the above instances, with the exception of Mk. iii. 7, 8 and Acts xiv. 21, with WH, and has in addition, Mk. v. 1, vi. 26 (= Mt. xiv. 9), 36 (direct speech), viii. *31*, xiv. 43. Wensinck, who drew attention to this Semitism in Luke,[1] noted Lk. ii. 34 (dialogue), 44, vii. 17. Out of fifteen examples, two come from sayings of Jesus, two from direct speech or dialogue, and no less than eleven instances from Mark alone.

Most of the other cases of Semitisms in the use of prepositions occur in constructions after certain verbs. The following examples are either hitherto unattested from Aramaic or additional to the well-known cases.[2]

Διά. Mt. xi. 2, *πέμπειν διά*, is claimed by Wellhausen, but whether as Hebraism or Aramaism is not clear.[3] It is regarded as either Hebraism or Aramaism by Howard, but apparently on Wellhausen's authority alone. I have not so far been able to find the expression in Aramaic, but it occurs in the Palestinian Talmud in Hebrew, viz. *Bikk.* i. 6, f. 64*a*, lines 45, 48, 55; *Makkoth*, ii, f. 31*d*, line 53.

Εἰς. A quite extraordinary use of *εἰς* is found in Lk. xix. *44* (D), *οὐκ ἔγνως εἰς καιρὸν ἐπισκοπῆς σου*: the strange preposition is reproduced in the Latin *d*, 'non cognovisti *in* tempus visitationis tuae'. The first explanation which occurs to one on examining the Bezan text is that the *εἰς* has come into this verse from verse 45, *εἰσελθὼν εἰς τὸ ἱερόν*: similarly in Acts i. 6 (D), *ἀποκαθιστάνεις εἰς τὴν βασιλείαν*, the second *εἰς* is a dittograph of the last syllable of the verb. Lk. xix. *44* (D), however, is Semitic Greek and a saying of Jesus, so that the alternative cannot be overlooked that we have here a translation version of an Aramaic saying.[4] Moreover, something may be made of

[1] *Semitisms*, p. 15 f.

[2] Cf. Moulton, *Prol.*, p. 104 and Howard in *Gramm.* ii, p. 460 f.; Lagrange, *S. Matthieu*, p. cviii; Nestle in *Z.N.T.W.*, 1906, p. 279 f.

[3] *Einl.*[1], p. 31.

[4] For the Aramaic construction, see *supra*, p. 80, n. 2.

the intolerable Greek, perhaps, 'Thou hast not recognized with regard to the time of thy visitation'.

In Lk. xvi. *16*, *πᾶς εἰς αὐτὴν βιάζεται*, usually understood as 'everyone forces himself into it', if *βιάζεται* is taken as a transitive middle, we get the same Aramaism, 'everyone oppresses it', which brings Luke into harmony with Mt. xi. 12.[1]

Ἔμπροσθεν. The prepositional phrase in Lk. xix. 4, *προδραμὼν εἰς τὸ ἔμπροσθεν*, as Wensinck pointed out,[2] is a well-known Biblical one, Hebrew *liqrath*, Aramaic *l^eqadhmutheh* (or *l^e'ur'eh*); Gen. xxix. 13, '. . . he ran to meet him' (in the Palestinian Pentateuch Targum, E, *l^eqadhmutheh*). Wensinck may be right in thinking that לקדמותא(ה) in Lk. xix. 4 contained the suffix and should have been rendered 'to meet him'.

Ἐν. In Lk. xii. *52* (D), *τρεῖς διαμεμερισμένοι ἐν δυσί*, the preposition in WH is correctly *ἐπί*. The Bezan variant reflects a Semitic use of *b^e*, exemplified by the reading of the Targum of Lev. xx. 6 (not a rendering of the Hebrew), '*against* (*b^e*) that man'; cf. also Sy^pal. to Exod. ix. 17.

Ἐπί. A thoroughly Semitic use of this preposition is found in Lk. ix. 16 (D) after the verb *εὐλογεῖν*, *ηὐλογήσεν ἐπ' αὐτούς*: it corresponds to the Hebrew or Aramaic ברך על, and is attested frequently in the Palestinian Talmud, e.g. *Berach.* vi, f. 10*a*, lines 39, 53, 55, 57. Wensinck called attention to this Bezan Semitism.[3]

Κατέναντι. In Mk. vi. 41 (D), *ἵνα παραθῶσι κατέναντι αὐτῶν*, WH has the idiomatic Greek *παρατιθῶσιν αὐτοῖς*: D retains a Semitic construction. It occurs, e.g., in the Targum to Prov. xxiii. 1, 'If thou sittest down to eat with the powerful, give heed to what is set before thee' (*man d^esim q^odhamakh*); the Hebrew has simply, '. . . give heed to that which is before thee'.

[1] It seems very unlikely that Jesus said '*everyone* oppresses it'. The verbs *βιάζεσθαι*, *ἁρπάζειν* in Matthew go back to the same Aramaic (Dalman, *Worte Jesu*, p. 115 f.). Perhaps the original was simply 'violent men oppress it' (*'anosin 'an^esin lah*), which gave rise, in oral transmission, to a variant form, 'men oppress it' (*'enashin 'an^esin lah*). There may be a play on *Ἰωάννης*: in the following verse 14, Elijah is *'ilya* or *'elya*, Sorrow (*Genesis Rabbah*, 15, end).

[2] *Semitisms*, p. 40.

[3] *Semitisms*, p. 17.

Πρός. A most difficult *πρός* intrudes in the WH text of Mt. xxvii. 14 (it is omitted in D), *καὶ οὐκ ἀπεκρίθη αὐτῷ πρὸς οὐδὲ ἓν ῥῆμα*. The expedients to which resort has been taken to make something of it are too well known to be recapitulated.

A not dissimilar preposition occurs with the Aramaic verb 'to answer' in the idiomatic phrase 'to answer back', 'to gainsay', viz. *l^equbhla*; the phrase renders Isa. x. 14, *καὶ οὐκ ἔστιν ὃς . . . ἀντείπῃ μοι* in Sy^pal. But we should then expect *πρὸς αὐτόν*, not *αὐτῷ πρός*.

The not infrequent use of *παρά* for *ἤ* in comparison in the Gospels is commented on as a Semitism by Jeremias (*Abendmahlsworte Jesu*², p. 115), e.g. Lk. xiii. 2, 4. Especially and idiomatically Semitic is the use of *παρά* or *ἤ* = *min* in an exclusive sense, e.g. Acts iv. 19, v. 29 ('one must obey God, *not* (ἤ) men'); cf. also Rom. i. 25, Lk. xviii. 14, *δεδικαιωμένος ἢ ἐκεῖνος*, i.e. this man went down justified, *but that one did not*; Jeremias compares LXX Gen. xxxviii. 26, *δεδικαίωται Θάμαρ ἢ ἐγώ*. Cf. further his *Unbekannte Jesusworte* (Gütersloh, 1951), pp. 74 ff.; Wellhausen, *Einl.*¹, p. 28; 2nd edit. p. 21; Moulton, *Gramm.* ii, p. 467.

Comparative and Superlative

The Semitic languages, with the exception of Arabic, have no special forms for comparative and superlative, the positive being used for both. The comparative is used for the superlative in the Koine,[1] but there does not appear to be any parallel in Greek to the Semitic positive for comparative or superlative. Wellhausen noted this Semitism in the Gospels and gave the following examples: Mk. ix. *43*, *45*, *47* (= Mt. xviii. *8*, *καλόν*, 'better'), xii. 28 (*πρώτη*, = Mt. xxii. 36, *μεγάλη*, 'greatest') (dialogue); Lk. v. *39* (*χρηστός*, 'best').[2] The following cases also occur: Mt. ii. 16 (D, *κάτω*; WH *κατωτέρω*); Mk. xiv. *21* (= Mt. xxvi. 24, *καλόν*, 'better'); Lk. ix. *48* (*μέγας*, 'greatest'), xvi. *10* (D, *ἐν ὀλίγῳ*; WH *ἐν ἐλαχίστῳ*, 'in least'); Jn. i. 15 (*πρῶτός μου*, 'before me') (Baptist), ii. 10 (*καλόν*, 'best') (dialogue). Out of eleven examples, seven occur in sayings of Jesus, three in

[1] Moulton, *Prol.*, p. 78.

[2] *Einl.*², p. 21.

dialogue, and one only, Mt. ii. 16 (D), in narrative. The construction appears most frequently in the Bezan text.

Repetition of an adjective or an adverb to express the elative is idiomatic Hebrew and Aramaic, and Wensinck claims Mt. xxi. 41, *κακοὺς κακῶς ἀπολέσει αὐτούς*, as an example of this Semitic usage.[1] He assumes that the Old Syriac, which renders by an iterative elative construction, read *κακῶς κακῶς*. But the construction is found in Greek, e.g. Sophocles, *Ajax*, 839; Euripides, *Medea*, 805. Moreover, in the parable of the vineyard, Matthew is dependent on Greek Mark and has nothing from an Aramaic source. The Syriac versions are simply transferring the Greek construction into the corresponding Aramaic.

In Jn. v. *36*, *ἐγὼ δὲ ἔχω τὴν μαρτυρίαν μείζω τοῦ Ἰωαννοῦ*, we have the idiom of *comparatio compendiaria*, where the second member of the comparison may be abbreviated: 'I have a witness greater *than John*' is a short and idiomatic way of saying, 'I have a witness greater than that of John', i.e. than the witness of John. The idiom occurs in both Hebrew and Aramaic: thus in Hebrew, Isa. x. 10, '. . . and their idols are more numerous than Jerusalem and Samaria', i.e. than the idols of Jerusalem and Samaria; Gen. xviii. *11*, 'a way like women', i.e. like the way of women.[2] A good example of the idiom in Aramaic occurs in the Elephantine Papyrus, i. 27. 28, 'And merit will be thine before YHW the God of heaven greater than (that of) a man (*min g^ebhar*) who brings an offering.'[3]

The Interrogative Particle

1. *Conditional Use of Interrogatives*

Joüon draws attention to a special use of interrogative *τίς* in conditional sentences in his *Notes philologiques*, xviii (1928), p. 349. Mt. xxiv. 45 'semble être une protase virtuellement

[1] *Une Groupe d'Aramaismes* (*supra*, p. 5, n.2, p. 10 (178).

[2] Cf. *Ges.-Kautzsch*, p. 430.

[3] Sachau in his edition of the papyri cites in illustration (p. 19) an example from the Arabic of Ḥarīrī's *Maqāmāt* '. . . he prefers the love of boys to maidens'. For classical examples, see Hom. *Il.* xvii. 51 and Horace, *Carm.* III. vi. 46.

conditionnelle dont le v. 46 est l'apodose. Je traduirais: "Quelqu'un est-il le serviteur fidèle et sage préposé par son maître à toute sa maisonnée pour donner à chacun sa nourriture aux temps fixés, (alors) heureux ce serviteur que son maître, arrivant, trouvera se conduisant ainsi."' Cf. Ps. xxv. 12. Another example occurs at Mt. xii. *11* = Lk. xiv. *5*.

2. *Ὅτι as (direct) Interrogative*

In his 'Notes on the Translation of the New Testament',[1] F. Field drew attention to a curious use of ὅτι (neuter indefinite pronoun) as an interrogative particle, a usage apparently confined to Mark. The discussion was taken an important step forward by C. H. Turner who adduced some extra-Biblical evidence for this peculiar usage.[2] As Field had shown, in his note on Mk. ix. 11, ὅτι as *indirect* interrogative can be supported by good classical authority; Turner cited Mk. viii. 16, 17 and xiv. 60 as other instances in Mark of this construction: Mk. viii. 16, 17 should be rendered 'they discussed with one another *why* they had no loaves'; and similarly we should no doubt render Mk. xiv. 60, 'Have you nothing to answer (to the question) *why* these people are testifying against you'. Though the construction can be supported, therefore, and is thus defensible as Greek, one wonders nevertheless whether it was ever widely used; Matthew, for instance, as Turner has shown, clearly disliked this ὅτι *interrogativum*; when he 'edits' Mk. viii. 16 he inserts λέγοντες to turn the Marcan ὅτι into a ὅτι *recitativum*.

The situation is quite different, as Turner emphasizes, with the case of ὅτι *as a direct interrogative*. Here there is no classical parallel or precedent, and, it would seem, only very slight support is forthcoming from Hellenistic writers. The Revised Version sought to get rid of it by various expedients in the three Marcan passages (ii. 16, ix. 11, 28) where the external evidence is clearly in favour of ὅτι, e.g., ii. 16, 'The scribes of the Pharisees . . . said unto his disciples He eateth and drinketh

[1] Cambridge, 1899, p. 33.

[2] 'Marcan Usage: Notes, Critical and Exegetical, on the Second Gospel (cont.)', *J.T.S.* xxvii, pp. 58 ff. Cf. also K. van Leeuwen Boomkamp, 'τί et διατί dans les Évangiles' in *Revue des Études grecques*, xxxix, pp. 327 ff.

with publicans and sinners'; ix. 11, 'And they asked him, saying, The scribes say that Elijah must first come'; ix. 28, 'His disciples asked him privately, *saying*, We could not cast it out'. Turner's comment is: 'Of these three renderings in the text of R.V. (there is a relative return to sanity in the margin in each case) the first makes just tolerable sense, the other two are quite impossible, or in Field's language 'simply intolerable'. Classical prepossessions must be frankly thrown overboard when they lead us to such an *impasse*. Even if no authority could be found outside St. Mark for the direct interrogative use of ὅτι, Field is certainly right that 'these two instances, occurring in the same chapter of St. Mark, must be held mutually to support and sanction each other'. (Cf. A. T. Robertson, *Grammar of the Greek N.T.*, p. 729, J. H. Moulton, *Prol.* p. 94, line 3.) The New English Bible recognizes the ὅτι *interrogativum* in the second two cases, viz. (ix. 11) 'And they put a question to him: 'Why do our teachers say that Elijah must be the first to come?': (ix. 28) '. . . and his disciples asked him privately, '*Why* could not we cast it out?'[1]

The only support which had hitherto been adduced for this very unusual use of ὅτι had been a single instance, cited by Field, from the LXX, viz.,

> 1 Chron. xvii. 6: εἰ λαλῶν ἐλάλησα πρὸς μίαν φυλὴν τοῦ Ἰσραὴλ τοῦ ποιμαίνειν τὸν λαόν μου λέγων Ὅτι οὐκ ᾠκοδομήκατέ μοι οἶκον κέδρινον; . . .

Turner drew attention to some further examples from the *Similitudes of Hermas*, the *Epistle of Barnabas*, and Irenaeus's *Adversus Haereses*. There seemed, in general, to be a similarity of style between *Hermas* and the Gospel of Mark, and Turner suggested that it might be profitable to compare the Greek of Hermas with the Greek of Mark in some detail: particularly striking was the Semitism at *Sim.* viii. 2. 8 τάγματα τάγματα, exactly parallel to the Marcan συμπόσια συμπόσια (vi. 39). Turner asked 'Shall we be told that "the construction" (ὅτι as direct interrogative) in Hermas is "Hebraistic"?'

[1] Turner includes Mk. ii. 7 and viii. 12 in this category. For alternative suggestions, see *infra*, pp. 122 ff.

In fact, the construction does occur in the LXX and 1 Chron. xvii. 6 is not an isolated instance. It is true, the construction still appears to be a rare one, so that it is doubtful if it could be described as a Septuagintalism: nevertheless it does appear to be peculiar to 'translation Greek' (or 'Jewish Greek').

I have noted the following instances in a survey of LXX interrogative clauses which was by no means an exhaustive one:

Gen. xii. 18: *καλέσας δὲ Φαραὼ τὸν Ἀβραὰμ εἶπεν τί τοῦτο ἐποίησάς μοι Ὅτι οὐκ ἀπήγγειλάς μοι . . .;*
(*ὅτι*= לָמָּה).

Gen. xviii. 13: *καὶ εἶπεν κύριος πρὸς Ἀβραὰμ Ὅτι* (D *τί ὅτι*) *ἐγέλασεν Σάρρα ἐν ἑαυτῇ λέγουσα . . .;*
(*ὅτι*= לָמָּה זֶּה).

Jer. xxii. 28: *Ὅτι ἐξερίφη καὶ ἐξεβλήθη εἰς γῆν ἣν οὐκ ᾔδει . . .*
(*ὅτι* = מַדּוּעַ). [A.V. (Is this man Coniah a despised broken idol? is he a vessel wherein is no pleasure); *wherefore* are they cast out, he and his seed, and are cast into a land which they know not?]

The following example is of an indirect interrogative *ὅτι*:

Exod. iii. 3: *εἶπεν δὲ Μωΰσης Παρελθὼν ὄψομαι τὸ ὅραμα τὸ μέγα τοῦτο ὅτι οὐ κατακαίεται ὁ βάτος; . . .*

The rarity of the direct construction even in Biblical Greek is an indication of how unidiomatic it was felt to be. The most plausible explanation of it would seem to be that it represents an illiterate extension of interrogative *ὅτι* in indirect questions to direct questions; and this seems most likely to have been the creation of a foreigner translating Hebrew or Aramaic into his own very imperfect kind of Greek.

3. *Miscellaneous Uses*

An idiomatic use of the Semitic interrogative particle is to introduce a rhetorical question expressing wonder or indignation. Examples from Aramaic are common: thus from the Palestinian Talmud, *Kil'aim*, ix. 4, f. 32*b*, line 7, 'Can it be then (*mah*)[1] thou art superior to thy master?' The question expresses

[1] The particle is, of course, the opening word in the question; cf. the third example above.

strong sarcasm. In the same passage from *Kil'aim*, at ix. 4, f. 32*b*, line 54, there is a question that expresses shocked indignation, 'Did he really (*mah*) study the Law more than I have?' Another example occurs in *Shebi'ith*, vi. 4, f. 37*a*, line 8, 'Did this one then sin (*mah ḥ*ᵃ*ta den*) more than all the other plants?'[1]

The use of τί in this way was pointed out by A. J. Wensinck, who gives as examples in the Gospels Lk. v. 22 (D), vi. 2.[1] Had he consulted the parallels, he would have discovered that it is not the Bezan text of Luke that has preserved the idiom; the construction is found in all texts of Mark.

Mk. ii. 7 (cf. Lk. v. 21) reads *τί οὕτως λαλεῖ βλασφημεῖ*, in which an Aramaism is probably already present.[2] Assuming that this Semitic idiom lies behind the Marcan *τί*, we get the rhetorical question, expressing horrified indignation, 'Can it be that he thus blasphemes?' An idiomatic English translation would be, 'Why! He thus blasphemes!' If *οὗτος* was the original reading, we get a contemptuous as well as a horrified, 'Why! this fellow blasphemes!' The WH reading in Lk. v. 21, *τίς ἐστιν οὗτος ὃς λαλεῖ βλασφημίας*, is a quite superfluous question. Alternatively, we may take the *τί* here in the sense of מָה exclamatory, 'How this fellow thus blasphemes!'.

In Mk. ii. *8*, *τί ταῦτα διαλογίζεσθε ἐν ταῖς καρδίαις ὑμῶν*, is, 'Can it be that ye think these things in your minds?' The question is purely rhetorical and expresses dismayed surprise. There was no reason for Jesus to ask what they were thinking; He already knew their thoughts.

In Mk. ii. 24, *ἴδε τί ποιοῦσιν τοῖς σάββασιν ὃ οὐκ ἔξεστιν*, the Pharisees are hotly indignant at what they see the disciples of Jesus doing; they ask, 'Are they then doing what it is unlawful to do on the Sabbath?' Mark further strengthens the indignant *τί* by prefacing *ἴδε*.

The following passages contain further examples where this idiom might be claimed: Mk. iv. *40* (= Mt. viii. *26*), *τί δειλοί ἐστε οὕτως*: x. *18* (= Lk. xviii. *19*), *τί με λέγεις ἀγαθόν*: xv. *34*

[1] I owe these examples to Wensinck, *Semitisms*, pp. 20 ff.

[2] *Supra*, p. 65.

(= Mt. xxvii. *46*), εἰς τί με ἐγκατέλιπες:[1] Lk. xxii. *46*, τί καθεύδετε. Mk. x. *18* (and parallel) may not be wholly rhetorical; it is not always possible to decide when an indignant or surprise question is not also a real question expecting an answer. The construction occurs in sayings of Jesus only and in dialogue, but there is no other place for questions. The predominance of the Semitic idiom in Mark is significant.

This same Semitic particle performs the function of exclamation as well as interrogative; the Hebrew (and Targum) of Ps. cxxxix. 17 may serve as illustration, '*How* (*mah*) precious also are thy thoughts unto me, O God! *how* great is the sum of them!' (A.V.).

There is one clear instance of interrogative τί used in this quite un-Greek way in Lk. xii. *49*, καὶ τί θέλω εἰ ἤδη ἀνήφθη.[2] Commentators occasionally render, '*How* I wish it were already kindled!', but as Plummer in his Commentary in loc. rightly remarks such a rendering 'does rather serious violence to the Greek'. Torrey emphasized that the solecism is unknown in the LXX; it is not just 'Aramaic-Greek', but mistranslation of an Aramaic original. Such Greek, however, would be at once understood by a Jew. The construction occurs in a saying of Jesus, and is probably best explained as translation Greek. The Semitism has been accepted by the New English Bible which renders: 'I have come to set fire to the earth, and how I wish it were already kindled!'

In Mk. viii. *12*, τί ἡ γενεὰ αὕτη ζητεῖ σημεῖον; the question may be rhetorical and reflect the idiom discussed above; we may perhaps render, 'Must this generation seek a sign?' The τί may be taken, however, as exclamatory, '*How* doth this generation seek a sign!'

An example similar to the illustration from the Psalm given above may be the reading τί in Mt. vii. *14*, τί στενὴ ἡ πύλη, '*How* narrow (is) the gate . . .': WH adopt the reading of Bא, ὅτι, but

[1] These words provide a good example of translation Greek: the original Hebrew or Aramaic is given; *lamah* or *l^ema* is εἰς τί.

[2] Attention was drawn to the Semitism by Torrey, *Our Translated Gospels*, pp. 31 and 34, and R. H. Connolly, in *J.T.S.* xxxvii, p. 376.

a good case can be made out for τί, the reading of the correctors in א and B; it is the reading of all Greek manuscripts of any moment, with the exception of B and א; several folios are missing at this point in D, but the allies of D, the Latin and Syriac versions, support the reading.

It will have been noted that all the examples which may be claimed for this Semitism come from sayings of Jesus.[1]

Numerals and Distribution

The use of cardinals for ordinals in dates has been frequently noted as a Gospel Semitism. The Semitism was queried by Moulton,[2] but there is no need to ransack the papyri to explain the Hebrew or Aramaic phrase, Mk. xvi. 2, τῇ μιᾷ τῶν σαββάτων, 'on the first day of the week'; the Semitism occurs in Mt. xxviii. 1; Lk. xxiv. 1; Jn. xx. 1, 19; Acts xx. 7; 1 Cor. xvi. 2. It is Jewish Greek.

Greek instances of distributive repetition have been adduced, but they are not normal Greek and are decidedly rare. All things considered, the case against Mark's συμπόσια, συμπόσια (vi. 39), πρασιαὶ, πρασιαί (40), as Semitisms is not very impressive.[3]

No Greek parallel has been produced to the Semitism in Mk. iv. *8*, *20* (D), ἓν ἑξήκοντα καὶ ἓν ἑκατόν, i.e. 'sixty-fold and a hundred-fold'. Allen, who drew attention to it, illustrated from Dan. iii. 19, and the Targum of Gen. xxvi. 12.[4] An example occurs in the Elephantine Papyrus, i. 3, *ḥadh 'ᵃlaph*, 'a thousand-fold'. The variations and combinations of εἷς, εἰς, and ἕν in the manuscripts of Mark and the corrections in Matthew and Luke show how foreign the construction was felt to be in Greek.

[1] For an un-Greek (and characteristically Aramaic) confusion of a neuter interrogative with a masculine at Acts xiii. 25 see Wilcox op. cit., p. 153.

[2] *Prol.*, p. 95 f.

[3] For illustrations, see I. Abrahams, *Studies in Pharisaism and the Gospels*, ii, p. 210 f.; Wensinck, *Semitisms*, p. 24.

[4] In *Expository Times*, xiii, p. 330.

The Verb

1. *Inchoative and Auxiliary Use*[1]

Characteristic Semitic inchoative or auxiliary verbs are listed and discussed by Dalman.[2] Such introducing or auxiliary verbs have often no special significance in themselves except as introductory forms of speech or in giving special emphasis to the main verb; the meaning of their Greek equivalents cannot therefore be pressed. To the examples discussed or given by Dalman, there should be added the use of an auxiliary *λαμβάνειν*, e.g. Mt. xiii. *31*; *ὃν λαβὼν ἄνθρωπος ἔσπειρεν*, xiii. *33* *ἣν λαβοῦσα γυνὴ ἐνέκρυψεν*. Cf. Jeremias (*Die Abendmahlsworte Jesu*², pp. 88 ff.) to whom I am indebted for this note and the following list of examples. The frequency of the construction is a clear indication that it reflects such an idiomatic Semitic auxiliary usage. Mt. xiv. 19; xv. 36; xvii. *27*; xxi. *35, 39*; xxv. *1*; xxvi. 26, 27; xxvii. 24, 48, 59; Mk. vi. 41; viii. 6; ix. 36; xii. 3, 8; Lk. vi. *4*; ix. 16; xiii. *19, 21*; xxiv. 30, 43: Jn. vi. 11; xiii. 4, 26; xix. 1, 6, 23, 40; xxi. 13: Acts ix. 25; xvi. 3; xxvii. 35; 1 Cor. xi. 23; Rev. viii. 5.

As in the case of *ἐλθών* above, the full use of the expression shades off into the auxiliary use and it is not always possible to distinguish the two; at Mt. xiv. 19, xv. 36, e.g., *λαμβάνειν* is probably used in its literal and usual sense. But in most other cases '*λαμβάνειν* gehört zu denjenigen Verben, die im Semitischen in einer für unser Sprachgefühl überflüssigen und umständlichen Weise eine Bewegung (oder Haltung) umschreiben, die die Handlung vorbereitet, auf der der Ton liegt; das gilt sowohl für hebräische לָקַח, נָטַל wie für aramäisch נְסַב'. (Jeremias, op. cit., pp. 88 ff.)

Lagrange protested that not all examples which have been claimed for this Semitism are to be so explained; in Mk. v. 23, vii. 25, xiv. 39, 45, xvi. 1, 'le part. *ἐλθών* est plus charactéristique'.[3] Similar objection has been taken to Dalman's explanation of the frequent *ἤρξα(ν)το* as an Aramaism. Thackeray, who

[1] Cf. Wilcox, op. cit., pp. 124 ff.

[2] *Worte Jesu*, p. 16 f.

[3] *S. Marc*, p. lxxxvii.

noted the frequency of the verb in Josephus, maintained that the locution is good colloquial Greek, and questions whether it is legitimate to speak of 'Aramaism'. He has to admit, however, that the possibility of Aramaic influence in Mark and Josephus cannot be excluded, and concludes that the Marcan use is an 'overworking of a form of expression, correct but unusual in good Greek, because it happened to correspond to a phrase that was frequent in the Semitic language'.[1]

Especially common in Aramaic is the auxiliary *'ᵃzal* (ἔρχεσθαι). In emphasizing the main verb, no idea of 'going' need be present at all, e.g. *Bereshith Rabbah*, 17, '. . . she went (*'ᵃzalath*) and got married'; other examples are *Ma'aser Sheni*, iv. 9, f. 55*c*, line 17; *Kil'aim*, ix. 4, f. 32*c*, lines 38, 42, 45, and passim in the Palestinian Talmud. Besides the Synoptic use of ἐρχόμενος, ἐλθών, in this way, the Johannine ὑπάγειν conforms to this idiom: Jn. xii. 11, ὑπῆγον . . . καὶ ἐπίστευον; xv. 16, ἵνα ὑμεῖς ὑπάγητε καὶ καρπὸν φέρητε. For a possible auxiliary (and adverbial) use of στρέφειν = *shubh*, *tubh*, expressing simply 'again', Joüon cites Mt. xviii. 3, *Notes philologiques*, p. 347: 'Je me demande si στρέφω peut bien avoir le sens de "changer". . . . Le sens "si vous ne redevenez comme les enfants" admis par quelques auteurs, est excellent. Nous avons ici tout simplement la manière hébraïque (*šub*) et araméenne (*tubh*, *hᵉfak*) d'exprimer l'idée de *re*. Il faut avouer que ce sémitisme est un peu gros, mais il ne semble pas possible de le nier.'

2. *The Impersonal Plural*

The passive is less frequently used in Aramaic than in Greek, its place being taken by an impersonal construction, uncommon in Greek apart from λέγουσι, φασί. In the appearance of this impersonal construction in the Gospels, Wellhausen detected the influence of Aramaic.[2] An examination of the distribution of the construction in the Gospels confirms his view: it predominates in sayings of Jesus, and, with the exception of Mt. i.

[1] 'An Unrecorded "Aramaism" in Josephus', in *J.T.S.* xxx, p. 370. The study is of importance, since it establishes a stylistic similarity due to Aramaic between Mark and Josephus. Cf. further Wilcox, op. cit., p. 125.

[2] *Einl.*², p. 18. See now further Wilcox, op. cit., pp. 127 ff.

23 (an Old Testament quotation) and Jn. xx. 2, those examples which are not in sayings of Jesus come from Mark's Gospel.

Mt. i. *23*, v. *15*, vii. *16*, ix. *17*, xxiv. *9*; Mk. v. 35, vi. 14, x. 13 (= Lk. xviii. 15), xiii. *26* (= Mt. xxiv. *30*, Lk. xxi. *27*), xv. 27;[1] Lk. vi. *44*, xii. *20*, *48*, xiv. *35*, xvi. *9*, xvii. *23*, xviii. *33*, xxiii. *31*; Jn. xv. *6*, xx. 2; Acts iii. 2, xix. 19, xiii. 28 (see Wilcox, pp. 127 ff.).

C. H. Turner has called attention to a characteristic Marcan usage, an 'impersonal plural' (so described by Turner) where the reference appears invariably to be to the Twelve; Matthew and Luke replace such plurals by a singular with Jesus as subject. This apparent mannerism of Mark loses its awkwardness when we turn these recurring third plurals into first plurals, and Turner (following a suggestion of Godet) was convinced that these third plural verbs reflect verbs in the first person plural in Peter's Memoirs.[2]

But there is no need to resort to such an explanation. Such a monotonous repetition of third plural or third singular verbs referring to a subject which has once been mentioned or is too well-known to require mentioning again is characteristic of simple Semitic narrative. Frequently in a Semitic story no care is taken to indicate change of subject; the identification is left to the attention and intelligence of the reader; in Arabic narrative the identification is not always obvious.

In the Aramaic story of Yoḥanan ben Zakkai's escape from beleaguered Jerusalem, told in *Midrash Echa*, i. 31, we have an instance of this kind of Semitic narrative.

Rabbi Yoḥanan ben Zakkai went out to walk in the city and saw people soaking straw and drinking the water. *He* said, 'People who soak straw and drink the water, can they stand against the forces of Vespasian? I will go out of here.' *He* said to ben Batiah, 'Bring me out of here'. *He* (ben Batiah) said to him, 'I cannot bring you out of here except as a corpse'. *He* (Rabbi Yoḥanan) said to him,

[1] Another possible instance in this chapter occurs at verse 8, καθὼς ἐποίει αὐτοῖς, 'just as one was wont to do for them', i.e. 'just as was customarily done for them'; cf. Sy$^{\text{vet.}}$ and the Arabic Tatian, which has, 'And all the people shouted and began to ask, as was the custom, that he should do for them. . . .'

[2] 'Marcan Usage', in *J.T.S.* xxvi, p. 225 f.

'As a corpse bring me out of here'. *He* pretended to be dead, and his disciples put him in a coffin; Rabbi Eliezer carried him at his head and Rabbi Yehoshua at his feet and ben Batiah walked in front of him, his garments rent. As soon as *they* arrived in front of the gate, *they* sought to get him through. *They* (the Romans at the gate) said to them, 'What are ye who are enemies seeking to do?' *They* (the Jews) said that even their Rabbi *they* (the Romans) did not spare. As soon as *they* (the Jews) had brought him out, *they* put him in a certain cemetery and returned to the city. As soon as *they* had returned, Rabbi Yoḥanan went to the forces of Vespasian.

Examples of such an 'impersonal plural' in Mark given by Turner are: i. 21, 29, 30; v. 1, 38; vi. 53, 54; viii. 22; ix. 14, 30, 33; x. 32, 46; xi. 1, 11 (*Θ*, *i*, *k*), 12, 15, 19, 20, 27; xiv. 18, 22, 26, 32. Examples which occur together, e.g. in ix, xi, xiv, provide the best illustration of the usage. The construction yields a criterion for the primitive text of Mark; thus in the group in xi, that text is preserved in *Θ* and the Old Latin.

3. *Generalizing Plural*

A 'generalizing' plural has been claimed by Joüon as a Semitism, and he is followed by Jeremias; e.g. Mt. xxii. 7, *τὰ στρατεύματα αὐτοῦ*, 'his army'. See Joüon, *L'Évangile*, p. 135; Jeremias, in *Z.N.T.W.* xxxviii (1939), pp. 115 ff.; *Die Gleichnisse Jesu*[2], p. 7 (note 2), p. 52 (note 2).

4. *Tense*

(*a*) *Aorist for the Semitic Perfect*

Many explanations have been offered of the aorist *ἐκάθισαν* in Mt. xxiii. 2, but the tense defies analysis on Greek lines.[1] It finds its true explanation in the light of Mk. i. 11, *εὐδόκησα*, which alludes to Isa. xlii. 1, *ὃν εὐδόκησεν ἡ ψυχή μου*, where the Greek aorist renders a Hebrew stative perfect, 'delighteth'. Mt. xxiii. 2, *ἐκάθισαν*, as Wellhausen observed,[2] is a Greek aorist used with the force of a Semitic perfect: the latter corresponds, not only to the aorist, but to the perfect and present tenses, in the latter use of present states or general truths. A similar instance is Mk. i. 8, *ἐβάπτισα*, the equivalent of a Semitic perfect,

[1] Cf. G. C. Richards, in *J.T.S.* x, p. 284.

[2] *Einl.*[2], p. 18.

used either of a general truth or an immediately completed act; the parallel in Mt. iii. 11 has correctly βαπτίζω; Mt. xiv. 31, ἐδίστασας, is similar, 'Why dost thou doubt?' Other examples are Mt. x. 25, ἐπεκάλεσαν (D correctly, καλοῦσι), Lk. xi. 52, ἤρατε (cf. *infra*, p. 260), and Jn. xi. 14, ἀπέθανεν. Joüon (*L'Évangile*, ad Mt. vi. 12) draws attention to another aorist of this type: 'Comme nous remettons en ce moment même; l'action est déjà accomplie au moment où l'on parle. C'est la valeur de l'aoriste ἀφήκαμεν, qui répond à un parfait araméen.' The tense of ἠγαλλίασε at Lk. i. 46 corresponds to a Stative Perfect, and should be rendered by a present (*infra*, p. 151). The other verbs in the Magnificat all correspond to Semitic Perfects, and may be rendered as perfects in English. So also Lk. xiv. 18, 20, ἀγρὸν ἠγόρασα, γυναῖκα ἔγημα, of immediately completed acts, and Lk. vii. 47, ἠγάπησε, a Stative Perfect, to be translated by a present, 'loves (much)'. Matthew's ὡμοιώθη (xiii. 24, xviii. 23, xxii. 2) is a Semitic Perfect (of general truths); cf. LXX παρασυνεβλήθη Ps. xlviii. 13, 21 (*nimshal*); Mt. vii. 24, 26 give a future ὁμοιωθήσεται. Other possible cases are the three aorists in Lk. xi. 52 (*infra*, p. 194).

A number of other cases are more doubtful, but deserve to be noted as possibly coming within this category of 'Semitic' Aorists.

The more difficult reading at Lk. i. 78 (Benedictus) is ἐπεσκέψατο, CDK for Bℵ ἐπισκέψεται which looks very like a grammatical correction: the correct rendering (if it is a Hebrew-type aorist) should be 'has visited us (now)'. The Latin versions prefer *visitavit*. On the other hand, it may be argued that ἐπεσκέψατο is a probably accidental (and unreflective) assimilation of the tense of the verb to the aorists in the context. The reading at Mt. xxii. 4 ἡτοίμασα (Θ, Koine) for ἡτοίμακα seems very probably a case of assimilation to other aorists in the context, especially in view of the following perfect τεθυμένα (ἐστιν) which supports ἡτοίμακα. (The variant, in any case, may be a scribal slip, σ for κ.) A more certain instance would seem to be Mk. x. 28 par. where ℵΘ, &c., read ἠκολουθήσαμεν against BCD, &c. ἠκολουθήκαμεν. Again it may be argued that the aorist is a mistaken assimilation to the preceding aorist *ἀφή-καμεν*. Since *ἀφήκαμεν* itself, however, seems to belong to the class of aorist ('we have (just) left, &c.'), we would expect an aorist of this type to follow, not a perfect.

The distribution of these anomalous tenses supports the source or translation Greek hypothesis.

Mt. vi. *12*, x. *25*, xiii. *24*, xiv. *31*, xviii. *23*, xxii. *2*, *4*, xxiii. *2*.
Mk. i. 8, 11, x. 28.
Lk. i. 46, i. 78, vii. *47*, xi. *52*, xiv. 18, 20.
Jn. xi. *14*.

(*b*) *Periphrastic Tenses: Participial Present or Imperfect*

Burney has noticed the frequency of the historic present in Mark and John, and attributed it to Aramaic influence.[1] But apart from its over-use in these two Gospels, there is nothing specially Semitic about the tense. The same applies to the frequent use in Mark and John of the imperfect and of the periphrastic tenses. The use of the participle with the verb 'to be' to express a continuous or progressive tense, though specially characteristic of Aramaic, is also a feature of the Koine. The use of *γίνεσθαι* for *εἶναι* with a participle has been claimed as an Aramaism by Allen, who compares the LXX's rendering of the Hebrew construction in Lam. i. 16.[2] Such a use of *γίνεσθαι* with no special force of its own is certainly not to be found in the Koine,[3] but in many (if not all) of the New Testament instances claimed by Allen, *γίνεσθαι* may be pressed; Rev. iii. 2, *γίνου γρηγορῶν*, is not 'be watchful', but 'become watchful'; so also Mk. i. 4, ix. 3, 7. We should require more examples from the Gospels in order to reach a definitive conclusion.[4]

The use of the participle alone in Hellenistic Greek as an indicative has already been noted.[5] But while the usage is occasionally found in the Koine, it is an especially characteristic Aramaic tense, the participial present or imperfect; examples will be found in the passage in the Palestinian Talmud, *Kil'aim*,

[1] *Aramaic Origin*, p. 87; cf. W. C. Allen, *Expository Times*, xiii, p. 329.
[2] Op. cit., p. 330.
[3] Cf. Mayser, *Gramm. der griech. Papyri*, ii, p. 223.
[4] Cf. Wilcox, op. cit., pp. 123 ff.
[5] *Supra*, p. 68.

ix. 3, f. *32b*, lines 44–46.[1] In the Gospels the construction is practically confined to Codex Bezae, and Moulton agreed with Wellhausen that, in D, '. . . we find this usage apparently arising from the literal translation of Aramaic'.[2]

Where one part of the verb 'to be' is already present in the same sentence or clause, the construction is in no way irregular, but is scarcely literary Greek; examples are, Mt. xxiv. *41*; Mk. i. 13 (D); Lk. i. 18, xvi. 19 (D); Acts viii. 13 (D).[3] The participle alone as an indicative occurs in Mk. iii. 6 (D), vii. 25 (D), ix. 26 (D); Acts v. 26 (D). A typical example is found in Mt. xxvii. 41 (D) (= Mk. xv. 31),[4] ὁμοίως δὲ καὶ οἱ ἀρχιερεῖς ἐμπαίζοντες μετὰ τῶν γραμματέων καὶ Φαρισαίων λέγοντες, 'Likewise also the chief priests (were) mocking with the scribes and Pharisees, saying . . .' WH read ἔλεγον, but by making this the main verb and subordinating ἐμπαίζοντες to it, the natural emphasis is lost: the chief priests and Pharisees were not saying, mocking; they were mocking, saying. Wilcox (op. cit., pp. 121 ff.) gives Acts x. 19, xiv. 3 as further examples of this usage.

Examples of this usage where it occurs in characteristic Semitic clauses are found in the following passages, all from D: Mk. vii. 25, ὡς ἀκούσασα περὶ αὐτοῦ, 'when she heard about him'; Lk. i. 36, καὶ ἰδοὺ Ἐλισάβεθ ἡ συγγενίς σου καὶ αὐτὴ συνειληφυῖα υἱὸν ἐν γήρει αὐτῆς, καὶ οὗτος μὴν . . ., 'And behold, Elizabeth thy kinswoman, she too has conceived a son in her old age'; a new sentence begins with καὶ οὗτος, so that συνειληφυῖα must be regarded as equivalent to a perfect indicative; WH, συνείληφεν. Lk. ii. 36 contains an example of a circumstantial clause, καὶ Ἄννα προφῆτις . . . καὶ αὐτὴ προβεβηκυῖα ἐν ἡμέραις, 'Now Anna the prophetess . . . she too is advanced in years . . .'

In addition to the uses of the participle noted, its employment to express a future tense in Aramaic is reflected in a number of passages in the Gospels. Dr. Joachim Jeremias gives the following list (*Abendmahlsworte Jesu*², p. 91):

[1] Other examples will be found in Burney, *Aramaic Origin*, p. 88 f., and Allen, op. cit., p. 329.

[2] *Prol.*, p. 224.

[3] An exhaustive list appears in Moulton, *Gramm.* ii, p. 452.

[4] Mt. xxvii. 41 (D) may preserve the primitive Marcan text.

Mk.: x. *30*; xiv. *24*.
Mt.: iii. 11 (dial.); xi. 3 par. (dial.); xxvi. 25, *28*.
Lk.: i. 35 (dial.); xxii. *21*.
Jn.: i. 29; xii. *25*; xiii. 11; xvi. *13*; xvii. *20*; xviii. 4; xxi. 20 (dial.).

Cf. further Burney, *Aram. Origin*, pp. 94 ff.; Joüon, *L'Évangile*, p. 69; W. B. Stevenson, *Grammar of Jewish Palestinian Aramaic*, § 21. 9; and Blass–Debrunner, § 339. *2a–c*.

At Jn. ii. 22, Joüon suspects (as does Burney, op. cit., p. 108) that behind ἔλεγεν lies a Semitic pluperfect (*Quelques aramaïsmes*, pp. 216 ff.). So also ἔλεγεν at Mt. ix. 21 (*Quelques aramaïsmes*, xvii (1927), p. 217). At Lk. iv. 16, ἦν τεθραμμένος we have a true Semitic Pluperfect. Mt. vii. 4 ἐρεῖς is cited by Joüon as a future with the sense of 'can' (as in Semitic Imperfects); Lk. vi. 42 has δύνασαι λέγειν; see his *L'Évangile*, in loc.

Vocabulary

In his brief but important study of the vocabulary of the Gospels[1] Wellhausen distinguishes between technically religious terms, words found in the LXX, and others influenced by Aramaic. In the first class there does not seem to be any sufficient reason for tracing πειράζειν, βαπτίζειν, ἀναστῆναι, 'to rise from the dead', or σώζειν, 'to keep alive' and hence 'to heal', to a specifically Semitic source or influence. Words from the second class may have come into the Gospels through the influence of the LXX.

In the third class, πρόσκαιρος in Mk. iv. 17 is a natural extension of common Greek usage, and ὀλιγόπιστος, while it may reflect an Aramaic compound, is not an unusual Greek formation. A number of expressions in this third class are, in fact, also found in the LXX; the phrase ἄρτον φαγεῖν, 'to eat', occurs in Gen. iii. 19, xliii. 16; Exod. ii. 20. The verb διακρίνειν occurs in Zech. iii. 7, rendering Hebrew *din* in the sense 'to govern', but such a meaning for κρίνειν in Mt. xix. 28 = Lk. xxii. 30 is doubtful. Similar well-known Semitisms are δοῦναι, 'to make, set or place'; it is found in Aramaic in *Midrash Echa*, i. 31 (in the story of Yoḥanan ben Zakkai translated above), '. . . his disciples placed him in a coffin'; *Kil'aim*, ix. 4, f. 32*b*, line 45,

[1] *Einl.*[1], p. 33 f.; 2nd edit., p. 17 f.

'. . . he put (*y^e^habh*) his finger upon it'.[1] The noun θάλασσα in the sense of λίμνη is thoroughly Semitic; we perpetuate the Semitism when we speak of the Sea of Galilee.[2] Uncertainty attaches to the sense of 'patch' for πλήρωμα (Mk. ii. 21).[3] The curious use of ὄρος, in the phrase used of Jesus going forth 'to the mountain' or 'to a mountain' to pray (e.g. Mt. xv. 29), suggests the influence of Aramaic *ṭura*, which in Palestinian Syriac has the twofold use of 'mountain' and 'country', the 'open country' as contrasted with inhabited places.[4]

In Lk. xiii. 24, for WH's οὐκ ἰσχύσουσιν, D reads οὐχ εὑρήσουσιν, a variant which Wellhausen traced to an ambiguous Aramaic *'ashkaḥ*.[5] But there is no instance hitherto adduced of this verb in the sense 'to be able' for Palestinian Aramaic; it means 'to find' only; it is in Syriac that it has the two senses 'to find' and 'to be able'. We cannot therefore infer, as has been done, that the Bezan variant is a 'Syriacism':[6] our knowledge of Palestinian Aramaic is still far from complete. But it does

[1] For δοῦναι in the sense of 'put or place', see further Joüon, *Notes philologiques*, p. 353, on Lk. vii. 44. Instead of rendering 'thou gavest me no water for my feet', Joüon suggests 'thou hast not poured water on my feet'; Simon himself ought to have performed this personal service as a token of courtesy and respect. (Cf., however, Klostermann, *Komm.* in loc.) Another example is Lk. xii. 51, εἰρήνην . . . δοῦναι, 'to set peace on earth'. D has ποιεῖν for δοῦναι here, and 'to make peace' is also a Semitic idiom; cf. Targ., Josh. ix. 15. Cf. Mk. xiii. 22 ποιήσουσιν *v.l.* ex LXX δώσουσιν. Wensinck cites in illustration Gen. xxvii. 40 (F), *y^e^habh nir*, 'to set a yoke on . . .'.

[2] Aristotle refers to 'the lake under the Caucasus which the inhabitants there call "sea" ' (*Meteor.* I. 13). The language was probably Syriac.

[3] One use of the Syriac verb *m^e^la* is 'to patch' and *malaya* is a 'tailor' (*Anecdota Syriaca*, ii. 269. 7).

[4] It is the equivalent of Hebrew *sadheh* and renders ἀγρός as well as ὄρος in the Gospels; Gen. ii. 5, 19, iii. 18; Deut. xi. 15; Isa. xliii. 20; Mt. vi. 28, 30, xiii. 36, 38, 44; Mk. xv. 21. See further Joüon, *Notes philologiques*, p. 349, on Mt. xxiv. 16: 'La Judée étant un pays montagneux, les ὄρη où il faut fuir sont des montagnes qui connotent le désert. On peut penser à des régions montagneuses désertiques au delà de la mer Morte. Là où Matthieu (18, 12) dit ἐπὶ τὰ ὄρη, Luc (15, 4) dit ἐν τῇ ἐρήμῳ. "Montagne" et "désert" sont connexes. En éthiopien et en arabe *dabr* est "montagne", en hébreu *midbr* est "désert". En araméen juif *ṭura* signifie à la fois "Berg", et "freies Feld" (Dalman, *Aramäisch-neuhebr. Wörterb.*).' Moulton–Milligan claim that ὄρος has also the sense of 'desert' in the Papyri.

[5] *Einl.*^2^, p. 17. *Gen. Apoc.* xxi. 13.

[6] F. H. Chase, *The Syro-Latin Text of the Gospels*, p. 44.

not so far support Wellhausen's Aramaism, so far as the Palestinian dialect is concerned. Wensinck claims Gen. iv. 7 (F) (ed. Ginsburger, p. 72, line 5) as a case where *'ashkaḥ* has the meaning 'to be able' in Jewish Palestinian Aramaic. G. D. Kilpatrick suggests that the source of the Bezan variant is the parallel in Mt. vii. 14. If Wensinck's claim is allowed, an original (ambiguous) Aramaic *'ashkaḥ* may be the source of the Synoptic variant; alternatively Matthew's 'find' may be a 'Syriacism', i.e. a rendering of the original in the light of Syriac, not Palestinian Aramaic usage. Does Lk. vi. 7, *εὕρωσιν*, mean 'be able'?

Ἀναστῆναι (*ἐν τῇ κρίσει*) *μετά* (Mt. xii. *41* = Lk. xi. *32*)

The expression was recognized as a Semitism by Wellhausen;[1] it is attested in the Palestinian Talmud, *Shebi'ith*, x. 9, f. 39*d*, 15 lines from foot of column, 'Rabbi Jose *disputed with* Rabbi Jacob' (*qam* R. Jose *'im* R. Jacob); *Terumoth* viii. 5, f. 45*c*, line 37. In the Gospel passages *ἀναστῆναι μετά* and *ἐγείρεσθαι μετά* are synonymous terms. In the Aramaic phrase there is nothing corresponding to *ἐν τῇ κρίσει*, and it is probable that these words represent a purely Greek addition to make an otherwise foreign idiom intelligible. It is noteworthy that they are omitted in Lk. xi. 31 in Codex Bezae, which thus gives the Aramaic phrase (verse 32 is omitted in D).[2] Joüon adds Mt. x. 21 (*Notes philologiques*, p. 346) and Lk. xxi. 36 (ibid., p. 355) for a similar legal sense of *ἐπανίστημι* and *σταθῆναι ἔμπροσθεν*. (*a*) Mt. x. 21: '*Ἐπανίστημι*, c'est prendre la position de l'accusateur (cf. Acts. 6, 13; Ps. 27, 12; Job 16, 8, et comparer Mt. 12, 41)'[3] (*b*) *Σταθῆναι ἔμπροσθεν τοῦ υἱοῦ τοῦ ἀνθρώπου*. 'C'est un hébraïsme qui signifie "se maintenir"; ici c'est pratiquement ne pas succomber, ne pas être condamné, puisque le Fils de l'homme vient pour juger.' He compares Ps. v. 5, 'The arrogant shall not stand (*lo yithyaṣṣ^ebhu*) in thy sight.'

[1] *Einl.*[1], p. 34; 2nd edit., p. 17.

[2] Cf. Wensinck, *Semitisms*, p. 35.

[3] *Παραδίδωμι* here (Mt. x. 21) and at x. 19 is taken to mean 'livrer au juge en vue d'une condamnation', and *θανατόω* 'a ici un sens causatif large: ce n'est pas "faire mourir" ni même "condamner à mort", mais "faire condamner à mort" par son accusation, "faire mettre à mort".'

'Απέχειν (Mk. xiv. *41*)

(See *infra*, p. 225.)

Αὐξάνειν (Mt. xx. *28* D; Lk. xxii. *28* D; Jn. iii. 30)

(See *infra*, pp. 173, 229.)

'Εθνικός (Mt. v. *47*, vi. *7*)

(See *infra*, p. 176 f.)

'Εκβάλλειν (Lk. vi. *22*; cf. Mt. v. *11*; Lk. x. *35*)

This first verse in Luke generally receives the interpretation, '. . . throw your name contemptuously away, reject it with ignominy as an evil thing'; so Plummer in his Commentary in loc. But it is very doubtful if the word has any such meaning in the context in Greek, and its simple and literal Semitic equivalent certainly did not. Wellhausen pointed out that it corresponded exactly to the Hebrew *hoṣi'* in one of its idiomatic uses, 'to give out', 'to make known', 'to publish abroad':[1] parallel to the Lucan verse is Deut. xxii. 14, 19, '. . . and shall give out, publish abroad against her an evil name'; we may compare further Num. xiii. 32, xiv. 36, 37; in the Palestinian Talmud, *Kethub*. iv. 2, f. 28*b*, line 55.

In the Koine, and especially in the papyri, the Greek verb has, in several of its uses, lost altogether the idea of violence; it may mean, e.g., 'to send out', 'to put away', and hence 'to divorce'. The verb has the same weakened sense in the LXX as a standing equivalent for *hoṣi'*,[2] but it is nowhere found either in the Koine or in the LXX meaning 'to give out', 'to publish abroad' of a name or reputation. In the LXX of Deut. xxii. 14 καταφέρειν is used, and in Num. xiii. 32 ἐκφέρειν. The expression 'to cause an ill name to go out' is idiomatically Semitic: the Aramaic *'appeq* is used exactly as the Hebrew verb in this sense; Lk. vi. 22 is rendered by this idiomatic expression in the Old Syriac, '. . . and give out, publish against you an evil name'. In Jewish Palestinian Aramaic, in the Jerusalem Targum of

[1] *Evangelium Lukae*, in loc.

[2] We may compare in the Gospels, Mt. xii. 35, xiii. 52; Jn. x. 4.

Gen. xxxiv. 30 (where a different phrase occurs in the Hebrew), we find this expression, '. . . in order to spread abroad (*l^emap-paqa*) an ill report about me'; so also the same Targum renders Num. xiii. 32, '. . . they spread abroad an evil report'; cf. further Targum Prov. x. 18 and in the Palestinian Syriac version, Lk. vi. 22 itself.

In Mk. i. 28, Lk. vii. 17, ἐξῆλθεν corresponds to the simple form of the verb in this sense, 'to go out' and hence 'to be published abroad'. In Aramaic an example occurs in *Vayyikra Rabba*, 27, '. . . and shouldest thou conquer us, thy name would go forth, be published abroad (*napheq*) in the world'. The Syriac expression *n^ephaq ṭebha* corresponds exactly to Mark's ἐξῆλθε . . . ἡ ἀκοή . . . (i. 28); cf. *Doctrine of Addai*, ed. Phillips, ܟ, line 6.

A second idiomatic use of this verb is assumed in Lk. x. 35, ἐκβαλὼν δύο δηνάρια; both the Hebrew and Aramaic words correspond to δαπανᾶν, 'to expend'; thus in 2 Kings xii. 11, 'And they gave the money . . . and they *laid it out* to the carpenters and builders . . .' The Aramaic verb appears in the Palestinian Talmud in this sense in *Gittin*, v. 3, f. 46*d*, line 27, '. . . he paid out (*'appeq*) four dinars'. The Palestinian Syriac version so renders ἀποδιδόναι in Mt. v. 26.

Ἐμβριμᾶσθαι τῷ πνεύματι (Jn. xi. 33, 38)

(See *infra*, p. 240 f.)

Ἐπιούσιος (Mt. vi. *11* = Lk. xi. *3*)

(See *infra*, p. 203 f.)

Ἐπιφώσκειν (Mt. xxviii. 1; Lk. xxiii. 54)

A Semitic use of this verb has been claimed for Mt. xxviii. 1 and Lk. xxiii. 54:[1] it is said in both passages to have the force of the Hebrew *'or*, Aramaic *n^egah*, idiomatically used of the 'breaking' of the Jewish day at sunset,[2] or as referring to the 'drawing on' of the following day any time after sunset, the evening and

[1] A. Geiger, in *Z.D.M.G.* xii, p. 365; G. F. Moore, 'Conjectanea Talmudica', in *Journal of American Oriental Society*, xxvi, pp. 323–9.

[2] Burkitt in *J.T.S.* xiv, p. 539, suggested that *n^egah* originally referred to the rising of the evening star (*nugha* in Syriac is Venus).

the night belonging, according to the Jewish reckoning, to the day which they usher in.

The word is rare in Greek, but in the two or three instances where it does occur in profane Greek it is always used of the real dawn.[1] In ecclesiastical Greek it has the sense claimed for the two Gospel passages: from an examination of the use of the verb in the Apostolic Constitutions, the Didascalia, and in Epiphanius, F. C. Burkitt concluded that we have here 'a real example of that "Jewish Greek" which the discoveries of the Egyptian Papyri have reduced to such a restricted compass'.[2]

A Jewish reader of Mt. xxviii. 1 would certainly understand τῇ ἐπιφωσκούσῃ of the 'drawing on' of the first day of the week on the late evening of the Sabbath: the same applies to Lk. xxiii. 54; it was on the evening of the Day of Preparation, when the Sabbath was drawing on, that Jesus was buried. In the *Gospel of Peter*, 2, Pilate receives the assurance from Herod that the burial of Jesus would have been carried out even if Pilate had not asked (on the request of Joseph of Arimathaea) for the body to be sent to him, 'seeing that it is the Sabbath that is drawing on (ἐπεὶ καὶ σάββατον ἐπιφώσκει), for it is written in the Law: Let not the sun go down on a slain man'. 'At what exact moment of the day he (Peter) may be supposed to place the conversation between Pilate and Herod on the subject of the burial, the moment to which the conversation looks forward can only be sunset: "that Sabbath is dawning" and "that the sun may not set on the corpse of a criminal" exposed on the gallows, are two parallel and mutually complementary parts of the argument.'[3]

If this is the meaning of the verb in Mt. xxviii. 1, how are we to reconcile it with Mark's quite unambiguous ἀνατείλαντος τοῦ ἡλίου? G. F. Moore thought that Mark's version 'may have originated in the desire to make clearer or to put into better

[1] Cf. Moulton-Milligan, *Vocabulary of the Greek New Testament*. The discovery of the verb in a papyrus does not necessarily mean that there was no Jewish Greek use of the word; in the papyrus the real dawn is meant.

[2] Op. cit., p. 546.

[3] C. H. Turner, in *J.T.S.* xiv, p. 189.

Greek such an expression as τῇ ἐπιφωσκούσῃ which we have in Matthew'.[1] We should require, in that case, to assume that Matthew is here independent of Mark, drawing on the original tradition which Mark, perhaps through a misunderstanding, is seeking to 'improve'; John's σκοτίας ἔτι οὔσης would go back to the same tradition as Matthew.

Such a view helps to resolve the contradictions in the several accounts of the Evangelists. The order of events might then be: Jesus was crucified on the Day of Preparation for the Passover, which fell that year on a Sabbath; He was buried in the late afternoon or early evening of the same day, before sunset. A full day later, late on the Sabbath in our reckoning but early on the first day of the week, i.e. late Saturday afternoon or evening, in the Jewish, Mary Magdalene and the disciples went to the Tomb: Mary had waited till the Sabbath was officially over, then without delay, on the Saturday evening, made her way to the Garden.[2]

Καρπὸν ποιεῖν

An idiomatic use of Hebrew *'asah*, 'to make', is 'to yield', 'to produce', e.g. of grain yielding meal (Hos. viii. 7), of a vineyard, grapes (Isa. v. 2, 4, 10), and of a tree, fruit; the LXX renders the Hebrew expression, 'to make fruit', either literally by καρπὸν ποιεῖν (Gen. i. 11, 12; 2 Kings xix. 30; Jer. xii. 2, xvii. 8; Ezek. xvii. 23), or by the more idiomatic καρπὸν φέρειν (Hos. ix. 16). The same idiom, 'to make fruit', meaning to yield or produce fruit, is found in Aramaic, perhaps in imitation of the Hebrew: the Targum has *'ᵃbhadh pira* in Gen. i. 11, 12, Jer. xvii. 8; the Jerusalem Targums have the same expression in the Genesis

[1] Op. cit., p. 328.

[2] Mk. xiv. 12 (and dependent parallels) is a familiar crux. It is very probable that τῇ πρώτῃ τῶν ἀζύμων is a misunderstanding of the Aramaic for 'on the day before the Feast of Unleavened Bread (the Passover)', i.e. the Day of Preparation. No Jew would make ready the Passover on the first day of the Feast! The rest of Mk. xiv. 12 provides further confirmation that this was the original text: the *Gospel of Peter*, 2, preserves the true tradition, πρὸ μιᾶς τῶν ἀζύμων: cf. Allen, *Mark* (Oxford Church Commentary), p. 170 f.; Chwolson, *Das letzte Passamahl* (1908), p. 133 f. Cf. further G. R. Driver in *J.T.S.* vol. xvi, pp. 327 ff.

passage, as has also the Palestinian Syriac. The Semitism may have come from the LXX. It occurs in Rev. xxii. 2. Its distribution in the Gospels is as follows:

Mt. iii. 10 (= Lk. iii. 9) (Baptist), vii. *17–19* (= Lk. vi. *43*); xiii. *26*; Lk. viii. *8*, xiii. *9*.

Κορβᾶν (Mk. vii. *11*, *12*; cf. Mt. xv. *5*)

The words 'Let it be *Korban* whereby I am profitable to thee' is a form of solemn prohibition found, word for word as in the Gospel, in the Talmud.[1] The meaning is, not that such alienated goods or services were really dedicated as an 'offering', but that they were to be regarded as if they had been so dedicated.

The passage has been illumined from the Jewish side by J. Levy, who cites the relevant parallels from the Babylonian Talmud, *Nedar*. i. 4, ii. 2, and iii. 2. In the last passage there is a close parallel to Mk. vii. 11:

> 'If anyone sees several persons eating figs that belong to him and says, "They are Korban with regard to you" (i.e. they are forbidden you), but afterwards discovers that as well as strangers his father and brothers are among them, then, according to the School of Shammai, his relatives are not bound by the Korban, but may partake of the figs; the strangers are bound by it. According to the School of Hillel, on the other hand, the relatives also are bound, even though the Korban has been pronounced with regard to them in error. *And if anyone expressly lays such a Korban on his relatives, then they are bound by it and cannot receive anything from him that is covered by the Korban.*'[2]

Μαμωνᾶς (Mt. vi. *24*; Lk. xvi. *9*, *11*, *13*)

The word is attested in the Targums and the Babylonian Talmud (*Berach.* 61*b*) in the sense of 'profit', 'money'. It is found in the Palestinian Pentateuch Targum to Gen. xxxiv. 23 (C) as a rendering of Hebrew *miqneh*, 'cattle', the 'wealth' of the Hebrew farmer. It occurs frequently in the Palestinian

[1] J. Lightfoot, *Horae Hebraicae*, ii, p. 227.

[2] I have freely paraphrased the note in Levy's *Chaldäisches Wörterbuch* (1867), ii, p. 385 f.

Talmud, e.g. *Nazir*, v. 4, f. 54*b*, line 12; *Sanhedrin*, viii. 8, f. 26*c*, lines 20, 21.[1]

Μωραίνεσθαι (Mt. v. *13* = Lk. xiv. *34*)

(See *infra*, p. 166 f.)

Ὀφείλημα, ὀφείλειν (Mt. vi. *12* = Lk. xi. *4*; cf. *ὀφειλέτης*, Lk. xiii. *4*)

It has for long been recognized that this word in the Lord's Prayer corresponds to Aramaic *ḥobha*, 'debt' or 'sin';[2] *ὀφειλέτης* in Lk. xiii. 4 is the equivalent of *ḥayyabha*, 'debtor' or 'sinner'; in xi. 4 Luke has correctly *ἁμαρτία*.[3] 'Sin' was conceived of in terms of a debt; we may compare the parable of the Unforgiving Debtor. Examples of the words in these senses are common: the following are taken from the Samaritan Liturgy, ii, p. 453, f. 76, line 14; i, p. 20, f. 28, line 7: the latter is a proverb,

> Whoever receiveth sinners (*ḥayyabhin*)
> Condoneth their sin (*ḥobhyon*).

Παραδιδόναι (Mk. iv. *29*)

(See *infra*, p. 163 f.)

Πιστικός (Mk. xiv. 3; cf. Jn. xii. 3)

(See *infra*, p. 223 f.)

Πληρωθῆναι (Lk. xxii. *16*)

(See *infra*, p. 230 f.)

Ποιεῖν (Mk. iii. 14)

The use of *ποιεῖν* at Mk. iii. 14 in the sense of 'appoint' is generally explained as due to LXX influence or as a Biblicism,

[1] On *Μαμωνᾶς* cf. further A. M. Honeyman, 'The Etymology of Mammon' in *Archivum Linguisticum*, vol. iv, fasc. 1, pp. 60 ff.

[2] J. T. Marshall, in *Expositor*, Ser. IV, iii, pp. 124, 281.

[3] Cf. Gen. iv. 23 (*ḥobh*, P-J), xviii. 23 (*ḥayyabh*, P-J). Cf. further, Joüon, 'La pécheresse de Galilée et la parabole des deux débiteurs', in *Rev. de science rel.*, xxix (1939), p. 616. *Infra*, p. 194. An example of *ἁμάρτημα* in another sense of *ḥubh* occurs in Mk. iii. *29*. It probably corresponds to *ḥiyyubha, condemnatio.* The Pa'el means 'to declare guilty' and the noun the state of being condemned, 'guilt'; Syriac *ḥuyyabha* has the same meaning and is equivalent to *κατάκριμα, καταδίκη*. Cf. J. T. Marshall, in *Expositor*, Ser. IV, iii, p. 282 f.; W. C. Allen, Oxford Church Commentary on Mark, in loc.

and this could be true. Cf., e.g., V. Taylor, *Commentary on Mark*, in loc.: examples are I Kings xii. 31, II Chron. ii. 18. But the usage may be due to Aramaic influence (or to an Aramaic source): the corresponding Syriac verb is idiomatically used in this sense (see P. Sm. Col. 2766). Cf. also Targum I Kings xii. 31 and Levy, *Chald. Wört.*, s.v.

Συναλίζεσθαι (Acts i. 4)

There is little that needs to be added to the full discussion of this very rare word by Wilcox:[1] the explanation that it is a rare (poetical) Biblical Greek term meaning 'to dine' and 'to feast' seems to me preferable to theories of an Aramaic original. The context, describing a post-Resurrection Meal of the Risen Lord with His disciples (similar to that described at Lk. xxiv. 30 ff.) would call for a special term of this kind.

Attention was first drawn to this possibility by Professor C. F. D. Moule in an article on 'The Post-Resurrection Appearances in the Light of Festival Pilgrimages'.[2]

Ὑψωθῆναι (Jn. xii. *32*, 34, dialogue; iii. *14*)

Several scholars have pointed out that the Syriac equivalent of *ὑψωθῆναι*, *'ezdeqeph*, has the special meaning 'to be crucified'; in its use of the word in this meaning the Fourth Gospel reveals the influence of Syriac.[3] Gerhard Kittel, however, pointed out that the same verb appears in this sense in Palestinian Aramaic: e.g. in Ezra vi. 11, and in the Targums of I Chron. x. 10, Esther I, ix. 13, II, vii. 10 (in the last example both *zeqaph* and *ṣelabh* are used without distinction).[4] The Johannine use is therefore an Aramaism.

The more general results of this chapter may be summarized:

1. As far as the distribution of Semitisms could be observed, it confirms the conclusion reached on similar evidence in earlier chapters that behind the sayings of Jesus there lies an Aramaic tradition.

[1] Op. cit., pp. 106 f.

[2] *New Testament Studies*, iv, p. 60, n. 4.

[3] E. Hirsch, *Studien zum vierten Evangelium* (1936), p. 51.

[4] In *Z.N.T.W.* xxxv, p. 282 f. Cf. further, *Bulletin of John Rylands Library*, Vol. 45, pp. 315 ff. and *infra*, p. 329.

2. It is doubtful whether the evidence is extensive or impressive enough to allow of the inference to Aramaic sources outside of the sayings. That inference some may be prepared to make, especially on the basis of the evidence of Aramaisms in Mark, and the recurrence of Aramaisms in direct speech or dialogue.

3. In both places, sayings-tradition and narrative, the result is negative as to the nature of the probable sources, whether documentary or oral. The Aramaic sayings-tradition of Jesus may either have been mediated by a written collection of the sayings in Aramaic or in translation Greek, or by a fixed oral tradition; and the importance of the latter among Eastern peoples makes it no less probable than the former. We do not know.

4. The Bezan Uncial is more often and more consistently stained by Semitisms than either B or א: the text represented by it stands nearer to the Greek of Asia Minor or Palestine of the Apostolic period than that of the Vatican or Byzantine recensions.

ADDITIONAL NOTE

Confusion of h^awa and hu'

Torrey has called attention to several instances in the Gospels where he claims that *h^awa*, 'he became', 'he was', has been confused with the pronoun *hu'* in its use as the copula 'is', 'was'.[1] For example, in Jn. xiv. 22 (WH), τί γέγονεν ὅτι . . ., renders *ma hu' d^e*, 'How is it that . . .', as if it had been *ma h^awa d^e*. It must be noted in this case, however, that Greek γέγονα in the Koine has come to be practically synonymous with εἰμί, so that this verse of John may be rendered as it stands, 'What is it that . . .' (the rendering 'how' is doubtful); D has τί ἐστι ὅτι.

In the Palestinian Talmud the Aramaic phrase *ma hu'*, generally contracted to *mahu*, means 'What does it mean'; an example occurs in *Yoma*, iii. 1, f. 40*b*, line 20.[2] In the light of this Aramaic use we may perhaps understand Jn. xiv. 22 as '*What does it mean*, Thou art going to reveal thyself unto us and not to the world?'

[1] *Our Translated Gospels*, p. 115 f.

[2] Cf. *Vayyikra Rabba*, 22, and Dalman, *Gramm.*[1], p. 88; 2nd edit., p. 119. Dalman records the construction with *d^e* after *mahu*.

PART III

SEMITIC POETIC FORM

CHAPTER VII

THE FORMAL ELEMENT OF SEMITIC POETRY IN THE GOSPELS

Parallelism of Lines and Clauses

In his *Poetry of our Lord* C. F. Burney has shown that the sayings of Jesus are cast in the form of Semitic poetry, with such characteristic features as parallelism of lines and clauses, rhythmic structure, and possibly even rhyme. Parallelism and rhythm are more easily discernible than rhyme, the recognition of which is almost wholly conjectural. Parallelism of lines and clauses can be readily detected and studied even in translation.

Burney noticed four types of parallelism in the Gospels:[1] (1) synonymous, where there is 'a correspondence in idea between the two lines of a couplet, the second line reinforcing and as it were echoing the sense of the first in equivalent, though different, terms'; (2) antithetic, a 'contrast of the terms of the second line with those of the first'; (3) synthetic or constructive, where 'the thought of the second line supplements and completes that of the first'; (4) and climactic, where the second line is not a complete echo of the first, 'but adds something more which completes the sense of the distich, thus forming, as it were, its climax'.[2]

All these forms of parallelism are to be found in the poetry of Jesus and the Gospels which has been examined by Burney. But they also occur, sometimes in conjunction with other characteristic features of Semitic poetry, outside of the sayings of Jesus in non-dominical sayings or in the dialogue of the Gospels.

In the examples which follow I have given, except where indicated, the translation of the Authorized Version, arranging

[1] Op. cit., pp. 16, 20, 21.

[2] *Aramaic Origin*, p. 42.

its verses in parallel lines. To illustrate the rhythmic structure of the poetry, I have translated into Aramaic the simplest lines where construction and vocabulary present no difficulties.

The Sayings of the Baptist

In the sayings of the Baptist in the Synoptics, Mk. i. 8 gives a clear instance of antithetic parallelism:

> I indeed have baptized (I indeed baptize)[1] you with water:
> But he shall baptize you with the Holy Ghost.

The couplet is followed in Q (Mt. iii. 12 = Lk. iii. 17) by two synonymous lines completed by two antithetic lines:

> Mt. iii. 12 Whose fan is in his hand,
> And he will throughly purge his floor,
> And gather his wheat into the garner;
> But he will burn up the chaff with unquenchable fire.

Mk. i. 7 also gives two lines in synonymous parallelism which, followed by the antithetic lines in verse 8, fall into the same scheme, *s s*: *a a*:

> There cometh one mightier than I after me, (*'athe bathrai ḥayyol minni*)
> The latchet of whose shoes I am not worthy to stoop down and unloose.[2]

Perhaps the order in the original prophecy was, Mk. i. 7, 8; Mt. iii. 12 (= Lk. iii. 17), *s s*, *a a*: *s s*, *a a*.

In the earlier Baptist pericope from Q, Mt. iii. 7–10 (= Lk. iii. 7–9), there are two synonymous lines in verse 10 and two antithetic lines in verse 9. In verse 7 φυγεῖν is *'ᵃraq*, and in verse 10 ῥίζα is *'iqqar*; if the word-play was to be effective, verse 10 must have followed directly on verse 7, thus giving an appropriate setting for verse 8, following verse 10. Perhaps, balancing verse 8 with its strong imperative, the Baptist's saying at verse 2, 'Repent ye: for the kingdom of heaven is at hand',

[1] *Supra*, p. 128.

[2] Luke's shorter form (iii. 16), 'the latchet of whose shoes I am not worthy to unloose' goes into simple rhythmic Aramaic:

דערקתא דשווירהי
לא שוא אנא דאשרי

The rendering adopted for ὑπόδημα is that of the Palestinian Syriac.

followed immediately on verse 7;[1] it makes a most attractive transposition. The verses from Mark and Q discussed above may have formed the continuation and completion of the original prophecy.[2]

(7) O generation of vipers, who hath warned you to flee from the wrath to come (*l^{e}meʿraq min rugza d^{e}'athe*)?
(2) (Repent ye: for the kingdom of heaven is at hand.)
(10) And now also the axe[3] is laid unto the root (*ʿiqqar*) of the trees:
Therefore every tree which bringeth not forth good fruit is hewn down (*ʿ^{a}qar*), and cast into the fire.
(8) Bring forth therefore fruits meet for repentance:
(9) And think not to say within yourselves, We have Abraham to our father:
For I say unto you, that God is able of these stones to raise up children unto Abraham (*d^{e}yakhel '^{e}laha min 'abhnayya hallen la'^{a}qama b^{e}nayya l^{e}'abhram*).

Burney has called attention to the parallelism in the Johannine Prologue. The last three verses are there attributed to the Baptist and contain examples of Semitic parallelism. In view of its contents, it is doubtful whether verse 18 can be regarded as a genuine saying of the Baptist's, but it furnishes an example of antithetic parallelism;

No man hath seen God at any time;
The only begotten Son, which is in the bosom (*ʿubba*) of the Father (*'abba*), he hath declared him.

In verse 15 (30), either of the clauses ἔμπροσθέν μου γέγονεν or πρῶτός μου ἦν gives a half-line in antithetic parallelism to the previous 'He that cometh after me'. They may be understood to refer either to Jesus' priority in time to John, His pre-existence as the Logos, or to His precedence in rank and authority. If they are not to be tautologous, we must assume that one refers to the first, the other to the second; the A.V. renders, 'He that cometh after me is preferred before me: for he was before me'.

[1] If we could assume that ἐχιδνῶν in verse 7 is a Greek translation of *ʿaqrabbin*, 'scorpions', we should obtain an effective word-play with ἤγγικεν, *q^{e}rabh*, in verse 2.

[2] The word-play, *ʿ^{a}raq*, 'flee', *ʿiqqar*, 'root', is continued in *ʿarq^{e}tha*, 'thong'.

[3] Hebrew *garzen*.

This distinction between priority in time and precedence in rank can only be maintained in the context of the Prologue. It could not come from John the Baptist himself, for John had no theology of the pre-existent Logos and could hardly claim that his great contemporary (and his junior in years) had existed before him. We are not bound to infer, however, that this verse is John the Evangelist's own. The two clauses go back into the same Aramaic: 'he is superior to me' (קדמי הוא) might be read and interpreted 'he was before me'. A genuine saying of the Baptist may have been interpreted by the Evangelist and incorporated in his theological Prologue. If the saying was originally John the Baptist's, it can only have read:

> 'He that cometh after me (*'athe bathrai*)[1]
> Is superior to me.'

Further traces of parallelism are discoverable in the long reply of the Baptist in iii. 27–36. The direct speech of the Baptist in verses 27, 28 gives two lines in synthetic or constructive parallelism, followed by other two which might be regarded as either synthetic or antithetic:

> (27) A man can receive nothing,
> Except it be given him from heaven.
> (28) I am not the Christ,
> But . . . I am sent before him.

Synthetic or synonymous parallelism reappears in verse 35:

> The Father loveth the Son,
> And hath given all things into his hand.

Verse 36 contains two lines in antithetic parallelism followed by a third line that forms a climax to the whole verse:

> He that believeth on the Son hath everlasting life:
> And he that believeth not the Son shall not see life;
> But the wrath of God abideth on him.

[1] This expression is the equivalent of ἀκολουθεῖν, so that the Aramaic lines may contain the oxymoron, 'He that is my follower is my superior'. They would be naturally so understood in Aramaic, and if the saying is genuinely the Baptist's, might be held to support the view that Jesus began His career as a disciple of John. But the saying may be no more than an alternative version or tradition of Mk. i. 7. See further *infra*, p. 195.

The same scheme of two antithetic lines followed by a concluding climactic line can be detected in the simile of the Bridegroom and the Friend of the Bridegroom[1] in verse 29, when we render it back into Aramaic. To obtain the parallelism we require to make 'he that standeth and heareth him' subject of a clause with '(is) the friend of the bridegroom' as its predicate, the last clause being attached ἀσυνδέτως. So to construe the verse in Aramaic is not only legitimate, but gives the natural order and meaning.

He that hath the bride is the bridegroom (*hu' d^{e}leh kall^{e}tha ḥathna hu'*):
He that standeth and heareth him (is) the friend of the bridegroom (*hu' d^{e}qa'em shama' leh shoshbin hu'*)
(And) rejoiceth greatly because of the voice of the bridegroom (*qaleh d^{e}ḥathna*).

There follows a single line and two antithetic lines; if we transpose we restore the parallelism, *a a c*:

He must increase,
But I must decrease (*q^{e}lal*)
This my joy therefore is fulfilled (*k^{e}lal*).

The word-play, *kall^{e}tha* (νύμφη), *qala* (φωνή), *q^{e}lal* (ἐλαττοῦσθαι),[2] and *k^{e}lal* (πεπλήρωται, 'is perfected')[3] is maintained throughout the simile and supports the proposed reconstruction of the last three lines.

The same type of parallelism may be restored in verses 31, 32. 'He that cometh from above' and 'He that cometh from heaven' are alternative renderings of the same Aramaic; the latter makes explicit in Greek what is implicit in the Semitic idiom in the first form, thus preventing any possible misunderstanding of what was meant by 'from above'. The Aramaic of the more literal translation (*mill^{e}'el*) gives a word-play with the original of ἐπάνω (*'ilawe*). In Aramaic, no less than in Greek or English, 'he that is of the earth is of the earth' is pure tautology and

[1] For the *Shoshbin* or Groomsman, see I. Abrahams, *Studies in Pharisaism and the Gospels*, ii, p. 213.

[2] *Infra*, p. 173.

[3] *Infra*, p. 230 f. The Old Syriac renders by *ṭ^{e}laq*, 'is finished'.

has no meaning: but if, instead of reading a second מן ארעא (ἐκ τῆς γῆς), we read מן לארעיה (מלרעיה), the meaning is 'he that is of the earth *is inferior to Him*'; the similarity of the prepositional phrase in Aramaic with the original of ἐκ τῆς γῆς has obviously been the cause of the mistranslation.[1] We thus obtain the required parallel and contrast to 'is above all'.

      a   b
He that is of the earth is inferior to Him,
a (He that is from beneath is beneath Him)
      c
And speaketh of the earth.
      a   b
a He that cometh from above (*mill*^{e}*ʿel*) is above all (*ʿilawe kulla*),
      c
And what he hath seen and heard that he testifieth;
c And (But) no man receiveth his testimony.

Between verses 33 and 34 there is not only an absence of any true parallelism, but even a logical connexion is wanting in the Greek. Verse 33, which comes at the culmination of the Baptist's testimony to Jesus, 'neither brings a conclusion derived from the preceding verses, as its opening words lead us to expect, nor does it give the ground of the following doctrine, which professes to rest on it'.[2] A simple conjecture restores both the parallelism and the connexion with what precedes and follows: it is that an Aramaic verb שדריה, 'sent him', has been misread as שרירא, ἀληθής. We have then two lines in synthetic or constructive parallelism followed by the usual climactic line.

He that hath received his testimony
Hath set to his seal ('^{a}*shar*)that God *sent him*;

[1] For the phrase in Aramaic, Jerusalem Targum I, Gen. xxvii. 28; in Jerusalem Targum II of Gen. xl. 23, 'the grace that is from beneath (חסדא דלרע)', i.e. human grace, is contrasted with 'the grace that is from above (חסדא דלעיל),' divine grace.

[2] *Our Translated Gospels*, p. 145. Torrey conjectures an original, 'he who receives his witness attests that *truly he is divine*' (*qushta* '^{e}*lah*(*a*) '*ithohi*): if '^{e}*laha* is read instead of '^{e}*lah*, the result is our Greek text. But how could ἀληθής come out of an Aramaic adverb? And where do we find '^{e}*lah*, 'divine', attested in Palestinian Aramaic? Torrey's Aramaic could only mean 'that truly he is a god', and it is doubtful if any Jew or Christian could ever have made such a statement.

For he whom God *hath sent*
Speaketh the words of God:
For God giveth not the spirit by measure.

It is possible that these two synthetic lines stood by themselves, and that the climactic line belongs to the following verse, where it is equally, if not more, appropriate:

The Father loveth the Son,
And hath given all things into his hand,
For God giveth not the spirit by measure.

Verses 35 and 36, which conclude the Baptist's reply, like verse 18 at the end of the Baptist's testimony in the first chapter of John, would be much more appropriate if spoken by Jesus in the Fourth Gospel than by John the Baptist. It may be that these verses are Johannine additions, though their poetic structure points to the same source as the rest of the poem. At any rate, it is clear that the Fourth Gospel is, in the sayings it attributes to the Baptist, a Greek translation of an Aramaic poem or prophecy; and it is equally certain that the Fourth Evangelist is not entirely inventing sayings for the Baptist, as a comparison of verses 23–8 of his first chapter with their Synoptic parallels shows. Perhaps a Greek sayings-group, translated from Aramaic sayings of the Baptist, was used by St. John.

Sources in the Fourth Gospel

The hypothesis of sources behind St. John's Gospel is now being seriously discussed by scholars who make little if any appeal to Aramaic. In his *Ego Eimi*, published in 1939,[1] Eduard Schweizer reached the conclusion (described as a well-grounded working hypothesis only, not a definitive result) that the Fourth Gospel was not an entirely free creation, but written on the basis of a tradition, which had already assumed a written form; it is also conceivable that the Evangelist made use of two distinct sources, a narrative and a sayings collection. The Gospel as a whole, however, bears the impress of the mind and

[1] *Ego Eimi ... ein Beitrag zur Quellenfrage des vierten Evangeliums* (Göttingen).

style of a single author, and this makes it difficult to analyse out any earlier sources.[1]

These tentative and cautious statements have been endorsed in language less guarded, and from a more authoritative quarter, in the new commentary on the Fourth Gospel by Rudolf Bultmann.[2] Bultmann distinguishes a *Redenquelle* (RQ) from a narrative *Semeiaquelle* (SQ, a collection of miracle stories), and 'the original language of RQ was either Aramaic or Syriac, as is shown by occasional obscurities best explained by defective rendition into the Greek'.[3]

This last result is striking confirmation of conclusions which have been arrived at by scholars interested in the Aramaic background of the Gospel. Few have been prepared to accept C. F. Burney's theory of an Aramaic original for the whole of John, but a recent examination of the distribution of Burney's Aramaic element by T. W. Manson leads to a result which runs parallel to the Bultmann–Schweizer analysis: a narrative source, with points of contact with the Synoptics, and where distinctive Aramaic colouring is absent, can be distinguished from a sayings source characterized by an Aramaizing style and other source phenomena.[4]

If Bultmann is right in his analysis, the *Redenquelle* (a Johannine Q) covers a large area of the discourse material (the passages in question are detailed by Easton). It is preceded by a group of sayings of the Baptist as in the Synoptic Q, where there is the same evidence of source. The difficulty will probably be (as with the other Q) the delimitation of the source, and it is complicated by the unity of the Johannine style and the absence of a 'double tradition'.[5] But it is a significant result to be able to speak at all about a Johannine Q.

[1] Op. cit., pp. 107, 108.

[2] *Das Evangelium des Johannes* (Göttingen, 1952), pp. 4 n. 5, 559 f.

[3] B. S. Easton, in a valuable review article in the *Journal of Biblical Literature*, lxv, p. 80.

[4] *Bulletin of the John Rylands Library*, xxx, pp. 2, 13 f.

[5] The Egerton Papyrus may supply us with material for comparison, however fragmentary; cf. Bell and Skeat, *Fragments of an Unknown Gospel*, p. 361, and *Revue biblique*, liv (July 1947), p. 442.

It was Streeter who coined the phrase 'interpretative transformations' to describe the Johannine discourses. An inspired 'targumizing' of an Aramaic sayings tradition, early committed to a Greek form, is the most likely explanation of the Johannine speeches, but, in that case, it is no different in character from the literary process which gave us the Synoptic *verba Christi*. For the extent of this process of 'transformation' we must await the results of further study, but in the light of recent work it would appear to be becoming a gradually diminishing area: the rabbinical character of the discourses and their predominantly poetic form certainly do not discourage the belief that much more of the *verba ipsissima* of Jesus may have been preserved in the Fourth Gospel—with John the Apostle as inspired 'author' —than we have dared believe possible for many years.

The Lucan Hymns[1]

The Magnificat

Verse 46, as it stands, is a couplet with synonymous clauses,

My soul doth magnify (*m^{e}rabbya*) the Lord, and my spirit hath rejoiced in God my Saviour.

The Aramaic verb in the first clause is taken up by μεγάλα (*rabhr^{e}bhatha*) in verse 49, and the word-play suggests that, in the original, this verse followed more closely on verse 46. Perhaps verse 49 came immediately after verse 46; in verses 46, 49, 47, 48*a*, we then obtain two couplets in synonymous parallelism:

My soul doth magnify the Lord, for he hath done to me great things (*m^{e}***rabbya** *naphshi l^{e}mara da'^{a}bhadh li* **rabhr^{e}bhatha**),
And my spirit hath rejoiced (*ḥadh^{e}yath ruḥi*, my spirit doth rejoice) in God my Saviour,
For he hath regarded the low estate of his handmaiden.

The best proof that some such scheme of exactly parallel lines and clauses was original in the first five verses is the exact

[1] Recent studies include N. Turner, 'The Relation of Luke i and ii to Hebraic Sources and to the Rest of Luke–Acts', in *N.T.S.* ii, pp. 100 ff.; P. Winter, 'The Birth and Infancy Stories of the Third Gospel', *N.T.S.* i, pp. 111 ff.; R. A. Martin, 'Syntactical Evidence of Aramaic Sources in Acts i–xv', *N.T.S.* x, pp. 38 ff.

parallelism of lines and clauses in the remainder of the hymn: two synonymous lines are followed by two couplets in antithetic parallelism.

He hath shewed strength with his arm (*bi*d^{e}ra'*eh*);
He hath scattered (**z^{e}raq**; cf. Targum, Isa. li. 20) the proud in the imagination of their hearts (*b^{e}***tar'***ithe libbehon*).
He hath put down the mighty from their seats,
And exalted them of low degree.
He hath filled the hungry with good things;
And the rich he hath sent empty away.[1]

The last two couplets are in synthetic parallelism, with synonymous clauses:

He hath holpen his servant Israel, in remembrance of his mercy;
As he spake to our fathers, to Abraham, and to his seed for ever.

The Benedictus

An Old Syriac variant in verse 71 gives a full line in synonymous parallelism with verse 69; for σωτηρίαν it reads, 'and he hath snatched us away to salvation from the hand of our enemies'. If the Old Syriac reading is original, we obtain, in verses 68, 69, and 71, three couplets with parallel clauses, the last two couplets in synonymous parallelism:

68 Blessed be the Lord God of Israel; for he hath visited and redeemed his people.
69 And hath raised up an horn of salvation for us in the house of his servant David;
70 As he spoke by the mouth of his holy prophets, which have been since the world began.
71 *And hath snatched us away to salvation* (*w^{e}'***a'dain** *l^{e}ḥayyin*) from the hands (**'idhe**) of our enemies.

[1] The variants 'poor' and 'hungry' may go back to a common *ḥ^{a}sirin*, 'indigent', giving a word-play with *'^{a}thirin*, 'rich'. The phrase 'to fill with good' occurs in both Hebrew and Targum of Ps. cvii. 9: an antithesis in the second half-line would be *'arḥeq*, 'to send away', especially in the moral sense 'to reject'; the verb can also account for the addition κενούς, for it gives a pun with *'areq*, 'to empty'; the words, with the suppression of the guttural, would be identical in pronunciation. The Old Syriac 'despise' (*shaṭ*), which it is difficult to get out of *shallaḥ* (so Burkitt, *Evangelion da-Mepharreshe*, in loc.), is also a representation of *'arḥeq*; cf. the Targum of Job xxx. 10, 'they *despised* me'.

From verse 76 to the end the parallelism of lines and clauses is without complications in the Greek:

76 And thou, child, shall be called the prophet of the Highest:
For thou shalt go before the face of the Lord to prepare his ways;
77 To give knowledge of salvation unto his people by the remission of their sins,
78 Through the tender mercy of our God; whereby the dayspring from on high hath visited us,
79 To give light to them that sit in darkness and in the shadow of death, to guide our feet in the way of peace.

The Nunc Dimittis and the Prophecy of Simeon

The present indicative in verse 29, ἀπολύεις, would translate an Aramaic participle (שרי), which should perhaps have been read as an imperative; for *sheri* in this sense cf. Mt. xv. 23 in the Palestinian Syriac. The Old Syriac version gives a more balanced parallelism of clauses in verse 29 than the Greek, but it does not presuppose any variants:

Henceforth thou dost dismiss him, my Lord, in peace, thy servant, even as thou hast promised.

For the Old Syriac variant, 'thy mercy' for τὸ σωτήριόν σου, in verse 30, see below, p. 248.

29 Lord, now suffer thou thy servant to depart in peace, according to thy promise:
30 For mine eyes have seen thy salvation, [31] which thou hast prepared before the face of all people;
32 A light to lighten the Gentiles, and the glory of thy people Israel.

In the prophecy of Simeon which follows the Nunc Dimittis there is a parallelism of a very rudimentary nature. The verses are among the most difficult in the Greek Bible; it is virtually impossible to find a logical connexion of thought running through the passage. How, for instance, are we to connect the first and second parts of verse 35? There has, I believe, been a decided failure in the Greek rendering of the original Aramaic (or

Hebrew) prophecy, and on this ground alone conjectural restoration may be justified.

Behind the thought of verse 34*a* there probably lie the two texts of Isaiah about the stone of stumbling and the precious corner-stone (Isa. viii. 14, xxviii. 16; cf. Rom. ix. 33, Mt. xi. 6, 1 Cor. i. 23): κεῖται may be given the (classical) sense 'is destined'. We may render: 'Behold, this (child) is destined for the down-fall and up-rising of many in Israel.' 'This child is appointed for a mission which will cause many to fall and many to rise in Israel.' (Creed, *The Gospel according to St. Luke*, in loc.)

The 'sign' is used in a familiar Biblical sense (cf. e.g., Lk. xi. 29): but Jesus will be a σημεῖον which will be a subject of dispute, ἀντιλεγόμενον (the participle may bear a future meaning, *infra*, p. 131).

These first two lines fall naturally into a two-line couplet with synthetic parallelism:

a Behold, this (child) is destined for the down-fall and up-rising of many in Israel,
b And for a Sign to be disputed.

In the following verse we would expect another two-line couplet parallel to *ab*. This can be obtained if we refer σοῦ αὐτῆς τὴν ψυχήν, not to Mary, but to Israel. So far as Semitic idiom is concerned and apart from the gender of αὐτῆς, there is no difficulty in so doing: sudden change of person is a familiar idiom in Semitic poetry.[1] Thus, Deut. xxxii. 15:

But Jeshurun waxed fat, and kicked:
Thou art waxen fat, thou art grown thick, thou art become sleek:
Then he forsook God which made him,
And lightly esteemed the Rock of his salvation. (R.V.)

The source of καὶ σοῦ αὐτῆς τὴν ψυχὴν διελεύσεται ῥομφαία is almost certainly to be traced to Ez. xiv. 17 (LXX ῥομφαία διελθάτω διὰ τῆς γῆς), where the reference is to Israel. This same verse has also inspired Orac. Sib. iii. 316, ῥομφαία γὰρ διελεύσεται διὰ μέσον σεῖο (Egypt).[2]

[1] Ges.–Kautzsch, *Gramm.*, § 144 p.

[2] Cf. J. Geffcken, *Orac. Sib.* (*Griech.-christliche Schriftsteller der ersten drei Jahrhunderte*), p. 64.

We are left with the difficulty of αὐτῆς; Luke clearly is thinking of Mary. But may this not have arisen through a failure to recognize the idiom? And is σοῦ αὐτῆς τὴν ψυχήν not a rendering of reflexive *naphsha* (*supra*, p. 76), or of the use of this word as an emphatic personal pronoun? Cf. Isa. xliii. 4 (of Israel): '. . . therefore will I give men for thee, and peoples for thy life (*naphshekha*)'.

The concluding verse, 'that the thoughts of many may be revealed', does not give a parallel with anything that precedes it. A variant reading, however, assumed by Ephrem's Commentary on the Diatessaron, does:[1] 'that the minds of many may be *divided*'. We may compare the saying of Jesus in Mt. x. 34 in the form in which it occurs in the Old Syriac:

I have not come to set peace on earth,
But *division of minds* and a sword.

We thus obtain the parallel couplets:

a Behold, this (child) is destined for the down-fall and up-rising of many in Israel,
b And for a Sign to be disputed:
a Through thee thyself, (O Israel), will the sword pass,
b That thoughts may be revealed from many minds (that the minds of many be divided?).

Additional Note on the Original Language of the Lucan Hymns

The choice appears to lie between a theory of Hebrew or Aramaic sources translated or found in Greek translations by Luke, or of simple Lucan composition in Semitic Greek, owing much, if not everything, to the LXX. That Luke can write an excellent 'pastiche of Septuagintal Greek',[2] and the obvious indebtedness of the Lucan hymns to the LXX, appear to favour the second hypothesis. On the other hand, it is difficult to believe that a Greek writer, who can compose the rhythmic Attic prose of the Preface and the idiomatic and quite un-Semitic Hellenistic Greek of the second half of Acts, should

[1] Burkitt, *Evangelion da-Mepharreshe*, ii, p. 190; J. Rendel Harris, *Ephrem*, p. 34.

[2] Cf. C. H. Dodd, in *Journal of Roman Studies*, xxxvii (1947), pp. 47–54.

adopt the Biblical Greek *pasticcio* in certain parts of his two-volume work, except for reasons such as the source-hypothesis supplies; and there is no doubt that Luke is dependent on sources elsewhere. The two views need not be incompatible; the LXX may have been the only 'aid' the Greek translator-author(s) had for their work of translation.

A decision as between Hebrew and Aramaic is difficult to make, though the tendency now appears to be to assume the former. So far as parallels are concerned, composition of hymns in either Hebrew or Aramaic, especially set pieces in the latter for the festivals, appears to go back to a very early period. Cf. further Appendix D, 'The Aramaic Liturgical Poetry of the Jews', p. .

The Beatitudes (Mt. v. 3 ff. = Lk. vi. 20 ff.)

That our Lord's Beatitudes were originally cast in poetic form, in Hebrew or Aramaic, is obvious from the parallelism of lines and clauses still discernible in both Matthew and Luke, and the presence of at least one obtrusive Aramaism in Luke's ἐκβάλωσιν τὸ ὄνομα ὑμῶν (verse 22).[1] Can we reconstruct, on the basis of the Greek versions which have survived, the original poetic form of at least some of the stanzas, and does a translation back into Aramaic contribute any fresh point to our understanding of the Beatitudes?

There is impressive textual support for taking Matthew's first and third Beatitudes together.[2] The third is an adaptation of Ps. xxxvii. 11, but not necessarily on that account an addition of Matthew's. Together these verses form a four-line stanza, each couplet containing two lines in synthetic parallelism, and the second couplet in synonymous parallelism with the first. The πτωχοί (*'anayyin*) and the πραεῖς (*'anawin*) are parallel terms describing the 'poor men of God', the afflicted saints:

Blessed are God's poor,
For theirs is the kingdom of God.
Blessed are God's humble,
For they (shall) inherit (possess) the earth.

[1] Cf. *supra*, p. 135.

[2] The evidence is set out in Gregory's *Proleg.* (1884), p. 174.

Zahn detected in these verses a fulfilment of Isa. lxi. 1, *εὐαγγελίσασθαι τοῖς πτωχοῖς*: this is the good news for the 'poor'.[1]

It is usually suggested that Matthew's second Beatitude is a softened form of Luke's third. But again we may have two separate but synonymously parallel couplets of a four-line stanza, one half of which has been preserved in Matthew, the other half in Luke:

Blessed are they that mourn,
For they shall be comforted.
Blessed are ye (they) that weep now,
For ye (they) shall laugh.

(As Luke preserves the more primitive form of Q and in both Matthew and Luke the words are addressed to the disciples, the second person may have been original throughout.) The blessing on the mourners is clearly again inspired by Isa. lxi. 1 ff.

A similar four-line stanza with parallel couplets is obtained when Mt. v, verses 7 and 9 are taken together:

Blessed are the merciful,
For they shall obtain mercy.
Blessed are the peacemakers,
For they shall be called the sons of God.

Beyond this point, it is precarious to proceed. The reference to hunger and thirst in Matthew does, however, suggest that a second couplet has been compressed into a single verse:

Blessed are ye that hunger,
For ye shall be filled,
(Blessed are ye that thirst,
For ye shall be sated.)

That the hunger and thirst were for the spiritual food and drink for which God's poor men longed is rightly brought out by Matthew's *δικαιοσύνη* (as earlier the character of the *πτωχοί*, by his *τῷ πνεύματι*). *Δικαιοσύνη* is certainly more than 'goodness' (Moffatt): it is the vindication of the cause of the afflicted saints, the fulfilment of Isa. lxi. 3, the acceptable year of the Lord.

[1] Matthäus, in loc.

Verses 10, 11, 12 have a unity of subject, the persecution of the saints, but any restoration of parallelism must be purely conjectural,[1] while verse 8 is difficult to associate logically with any of them or of the preceding verses, and there is nothing corresponding in Isa. lxi.[2]

Verse 12, however, with its parallel in Lk. vi. 23, contains an unnoticed Aramaism: (*duṣu* = ἀγαλλιᾶσθε Matthew) is associated with movement and dancing (= Luke σκιρτήσατε).[3] Again the thought of exultation is close to Isa. lxi. 3.

The evidence together does point to the importance of Isa. lxi as the inspiration of the Beatitudes. Jesus, according to Lk. iv. 16, opened His public ministry by reading these verses, and He replied in these same verses to the question of the disciples of John at Mt. xi. 5 = Lk. vii. 22. His quotation from Isaiah was immediately followed by *καὶ μακάριός ἐστιν, ὃς ἐὰν μὴ σκανδαλισθῇ ἐν ἐμοί*. Was this the occasion when the Beatitudes were addressed to the disciples? And was this their conclusion? It certainly follows closely on the thought of Mt. v. 11 = Lk. vi. 22.

Dialogue

Lk. vii. 6 f. (cf. Mt. viii. 9 f., Q: Healing of the Centurion's Servant) contains several examples of parallel lines and clauses in the words of the Centurion:

Lord, trouble not thyself:
For I am not worthy that thou shouldest enter under my roof:
Wherefore neither thought I myself worthy to come unto thee:
But say in a word, and my servant shall be healed.

In verse 8 a couplet in antithetic parallelism is followed by three lines in synonymous parallelism:

[1] Cf. *infra*, p. 192.

[2] The rendering of καθαροὶ τῇ καρδίᾳ into Aramaic gives דכי לב an expression which comes very near, so far as consonants go, to an Aramaic equivalent of Isaiah's *nishbere lebh* (דכיכי לב?), the 'broken-hearted' (cf. Ps. xxxiv. 19). Was it the 'contrite' who were to 'see God'?

[3] Cf. *infra*, p. 193.

For I also am a man set under authority,
Having under me soldiers,
And I say unto one, Go, and he goeth;
And to another, Come, and he cometh;
And to my servant, Do this, and he doeth it.

In the antithetic lines it is stated that the Centurion is a man under authority and at the same time that he has charge of soldiers, evidently someone vested with authority. Perfect synonymous parallelism, in this couplet as in the rest of the Centurion's speech, is found in the Old Syriac:

For I also am a man *that hath authority,*[1]
And soldiers are under my charge.

The point then of the Centurion's comparison of Jesus with himself is that the latter's authority is as absolute as his own; He has only to speak the word, and His command will be executed. The Old Syriac may well have preserved the true translation of the original Aramaic.[2]

Most other examples of parallelism in dialogue are from Mark:

xi. 9, 10 . . . Blessed is he that cometh in the name of the Lord:
Blessed is the kingdom of our father David.

Lk. xix. 38 adds the line,

Peace in heaven, and glory in the highest,

parallel to his

Blessed is the King that cometh in the name of the Lord.
xi. 28 By what authority doest thou these things?
And who gave thee this authority to do these things?
xii. 14 Master, we know that thou art true, and carest for no man:

[1] A different Syriac version of the same variant is found in the quotation of the verse in the Syriac *Theophany* of Eusebius, 'and I also am a man *in* authority' (Book iv, ܦ: edit. Lee, 1842). A reminiscence of the Syriac reading appears in the Liége Diatessaron, 'For I also am a man invested with secular power.'

[2] A clause, 'a man to whom there is authority (*d*^{e}*'ith shulṭana li*)' may have been corrupted to 'a man who is under authority (*d*^{e}*ith t*^{e}*ḥoth shulṭana*)', the preposition coming from *t*^{e}*ḥothi* (ὑπ' ἐμαυτοῦ).

For thou regardest not the person of men, but teachest the way of God in truth.

xiii. 4 Tell us, when shall these things be?
And what shall be the sign when all these things shall be fulfilled?

xv. 29 Ah, thou that destroyest the temple, and buildest it up in three days,
Save thyself, and come down from the cross.

Two examples occur in the dialogue with Nicodemus in the Fourth Gospel:

iii. 2 Rabbi, we know that thou art a teacher come from God:
For no man can do these miracles that thou doest, except God be with him.

4 How can a man be born when he is old?
Can he enter the second time into his mother's womb and be born?

Alliteration, Assonance, and Paronomasia

Alliteration, assonance, and paronomasia, the latter including not only the pun proper but word-play in general, the opposition and juxtaposition of similar sounding words, are characteristic features of all early poetry. They are especially prominent in the poetry of the Semites: the pun, in particular, which is completely out of favour in modern literature, was regarded as an almost indispensable feature of good literary style. Paronomasia is common in the Old Testament, especially in the prophets, and it occurs frequently, and for our taste much too frequently, in all strata of Hebrew literature, including modern Hebrew. A well-known Biblical example is Isa. v. 7:[1]

. . . and he looked for judgment (**mishpaṭ**),
But behold, oppression (**mispaḥ**);
For righteousness (**ṣ^e^dhaqah**),
But behold, a cry of distress (**ṣ^e^ʿaqah**).

[1] Other well-known examples are Jer. i. 11, xlviii. 2; Amos viii. 1–3. Dr. M. Wallenstein, of the Semitics Department of Manchester University, has drawn my attention to two striking examples in Isa. xxvii. 12, xxxii. 14 (cf. 1 Sam. xxii. 1). Two other instances from Isa. x. 15, li. 6, have been recognized by Professor Edward Robertson in his 'Points of Interest in the Massoretic Text', *Journal of Near Eastern Studies*, ii, No. 1, p. 38 f.

The Targum of Esther (II) ii. 5 gives an example of the common pun on a proper name; Mordecai is said to be *mera dakhya,* 'pure myrrh'. The Midrash *Genesis Rabbah* comments on Ps. xxxii. 1, 'Blessed is he whose transgression is forgiven', 'Blessed is the man who is exalted (גבוה) above his transgression, and not his transgression exalted (גבוה) over him', i.e. in control of him.[1] The following example is from the Babylonian Talmud, *Megilla 7b*: 'Though a yokel (חקלאה) become a king, the basket (דיקולא) comes not off his shoulder.'

Examples of striking word-play have been noted in the Syriac versions of the Gospels[2] and have been, in some cases, claimed as reproducing the original Aramaic paronomasia. Mt. xi. 17,

We have piped unto you, and ye have not danced;
We have mourned unto you, and ye have not lamented . . .

is rendered in both the Peshiṭta and the Old Syriac:

zᵉmarn lᵉkhon wᵉla **raqqedhton**
wē'lain lᵉkhon wᵉla **'arqedhton.**

Antithetic parallelism, rhythm, and even rhyme are to be found in the Syriac couplet. A similar example is the rendering of Mt. x. 30 in the Sinaitic Syriac,

But the very hairs of your head are all numbered.
mene *dᵉsa'rᵉkhon kullhen* **manyan** *'ᵉnen*
(The locks of your hair are all numbered.)[3]

The poetic rendering, 'the locks of your hair', for *ὑμῶν . . . αἱ τρίχες τῆς κεφαλῆς*, has been selected for the word-play. In Mt. vi. 24 (Lk. xvi. 13), the saying about serving two masters, the Palestinian Syriac version has, 'Either he will endure (*yᵉsauber*) the one or despise (*yibhsor*) the other'; it assumes *ἀνέξεται* for *ἀνθέξεται*. The Commentary of Ephrem on the Diatessaron cites as an addition to Matthew's 'an eye for an eye, and a tooth for a tooth' (v. 38) the phrase from Exod. xxi. 25, from which the quotation comes, 'a slap for a slap', which would be in Syriac *pakka ḥᵃlaph pakka*; the following verse in Matthew continues,

[1] I am indebted to M. Wallenstein for this example.

[2] See Meyer, *Jesu Muttersprache*, p. 81.

[3] See A. S. Lewis, *A Translation of the Four Gospels from the Syriac of the Sinaitic Palimpsest*, p. xv.

'but whosoever shall smite thee on thy right *cheek* (*pakka*), turn to him the other also'[1]

When we translate the Greek of the sayings of Jesus and of some of the non-dominical sayings back into simple Palestinian Aramaic, similar examples of this formal element in the poetry of the Gospels come to light. The examples which follow occur where alliteration, assonance, and word-play are reproduced in well-known Aramaic words; where less well-known words are suggested, their attestation is given in a note.

1. *Predominant Laryngals* (', ʿ) *and Palatals* (*k*, *q*)

Mk. iv. *1–9* (Parable of the Sower), *26–9* (the Seed growing Secretly), *30–2* (the Mustard Seed); Mt. xiii. *1–9*, Lk. viii. *4–8* (Sower); Mt. xiii. *31–2*, Lk. xiii. *18–19* (Mustard Seed).

In this group of parables, for which Mark is the main source, the key-sounds are laryngals and the sonant Rish.

In his *Evangelium Marci*, in loc., Wellhausen remarked that in Mk. iv. 4 'One would expect "*on* the road", not "*beside* the road"': Torrey pointed out that Aramaic *ʿal 'urḥa* is ambiguous;[2] Luke's κατεπατήθη, 'is trodden down', i.e. by wayfarers, is confirmation that it was '*on* the road' that the seed fell. Luke's verb is in Aramaic an intensive form of *r^eʿaʿ*; e.g. the same Greek verb is so rendered in Isa. lxiii. 3 by the Palestinian Syriac version. For ἐξανατέλλειν in verse 5 in Mark, we may put *y^eʿa* (or *yiʿa*); τὸ πετρῶδες is *shuʿa*; ἰκμάς in Luke, verse 6, is *leḥa*, the rendering giving by the Palestinian Syriac. The phrase for καρπὸν διδόναι is discussed below in the parable of the Seed growing Secretly.

Mk. iv. 3 . . . Behold, there went out a sower to sow (Luke adds, his seed)
(*ha n^ephaq* **zaroʿa l^emizraʿ** (**zarʿeh**)):

4 And it came to pass, as he sowed, some fell *on the road*
(*wah^awa kadh* **zaraʿ** *'ith din^ephal ʿal* **'urḥa**),
(Luke, And it was trodden down,) and the fowls of the air (came and, Luke omits) devoured it up

[1] In some of the above instances the Syriac may have reproduced the *Urlaut*. See further *infra*, pp. 247 ff.

[2] *Our Translated Gospels*, p. 7 f.

((*w^e*ra'ra'*unneh*, and men trampled it down) *wa 'akhalunneh 'ophe sh^emayya*).

5 And some fell on stony ground, where it had not much earth
(*w^e'ith din^ephal 'al* shu'a *han d^eleth* 'ar'a *saggi'ah*);
And immediately it sprang up, because it had no depth of earth
(*w^ebah* sha'atha yi'a *d^eleth leh 'umqa d^e'*ar'a):

6 But when the sun was up, it was scorched
(*w^ekadh d^enaḥ shamsha 'itt^e*ḥar);
And because it had no root (Luke, moisture), it withered away
(*wid^eleth leh 'iqqar* (*leḥa*) *y^ebhash*).

7 And some fell among thorns, and the thorns grew up
(*w^e'ith din^ephal 'al* kubb*in wis^elaqu* kubb*in*),
And choked it, and it yielded no fruit
(*w^eḥan^equnneh w^ela* y^ehabh 'ibba(*eh*)).

8 And other fell on good ground
(*w^e'*uḥran *n^ephal 'al* 'ar'a *ṭabh^etha*),
And did yield fruit that sprang up and increased,[1] some thirty, and some sixty, and some an hundred[2]
(*ḥadh t^elathin, ḥadh shittin, w^eḥadh m^e'ah*).

In the parable of the Seed growing Secretly, *ὁ σπόρος* is *zar'a*, *γῆ*, *'ar'a*, *ἐγείρεσθαι*, *'itt^e'ar*, and *μηκύνεσθαι*, *'arikh*.

Verse 29 contains a well-known philological *crux*, *παραδοῖ*. The closest parallel is found in the LXX variant for *καρποφορήσει* in Hab. iii. 17, *ἡ συκῆ οὐ μὴ παραδῷ τὸν καρπὸν αὐτῆς* (the variant is to be found in the Complutensian text). But the verb here, as we should expect it to be, is transitive; there is no instance of *παραδοῦναι* used intransitively and apparently meaning 'to be produced' of the fruits of the earth. The best attested Greek use of the verb, which does not, however, give a very satisfactory sense, is 'to permit', 'to allow', of circumstances, times or seasons, e.g. Polyb. xxii. 24. 9.

One instance has been adduced of the aorist *παρέδωκεν* used intransitively and meaning 'to yield itself up', 'to surrender',

[1] Cf. Torrey, op. cit., p. 8.

[2] *Supra*, p. 124.

namely LXX Joshua xi. 19;[1] there is a considerable difference, however, between a city 'yielding itself up' and the earth 'yielding' fruit; the verb in Joshua is an example of bad translation Greek; it corresponds to an intransitive use of the Hebrew Hiphil. Such translation Greek, however, points to translation of Aramaic in Mk. iv. 29.

Professor T. W. Manson has suggested that an original Aramaic, 'and when the fruit is fully mature (*yishlam*)', has been mistranslated by ὅταν παραδοῖ (*yashlem*) ὁ καρπός.[2] The verb *sh^elem*, however, which means 'to be whole, complete', is not found in this sense; the only support Dr. Manson finds for it is in the Syriac phrase 'an *adult* (*shal^ema*) male'. There is, however, another verb with the same consonants which may have this meaning. The Peshiṭta renders πλήρη (σῖτον) in verse 28 by a form of *m^ela* (Shaphel passive participle, *m^eshamlai*). Hebrew *male* is similarly employed of 'ripe' grain. But the Shaphel of *m^ela* is not attested for Palestinian Aramaic. If we could assume its use, then a mistranslation might account for παραδοῖ, *m^eshamlai* misread as *mashlem*. The most serious objection, however, to the conjecture is the incredible sense which the translator made of his original, either 'when the fruit *betrays*' or '*submits itself*' as a captive to its conqueror.

The phrase καρπὸν ποιεῖν has already been discussed; synonymous with it is καρπὸν διδόναι,[3] used in the Old Testament especially of the 'fruits' of the earth as contrasted with the fruit of trees. The Semitism is familiar in Aramaic; the phrase 'to give fruit (*pira*)' occurs in the Pseudo-Jonathan Targum of Lev. xxvi. 4. For the 'fruits' of the earth the Aramaic is *'ibba*, 'crop', and 'to produce or yield' this kind of 'fruit' is *y^ehabh 'ibba*, 'to give crops'; it will be found, e.g., in the same Targum of Lev. xxvi. 4. It is this phrase which lies behind Mark's παραδοῖ ὁ καρπός. The original would read either 'when it (the earth) has yielded fruit (*y^ehabhath 'ibba*, or *'ibbah*, its fruit)' or 'when the fruit has been produced (*y^ehibha 'ibba*(*h*))'. The translator's choice of a verb was probably dictated by the desire to give a

[1] Swete, *Mark*, in loc.

[2] In *J.T.S.* xxviii, p. 399 f.

[3] Cf. *Einl.*[2], p. 17.

literal or near equivalent of the Aramaic, and he no doubt meant 'when the fruit allows'. The paronomasia is continued in the last clause of the verse; παρέστηκεν means 'is ripe', corresponding, in the LXX, to Hebrew *'abhibh*, e.g. Exod. ix. 32; *'abbibh* is used in the same sense in Aramaic.

Mk. iv. 26 . . . So is the kingdom of God,
As if a man should cast seed (**zar'a**) into the ground (**'ar'a**):
27 And should sleep, and rise (**'itt^{e}'ar**) night and day,
And the seed (**zar'a**) spring and grow (**'^{a}rikh**), he knoweth not how.
28 For the earth (**'ar'a**) bringeth forth fruit (**par^{e}'a**, sprouteth)[1] of herself,
First the blade, then the ear, after that the full corn in the ear.
29 But when *its crop is ready*
(*kadh* **y^{e}hibha 'ibbah**),
He putteth in the sickle, for the harvest is ripe
(*shallaḥ magla daḥ^{a}ṣadha* **'abbibh**).

In the parable of the Mustard Seed the words for 'sowing' (*z^{e}ra'*) and 'growing' (*r^{e}bhi*) give the key-sounds and are the basis of the paronomasiae; the grain of mustard seed is 'less' (μικρότερον, *z^{e}'er*) than all seeds (*zar'in*), but when it 'grows' (Matthew and Luke, αὐξάνειν, *r^{e}bhi*) it becomes 'greater' (*rabba, rabhr^{e}bha*) than all herbs, perhaps *z^{e}ro'in*.

The clause ὅταν σπαρῇ occurs twice in Mark, verses 31 and 32, in two parallel lines; its repetition destroys the antithetic parallelism, which is, however, intact in the corresponding clauses in Matthew (verse 32), 'but when it grows, it is the greatest among herbs'. An original 'but when the seed is grown' (*kadh* **zar'a** *m^{e}rabba*) may have been mistranslated 'but when it is sown and grows' (*kadh* **z^{e}ri'** *m^{e}rabba*). In verse 32, for 'branches', κλάδοι, the Palestinian Syriac has the noun *'anpa*, probably to be pronounced *'appa*; τὰ πετεινά is *'ophin, 'ophayya*.

Mk. iv. 30 . . . Whereunto shall we liken the kingdom of God?
31 It is like a grain of mustard seed,
Which, when it is sown in the earth, is less than all seeds that be in the earth
(*di kadh* **z^{e}ri'** *b^{e}*'**ar'a z^{e}'er** *hu' min kullhon* **zar'***in dib^{e}*'**ar'a**):

[1] Cf. LXX Hab. iii. 17.

32 But *when the seed is grown*, it becomes greater than all herbs
(*w*^{e}*kadh* **zar'a** *m*^{e}**rabba** *h*^{a}*wa* **rabhr**^{e}**bha** *min kullhon* **z**^{e}**ro'in**),
And shooteth out great branches (**'anpin rabhr**^{e}**bhin**); so that the fowls (**'ophin**) of the air may lodge under the shadow of it.

Mt. v. *13*; Lk. xiv. *34, 35*; Mk. ix. *50*

An Aramaic parallel to the saying about the Salt that loses its Savour is to be found in the Babylonian Talmud, *Bechor.* 8*b*, 'Salt, if it become putrid (*s*^{e}*ri*), wherewith shall it be salted?' We appear to have to do with a well-known saying, perhaps even a popular proverb.[1] But the words in the Talmud do not help us to account for the language or variants of the Gospel saying.

Lightfoot pointed out, in a note on Lk. xiv. 34, that '*μωρανθῇ* suits very well with the Hebrew תפל, which signifies both *unsavoury* and a *fool*'.[2] The word occurs in the Palestinian Talmud in at least one passage where the language is Aramaic as well as Hebrew;[3] it was probably the only Semitic word for the thing signified and in common use among Aramaic-speaking Jews. As Lightfoot noted, the Hebrew word is idiomatically used of persons lacking sense, and, if it was the original word used by Jesus, we can then account for Mark's version as the literal translation (Aquila renders the Hebrew word by *ἄναλος* in Ezek. xiii. 10, xxii. 28): the rendering of Q, *μωρανθῇ*, represents an interpretation; the 'insipid' salt refers to foolish disciples. A further confirmation that the word was original is that it gives a word-play with the Aramaic for 'salted', 'seasoned' (*tabbel*).

In verse 35 in Luke, which follows this saying, Friedrich Perles has suggested that 'It is neither fit for the land (*εἰς γῆν*), nor yet for the dunghill (*εἰς κοπρίαν*)', is a mistranslation of 'It is neither fit for seasoning (*l*^{e}*thabbala*) nor for dunging (*l*^{e}*zabbala*)': the Hebrew word *tebhel*, used in the Targum, is occasionally

[1] Cf. I. Abrahams, *Studies in Pharisaism and the Gospels*, ii, p. 183.
[2] iii, p. 152.
[3] *Terum.* x. 7, f. 47 *b*, line 20.

rendered in the LXX by γῆ.[1] This Hebrew word might conceivably have been the original of γῆ in 'Ye are the salt of the earth (world)', and the occurrence of the same consonants in a following line may have misled a translator to render לתבלא by εἰς γῆν. But 'Ye are the salt of the earth' is not in Luke; we should require to assume that this group of sayings was rendered together and by the same translator. Besides, the Hebrew *tebhel* is invariably used of the 'world' or the inhabited 'earth' (its usual LXX equivalent is οἰκουμένη), so that we should require to make the further assumption that the words were understood by the translator 'It is neither fit for the world nor for dung', an incongruous pair and an incredible blunder.

The verse continues in Matthew, 'it is thenceforth good for nothing but to be cast forth, and to be trodden underfoot of men (καταπατεῖσθαι ὑπὸ τῶν ἀνθρώπων)'. The Aramaic equivalent of the last verb is an intensive form of רעע, thus giving a word-play with *'ar'a* (γῆ). Luke's οὔτε εἰς γῆν οὔτε εἰς κοπρίαν continues the paronomasia; εἰς γῆν is *l^e'ar'a*, and εἰς κοπρίαν, *l^erē'a*; the last word is confined to the Pseudo-Jonathan and Jerusalem Targums and the Targum to the Hagiographa,[2] e.g. in the Pseudo-Jonathan Targum, Exod. xxix. 14, 'But the flesh of the bullock, and his skin, and his dung (*rē'a*), shalt thou burn with fire without the camp . . .'.

The verses are arranged in two synthetic lines followed by two synonymous lines. Verse 35 in Luke has an idiomatic impersonal plural, 'men throw it out'; parallel to this we may perhaps set, '(and men) trample it underfoot'.

Ye are the salt of the earth (*'attun m^elaḥ* **'ar'a**),
But if the salt have lost its savour, wherewith shall it be salted (*'in* **taphel** *m^elaḥ b^ema* **tabb^el***unneh*)?
It is neither fit for the ground, nor yet for dung (*la l^e'***ar'a**, *'aph la l^e***rē'a** *kashar*),
(But) men throw it out (and) trample it down (**ra'ra'***unneh*).

[1] In *Z.N.T.W.* xix, p. 96; cf. Abrahams, l.c.
[2] Cf. Levy, *Chaldäisches Wörterbuch*, ii, p. 431 f.

Lk. ii. 8–14

In the story of the Shepherds verse 14 is arranged in antithetic parallelism; when rendered into Aramaic it falls naturally into rhythmic structure, and, with the earlier words for *ποιμήν*, *ποίμνη*, *γῆ*, preceding *εὐδοκία*, there is an example of paronomasia: the guttural and the Rish sounds, as will be seen, are also prominent in verse 12.

8 And there were in the same country (*bah* **'ar'a** ?)[1] shepherds (**ra'watha**) . . . keeping watch over their flock (**mar'itha** *dil*^{e}*hon*) by night.
12 And this shall be a sign unto you; ye shall find the babe wrapped (**m**^{e}**kharakh**) in swaddling clothes, lying in a manger (**'urya**).
14 Glory to God in the highest (*sh*^{e}*bhaḥa le'*^{e}*laha b*^{e}*ruma*)
And on earth peace to men of good will (*b*^{e}**'ar'a** *sh*^{e}*lama le'*^{e}*nashe* **r**^{e}**'utha**[2]).

The same word-play is found in Lk. xii. *32*:

Fear not, little flock (**mar'itha**);
For it is your Father's good pleasure (*d*^{e}**ra'e** *'*^{a}*bhukhon*) to give you the kingdom.

Lk. xiv. *5*

Jesus' reply to the scribes and Pharisees who challenged Him for healing on the Sabbath contains a pun on the words for 'son', *b*^{e}*ra*, 'ox', *b*$^{e'}$*ira*, and 'well', *bēra*.

Which of you shall have a son (**b**^{e}**ra**) or an ox (**b**$^{e'}$**ira**) fallen into a pit (**bēra**)
And will not straightway pull him out on the Sabbath day?

The combination of 'son' with 'ox' (or, with א, *ὄνος*, or D, *πρόβατον*) may seem to some unusual, if not incongruous. The usual pair is 'an ox and an ass', and the latter may be described as *bar ḥamra* (cf. Mt. xxi. 5, *υἱὸς ὑποζυγίου*), so that perhaps the original ran, 'Which of you shall have an ox (*b*$^{e'}$*ira*) or an ass (*bar ḥamra*) fallen into a well (*bēra*) . . .'.

[1] *Supra*, p. 96 f.

[2] It is this word which is used in the Old Syriac, though it belongs to the Palestinian dialect of Aramaic and is otherwise unknown in Syriac. See *infra*, p. 281.

To this suggestion it has been objected[1] that the word *be'ira* does not mean specifically 'an ox', but any beast of burden.

The word *bᵉ'ira* is the *generic* word, but that it was nevertheless the original expression at Lk. xiv. 5 the following considerations show, I believe, conclusively.

The 'case' posited by Jesus here, with reference to the sabbath, is one which falls under the Law codes at Deut. xxii. 4, Exod. xxiii. 5; cf. xxi. 33 f. The animals there concerned are 'ox', 'sheep', and 'ass', described generically as *bᵉ'ir* in the Massoretic text at Exod. xxii. 4. If we assume the original first line of the simple Aramaic couplet at Lk. xiv. 5 to have read: Which of you shall have a *beast* (*bᵉ'ira*) fallen into a pit (*bēra*) . . ., we can account for two things: (*a*) the variations in the Greek readings, *βοῦς, ὄνος, πρόβατον*, (D, ex Mt. xii. 11, a synoptic variant); they are Greek explications of the Aramaic, no doubt in the light of the Old Testament passages; (*b*) the presence of the incongruous *υἱός* in such a context: it is a misreading of *bᵉ'ira*.

Mk. ix. *38–41*; Lk. ix. *49–50*; Mk. ix. *42–8*; Mt. xviii. *6–9*; Lk. xvii. *1–2*

Evidence that an Aramaic source lies behind the saying of the disciple John in Mk. ix. 38 has already been discussed;[2] a further indication of such a source is to be found in the Bezan variant in the parallel in Matthew (x. 42) to Mk. ix. 41.[3]

But the most remarkable feature and clearest proof of source for this group of sayings is their poetic form in Aramaic. The key-sound in the sayings about Offences is QL; the first sound is the hard Semitic Qoph, and in its repetition and the guttural 'E which occasionally replaces it, we have a fitting expression for the powerful utterances which this sayings-group contains. In the sayings about Offences we have to do with a longer connected passage, and can thus study this formal poetic element over a series of verses.

[1] Dom Connolly, in *Downside Review*, lxvi, p. 203. Cf. L. S. Thornton, *The Dominion of Christ*, p. 69 f.

[2] *Supra*, p. 71.

[3] *Infra*, p. 245.

In Mk. ix. 38, 39, *κωλύειν* is *k^e li*, *δύναμις*, *ḥela* (so Sy^{pal.}), and *δυνήσεται*, *yakhel*: *κακολογεῖν* is *'aqqel*; in the Palestinian Talmud, *Demai*, i. 3, f. 22*a*, line 19 f., Pinchas ben Yair, while passing through a river, said to his disciples, 'Who knows for certain that he has never in his life reviled (*'aqqel*) an Israelite, let him pass over unharmed.' Also in verse 39, for *ταχύ*, we may put *b^e qallilu*; the adverb occurs, e.g. in the Pseudo-Jonathan Targum of Gen. xxix. 1; it may not be original in verse 39, but have arisen through a misunderstanding of the verb; we may compare Isa. ix. 1, where the R.V. renders the Hebrew *heqal* correctly, 'he brought into contempt', but the LXX has *ταχὺ ποίει*.

In the sayings about Offences, *σκανδαλίζειν* is *'athqel*[1] (verse 42); in verses 43, 45, and 47, *εἰσελθεῖν* is *'al*, and in verse 45, *χωλός* is *maṭlaḥ*; for the last word, we may compare the Pseudo-Jonathan Targum of Gen. xxxii. 32. At verse 48 (or previously, with the Received Text, at verses 43 and 45), *σκώληξ* is *tola'ta*. A less well known but fully attested word for *βάλλειν* in Mk. ix. 42 and Mt. xviii. 8 and 9 is *ṭ^e laq* in its intensive forms: it is a poetic word and a strong one, not just 'throw', but 'hurl', and is particularly appropriate to Mt. xviii. 8, 9 and Mk. ix. 42; a parallel to the latter is the Targum of Job iii. 5, '. . . when he was hurled (*b^e 'iṭṭallaqutheh*) into the sea'.

Mk. ix. 38 . . . Master, we saw one casting out devils in thy name . . . and we forbad him (**k^e laineh**) . . .

39 But Jesus said, Forbid him not (*la* **tikhloneh**):
For there is no man that shall do a miracle in my name, that can lightly speak evil of me.
(*d^e leth bar '^e nash d^e 'abhedh* **ḥela** *bish^e mi d^e* **yakhel** *b^e*-**qalliluth** *l^e* **'aqqaluthi**).

42 And whosoever shall offend (**yathqel**) one of these little ones that believe in me,
It is better for him that a millstone were hanged (**t^e li**) about his neck, and he were cast (**'iṭṭallaq**) into the sea.

43 And if thy hand offend thee (**'athq^e l***athakh*),
Cut it off (**q^e ta'***innah*; Matthew adds 'and cast it from thee,' *w^e* **ṭall^e q***innah minnakh*):

[1] Cf. Lagrange, *S. Matthieu*, p. cviii.

It is better for thee to enter into life maimed (*ṭabh hu' lakh di*q^{e}ti' te'ol *l^{e}ḥayyin*),
Than having two hands to go into hell, into the fire that never shall be quenched.
44 (T.R.) Where their worm (**tola'***ta*) dieth not, and the fire is not quenched.
45 And if thy foot offend thee (**'athq^{e}l***athakh*),
Cut it off (and cast it from thee, *w^{e}***ṭall^{e}q***innah minnakh*):
It is better for thee to enter halt into life (*ṭabh hu' lakh d^{e}***maṭlaḥ te'ol** *l^{e}ḥayyin*),
Than having two feet to be cast (*l^{e}'***iṭṭallaqu**) into hell . . .

Jn. viii. *34*

In her *Light on the Four Gospels from the Sinai Palimpsest* (London, 1913), Mrs. Agnes Smith Lewis pointed out that in this verse there 'is a play on two Aramaic words *'abed* "to do" and *'abd*, "a slave"', and added: 'This is supposed to be an indication that our Lord was speaking Aramaic, i.e. Syriac.'

The word-play is found in the Syriac versions and is also present when we render the words into Palestinian Aramaic:

kul(man) d^{e} 'abedh ḥeṭ'ah
'abhda(ah) hu' d^{e}ḥeṭ'a

D omits τῆς ἁμαρτίας, and Mrs. Lewis thought the passage gained in force by the omission. We certainly in this way obtain a short pithy saying:

kul(man) d^{e}'abedh ḥeṭ'ah
'abhda(ah)
'Everyone who does sin is (its) slave.'

Mt. xx. *28* f. D, Sy$^{c.phil.}$; Lk. xiv. *7–10*

Luke's parable of the Wedding Guest is found in one of the best known and longest of the Bezan 'interpolations', the same in substance as in Luke (there is nothing in D about a wedding), but differing considerably in form and language. It is generally explained as an ancient gloss, based on Luke, and 'interpolated' in the Western text of Matthew. Scrivener, while conceding its antiquity, rejected it as spurious, among other reasons, for its crude and unliterary Greek, unworthy of St. Matthew.[1]

Unliterary Greek may be translation Greek, and the Bezan passage shows evidence of translation of Aramaic. This was first noticed by F. H. Chase, who compared D with the Curetonian Syriac and concluded that the former was a rough and not always accurate translation of the Syriac.[2] Chase's main argument is that the awkwardness of the Greek points to retranslation; the simple and forcible nature of the Syriac is proof of its originality.

The Greek of D, however, is no more awkward here than in other parts of the Western text of Matthew (cf. x. 11 f., *supra*, p. 101), and the Old Syriac is well-known as a translation of high literary merit. It only appears to be the original of D; there is no support whatever elsewhere for the introduction into a Greek manuscript of a Greek translation of a gloss written originally in the language of a version. Here, as elsewhere, the Curetonian Syriac is a rendering of a Greek text of the same Western type as we find in D.

But D is itself a rendering, in awkward translation Greek, of the Aramaic parable of Jesus. This becomes clear when we retranslate it into Aramaic, where the poetic form of the parable, parallelism of lines and clauses with the accompanying features characteristic of the poetry of Jesus, comes to light.[3] Even in the Syriac version there is discernible a rhythmic cadence,

[1] *Bezae Codex Cantabrigiensis*, p. xlix.

[2] *Syro-Latin Text of the Gospels*, p. 9 f.

[3] In view of the contents of another remarkable 'interpolation' of D, at Lk. vi. 5, the story of the man whom Jesus found working on the Sabbath, one hesitates to make the same claim as is here made for the authenticity of the Bezan parable of the well-behaved guest. But it is worth noting that the saying of Jesus in this interpolation also falls into rhythmic lines in antithetic parallelism, and there may be more than one paronomasia: 'On the same day, seeing a certain man working (*'abhedh*) on the Sabbath, he said to him,

> Man, if thou knowest what thou doest, blessed art thou
> (*'in y^{e}dha't ma* **'abhedh** *'att*, **b^{e}rikh** *'att*);
> If thou knowest not, accursed art thou, and a transgressor of the Law
> (*'illa y^{e}dha't*, **'^{a}rur** *'att, w^{e}* **'abhar 'orayy^{e}tha**).'

For *'^{a}rur* in Aramaic, Targum, 2 Kings ix. 34. The form *'arira* occurs in the Palestinian Talmud, *Hagiga*, ii. 1, f. 77 *c*, lines 47 and 49.

absent altogether in the translation of the parable in Luke; when rendering their Greek text of the passage the Syriac translators involuntarily reproduced something of the original rhythmic structure.

The didactic point which the parable illustrates, placed at the end in Luke, comes first:

ὑμεῖς δὲ ζητεῖτε· ἐκ μικροῦ αὐξῆσαι
καὶ <μὴ> ἐκ μείζονος ἔλαττον εἶναι.

The words are meaningless till a μή has been inserted, with the Curetonian Syriac, before ἐκ, giving, it is true, an intolerable καὶ μή, which probably accounts for the removal of the negative; but it is what we would expect in a literal translation of Aramaic. We have then a simple and effective couplet in antithetic parallelism:

And ye, seek from little (**qallil**) to become great (**l^{e}mirbe**), and not from great (**rabh**) to become little (**l^{e}meqal**).

The word *qallil* (μικρός) is usual in the sense of 'unimportant', as is also the verb *q^{e}lal*; cf. Gen. xvi. 4, 5, in the Targum, 'and I am unimportant (*qaleth*) in her eyes'; it is also the word for ἥττων at the end of the parable. The verb *r^{e}bhi* is the equivalent of αὐξάνειν meaning 'to increase', but here it has the sense 'to become great', 'vornehm werden'; the Greek verb, in this sense, is translation Greek; we find it similarly used in the saying of the Baptist in Jn. iii. 30 in antithesis to ἐλαττοῦσθαι (*q^{e}lal*). In the following verse, μὴ ἀνακλίνεσθε, is *la tirb^{e}'un*; this verb, *r^{e}bha'*, 'to recline at table', thus gives a paronomasia with the previous *r^{e}bhi*, *rabh*;[1] the same word is continued in the Aramaic of εἰς τοὺς ἐξέχοντας τόπους (Luke, εἰς τὴν πρωτοκλισίαν), the latter being rendered in the Palestinian Syriac version by *b^{e}rishe marbu'in*; for the phrase in D we may put *b^{e}marbu'in yaqqirin*, 'in the places of honour'. The last word is taken up by the following ἐνδοξότερος, *yaqqir*; the Targum of Isaiah (xxiii. 8, 9) speaks of the 'élite of the earth (*yaqqire 'ar'a*)'; cf. Targum, Num. xxii. 15, '. . . more and worthier men (*yaqqirin*) than these'. In the corresponding verse in Luke, μήποτε ἐντιμότερός

[1] Cf. *infra*, p. 229.

σου ᾖ κεκλημένος, is *dil*^e*ma* **yaqqira** *minnakh yith*q^e**ri**. The phrase ὁ σὲ καὶ αὐτὸν καλέσας in Luke (verse 9) goes into simple Aramaic; here it is the Bezan Matthew which gives an unusual (and more literary) rendering.[1]

In the last verse of the Bezan passage the banal καὶ ἔσται σοι τοῦτο χρήσιμον corresponds to Luke's τότε ἔσται σοι δόξα ἐνώπιον πάντων τῶν συνανακειμένων σοι. The Curetonian Syriac 'interpolation' preserves a variant which gives a sense parallel to Luke's and furnishes the clue to the reading of D; it reads:

'And there will be to thee *excelling honour* (*teshboḥta m*^e*yattarta*) in the eyes of the guests.'

The use of Hebrew *yether* and *yithron* in such a connexion, meaning 'abundance', and hence 'superiority' or, as our A.V. renders, 'excellency' is familiar from Gen. xlix. 3, 'the excellency (*yether*) of dignity, and the excellency of power', and from Eccles. vii. 12, 'the excellency (*yithron*) of knowledge'. In an Aramaic original behind the Curetonian variant either the verb *yattar* or the noun *yithron* would be employed, as the latter is, e.g., in the Palestinian Syriac version of Eccles. vii. 12; 'excelling honour' is either *sh*^e*bhaḥa m*^e*yatt*^e*ra* or *yithron sh*^e*bhaḥa*, 'abundance of honour'. But in Palestinian Aramaic, as in Syriac,[2] the word *y t r* bears also the meaning of 'advantage', 'usefulness', 'profit': Targumic *yuthran* appears to be used exclusively in this sense, e.g., Prov. xxi. 5, 'the plans of the diligent are profitable (*l*^e*yuthrana*)'. In the Aramaic text or source which D is rendering the word for δόξα has been omitted, and the translator made the best he could of *m*^e*yatt*^e*ra* or *yithron* by itself.

The verses fall into parallel rhythmic lines. The didactic point which the parable illustrates is a rhythmic couplet in antithetic parallelism. The parable itself contains two verses, each verse having two lines (with parallel clauses) in synthetic parallelism, concluding with a climactic line.

[1] The word δειπνοκλητόριον is found, but δειπνοκλήτωρ is unknown; cf. Nestle, *Einführung*, edit. 1899, p. 217; English edit., p. 257.

[2] The same explanation of χρήσιμον was given by Chase, but from Syriac; op. cit., p. 13.

But ye, seek from little to become great (*w^{e}'attun b^{e}'on min* **qallil l^{e}mirbe**), and not from great to be made small (*w^{e}la min* **rabh l^{e}meqal**).
When ye enter as guests to dinner, recline not in the seats of honour (*la ti***rb^{e}'***un b^{e}ma***rbu'***in* **yaqqir***in*),
Lest a more honoured guest than thou come *invited* (*dil^{e}ma* **yaqqira** *minnakh yethe yith***q^{e}ri**), and thy host approach and say to thee, 'Still lower down!'
And thou art affronted (Sy^{c} adds, in the eyes of the guests).
But if thou reclinest in a less honoured place, and a less honoured guest than thou should come (*'in tirbo' b^{e}marbo'* **qallil** *w^{e}***qallil** *minnakh yethe*),
The host will say to thee, 'Go up yet higher!'
(Sy^{c}) Then thou wilt have great honour in the eyes of the guests (*w^{e}yihwe lakh yithron sh^{e}bhaḥa b^{e}'ene r^{e}bhi'in*).

In comparison with the Bezan translation, Luke is clearly a literary version of the parable. Moreover, from such a comparison we are in a position to judge the character of the 'translation' which we find in Luke, in particular in his parables. So far is it from being a literal translation, that it is doubtful if we have the right to call it a translation at all; Luke's parables are literary productions, perhaps based on such crude translation Greek parables as has here been preserved in D. Whether the passage in D ever formed part of the canonical Matthew, it is difficult to say.[1] The reasons for its rejection from the other great Uncials were no doubt connected with its unliterary Greek and general inferiority in this respect to the Lucan form of the parable. But it may have come from the Greek Q.

Mt. xxiii. *24*

An interesting suggestion has been made by A. T. Olmstead (*Journal of Near Eastern Studies*, i, p. 74) who renders this verse:

'. . . who strain out the louse (*qalma*) and swallow the camel (*gamla*).

Mt.'s κώνωψ means a 'gnat' or a 'mosquito', but so too, it would appear, can *qalma* (or *kalma*, *kalm^{e}tha*); it is the Targum's

[1] Cf. Kenyon, 'Western Text in Gospels and Acts', in *Proceedings of the British Academy*, xxiv, p. 315.

rendering of *kinnam* (*kinnah*) at Exod. viii. 12 f. (LXX κνῖφος, Philo, *de vita Mos.*, i, p. 97 M., σκνῖπες, Slav. *sknipa*, 'gnat'):

2. *Predominant Sibilants and Palatals*

Mk. xi. *17*; Mt. xxi. *13*; Lk. xix. *46*

Another possible example of paronomasia occurs in the Word of Jesus in the incident of the cleansing of the Temple: προσευχή is *ṣ*ᵉ*lutha,* and the Greek word λῃστής is found frequently in Aramaic, e.g. in the Palestinian Talmud, *Sota,* ix. 10, f. 24*a*, line 37, Targum, Job iv. 11, v. 5.

. . . My house shall be called of all nations the house of prayer (*beth* ṣᵉlutha *yithq*ᵉ*re*),
But ye have made it a den of thieves (*m*ᵉ*ʿarta d*ᵉlesṭin).

Mt. vi. *1–8*

A difficult problem is raised by Matthew's ἐθνικοί in verse 7 (as also in v. 47; cf. vi. 32). There is scarcely need for Jews to be exhorted not to pray as Gentiles; for the Semitic mind the idea is incongruous. In the parallel in Lk. xi. 2 (D) we read, instead of ἐθνικοί, οἱ λοιποί. Nestle sought an explanation of the Bezan variant by tracing both words to a common Hebrew *ḥ*ᵃ*bherim*; the *Haberim* were the learned associates or 'fellows' of the Pharisaic guilds.[1] But by no stretch of language can *ḥ*ᵃ*bherim* be made to have the meaning of either Greek word.

F. H. Chase pointed out that in Paul οἱ λοιποί is practically synonymous with τὰ ἔθνη (1 Thess. iv. 13, v. 6; Eph. ii. 3).[2] He explained the phrase 'the rest', 'the rest of men' for Gentiles as a Syriac idiom. The full expression occurs in Rev. ix. 20, οἱ λοιποὶ τῶν ἀνθρώπων, in a context where it is the Gentiles which are meant.

By themselves the words need have no reference to non-Jews. In the parable of the Pharisee and the Publican the phrase occurs twice (Lk. xviii. 9, 11) to denote, not Gentiles, but all the non-righteous in the eyes of the self-righteous Pharisee;

[1] *Philologica Sacra*, p. 27.

[2] *Syro-Latin Text of the Gospels*, p. 93.

there is a contemptuous ring about it, similar to our use of *οἱ πολλοί*. The Bezan variant in Luke may be a literal Greek rendering of the same Aramaic as underlies *οἱ λοιποὶ* (*τῶν ἀνθρώπων*) in the parable, *sharka de'ᵉnasha*, meaning, in this context, all who were not disciples of Jesus. It is His disciples Jesus is teaching to pray, and He is making the contrast between what is to be their style of prayer and the prayers typical of 'the rest of men'; He makes the same distinction between His disciples and the outside world in Mk. iv. 11. Luke's rendering is then literal and correct; Matthew's *ἐθνικοί* is clearly Jewish interpretation. And this applies equally to his use of the expression in v. 47 and vi. 32.

Confirmation of Jesus' use of this expression, *sharka de'ᵉnasha*, in Mt. vi. 7, comes from a notable series of paronomasiae in the context. For *προσέχειν* a form of *zᵉhar* is the correct word; we may compare *Sanhedrin*, vii. 13, f. 25*b*, 20 lines from foot. An older Semitic word for *μισθός* is *sakhar*, attested for Aramaic by Lidzbarski;[1] some doubt would attach to its use here because of its rarity in Aramaic literature, were it not for the word-play throughout the passage. For *ὑποκριταί* in verses 2 and 5 the word is *shaqqarin* or *shaqqare*; *ῥύμαι* is *shuqin* and *ἐν ταῖς γωνίαις τῶν πλατειῶν*, *bᵉqarnath shᵉqaqe*; cf. Prov. vii. 12 in the Targum, 'at one time in the streets (*shuqe*), at another in the open places (*shᵉqaqe*)'. In verse 6 *κλείειν* is *sᵉgar* or *sakkar*, and in verse 8 the equivalent of *χρείαν ἔχειν* is a phrase with *ṣᵉrikh*. If we put *ḥaze* for *βλέπων* in verse 4, we obtain a paronomasia with *gaze*, *ἀποδώσει*; *ἐν τῷ κρυπτῷ* is *bᵉḥashai*[2] contrasted with *bigᵉlai*, *ἐν τῷ φανερῷ*, if that was the original reading in verse 6.

1 Take heed that ye do not your alms before men, to be seen of them
('**izdᵉharu** *dᵉla ta'bᵉdhun ṣidhqathekhon qᵒdham 'enashin lᵉ'ithḥᵃza'ah lᵉhon*):
Otherwise ye have no reward of your Father which is in heaven
(*'ilmale leth* **sakhar** (?) *lᵉkhon min 'ᵃbhukhon dibhishᵉmayya*).

[1] As verb, in *Handbuch der nordsem. Epigraphik*, p. 375; cf. *Pes.* 118*a*.

[2] Dalman, *Gramm.*², p. 211.

2 Therefore when thou doest thine alms, do not sound a trumpet (*la t^{e}qarnen*) before thee,
As the hypocrites do in the synagogues and in the streets (*hekhma da'^{a}bhadhu* **shaqqar***in bik^{e}nishatha ub^e***shuq***in*),
That they may have glory of men . . .
4 That thine alms may be in secret (*b^e***ḥash***ai*):
And thy Father which seeth in secret shall reward thee . . .
(*wa'^{a}bhukh d^e***ḥaze** *b^e***ḥashai gaze** *lakh* . . .)
5 And when thou prayest, thou shalt not be as the hypocrites (**shaqqarin**) are . . .
6 But thou, when thou prayest, enter thy closet, and when thou hast shut (**s^{e}gart** or **sakkart**) thy door . . .
7 But when ye pray, use not vain repetitions,[1] as the rest of men (**sharka** *de'^{e}nasha*) do . . .
Be not therefore like unto them, for your Father knoweth what things ye have need of (**ṣ^{e}rikh***in 'attun*) before ye ask him.

Mt. vi. *19–20, 25–34*; Lk. xii. *33–4, 22–31*

Alliteration and paronomasia both occur in the sayings about treasures; the key-sound is sibilant; the alliteration is reproduced fully in the Syriac translations. The most striking example of paronomasia is in Lk. xii. 34: ἐγγίζειν is *q^{e}rabh*; διαφθείρειν of the destruction wrought by the moth, *ruqba*, is *r^{e}qabh*; cf. the Palestinian Syriac translation of Exod. xxvi. 32, ἄσηπτοι, *d^{e}la marq^{e}bhin*.

Mt. vi. 19 Lay not up for yourselves treasures upon earth . . .
(*la th^{e}simun l^{e}naphsh^{e}khon simatha b^e'ar'a*)
20 But lay up for yourselves treasures in heaven . . .
(*simu l^{e}naphsh^{e}khon simatha bish^{e}mayya*)
Lk. xii. 33 . . . where no thief approacheth (**qarebh**),
Neither moth (**ruqba**) corrupteth (**marqebh**).

In the group of sayings on Cares, the same meaning may underlie Matthew's ἐθνικοί in verse 32, 'the rest of men', *sharka de'^{e}nasha*, as in v. 47, vi. 7; Jesus is again referring to the rest of the world as contrasted with the inner circle of His disciples. The alliteration and assonance is predominantly sibilant, especially the soft and melodious Shin, *shushanin*, 'lilies',

[1] A phrase with *s^{e}riq*? Cf. Targum, Ps. ii. 1.

Sh^e^lomoh, Solomon. In verses 28 and 29 in Matthew the Palestinian Syriac has a paronomasia which may well be original:

Consider the lilies of the field, how they grow (**shabh^e^ḥin**) . . .
. . . even Solomon in all his glory (**teshboḥteh**) was not arrayed like one of these.

In Luke's saying about the ravens (xii. 24) two examples of paronomasia are highly probable: 'ravens', *'or^e^bhin* and *rabbi*, *τρέφειν*. The sibilant predominates in *y^e^ṣaph*, *μεριμνᾶν*, and *'oseph* (Aphel of *y^e^saph*), *προστιθέναι*.

Consider the ravens (**'or^e^bhin**) . . . and God feedeth (**m^e^rabbe**) them.
And which of you with taking thought (**yaṣeph**) can add to (**'oseph**) his stature one cubit.

Lk. xxii. *36*

The equivalent of *μάχαιρα* in Aramaic is *say^e^pha*; *τελεσθῆναι* is *suph*, and *τὸ τέλος supha*; *ἱκανόν ἐστι* may be expressed by *s^e^pheq*.

. . . and he that hath no sword (*di d^e^leth leh* **say^e^pha**),
Let him sell his garment and buy one (*yizbon maneh*[1] *wiy^e^zabben* **say^e^pha**),
For I say unto you, that this that is written must yet be accomplished in me (*lim^e^***saph** *bi*) . . .
For the things concerning me have an end (*dil^e^dili* **supha**). . . . It is enough (**s^e^pheq**).

3. *Predominant Dentals and Labials*

Mt. v. *43–8*; Lk. vi. *27–36*

Alliteration, assonance, and word-play are all prominent features of the Aramaic of these verses. Considerations of parallelism suggest a different arrangement from what we find in the Gospels. Verses 27 and 28 in Luke go naturally together as four synonymous lines: verses 32 and 33, in synthetic parallelism, develop the thought of the first two synonymous lines and probably followed directly on verse 27; verse 28 is imperfectly continued in 29. Verses 27, 32, and 33 may therefore be taken together as forming a poetic unit.

[1] A less common word is *kissuya* (e.g. Esther II Targum, vi. 10); it would give a word-play with *kis*, *βαλάντιον*.

For ἀγαθοποιεῖν in verse 33 we may use *ṭayyebh*; the phrase ποία ὑμῖν χάρις ἐστί in verses 32 and 33 very probably reflects the Talmudic *ma(h) ṭebhu*; the latter occurs, e.g., in the Palestinian Talmud at *Kethub.*, Beginning, f. 24*d*, lines 13 and 17 (repeated as in the Gospel), and at *Ta'anith*, i. 4, f. 64*b*, line 50. In verse 32 ἁμαρτωλός is *ḥayyabh* which gives a paronomasia with *ḥabbibh* (or *'aḥebh*), ἀγαπᾶν.[1]

Lk. vi. 27 Love your enemies, do good to them which hate you . . .
32 For if ye love them which love you, what thank have ye?
(*'in* **ḥabbibh***ton m*^{e}**ḥabb**^{e}**bh***ekhon ma* **ṭebh***u l*^{e}*khon*)
For sinners also love those that love them.
(*d*^{e}**ḥabbibh***u 'aph* **ḥayyabh***in m*^{e}**ḥabb**^{e}**bh***ehon*)
33 And if ye do good to them which do good to you, what thank have ye?
(*'in* **ṭayyebh***ton m*^{e}**ṭayy**^{e}**bh***ekhon ma* **ṭebh***u l*^{e}*khon*)
For sinners also do even the same.
(*d*^{e}*'aph ken* **'**^{a}**bh**^{e}*dhu* **ḥayyabh***in*)

The same form of verse may be restored by taking verse 30 along with 34. The Aramaic equivalent of αἰτεῖν, *sh*^{e}*'al*, means 'to ask for a loan', 'to borrow', as well as simply 'to ask' (cf. the parallel, Mt. v. 42); *sh*^{e}*'al* gives a paronomasia with *sh*^{e}*qal* (αἴρειν). The Aramaic for δανείζειν is *'ozeph* (Aphel of *y*^{e}*zaph*), so that we get another word-play with *n*^{e}*sabh* (λαμβάνειν). Verse 29, which continues verse 28, in a different poetic unit, also contains a paronomasia.

30 Give to every one that *borroweth from thee* (*habh l*^{e}*khul '*^{e}*nash d*^{e}**sha'el** *minnakh*)
And of him that taketh away thy goods, ask them not again (*minneh d*^{e}**shaqel** *ṭabhathakh la* **tishal** *'adh*).
34 (And) if ye lend (**'ozaphton**) to them of whom ye hope to receive (**l**^{e}**missobh**), what thank have ye?
For sinners also lend (**'oz**^{e}**phu**) to sinners, to receive (*d*^{e}**yiss**^{e}**bhun**) as much again.
29 And unto him that smiteth thee on the one cheek, offer also the other (*leh* **m**^{e}**qappaḥ**[2] *lakh b*^{e}**pagga**(**kh**)[3] (*ḥ*^{a}*dha*) **habh** *'aph* **ḥabh***reh*.

[1] *Infra*, p. 182.

[2] Cf. Sy^{pal}. Ps. xlvi. 2.

[3] Sy^{pal}. Isa. l. 6.

One of the more interesting of the examples of paronomasia occurs in Mt. v. 47, 48: the regular Semitic expression for 'to greet' is 'to ask for the peace or welfare (*sh^elam*) of', and τέλειος is *sh^elim*; for the latter we may compare the Jerusalem Targum I's paraphrase of Lev. xxii. 27, with its reference to 'the virtue of the perfect man (*sh^elima*)'. The word corresponding to τέλειος in Luke is οἰκτίρμων, and Eberhard Nestle traced the variants to *sh^elim*, but the evidence for the identification of οἰκτίρμων with this word is of very doubtful value.[1] In the Pseudo-Jonathan Targum of Lev. xxii. 28 we find an almost verbal parallel to Lk. vi. 36; it reads, 'As our Father is merciful (*raḥman*) in heaven, so be ye merciful on earth'. The words occur in a typical Targumic expansion, and any suggestion of dependence on the Gospel saying is fanciful. But the saying in the Targum became well known; it is referred to and quoted in the Palestinian Talmud in *Berach.* v. 3, f. 9*c*, line 25; *Megilla*, iv. 9, f. 75*c*, line 14. It may have been familiarly quoted in the first century; we know that the Jerusalem Targums contain substantial portions of earlier Palestinian Pentateuch Targums.[2] Jesus may have been drawing on the Targum. In view of the word-play in Matthew, however, it seems more probable that the first Gospel has preserved the original form of the saying as spoken by Jesus, perhaps a modification of the popular form, and that it is to the influence of the Targumic form of the words that the Lucan variant is due.

Lk. vii. 36–50[3]

In the story of the Woman who was a Sinner the moral (and social) status of the woman is specially emphasized; she was a ἁμαρτωλή, *ḥayyabhta*. Jesus' parable skilfully plays on this

[1] *Philologica Sacra*, p. 12 f. Among the explanations of the name 'Solomon' given in Lagarde's *Onomastica Sacra* (174, 93) we find ἐλεήμων ἢ εἰρηνικός, and on the basis of this evidence, 'the last doubt disappears' that οἰκτίρμων is *sh^elim.*

[2] *Supra*, p. 21 f.

[3] Cf. Joüon, 'La pécheresse de Galilée et la parabole des deux débiteurs', in *Rec. de science rel.* xxix (1939), pp. 615 ff., and J. Jeremias, *Gleichnisse Jesu*², pp. 104, 122.

central word: the key-words are χρεοφειλέτης, *mar ḥobha*, δανειστής, *bar ḥobha* or *ḥayyabh*, ἁμαρτία, *ḥobha*, and ἀγαπᾶν, *ḥabbebh* or *'aḥebh*.[1]

41 There was a certain creditor which had two debtors
(*hawa ḥadh mar* **ḥobha** *deleh teren bene* **ḥobha** or **ḥayyabh***in*):
The one owed five hundred pence, the other fifty
(**ḥabh** *ḥadha ḥamesh me'ah dinarin 'uḥrana ḥamshin*).
42 And when they had nothing to pay, he frankly forgave them both.
Tell me therefore, which of them will love him most
(*'edhen ye***ḥabbebh***inneh yattir*)?

The antithetic parallelism after verse 44 is noteworthy.

44 Simon, seest thou this woman?
I entered into thine house, thou gavest me no water for my feet:
But she hath washed my feet with tears, and wiped them with the hairs of her head.
45 Thou gavest me no kiss:
But this woman since the time I came in[2] hath not ceased to kiss my feet.
My head with oil thou didst not anoint:
But this woman hath anointed my feet with ointment.

The second half of verse 47 draws a logical moral from the parable 'but to whom little is forgiven, the same loveth little': but these words are not parallel to the first part of the verse, and there is no proper antithesis. A very simple error in translation may have given rise to the confusion.

Wherefore I say unto you,
She whose many sins are forgiven, (that) she loveth[3] much.
(*dishebhiqin lah ḥobhaha saggi'ayya deḥabbibhath saggi'*)

The first *de*, a *relative*, has been taken as *de recitativum* (and omitted in Greek). The second *de* is not ὅτι, 'because', but *de recitativum* after 'I say'; the subject of the clause '(that) she loved much' is the earlier clause, 'she *whose* many sins are for-

[1] *Supra*, p. 180. On the word-play *ḥubh, ḥabbebh, 'aḥeb*, cf. E. Nestle, *Philologica Sacra*, pp. 49 ff.

[2] Probably 'since the time she came in'; cf. Torrey, *Our Translated Gospels*, p. 98 f.

[3] The aorist ἠγάπησεν corresponds to a Stative Perfect; *supra*, p. 129.

given', removed out of its own clause in an idiomatic hyperbaton to its present prominent and emphatic position in the sentence.[1] The translator, however, took the subordinate clause as the main clause, and by making the *d^e recitativum* a conjunction, 'because', made the main clause subordinate; with the latter he has wrongly construed *οὗ χάριν*, which goes along with 'I say unto you', and with these words only.

We are thus able to restore the antithetic parallelism. It may be that there was no reference to the woman at all in this verse, but a general statement of the moral of the parable (the suffixes being masculine):

Wherefore I say unto thee,
(*k^edhen 'amar 'ana lakh*)
One whose many sins are forgiven loveth much (*dish^ebhiqin leh* **ḥobh***in saggi'in d^e***ḥabbebh** *saggi'*), but to whom little is forgiven, the same loveth little.

It is no doubt possible in Greek to construe the *ὅτι ἠγάπησεν πολύ* as a *ὅτι recitativum* clause after *λέγω*, but the syntax is odd. In any case, it seems as if Luke intended us to understand, in spite of the logic of the parable, the words in the sense 'because she loved much', in order to enable him to go on to portray Christ granting the woman absolution (v. 48): because of this demonstration of gratitude (Luke intends us to understand) the woman's sins are being (or going to be) forgiven now. The alternative (and undoubtedly original) meaning places the absolution or forgiveness of the woman *in the past*—her demonstration of affection is a consequence of her having been forgiven. There is no doubt how the original Aramaic was construed.

Mt. xi. 28–30[2]

Arnold Meyer pointed out a paronomasia in these verses: the Aramaic of *ἀναπαύειν* is *'aniḥ*: *πραῦς* is *n^eyaḥ*; in the II Targum of Esther viii. 13, 'with a gentle spirit' is *b^eruḥa niḥ^atha*; *ἀνάπαυσις* is *niḥa*.[3] The prevailing sounds are all soft, smooth, and pleasant.

[1] Cf. *supra*, p. 53. Cf. Torrey, *Our Translated Gospels*, p. 98.

[2] On the Aramaic of Mt. xi. 28-30, see further Joüon, *Notes philologiques*, p. 346.

[3] *Jesu Muttersprache*, p. 84.

Come unto me, all ye that labour and are heavy laden
(*'ᵉtho lᵉwathi kullᵉkhon dᵉlahain uteʿinin* or *tᵉʿine mobhᵉlin*),
And I will give you rest (*wa'ᵃna* **'aniḥᵉ***khon*).
Take my yoke upon you and learn of me
(*qabbᵉlu niri* (*'oli* ?) *'ᵃlekhon ulᵉmadhu minni*);
For I am meek and lowly in heart
(*da'ᵃna* **nᵉyaḥ** *wᵉʿenwan bᵉlibba*(*i*)):
And ye shall find rest for your souls
(*wᵉtishkᵉḥun* **niḥa** *lᵉnaphshᵉkhon*).
For my yoke is easy, and my burden is light
(*dᵉnaʿim niri* (*ʿoli* ?) *wᵉqallil mobhᵉli*).

Mt. xviii. *12–14*; Lk. xv. *3–7*

The key-words in the parable of the Lost Sheep are 'one' (*ḥadh*), and the 'joy' (*ḥedhwa*) in heaven over the 'one' sinner that repenteth. The shepherd rejoices (*ḥᵃdhi*) over the recovery of the 'one' lost sheep that 'went astray', πλανηθῇ, Aramaic *tᵉʿi*, the same consonantal grouping as *ḥᵃdhi*. If Jesus used the word *ḥaṭya* for ἁμαρτωλός (Luke, verse 7) then there is a paronomasia with *ṭᵉʿi*.

Lk. xv. 2 And the Pharisees and scribes murmured, saying, This man receiveth sinners, and eateth with them (*gabhra den mᵉqabbel* **ḥaṭain** or **ḥaṭayyin** *wᵉ'akhel ʿamᵉhon*).

Mt. xviii. 12 . . . If a man have an hundred sheep, and one of them be gone astray (*wᵉ***ḥadh** *minnᵉhon* **ṭaʿe**) . . .

13 And if so be that he find it . . . he rejoiceth (**ḥadhe**) more over that sheep than of the ninety and nine that went not astray (*dᵉla* **ṭaʿain**).

Lk. xv. 7 . . . Likewise joy (**ḥedhwa**) shall be in heaven over one sinner (**ḥᵃdha ḥaṭya**) that repenteth.

Several general observations may be made in conclusion. The occurrence of formal elements of Aramaic poetry in non-dominical sayings or speeches and in the Gospel dialogue as well as in the sayings of Jesus, points to an Aramaic source or sources of a literary character in addition to the sayings-source. The clearest cases of parallelism of lines and clauses, with accompanying assonance and word-play, were found in the sayings of the Baptist, in the Fourth Gospel as well as in the Synoptics, and in the early hymns and narrative of St. Luke. The evidence supports the view that, if the Evangelist is not himself translating, he is making use of translated Aramaic hymns or poems, and turning them into literary compositions. Attempts to trace the sources of such hymns have not met with much success,[1] but the evidence points to their existence.

In the reconstruction into Aramaic which has been attempted above, no claim can be made to finality or absolute certainty in any single instance of a reconstructed original. Where we are dealing, however, with common words and expressions, there exists a high degree of probability that we have the original *Urlaut*. There certainly seems to me to be sufficient certain instances to show (*a*) that Jesus did employ the medium of alliteration, assonance, and word-play as well as parallelism and rhythm; and (*b*) that these phenomena are practically confined to the sayings of Jesus, the exceptions again being the speeches of the Baptist and the early chapters of Luke. In the sayings of Jesus, Mark and Q supply the bulk of the examples; the remainder come from Matthew's or Luke's special sources.

In one instance the paronomasia and predominant consonantal sounds can account for the order in which the sayings have been arranged. There is no connexion in subject-matter between the verses about the strange exorcist in Mk. ix. 38 f. and the following section on Offences. But there is a formal connexion in the poetic form and predominant sounds in both groups of sayings.

Jesus did not commit anything to writing, but by His use of poetic form and language He ensured that His sayings would not be forgotten. The impression they make in Aramaic is of carefully premeditated and studied deliverances; we have to do with prophetic utterance of the style and grandeur of Isaiah, cast in a medium which can express in appropriate and modulated sound the underlying beauty of the sentiment or the passion out of which the thought arose—soft and gentle in the kindly sayings, as in the promise to the heavy-laden, inexorable and hard in the sayings about Offences, strongly guttural and mockingly sibilant where hypocrites and 'the rest of men' are contrasted with the Christian disciples.

[1] Cf. Schaeder–Reitzenstein, *Studien zum antiken Synkretismus*, p. 326.

PART IV

TRANSLATION OF ARAMAIC

CHAPTER VIII

A. SYNOPTIC VARIANTS FROM ARAMAIC

EVERY student of the New Testament is indebted to Professor T. W. Manson's studies in Q with reference to the Aramaic.[1] Q is a single source that most probably represents a translation of an Aramaic document,[2] the original order and more primitive version of which is St. Luke's; at a later stage the Greek version was revised with reference to the Aramaic, and it is this revised version which St. Matthew edited.[3] The Aramaic Q probably took shape as a catechetical manual, consisting originally of sayings only and possessing a certain literary integrity; it is probably to be identified with the 'Logia' attributed by Papias to St. Matthew and said to have been composed by him 'in a Hebrew (Aramaic) dialect.'[4]

In his *Synoptische Studien*[5] Dr. Wilhelm Bussmann elaborated a more complex theory on the basis of a study of the Aramaic. Bussmann was impressed (as all students of Q have been) by the extent of differences within the source. In about half of the passages usually assigned to it, verbal agreement between Matthew and Luke is striking; in the other half, community of subject-matter rather than identity of language justifies our assigning them to the 'double tradition'. Various explanations,

[1] *The Teaching of Jesus* (1931), pp. 27 ff.; *The Sayings of Jesus* (1950).

[2] The following is perhaps the most striking illustration of a Q 'Aramaism', because it is still in everyday use. Whenever we repeat the Lord's Prayer in the form 'Forgive us our debts, as we forgive our debtors', we are perpetuating an Aramaic idiom, for it is in Aramaic, and not in Greek or Hebrew, that sin or guilt towards God or man is regularly conceived in terms of debt: Jesus, however, meant 'trespasses' or 'sins', as Luke renders. Cf. *supra*, p. 140.

[3] Cf. the *Expository Times*, xlvii. 1, pp. 7 ff.

[4] See especially *Bulletin of the John Rylands Library*, xxix. 2, pp. 4 ff. and 17.

[5] Halle, 1925.

by no means mutually exclusive, have been given of this perplexing fact.[1] Bussmann, by analysing out stylistic and other differences between the first group of passages and the second, concluded that Q^A (to simplify his *sigla*) represented a distinct source which had come into the Evangelists' hands as an already translated document; in Q^B, Matthew and Luke were themselves independently translating a different Aramaic collection, 'each as he was able'; Q^A contains narrative, Q^B 'logia' or sayings only, and it alone is to be identified with the Logia of Papias. It is in this second part of the theory that the appeal is made to Aramaic. So far as the 'two-source hypothesis' is concerned, it is extremely doubtful if Bussmann has made out his case.[2] The further 'bifurcation' of Q^B into two independent translations is supported by no less than one hundred and twenty-two alleged 'translation-variants'. The list contains evidence of Aramaic origin: that fact is not in doubt; it is similar to the evidence in Q^A and contains some of the most striking examples.[3] But *less than one-third* of the 'variants' need be so explained, and even there, there must always be some doubt. 'Variants' are mostly Greek synonyms, and when we compare them, it is impossible to avoid the conclusion that Matthew's Q is simply a Greek revision—he is doing for Q what he does for Mark. Luke is the more primitive Greek version.

But still more significant literary processes have been at work in producing Matthew's edition of Q. In more than half of Bussmann's 'variants', while the meaning is much the same in both Gospels, Matthew's 'version' resembles nothing so much as a free literary paraphrase; a comparison, for example, *inter alia*, of the two forms of the Beatitudes suggests that Matthew is doing some Greek 'targumizing' of Q on his own. Nothing certainly could be clearer, when Bussmann's parallels are compared one by one, than that Q in Matthew is not just a translation: *it is a Greek literary composition*. And it is not improbable,

[1] See V. Taylor in the *Expository Times*, xlvi. ii, pp. 70 ff.

[2] Cf. Taylor, op. cit., p. 73 f.

[3] Bussmann, op. cit., ii, p. 151 f.; cf. Manson, in the *Expository Times*, loc. cit.

in view of Matthew's known editorial methods, that Streeter is right in thinking that he has also collated 'parallel versions' of sayings which he found in his special source with Q sayings.[1] No other hypothesis can so satisfactorily account for the wide divergence in language in the Q^B passages.

This is to say nothing new: all these possibilities are allowed for in Dr. Manson's view of a revision of Q edited by Matthew.[2] But what of Luke? To what extent, if any, has the Greek literary process which we can detect in Matthew affected Luke's version of Q?

It seems to me to be reasonably certain that over large tracts of Q^A we have to do with a translated tradition, in the main a faithful rendering of an Aramaic source; the parallelism of lines and clauses, which Eduard Norden considered the most certain 'Semitism' in the New Testament,[3] is an indication that the literary structure of the original is behind the version.[4] Moreover, in one instructive example of a saying in Q which is preserved *in a different translation* in Mark, we can see at a glance that both versions are based on a single definitive Aramaic text, and are entirely faithful to it: Lk. xvii. 33 (= Mt. x. 39) is parallel to Mk. viii. 35; θέλῃ and ζητήσῃ translate the same Aramaic verb;[5] σώζειν, περιποιήσασθαι, and ζωογονήσει are all translation-variants[6]—here, if anywhere in the Gospels, is an example of 'each translating as he was able'. Other similar examples I have noted elsewhere.[7] The translations are literal ones: it is when we consult the parallels in Matthew and John (xii. 25) that it is impossible to speak (as Bussmann does for Matthew) of 'translation-variants'; both are literary 'targumiz-

[1] *The Four Gospels*, p. 238 f.

[2] It is difficult to maintain the distinction between an earlier revise of Q and Matthew's 'revise' of this revision. What is clear is that a great deal of the revision comes from the hand of the author of the Gospel.

[3] *Agnostos Theos*, p. 365. [4] Cf. *supra*, p. 143. [5] Cf. *infra*, p. 244.

[6] Of Aramaic *ḥaya*: in LXX Ezek. xiii. 18, περιποιεῖσθαι τὰς ψυχάς becomes in Symmachus περισώζειν (Theodotion has ζωῶσαι); Origen on Exod. xxii. 18(17) reports the variant ζωογονεῖν for περιποιεῖν—all go back to Hebrew *ḥaya*. Consult Field's *Hexapla*, in loc.

[7] In the *Expository Times*, lix. 1, p. 14 f.

ings' of the saying, using such familiar contrasts as 'seek' and 'find', 'love' and 'hate'.[1]

But there are other passages where we can detect a literary rewriting of a saying in the Lucan Q. I have noted above that it is only in Mark that we find anything resembling a literal translation of the parables (even there the 'translation' is, in many respects, more literary than literal).[2] If we compare the overlapping tradition of Mark and Q in the Parable of the Mustard Seed (Mk. iv. 30 f. = Lk. xiii. 18 f.: Mt. xiii. 31 f. is a conflation of Mark and Q), Q = Luke is faithful in all but language to the Aramaic behind Mark.[3] In the Beelzebub controversy (Lk. xi. 17 f. = Mk. iii. 23 f.), the underlying structure of the Marcan parallelism depends on the four times repeated (and rhetorically most effective) *δύναται* (verse 25 *δυνήσεται*, the same Aramaic); the structure has dissolved in Luke in a literary rewriting (with conspicuous hypotactic participles in marked contrast to the Marcan parataxis). The most instructive example, however, is Q = Lk. xii. 10, where the sin against the Holy Ghost is contrasted with a word against the Son of Man; Mark has nothing about the Son of Man, but he has the Aramaism 'sons of men' for men: the question of priority may be here debatable, but there can be no question in the rest of the saying where the Judaistic outlook of Mk. iii. 29 is replaced by an abridged version in Q, deliberately soft-pedalling the harsh sentiment retained in Mark.[4] (Matthew is faithfully 'targumizing' Mark as well as conflating with Q.)

[1] The alternative (and it is a serious one) is to assume that Matthew and John have independent sayings from the same discourse. But they cannot be *traced* to translation of Aramaic.

[2] *Supra*, p. 63.

[3] To assume, as I have done (*supra*, p. 123), an original *zera'* behind *σπείρειν* and *ze'er* as the original of *μικρότερον* is no more 'conjectural' than to translate in English by 'sow' and 'less'; these are the inevitable equivalents of common words. *No paronomasia is more certain in the Gospels.* But all this can be recovered from Mark only—it disappears entirely in Luke's literary *ὃν λαβὼν ἄνθρωπος ἔβαλεν εἰς κῆπον ἑαυτοῦ.* But Q is in touch with the Aramaic where Mark is not in *ηὔξησε* (ib.).

[4] Where *ἁμάρτημα* in its first occurrence is *ḥobha* '*sin*', and in the second, the consequence of the final Sin, is really = *κατάκριμα* (TR *κρίσεως*!). It is the same word which is used in Aramaic for *ἔνοχος*: *ἔνοχός* (*ḥayyabh*) *ἐστιν αἰωνίου ἁμαρτήματος* (*ḥiyyubha*), *obnoxius est condemnationis aeternae.* Cf. *supra*, p. 140. Mark is the all-too-literal translation, which disappears in Luke.

Much of Luke's editorial work consists of an accommodation of his 'Jewish' material to Gentile ways of thought; and some of this editing consisted in the removal of some passages and the simplification of others. Thus Lk. xi. 42 removes the reference to the 'weightier matters of the Law', while the Hebrew phrase in Matthew (xxiii. 23) 'mercy and faithfulness' becomes 'the love of God'. In the passage Lk. vi. 29 = Mt. v. 39, Matthew is thinking of an insult (ὅστις σε ῥαπίζει) and uses the term which is familiar for this kind of buffet in Biblical Greek (e.g. 1 Es. iv. 31, Hos. xi. 4). Luke thinks of an act of violence (τῷ τύπτοντί σε), as also in verses 29b and 30. Matthew's restriction of the sense to insult, legal action, and borrowing (verse 42a τῷ αἰτοῦντί σε par. to 42b, cf. *supra*, p. 180) may well be original. Luke has then, in the course of his interpretation imported ideas of active violence and robbery by violence into the thought of the passage.

In the light of such observations it is not possible to claim that the Lucan form of Q is always the more faithful to the Aramaic original, though it is for the most part the most primitive translation of the Aramaic. But again and again Matthew gives us a much fuller 'version' in Q as elsewhere in his special material of the sayings and teaching of Jesus, and much of it may be original. [1]

There are, of course, many 'variants' which are probably simply different translations of the Aramaic, without literary or interpretative factors unduly influencing the 'version'. Thus at Lk. xvii. *2* = Mt. xviii. *6* (= Mk. ix. *42*), the original of the variants καλόν ἐστι, συμφέρει, λυσιτελεῖ was almost certainly *ṭabh*, of which Mark gives the literal rendering; cf. LXX Job x. 3, καλόν σοι ἐὰν ἀδικήσω (*ṭobh*, verb), Jer. xxxiii (xxvi) 14, συμφέρει (*ṭobh*). But even here Luke's λυσιτελεῖ, a stronger expression, is probably the editor's deliberate literary choice. And sometimes it is Matthew who introduces the more literary turn of phrase (cf. Lk. xvii. 2 with Mt. xviii. 6, καὶ ἔρριπται εἰς

[1] Cf. B. C. Butler, *The Originality of St. Matthew* (C.U.P., 1951), pp. 37 ff., p. 45 (2nd par.).

τὴν θάλασσαν = καὶ καταποντισθῇ ἐν τῷ πελάγει τῆς θαλάσσης). This is Greek writing, not simple translation.

This evidence of 'non-translation Greek' in Q is just as important as the evidence of translation; and it points to something more than minor editorial improvements by the Evangelists. In the light of it, it is doubtful if we are justified in describing Q, without qualification, as a translation of Aramaic. Certainly it seems clear that the most the Aramaic element can *prove* is an Aramaic origin, not always translation of an Aramaic original; and *it is the Greek literary factor which has had the final word with the shaping of the Q tradition.*

The evidence from the Gospels themselves for the existence of an Aramaic document is necessarily speculative. But if a collection of Aramaic Logia did exist, as Papias claims, there is as much probably to be said for the theory that more than one cycle of the Greek sayings-tradition is indebted to it, especially in view of such overlapping 'logia' as we find in M and Q, and Mark and Q, as for its identification with a single collection such as Q; the latter theory has always to reckon with the narrative element in Q^A. Whether more has actually been made of the Papias tradition than it is worth is difficult to say; it is doubtful if it could have arisen, as Bacon has suggested, by a confusion of the original 'Hebrew' with the later Aramaic 'targums' of Matthew, which circulated among Jewish Christians in the second century.[1]

If the conclusion which has been set out above is sound, and the Greek literary factor has had the final word with the shaping of Q, attributing of Synoptic variants to Aramaic must be done with caution. Nevertheless there are a number of these about the ultimate Aramaic origin of which there can be no doubt.

Lk. vi. 22 = Mt. v. 11, ἐκβάλωσιν τὸ ὄνομα ὑμῶν ὡς πονηρόν = εἴπωσιν πᾶν πονηρὸν καθ' ὑμῶν. See *supra*, pp. 135 ff.

Lk. vi. 23 = Mt. v. 12, οἱ πατέρες αὐτῶν = τοὺς πρὸ ὑμῶν.

That the variants οἱ πατέρες αὐτῶν and τοὺς πρὸ ὑμῶν probably

[1] Cf. G. D. Kilpatrick, *Origins of the Gospel according to St. Matthew* (Oxford, 1946), p. 5.

go back to an Aramaic original קדמיכ[ה]ון, read in the one case (Matthew) with a 2nd person plural suffix and in the other (Luke) with a 3rd person plural suffix, was first suggested by Wellhausen.[1] In that case Matthew may be regarded as a mistranslation.

Mt. v. 11, 12 par. differ from the rest of the Beatitudes by the absence of parallelism. The original lines have clearly been overlaid with prose additions of the Evangelists. If we take as the original expressions those common to Matthew and Luke in v. 11, 'Blessed are ye when men reproach and revile you' (= Luke), we obtain an excellent parallel to Mt. v. 10a, the blessing on the persecuted. The actual line which was originally parallel to the blessing on the reproached and defamed may have been incorporated by Matthew in v. 11: 'Blessed are ye when men persecute you . . .'. Such a line is logically completed by v. 12b:

> Blessed are ye when men persecute you,
> For thus did they persecute the prophets before you.

It is just possible that Lk. vi. 23b, 'for thus did their fathers do to the prophets' is not a doublet of Mt. v. 12b, but the concluding line of Blessed are ye when men reproach and revile you:

> Blessed are ye when men reproach and revile you,
> For thus did their fathers do to the prophets.

We have thus a four-line stanza similar to that reconstructed above for other verses.[2] When we turn the lines into Aramaic, the equivalents of *οἱ πατέρες αὐτῶν* and *τοὺς πρὸ ὑμῶν* give a paronomasia and (if these words came at the end of the lines) a rhyme.

> Blessed are ye when men persecute you,
> For thus did they persecute the prophets before you.
> (*di kedhen rᵉdaphu nebhiin qadhmekhon*)
> Blessed are ye when men reproach and revile you,
> For thus did their fathers do to the prophets.
> (*di kedhen ʿabhadu lᵉnebhiin qadhmehon*)

[1] *Einl.*[1], p. 36 (omitted in 2nd edit.).

[2] *Supra*, pp. 156 ff.

In further support of this conjectured reconstruction, it may be noted that while οὕτως may be a variant of κατὰ τὰ αὐτά (an expression peculiar to Lk. vi. 23, xvii. 30) (Aramaic *hekhᵉdhen*, lit. 'according to this'), ἐδίωξαν and ἐποίουν are difficult to trace to the same verb.

Lk. vi. *23* = Mt. v. *12*, σκιρτήσατε = ἀγαλλιᾶσθε.

Luke's σκιρτήσατε clearly implies some outward (physical) expression of feeling, 'to leap, dance' which is entirely absent from Matthew's ἀγαλλιᾶσθε. The Hebrew and Aramaic verb *duṣ* has a range of meaning which covers both expressions. The Old Syriac renders σκιρτήσατε by ܘܕܘܨܘ, but there is a space before it which Burkitt thinks was occupied by ܘܪܘܙܘ (= Matthew's ἀγαλλιᾶσθε); *r u z* in Aramaic is synonymous with *d u ṣ* but with none of the associations with movement and dancing of the latter. If, however, the original was *r u z*, then Luke's σκιρτήσατε might be explained as a mistranslation, by reading a different set of consonants *d u ṣ*. If, on the other hand, as seems more likely, ודוצו stood in the original, then Matthew's is the correct rendering in the context, Luke's an individual interpretation of it.[1]

Lk. vi. *46* = Mt. vii. *21*, τί δέ με καλεῖτε· κύριε κύριε; = [οὐ] πᾶς ὁ λέγων μοι κύριε κύριε.

Matthew's expression recalls the use of Semitic אמר in the meaning 'to designate, name', e.g. 1 Sam. xvi. 3, LXX, ὃν ἐὰν εἴπω πρὸς σέ. In that case it is Luke who gives the more idiomatic Greek phrase; cf. Mt. xxiii. 8.[2]

Lk. x. *5* = Mt. x. *12*, λέγετε· εἰρήνη τῷ οἴκῳ τούτῳ = ἀσπάσασθε αὐτήν.

As Wellhausen noted,[3] Luke gives the Semitic form of greeting. Matthew translates it into its idiomatic Greek equivalent, but the words which follow in Matthew are only to be understood in the light of the Lucan form. Here Luke is clearly the primitive translation.

Lk. xi. 3 = Mt. vi. 11.

[1] See also *supra*, p. 158.
[2] Cf. Wellhausen, *Einl.*[2], p. 27.
[3] *Einl.*[1], p. 36; 2nd edit., p. 27. Cf. *supra*, p. 181.

If the view taken of the origin of ἐπιούσιος is sound (*infra*, pp. 203 ff.), then we must regard Matthew's τὸν ἐπιούσιον . . . σήμερον, and Luke's τὸν ἐπιούσιον as variants to the correct translation of the Aramaic idiom given by Luke as τὸ καθ' ἡμέραν.

Lk. xi. 4 = Mt. vi. 12, τὰς ἁμαρτίας ἡμῶν = τὰ ὀφειλήματα ἡμῶν. *Supra*, p. 140 f.

παντὶ ὀφείλοντι ἡμῖν = τοῖς ὀφειλέταις ἡμῶν. The παντί is probably Lucan.

ἀφίομεν = ἀφήκαμεν. Luke's version rightly renders the Semitic tense by a present. Cf. *supra*, p. 129.

Lk. xi. 41 = Mt. xxiii. 26, δότε ἐλεημοσύνην = καθάρισον. *Supra*, p. 2.

Lk. xi. 42 = Mt. xxiii. 23, πήγανον = ἄνηθον.

According to Matthew, the Pharisees are charged by Jesus as paying tithe of mint and *anise* (ἄνηθον, RV marg. dill) or cummin: in Luke the charge is that they tithe mint and rue (πήγανον) and every herb.

In a note in the *Expository Times*, xv (1904), p. 528, E. Nestle recalled that the Semitic names for these plants as given in Löw, *Aramäische Pflanzennamen* are (*a*) πήγανον = שַׁבָּרָא (*Peganum Harmala*); (*b*) ἄνηθον = שְׁבֶתָא (*Anethum graveolens*). (Löw, §§ 317, 318). 'Can there be any doubt that Luke used a Semitic source and misread in it שברא for שבתא, just as in the preceding verse, according to the beautiful discovery of Wellhausen, he took זכו as an imperative Peal and translated "give alms" instead of the Pael, "cleanse"?' The probability that Luke here represents the mistranslation is confirmed by the fact that whereas ἄνηθον was subject of tithing, there appears to be no evidence that πήγανον was.[1]

Lk. xi. 48 = Mt. xxiii. 31, ὑμεῖς δὲ οἰκοδομεῖτε = ὅτι υἱοί ἐστε . . .. Cf. *supra*, pp. 12 ff.

ἄρα μάρτυρές ἐστε = ὥστε μαρτυρεῖτε ἑαυτοῖς.

Lk. xii. *10* = Mt. xii. *32*, πᾶς ὃς ἐρεῖ λόγον εἰς τὸν υἱὸν τοῦ ἀνθρώπου = ὃς ἐὰν εἴπῃ λόγον κατὰ τοῦ υἱοῦ τοῦ ἀνθρώπου.

[1] Cf., for a different view, E. F. F. Bishop in *Expository Times*, lix. 3, pp. 80 ff.

The expression 'to say a word with regard to (*εἰς*) or against (*κατά*)' is a Semitism, and probably Aramaic in origin. The phrase occurs at Dan. vii. 25 in the form *millin lᵉṣadh* (*'illaya*) *mallel*, lit. 'to speak words against (the Almighty)', LXX, *ῥήματα εἰς τὸν ὕψιστον λαλήσει*, Theod., *λόγους πρὸς τὸν ὕψιστον λαλήσει*. The expression occurs again at Job ii. 9, *εἰπόν τι ῥῆμα εἰς* (A *πρὸς*) *κύριον*, where it is equivalent to MT ברך, 'curse'.[1]

In addition to the present passage, the expression occurs at Acts vi. 13, 11: *οὗτος οὐ παύεται ῥήματα λαλῶν κατὰ τοῦ τοπου ἁγίου*; cf. verse 11 (*ἀκηκόαμεν αὐτοῦ*) *λαλοῦντος ῥήματα βλάσφημα εἰς Μωσῆν καὶ τὸν Θεόν*.[2] Here it clearly has the same sense as in Dan. vii. 25 (to blaspheme). In Lk. xii. 10b, *βλασφημήσαντι* corresponds to Mt. xii. 32b *ὃς δ' ἂν εἴπῃ κατά*.[3]

Lk. xiv. 27 = Mt. x. 38, *ἔρχεται ὀπίσω μου* = *ἀκολουθεῖ ὀπίσω μου*.

Attention has been drawn more than once to the equivalence of *ἔρχεται ὀπίσω* and *ἀκολουθεῖ*; thus Joüon ('*Notes philologiques*', xviii (1928), p. 347): 'Les deux verbes *ἐλθεῖν ὀπίσω* et *ἀκολουθεῖν*, ont exactement le même sens "suivre"; seulement *ἐλθεῖν ὀπίσω* est un aramaïsme et un hébraïsme.' Cf. *supra*, p. 146 (note). The expression in Aramaic is *'ᵉtha bathar*. Matthew retains a relic of the original Aramaism in his *ὀπίσω μου* (instead of the normal dative case).

The variants *λαμβάνει* and *βαστάζει* suggest an original *shᵉqal*, which can have both meanings; for the first Targ. Prov. xvii. 8; the second is attested for Babylonian Aramaic and Syriac (Bab. Talmud, *Menach.* 85a, *B. Mes.* 99b, *Chull.* 105b). Cf. also Cook's *Glossary of Aramaic Inscriptions*, p. 109. According to Schulthess, however, the word is a borrowing from the northern dialect in Palestinian Syriac (*Lex.* s.v.), and the meaning 'to carry', though well attested for the northern dialect and

[1] Hatch and Redpath refuse to give the MT as the equivalent of the expression. Was there a *var. lect.* read by LXX? If there was, it may well have been an Aramaism.

[2] *Βλάσφημα* has clearly been added to bring out the meaning at v. 11.

[3] For other Aramaisms in this saying see *supra*, p. 189. Cf. Wilcox, op. cit., pp. 134 ff. Wilcox adds, as another possible example, Acts xiii. 45.

Syriac, is not represented in Levy's *Chald. Wörterbuch.* The same word may lie behind Mark's αἴρειν, viii. 34 = Lk. ix. 23, Mt. xvi. 24.

Lk. xvi. *16* = Mt. xi. 12, εὐαγγελίζεται = βιάζεται(?). *Infra,* p. 211 (note).

Synoptic Variant. Mk. ii. *17* = Mt. ix. *12*, Lk. v. *31*.

The variants οἱ ἰσχύοντες (Mark = Matthew) and οἱ ὑγιαίνοντες (Luke) have been explained by Jeremias as coming from an original Aramaic *bari'* which means either 'strong' or 'sound, healthy'.[1] The basic meaning of the verb given by Levy (*Chald. Wörterbuch,* s.v. *b^eri,* ii) is 'stark, kräftig sein'. Exod. iv. 7 (Jer. Targ.) supplies an example of the word in the Lucan meaning: in the story of Moses' leprous hand at Exod. iv, the words 'behold it was turned again as his other flesh' (v. 7) are paraphrased 'it has been restored to become whole (*barya*) like his flesh'.

[1] *Theol. Literaturzeitung,* 1949, Nr. 9, p. 532 (col. 2, top).

B. MISTRANSLATION AND INTERPRETATION OF ARAMAIC

With the exception of a few outstanding examples, the assumption of mistranslation of an original Aramaic has not proved the most successful line of approach to the Aramaic problem of the Gospels. From the very nature of such evidence the element of conjecture may be reduced but cannot be eliminated. This type of evidence, however, is not to be overlooked, but, as has already been emphasized, there are two demands we may make of it; for a mistranslation to be feasible, its conjectural basis must be possible and credible. Its value is to be assessed in comparison with alternative proposals from the Greek side; it may be found to offer the best available explanation of the difficulty, especially where there is a decided failure in the Greek.

It has already been noted on several occasions that the interpretation of Aramaic, giving rise to a Greek literary composition rather than a literal translation, sheds light on several passages in the Gospels; two further examples of this are considered below (Mk. iv. 11, 12; Lk. xxii. 16). The order followed is (1) Matthew's special material, (2) the source Q, (3) Mark, (4) Luke's special material, (5) John. I have not so far encountered any convincing examples of mistranslation in Acts.

Matthew

Mt. ii. 23

'And he came and dwelt in a city called Nazareth: that it might be fulfilled which was spoken by the prophets, He shall be called a Nazarene (*Ναζωραῖος*).'

Jesus was known as *ὁ Ναζωραῖος* or *ὁ Ναζαρηνός*, the second form of the name being practically confined to Mark, the first appearing in the other Gospels and in Acts, where the Christians were first described as *Ναζωραῖοι* (xxiv. 5).[1] On the strength of Mt. ii. 23, both forms are generally explained as equivalent to *ὁ ἀπὸ Ναζαρέθ* (Mt. xxi. 11; Jn. i. 45; Acts x. 38). 'A man from Nazareth' could be *Ναζαρηνός* or *Ναζαραῖος*,[2] but *Ναζωραῖος* is not to be derived from *Ναζαρέθ*, and it is this which is the commonest form of the name.

Mt. ii. 23 contains a punning allusion to Isa. xi. 1 (cf. Jer. xxiii. 5, xxxiii. 15): 'the Branch', *neṣer*, was a name applied to the Messiah. The Hebrew word for 'branch', however, does not help us to explain *Ναζωραῖος*, any more than does *Nazir*, Nazarite.[3] Mark Lidzbarski drew attention to the striking similarity between *Ναζωραῖος* and *naṣorayya*, one of the names of the Mandaeans (their usual name is *mandayye*), the Christian gnostic sect, with strong Jewish and Babylonian elements, whose descendants are still to be found practising their ancient rites of baptism and purification in Iran and Iraq.[4] The meaning of the name is no longer known by the Mandaeans themselves; Lidzbarski derives it from the Hebrew *naṣar*, 'to guard', 'to observe'; the *naṣorayya* are so called from their strict observance of certain rites and customs, in particular those of baptism and purification.

The Mandaeans derive their beliefs and customs from different sources, but they are traditionally connected, especially with regard to their baptismal rites, with John the Baptist. This connexion may or may not be historical. The earliest strata of extant Mandaean literature is not earlier than Islamic times, but it is in this earliest literature that John the Baptist is mentioned. What is said there may all come from our Gospels, but it is not yet possible to be so decisively certain as Lietzmann is that it does, or that the Mandaean rejection of Jesus in favour

[1] The first form occurs again in Mt. xxvi. 71 and in Lk. xviii. 37; Jn. xviii. 5, 7, xix. 19; Acts ii. 22, iii. 6, iv. 10, vi. 14, xxii. 8, xxiv. 5, xxvi. 9: the second form appears in Mk. i. 24, x. 47, xiv. 67, xvi. 6, and in Lk. iv. 34 (from Mark).

[2] Dalman, *Gramm.*[1], p. 141.

[3] Lightfoot (*Horae Hebraicae*, Mt. ii. 23) assumes that a nomen agentis, *nazor*, was in use.

[4] *Mandäische Liturgien* (Berlin, 1920), p. xvi f. On the Mandaeans, E. S. Drower, *The Mandaeans of Iraq and Iran*.

of the Baptist began with the opposition to Byzantine Christianity.[1] Mandaean tradition has roots which run deep into pre-Christian Persian and Babylonian thought; another root may have stretched westwards as far as the banks of Jordan and lie as deep as the first or second centuries.

We do not know by what name the followers of John the Baptist were originally known, but such a designation as *naṣorayya*, 'the guardians' or 'keepers' of a strict religious tradition or 'the observers' of certain rites,[2] is in agreement with what we know both of the Baptist himself and of his movement. The latter was one of considerable importance, and its influence was extensive in its time and for several generations afterwards. Aquila and Priscilla in Acts xviii. 24 f. met a Jew from Alexandria, by name Apollos, preaching in Ephesus, 'knowing only the baptism of John'. As late as A.D. 101 we hear of a prophet of some local fame east of Jordan, Alexis or Elxai, whose beliefs are a strange mixture of Christianity and Judaism, but the latter is the more prominent and in it rites of purification and baptism occupy a central position.[3] It would be surprising if a name for John's movement and followers had disappeared entirely from history.

It has possibly survived in the Mandaean name. It may also be preserved in the name of the Nazarenes, called *Ναζωραῖοι* by Theodoret[4] and by Epiphanius,[5] a Jewish-Christian heretical sect which has given us some fragments of an apocryphal Gospel. Among the seven pre-Christian Jewish sects described by Epiphanius (who is tracing their influence on Christianity), the Baptist's sect is mentioned, and he declares that it is the followers of the Baptist from whom the *Ναζωραῖοι* are descended:

[1] *Geschichte der alten Kirche* (Berlin, 1932), i, p. 33; but cf. Lidzbarski, op. cit., l.c.

[2] Zimmern pointed out that the Babylonian *nasir* was used as proper name for the 'protectors of the divine mysteries': he suggested that both Mandaeans and Christians have the name from Babylonian; *naṣorayya* is to be understood as 'keepers of the mysteries'. There may even be a connexion with the 'Ansar of the Qoran; the name is applied there to the disciples of Jesus as well as to the 'Helpers' of Mohammed (*Z.D.M.G.* lxxiv, p. 429 f.).

[3] Lietzmann, op. cit. i, p. 193 f.

[4] *Haer. Fab.* ii. 2.

[5] For the value of the evidence of Epiphanius, consult H. J. Schoeps, *Theologie und Geschichte des Judenchristentums*, pp. 17 ff.

the general ascetic practices of the Nazarenes, described by Epiphanius, agree with the picture of John in the Gospels.[1]

The earliest name given to the Christians may, therefore, have arisen through their popular identification with the followers and movement of John the Baptist. The religious cult of the Baptist, like the figure of its founder, has been overshadowed by Christianity, but the perspective of later history was not that of the first century: where we see the Christian movement, slowly gathering strength, contemporaries, and in particular Gentile contemporaries, may have seen only a widespread sect of Judaism, associated with the name of John the Baptist, and called *Ναζωραῖοι* on account of its peculiar tenets and customs.

This was, in actual history, how Christianity began: Jesus was baptized by John; the Gospels do not say that He was a follower or disciple of the Baptist, but He may nevertheless have begun His career as such.

Mark's preference for the second form of the name, *Ναζαρηνός*, is striking; the evidence elsewhere is overwhelmingly in favour of the first form. The Marcan form may be taken as original and as supporting the derivation from *Ναζαρέθ*. But Mark's Gospel may have been written and read at a time when its author was anxious to avoid the identification of Jesus and His followers with the movement of His great predecessor.

Mt. vii. 6

'Give not that which is holy (*τὸ ἅγιον*) unto the dogs, neither cast ye your pearls before swine, lest they trample them under their feet, and turn again and rend you.'

One of the earliest suggestions made towards the elucidation of the Gospels from Aramaic was that *τὸ ἅγιον* in this verse mistranslated קדשא, *q^edhasha*, Hebrew *nezem*, 'a ring', usually of gold, as *qudhsha*.[2] A suitable parallel is then obtained to 'pearls',

Give not a (precious) ring to dogs,
And cast not your pearls before swine.

[1] *Haer*. 29. 7. See further, *Bulletin of the John Rylands Library*, Vol. 41, pp. 298 ff.

[2] See A. Meyer, *Jesu Muttersprache*, p. 80 f.

Arnold Meyer recalled that *nezem* is applied by the Rabbis to the Law, the individual injunctions of which are its 'pearls'.[1] The conjecture was elaborated by Felix Perles, who noted that לא תתלון, *la thitt*[e]*lun* (μὴ δῶτε), may be read as *la thithlon*, 'Do not hang'; the verb in *w*[e]*la thirmon* (μηδὲ βάλητε) may be read as an Aphel, *tharmon*, the meaning then being, 'and do not adorn'; *b*[e]*'appe* (ἔμπροσθεν) may be taken literally as 'in the snout of'. To obtain exact parallelism with 'pearls', Perles proposed to read *q*[e]*dhashe*, a plural form in *e* as in Syriac: he could then render,

Hang not (precious) rings on dogs,
And adorn not the snout of swine with your pearls,

comparing, for the second line, the 'ring (*nezem*) in a swine's snout' in Prov. xi. 22.[2]

The assumption of a Syriac plural form for Palestinian Aramaic is, on the whole, unwarranted by the usage of that dialect; Aramaic for 'rings' is *q*[e]*dhashin*.[3] The second line of the couplet may perhaps be understood as Perles suggests, provided that the Aphel of *r*[e]*mi* can be shown to have the meaning 'adorn' in the Aramaic of Palestine.[4] The continuation of the verse in Matthew, however, 'lest they trample them under their feet, and turn again and rend you', assumes an earlier 'neither *cast* ye your pearls before swine'. Perles takes the view that these words represent a scribe's explanatory gloss in Greek, after the original 'and do not adorn' had been mistranslated 'and do not cast'. But the 'addition' is Matthew's own, and it may be the Evangelist's own expansion of the previously mistranslated saying. Moreover, τὸ ἅγιον may not just be a mistranslation; it may be an interpretation of the Aramaic (the Didache further interprets of the Eucharist). In Matthew we have the simple

[1] Ibid. For the abusive 'dogs', see I. Abrahams, *Studies in Pharisaism and the Gospels*, ii, p. 195 f.

[2] In *Z.N.T.W.* xxv, p. 163 f.

[3] A plural τὰ ἅγια is read by a few Greek MSS. and has patristic support.

[4] Perles cites *Peshiṭta*, Gen. xxiv. 47. The words μὴ δῶτε, as they stand, may be an Aramaism, 'do not put' (*supra*, p. 133), but they would require (as would also Perles's 'adorn') to be followed by the preposition *b*[e] or *'al*: **τοῖς κυσί** is *l*[e]***khalbin***.

saying emerging with new meanings and an imaginative addition. The original parallelism has the authentic ring of Semitic poetry.

Mt. xii. *33* (cf. vii. *17*, Lk. vi. *43*)

'Either make the tree good, and his fruit good; or else make the tree corrupt, and his fruit corrupt: for the tree is known by his fruit.'

What are we to make of this form of the saying? The parallels give a coherent sense: 'Even so every good tree bringeth forth good fruit; but a corrupt tree bringeth forth corrupt fruit' (Mt. vii. 17); 'For a good tree bringeth not forth corrupt fruit; neither doth a corrupt tree bring forth good fruit' (Lk. vi. 43).

Few of the commentators appear to be aware of any difficulty, with the exception of Wellhausen, who wrote: '*ποιήσατε τὸ δένδρον καλὸν καὶ τὸν καρπὸν αὐτοῦ καλόν* cannot be understood at all as it now reads in Greek.'[1] He sought to overcome the failure in the Greek by explaining *καί* as introducing a Semitic conditional parataxis; it had been misunderstood by the translator as the simple connecting particle, thus giving a following accusative after the verb; the clause after *καί* should have appeared in the nominative, *ὁ καρπὸς αὐτοῦ καλός*. The translation would then be, 'Either make the tree good, *then* its fruit will be good, &c.' Wellhausen compared Mt. xxiii. 26: '*καθάρισον τὸ ἐντὸς* (*ἵνα γένηται* is rightly omitted Lk. 11, 41) *καὶ τὸ ἔκτος καθαρόν*.'[2] The comparison would be apposite, if we could be certain that Matthew's *ἵνα γένηται* was not represented in an original Aramaic. It is omitted in Luke, as Wellhausen noted, but then Luke has *καὶ ἰδού*, not the paratactic *καί*. To explain the Greek in this way, however, certainly gives some meaning to it.

But it is not only the second accusative after *καί* that makes the sentence awkward in Greek; the use of the verb *ποιήσατε* (and in the imperative) in this connexion has its own difficulties: Wellhausen's rendering may no doubt be defended; he takes the verb in the sense of *ponite*, 'represent . . . as'.[3] Certainly the plain sense of 'make' is unintelligible.

[1] *Einl.*[1], p. 20; 2nd edit., p. 13.

[2] *Einl.*[2], l.c.

[3] *Evangelium Matthaei*, p. 61. So Alford and many others; Alford's comment is typical of the older exegesis: 'How *make*, the parable does not say: but let us

The parallels suggest a solution from Aramaic which is at once possible and credible: both Matthew and Luke have the Semitic phrase *καρπὸν ποιεῖν*, 'to make fruit' in the sense 'to produce fruit'; the more idiomatic Greek expression *καρπὸν φέρειν* occurs in Mt. vii. 18. The expression in Aramaic is *ʿᵃbhadh pira*,[1] and a translator who failed to recognize and understand the Aramaic idiom would at once get into difficulties with his translation. How he arrived at the text of Mt. xii. 33 is a matter of conjecture in detail, but once the credibility of the original blunder is allowed, the genesis of its Greek equivalent presents no great difficulties.[2]

The Source Q

Mt. vi. *11* (= Lk. xi. *3*)

'Give us this day our daily bread' (*τὸν ἄρτον ἡμῶν τὸν ἐπιούσιον*).

The unusual *ἐπιούσιος* has proved to be one of the most debated *ἅπαξ λεγόμενα* in the Gospels. Origen informs us that the word was not employed by any Greek writer; it was neither known to the learned nor in current use among ordinary people. He suggested that it had been coined by the Evangelists themselves, in order, as his words imply, to translate 'the Hebrew'.[3] Certainly in this Word of Jesus, if in any other, we can be confident that a Semitic, and presumably an Aramaic, original underlies the Greek, and this view of the origin of *ἐπιούσιος* is widely held.

Different attempts have been made to explain the word from Hebrew or Aramaic.[4] Arnold Meyer, taking the text of Luke as basis, suggested that the petition read in the original

remember, the Creator speaks, and sets forth a law of His own creation, with which our judgments must be in accord.'

[1] *Supra*, p. 138.

[2] 'A good tree produces good fruit' is *ʿabhedh* (עביד) *ʾillana ṭabha pira ṭabha*: the participle may have been read as עבדו, *ποιήσατε*.

[3] *De Oratione*, 27 (ed. Lommatzsch, tom. xvii., p. 208 f.). The word has been discovered in a papyrus, but whether meaning 'daily' or 'for the following day' is not clear; see in *J.T.S.* xxxv, p. 377.

[4] e.g. F. H. Chase in 'The Lord's Prayer in the Early Church', in *Texts and Studies*, i, p. 45 f.; Dalman, *Worte Jesu*, p. 321 f.

Aramaic, 'Bread which is sufficient for us (*laḥma d^e^missathna*), give us day by day': the expression 'my sufficient bread' (*laḥma missathi*, literally, 'bread, my sufficiency') is found in the Targum of Prov. xxx. 8 as a rendering of 'my apportioned bread' (*leḥem ḥuqqi*).[1] Meyer explained τὸν ἄρτον ἡμῶν τὸν ἐπιούσιον as a literal rendering of this Aramaic, ἐπιούσιος to be derived (with Origen) from ἐπὶ τὴν οὐσίαν, meaning 'zum Dasein gehörig', and hence 'necessary, needful'. So the Peshiṭta had understood ἐπιούσιος in Matthew and Luke when it translated 'the bread of our necessity'. Such a meaning for the word alone 'entspricht dem Geist des Gebets'.

But even if this abstruse meaning of the Greek adjective could be conceded, the two ideas, 'our sufficient bread' and 'our needful bread', however closely associated, are by no means equivalent, and ἐπιούσιος cannot be made to mean 'sufficient'. Besides, it is very doubtful if any Greek writer would have employed so unusual a compound for 'necessary', 'needful', for which there are simple and common Greek words available.

The natural and straightforward way of understanding ἐπιούσιος is to connect it with ἐπιέναι; ἡ ἐπιοῦσα with or without ἡμέρα is a not uncommon expression for 'the coming day', e.g. (without ἡμέρα) LXX Prov. xxvii. 1. In a context containing σήμερον or τὸ καθ' ἡμέραν, ἐπιούσιος was bound to be understood in the sense 'for', referring to, 'the coming day'; the Memphitic version renders 'the bread of the coming day'; and the reading of the Gospel to the Hebrews, 'bread of to-morrow', shows that the petition was understood in this way at a very early period.

Meyer's reconstruction, however, suggests the source of the Peshiṭta's rendering, 'the bread of our necessity', namely in Prov. xxx. 8. The Peshiṭta has the Targum rendering of this verse, 'Give me the life sufficient for me' (*messathi*): LXX reads τὰ δέοντα καὶ τὰ αὐτάρκη, the Vulgate has 'tribue tantum victui meo *necessaria*'. The rendering of ἐπιούσιος does not come directly from the Peshiṭta Old Testament into the New, but the latter has been influenced in its choice of an equivalent for it by the translation of Prov. xxx. 8 in the ancient versions.

[1] *Jesu Muttersprache*, p. 107 f.

Similarly, the version of the Curetonian Syriac, '*continual* bread' comes from Num. iv. 7.

Meyer gives as the Aramaic equivalent of Luke's τὸ καθ' ἡμέραν, *l*ᵉ*yoma b*ᵉ*yomeh*, a phrase modelled on *yoma b*ᵉ*yomeh*, corresponding to Hebrew *yom b*ᵉ*yomo*, and found, e.g., in the Targum of 2 Chron. viii. 13, 14. In rendering the different Hebrew expressions for 'day by day', 'daily', the Targum, as a rule, reflects the Hebrew word for word; for the frequent *yom yom*, we find *yom yom* in the Targum or else *yoma w*ᵉ*yoma*. But in the Jerusalem Targum of Gen. xxxix. 10, the Hebrew is rendered by *yoma den w*ᵉ*yomaḥra*, literally 'to-day and to-morrow', 'day by day' (LXX ἡμέραν ἐξ ἡμέρας). Similarly in the Targum of Esther iii. 4 we find the same phrase, in the form *yoma w*ᵉ*yomaḥra*, rendering *yom wayom*; the LXX here is καθ' ἑκάστην ἡμέραν.[1] The word *yomaḥra* (or *yomḥ*ᵃ*ran*) does not appear in the Targums to the Pentateuch and the Prophets associated with Onkelos and Jonathan, but it is attested in the Jerusalem Targum to the Pentateuch and appears at least once in the Targum to the Hagiographa;[2] it is also found in Palestinian Syriac.[3] The word probably belongs to the Palestinian stratum of Targumic Aramaic, and we have to recognize in the expression *yoma den w*ᵉ*yomaḥra* an idiomatic Aramaic one which has been replaced in the later canonical Targumim by the Hebraic *yom yom, yoma w*ᵉ*yoma*.

An important piece of evidence for the use of this expression by Jesus comes to light in Lk. xiii. 32, '. . . Behold, I cast out demons, and I do cures to-day and to-morrow (σήμερον καὶ αὔριον), and the third day I shall be perfected.' The 'three days' have been variously understood. There are two Old Testament parallels, Exod. xix. 11 and Hos. vi. 2: the first reads, 'And the Lord said unto Moses, Go unto the people, and sanctify them

[1] Some editions of the Esther Targum (e.g. Walton and the Paris Polyglot) have *yoma w*ᵉ*yoma*; the variant *yoma w*ᵉ*yomaḥra* was reported by J. Levy (*Chaldäisches Wörterbuch*, i, p. 330), and I have been able to confirm it in Bragadin's *Mikra Gedola*, the best of the Venice editions.

[2] Gen. xix. 34; Exod. xix. 10; Lev. vii. 16; 2 Chron. xx. 16.

[3] Jn. i. 29, *yoma ḥurana* (ἡ ἐπαύριον). The word is a compound of *yoma* and *'uḥran*, 'the other day', 'the next day', 'to-morrow'.

to-day and to-morrow . . . and be ready against the third day . . .' The words refer to two actual days, followed by the third day. But in Hos. vi. 2, 'After two days he shall revive us: in the third day he will raise us up', no two actual days followed by the third day are implied: an indefinite period, of longer or shorter duration, is to culminate at a certain but still indefinite time. The idiom is a common Semitic one, and examples in Aramaic are frequent.[1]

It is this idiom which we find in Lk. xiii. 32: no two definite days followed by a third day are implied, but a short indefinite period, followed by a still indefinite but imminent and certain future event.

But Jesus does not say 'after two days' like Hosea, but 'to-day and to-morrow'. The Aramaic *yoma den weyomaḥra* supplies the clue to the understanding of His words; they mean 'day by day'; 'Behold I cast out demons, and I do cures *day by day*, but *one day soon* I shall be perfected.'

The same expression occurs in the following verse 33, but in this case appears clearly to imply that two definite days followed by the third day are meant, *πλὴν δεῖ με σήμερον καὶ αὔριον καὶ τῇ ἐχομένῃ πορεύεσθαι*. There is, however, a very important variant text given by the Peshiṭta which reads a verb after *αὔριον*, so that *τῇ ἐχομένῃ* goes with *πορεύεσθαι*: 'But to-day and to-morrow I must needs *work*, and on the next day go my way.' Torrey has shown that in simple Aramaic the variant gives a clever paronomasia, 'To-day and to-morrow I must work (*leme'badh*),[2] and on the next day go my way (*leme'bar*)'; the last expression is a Semitic euphemism for death ('to pass on'); the same verb is employed in both Hebrew and Targum in this way in Job xxxiii. 18.[3] We thus get the idiom 'day by day' restored in the original in a two-line couplet exactly parallel to verse 32:

a
Behold I cast out demons, and I do cures day by day,
b
But one day soon I am perfected.[4]

[1] e.g. *Midrash Echa*, i. 4; *Bereshith Rabbah*, 63; *Vayyikra Rabba*, 12.

[2] The infinitive alone expresses δεῖ.

[3] *Our Translated Gospels*, p. 133.

[4] Torrey (l.c.) regards τελειοῦμαι as a mistranslation for παραδοθήσομαι, but

a
But day by day I must needs work,
b
Then one day soon pass on.

If we place this idiomatic expression in the Lord's Prayer, we get the simple petition,

Give us our bread (*habh lana laḥma*)
Day by day (*yoma den w^e^yomaḥra*).

A translator of the Aramaic who failed to recognize the idiom and felt constrained to give a Greek equivalent of the words he found before him would get into difficulties with his rendering of *yomaḥra*. Matthew's text preserves the mistranslation: compared with the above Aramaic, its difficulties are explicable; *σήμερον* is *yoma* (*den*), *τὸν ἐπιούσιον* corresponds to (*den*) *w^e^yomaḥra*.[1] Luke retains *τὸν ἐπιούσιον*, which he no doubt found in Q, but he has combined it with the true tradition, a correct rendering of the Aramaic, *τὸ καθ' ἡμέραν*.

Mt. viii. 22 = Lk. ix. 60

This saying in Q is usually interpreted as referring, in the first *νεκρούς*, to the 'spiritually dead', and perhaps to the other members of the man's family so regarded. 'In our ignorance of the circumstances this sounds somewhat harsh, though it may have been the incentive that the waverer needed.'[2] McNeile goes on to suggest that the Greek perhaps obscures an Aramaic proverb analogous to 'Let the dead past bury its dead'. No such proverb, however, has ever been discovered. The further suggestion that the infinitive *θάψαι* (Aram. *l^e^miqbar*) should be read as *lim^e^qabber*, 'Leave the dead to the undertaker (lit. to him that buries their dead bodies)' is banal.

In the course of reading the Palestinian Pentateuch Targum, I have noted the word *m^e^than*, 'to delay, put off', the pass. partc. of which, *m^e^thin*, is employed as a noun to describe an

the Greek verb is attested of the martyr's perfection by death (Eusebius, *H.E.* iii. 35, vii. 15; cf. Westcott, *Hebrews*, p. 64), and this gives the desired parallel. I suspect a form of *k^e^lal* behind *ἀποτελῶ* and *τελειοῦμαι* (cf. *infra*, p. 233 f.).

[1] I would suggest that דין ויומחרא has been misread as דין דיומחרא, *τὸν ἐπιούσιον*.

[2] A. H. McNeile, *The Gospel according to St. Matthew*, in loc.

individual who puts off making a decision for prudential or other reasons, e.g. Lev. xxiv. 12, Num. ix. 8, xv. 34. The equivalent Hebrew word *mathon* has a wider range: in the sense of 'slow (to decide)' it occurs in the Babylonian Talmud at *Yebam.* 63a, 'Be quick when you buy a piece of land, but *mathon* when you take a wife.' From 'slow' to 'sluggish', 'easy-going', 'weak' is a natural development, and in this sense the adjective describes the demoralized inhabitants of Sodom or the Amorites in the *Tosephta* (*Sabbath*, vii [viii.]). It thus shares the meaning of the Syriac *mathin*, used to translate *νωθρός*; cf. Payne-Smith, *Thesaurus Syriacus*, *s.v.* Payne-Smith quotes the phrase *talmidhe mathine, discipuli hebetes, segnes.* It is very probable that the Palestinian Aramaic *m^ethin* had the same sense and associations.

An original may have read,

> Follow me, and let the *waverers* (מתניין) bury their *dead* (מיתיהון).

The first word, instead of being read as *m^ethinin* has been translated from *mithin* (*νεκροί*).

Mark

Mk. i. *15*

The rendering of Mk. i. 15, *ἤγγικεν ἡ βασιλεία τοῦ θεοῦ*, as 'the Kingdom of God *has come*' first suggested by Professor C. H. Dodd,[1] still continues to attract expositors.[2]

So long, however, as we assume (with Dodd) an Aramaic *m^eṭa* (Hebrew *naga'*) as the original of *ἤγγικεν*, a serious difficulty stands in the way. There is no objection to taking *ἐγγίζω* as an equivalent of *m^eṭa* or *naga'* (as Dr. Dodd has abundantly illustrated from the LXX) in certain connexions. Where it does render these verbs, it is usually in the sense 'to

[1] See his *The Parables of the Kingdom*, p. 44. The view was challenged by J. Y. Campbell in the *Expository Times*, xlviii, p. 91, to which Dodd replied in the following number (xlviii, p. 138). See also Dodd's *According to the Scriptures* (London, 1952), p. 69 (note 2).

[2] E.g. A. M. Hunter, *The Work and Words of Jesus*, p. 73.

arrive *at*', 'to draw near *to*', seldom absolutely 'to arrive', 'to come'. These Semitic verbs, when so rendered, are always completed by a predicate, for example, Dan. iv. 8(11), 19(22), *mᵉṭa lᵉ*, 'to arrive at', 'to reach *to* (heaven)'; so also in the Targum of Gen. xi. 4, of the Tower of Babel whose 'top reaches *to* the clouds (*yimṭe lᵉʿanane*), or Job xx. 6, of the wicked whose 'head reaches *up to* heaven (*maṭe ʿadh ṣeth shimmayya*)'. In all the examples cited by Dr. Dodd for ἐγγίζω rendering *mᵉṭa* or *nagaʿ*, it is followed by the prepositions πρός, εἰς (= *lᵉ*) or ἕως (= *ʿadh*) with a noun or pronoun, or by a noun in the dative or genitive (Jonah iii. 6, Jer. xxviii (li). 4 (B), Ps. xxxi (xxxii). 6, Ps. cvi (cvii). 18, Sir. li. 6 (8, 9), Ps. lxxxvii. 9 (lxxxviii. 3), Dan. iv. 8, 19).

If the original of ἤγγικεν at Mk. i. 15 was *mᵉṭath* (or *nagᵉʿa*), standing alone and without any such complementary predicate, it seems doubtful if a translator would have gone out of his way to render by an equivalent (ἐγγίζω) which *mᵉṭa* (*nagaʿ*) only have elsewhere in the compound expression.

The case is quite otherwise at Lk. x. 9, ἤγγικεν ἐφ' ὑμᾶς ἡ βασιλεία τοῦ θεοῦ, for the verb does have the necessary predicate, and we can then assume an underlying *mᵉṭath lᵉ*. It is true the preposition ἐπί is not found elsewhere with ἐγγίζω to translate the Aramaic expression, but this is a minor difficulty. The main objection to taking ἤγγικεν ἐφ' ὑμᾶς here as a rendering of this expression is that it is nowhere employed elsewhere to express any comparable idea.

In all these circumstances it is worth looking about for alternative equivalents in Aramaic for ἐγγίζω.

The most natural equivalent of ἐγγίζω in Aramaic or Hebrew is the Semitic verb *q r b*.[1]

It seems surprising that a suggestion made some years ago in this connexion by M. Paul Joüon should not have received the attention it deserved.[2] M. Joüon pointed out that 'en hébreu la racine *q r b*, qui exprime la notion de proximité, s'emploie

[1] See Dalman, *Worte Jesu*, p. 87.

[2] 'Notes Philologiques sur les Évangiles' in *Recherches de Science Religieuse*, Tome xvii (1927), p. 538.

parfois aussi dans des cas où, la proximité étant absolue, nous disons, non plus "il est proche", mais "il est arrivé" '. 1 Kings viii. 59 is cited in support: 'And let these my words, wherewith I have made supplication before the Lord, be *present* (*qᵉrobhim*, RV 'nigh') unto the Lord our God day and night . . .'; so also Ps. cxix. 169, 'Let my cry be *present* (*tiqrabh*) before thee, O Lord.' At 1 Macc. ix. 10 M. Joüon detects the same idiom in the phrase *ἤγγικεν ὁ καιρὸς ἡμῶν*, RV, '. . . and if our time *is come*, let us die manfully for our brethren's sake'. Here the original is lacking, but Joüon compares Lam. iv. 19(18), *qarabh qiṣṣenu*, LXX *ἤγγικεν ὁ καιρὸς ἡμῶν*, which he renders *notre fin est arrivée*.

At first glance it might seem doubtful if we have any right to speak of an idiomatic use of *q r b* in this way. Where the word is used with reference to time, Brown, Driver, and Briggs give simply 'to draw near', and the phrase at 1 Macc. ix. 10, Lam. iv. 19(18) is clearly modelled on the familiar expressions of Gen. xlvii. 29, Deut. xv. 9, 1 Kings ii. 1.[1] The meaning 'to be near', 'to be imminent', can be given to all the examples cited by Joüon. At 1 Macc. ix. 10, the context perhaps justifies the translation of the RV (the time to do or die *had come* for Judas and his brethren), but it is still possible to retain the familiar sense of *q r b* and render 'and if our time is imminent'.[2]

Several further considerations, however, support M. Joüon's valuable observation. Both at Lam. iv. 19(18) and Ezek. vii. 6 f. (LXX 2, 3, 4), where a similar phrase occurs, the context bears out the meaning the 'time has come'. At Lam. iv. 19(18), the parallel phrases in the verse are 'our days are fulfilled' (a striking parallel to Mk. i. 15) and 'our end is come'; the LXX has ἐπληρώθησαν αἱ ἡμέραι ἡμῶν and πάρεστιν ὁ καιρὸς ἡμῶν; thus in the original Hebrew *q r b* appears to be synonymous with *male'* and *ba'* (*ba' qiṣṣenu* = *qarabh qiṣṣenu*). At Ezek. vii. 6 f., the

[1] Cf. Abel, *Les Livres des Maccabées* (Paris, 1949), p. 161.

[2] It is not only the RV, however, which understood ἤγγικεν here as 'came'; the Old Latin MS. B reads et si *venit* dies noster (D. de Bruyne, *Les anciennes traductions latines des Machabées*, p. 51) and the Syriac version *mᵉṭi*, 'arrived' (edit. Lagarde, 188).

expression is *qarobh hayyom*, LXX ἤγγικεν ἡ ἡμέρα; and it occurs side by side with *qeṣ ba'* (bis) (LXX πέρας ἥκει) and *ba' ha'eth* (LXX ἥκει ὁ καιρός); a third expression of the MT is *ba'ah haṣṣephira* (RV 'thy doom is come unto thee, O inhabitant of the land . . .') Lk. xxi. 8, ὁ καιρὸς ἤγγικεν, occurs in a similar context, where the parallels again support the meaning, 'the time has come'. (In this connexion, καιρός, as in the Old Testament passages, is almost a technical term for the time of the End.) Further confirmation for Joüon's claim may be found in the rendering of *q r b* by the Pseudo-Jonathan Targum at Gen. xxvii. 41 by *m^{e}ṭa*, 'unto the time when the days of mourning for the death of my father *arrive* (*yim^{e}ṭun*)'.

Even if the case for M. Joüon's view is felt by some to fall short of demonstrative proof, all these Old Testament passages make it clear that *q r b* in this connexion refers always to an *immediately* imminent event.[1]

The parallel at Mk. i. 15, πεπλήρωται (like the parallel at Lam. iv. 19(18)), may be taken to support the translation of ἤγγικεν = *q^{e}rabhath* (*malkuth '^{e}laha*) by 'The Kingdom of God *has come*'.[2]

Mk. iv. *12* (cf. Mt. xiii. *13* = Lk. viii. *10*)

'(And he said unto them, Unto you it is given to know the mystery of the kingdom of God: but unto them that are without, all these things are done in parables:)

[1] The phrase *'attah miqqarobh* at Ezek. vii. 8 (RV *Now* will I *shortly* pour out my fury upon thee . . .)' clearly refers to an immediately imminent event.

[2] Like Dodd, Joüon (loc. cit.) equates φθάνω (Mt. xii. 28) with Aramaic *m^{e}ṭa*, comparing Dan. iv. 21 (Theod.). In the other crucial passage (Mt. xi. 12 = Lk. xvi. 16, Q), a possible original of Matthew's βιάζεται might be represented by the Semitic root *p r ṣ* (*p ṣ r*) (see Hatch and Redpath, *s.v.* βιάζεσθαι); Luke's εὐαγγελίζεται is *b s r*. Hebrew *p r ṣ* is used idiomatically of Jahweh 'breaking in violently (in judgement) upon' (2 Sam. v. 20), or of a plague 'breaking out violently upon' (in judgement) (Ps. cvi. 29) (see *B.D.B. s.v. p r ṣ*). Did Christ speak of the 'kingdom' 'breaking violently in' on the world in judgement? That Luke's εὐαγγελίζεται is secondary tradition (and Luke's own word) is widely recognized (see Creed, *St. Luke*, in loc.). Mt. xii. 28 may also imply judgement (cf. Dan. iv. 21 Theod.). In such a notoriously *unheilbare Stelle* as Mt. xi. 12, we are thrown back on conjecture of this kind. The rest of the verse in Matthew and Luke (καὶ βιασταὶ ἁρπάζουσιν αὐτήν, καὶ πᾶς εἰς αὐτὴν βιάζεται) may represent further attempts to interpret the original expression. Cf. *supra*, p. 116 (note).

That (ἵνα) seeing they may see, and not perceive; and hearing they may hear, and not understand; lest at any time (μή ποτε) they should be converted, and their sins should be forgiven them (καὶ ἀφεθῇ αὐτοῖς).'

Many have felt the harshness of Mark's ἵνα in this verse. 'The stumbling-block here is the ἵνα. As the text stands it can only mean that the object, or at any rate the result, of parabolic teaching is to prevent insight, understanding, repentance, and forgiveness. On any interpretation of parable this is simply absurd.'[1] Professor T. W. Manson goes on to note that 'the quotation from Isa. vi. 9 f. ends with the words καὶ ἀφεθῇ αὐτοῖς, departing from the LXX καὶ ἰάσομαι αὐτούς, and the Hebrew וְרָפָא לוֹ, and agreeing with the Targum וישתביק להון'. The beginning of the quotation in the Targum reads, 'And he said: Go and say to this people, *who* hear indeed and do not understand, and see indeed and do not know. . . .' The Targum *de* is relative, and Dr. Manson suggests that 'the form in which the words were spoken by Jesus approximated to what we find in the Targum, and that the Marcan version rests on a misunderstanding of the Aramaic due mainly to the ambiguity of the particle ד'. The verse is to be rendered:

'To you is given the secret of the kingdom of God; but all things come in parables to those outside who
See indeed but do not know
And hear indeed but do not understand
Lest they should repent and receive forgiveness.'

The suggestion is an attractive one, but it takes liberties with Mark. The Marcan Greek states that those without are taught in parables in order that, though they see, they may not perceive, and though they hear, they may not understand: but Mark does not, like Luke, stop at that point; he goes on to add, 'Lest (if they were to perceive and understand) they may repent and obtain forgiveness.' The parabolic teaching is not simply to prevent perception and comprehension; more important still, it is to prevent their consequences, repentance, and forgiveness,

[1] T. W. Manson in *The Teaching of Jesus* (Cambridge, 1931), p. 76.

and it could not do so unless those without were taught in parables *in order that* they might not perceive and understand. Mark's μή ποτε clause, that is to say, logically depends on his ἵνα clause. To remove the first 'stumbling-block' by regarding it as a misunderstood *dᵉ* clause, which should have been relative, makes its dependent μή ποτε clause meaningless.

The same applies to the saying in Aramaic: the *dᵉ* would only be ambiguous were there no immediately following and dependent *dilᵉma* (μή ποτε) clause. It is, however, ambiguous in the Aramaic of Luke, who omits Mark's μή ποτε clause. Matthew, who departs from Mark altogether at this point, has, significantly, a ὅτι clause, where both Luke and Mark have ἵνα. Matthew's ὅτι is as much a stumbling-block as Mark's ἵνα: 'Therefore I speak to them in parables: because they seeing see not; and hearing they hear not, neither do they understand.' The reason given in Matthew for the use of parable ought surely to be a reason for the very opposite, plain speaking without parable. Everything points to a failure in the Greek. When *dᵉ* relative is assumed, the difficulty is removed. But only in the shorter form of the saying preserved in Matthew and Luke. That we have the right to assume an Aramaic original is clear from the variants ὅτι and ἵνα, both different interpretations of Aramaic *dᵉ*.

In Mark there is only one way in which the recalcitrant μή ποτε can be taken into the sentence as it stands and the ἵνα regarded as mistranslating a relative; it may be connected with the main clause and a comma placed at the end of the *dᵉ* clause: 'All things come to those without in parables, who seeing see . . . but do not understand, lest they should repent and obtain forgiveness.' The last clause alone then gives the reason for the parabolic teaching, the prevention of repentance and forgiveness. The stumbling-block remains.

Nothing is more certain than that Mark wrote and intended ἵνα . . . μή ποτε; his original purpose is clear from the ἵνα clause; it is continued and reinforced by the μή ποτε clause, which has been selected and adapted from the Old Testament quotation in order to be subordinated to the ἵνα clause. We are dealing not with direct quotation or misunderstanding of a quotation, but with intentional adaptation and interpretation of a quotation. Dr. Manson is probably right in suggesting that the words in the Old Testament passage on which the μή ποτε clause there depends, 'Make the heart of this people fat . . .', have been deliberately omitted by Mark, but not for the reason he gives (to avoid the implication that parable was intended to prevent forgiveness), but to enable the writer, by his adapted μή ποτε clause, to complete the main thought of the ἵνα clause, that the purpose of parabolic teaching was to prevent repentance.[1]

But while this is certainly what Mark intended, is it what Jesus Himself said? The Marcan interpretation leaves the impression of a later reflective and perhaps Hellenistic attitude towards the Jews: the judgement of God, preclusion from repentance, and forgiveness, were proclaimed by Jesus Himself. It is not difficult for a writer with such a prejudice to find support for it in the Old Testament quotation; it agrees with the harsh doctrine of the Hebrew verse, where God is called upon to make hard the people's minds lest they should repent and be forgiven.

In the interpretation of the verse found in the Targum, however, even more clearly than in the LXX, it is the people themselves who are to blame for their own blindness of perception and dullness of understanding, which they have culpably brought upon themselves, lest they should repent and be forgiven:

'And he said, Go and speak to this people, *who* hear indeed but do not understand, and see indeed but do not know. *Gross is the mind of this people, and its ears has it made heavy, and its eyes has it blinded, lest they should see with their eyes and with their ears should hear and with their minds should understand, and repent and obtain forgiveness.*'

[1] Cf. Wendling, *Ur-Marcus* (Tübingen, 1905), p. 5: 'Der Verfasser (Redaktor) geht von der secundären Theorie aus, die Gleichnisrede sei mystisch-allegorisch gemeint, ihr Verständnis deshalb dem Volke . . . verschlossen; . . . das Volk . . . solle nur die Worte hören, ohne den Sinn zu erfassen, damit ihm seine Sünden nicht vergeben würden.' Cf. further, *Marcus-Evangelium* (1908), p. 35 f.

It is upon such a Targum quotation that Mark or his source is drawing. That is clear from the Marcan variant *καὶ ἀφεθῇ αὐτοῖς*. No such Greek reading ever existed, for it is not a variant but a characteristic Targumic paraphrase of Hebrew *rapha'*, peculiar to the Targum of Isaiah; it occurs again as a paraphrase of the same verb in liii. 5, lvii. 18.[1]

Matthew's dependence on a source other than Mark is evidence that the quotation occurred in a genuine Word of Jesus. If Jesus cited the whole Targumic passage, it was probably in the form in which it has come down to us; it is most unlikely that He was in any way responsible for the grim adaptation of it which we find in Mark. The passage was a favourite quotation: it is cited in full by Paul in Acts xxviii. 26, but from the LXX.

In neither Matthew nor Luke can any support be found for the use by Jesus of the full quotation. Mt. xiii. 14 quotes, it is true, the whole verse, introducing it with the words, 'And there is fulfilled with regard to them the prophecy of Isaiah which says . . .', but the quotation which is then given (after the adapted form of verse 13) is from the LXX, and the insertion is so characteristic of Matthew, when he has the opportunity of introducing an Old Testament passage, that the whole verse from LXX Isaiah is probably Matthew's own expansion of the original saying.

But the shorter form of the words in Matthew and Luke may well be original and the quotation as cited by Jesus have stopped at *συνίωσιν*, the Aramaic *d*^{e} being the relative as in the Targum, to be rendered correctly by *οἵ* in Greek. In support of this it may be urged that Matthew and Luke are drawing, in this section, not only on Mark, but on the older document Q. Mt. xiii. 16 (= Lk. x. 23), from Q, discussed above,[2] follows immediately on this passage (verses 14 and 15 contain Matthew's LXX quotation). If, as has been suggested, Luke's version is the correct one, *μακάριοι οἱ ὀφθαλμοὶ οἱ βλέποντες ἃ βλέπετε*, then,

[1] The Targum reading occurs in the Peshiṭta of Isa. vi. 9 and in the Sinaitic Syriac of Jn. xii. 40; Sy^{s} is drawing on a Syriac Old Testament. Cf. Merx, *Johannes*, in loc.

[2] *Supra*, p. 70.

when a relative *d*[e] is read instead of ὅτι or ἵνα in Mt. xiii. 13, Lk. viii. 10, we get a contrast between the crowds without, *who*, while they see and hear, neither perceive nor understand, and the disciples, those within, *who* see with their eyes and understand, and are blessed on that account.

To sum up this discussion: so far as Mark is concerned, what we have in iv. 11, 12, in a 'saying of Jesus', is not a simple and straightforward translation of Aramaic, though that Mark is dependent on Aramaic sources is clear from his Targum reading: what is before us is a Greek literary work which is an author's own interpretation of a saying in an Aramaic source, at some idea of which in its original form we can fortunately arrive by a study of the Synoptic parallels.

Mk. vi. *8*, *9* = Mt. x. *10*, Lk. ix. *3*

Mistranslation of Aramaic has been claimed as the cause of the contradiction between Mk. vi. 8, *εἰ μὴ ῥάβδον μόνον*, and Mt. x. 10, *μηδὲ ῥάβδον* (Lk. ix. 3); and between Mk. vi. 9, *ἀλλὰ ὑποδεδεμένους σανδάλια*, and Mt. x. 10, *μηδὲ ὑποδήματα*. In the first case, *la* or *w*[e]*la* (*μηδέ*, *μητέ*) had been misread as *'illa* (*εἰ μή*), and in the second, *w*[e]*la* (*μηδέ*) as *'ella* (*ἀλλά*).[1]

But in the first example this explanation leaves one of the most important words in verse 8 of Mark unaccounted for; Mark's *μόνον* makes it clear that he intended and understood that the staff should be an exception; if *μόνον* was in the original Aramaic, 'not a staff only' is nonsense; 'except only a staff' alone gives good sense. In the second instance no account is taken by this theory of the participle *ὑποδεδεμένους*, which again makes Mark's meaning clear.

No example could make it plainer that Mark is not here simply translating or mistranslating; he is stating quite definitely that the staff was to be an exception. Perhaps the ultimate source of the contradiction may have been in the confusion in Aramaic of the words for 'neither' and 'except' or 'but' and 'neither'.[2]

[1] Cf. Wellhausen, *Ev. Marci*, in loc.; Torrey, *Our Translated Gospels*, p. 143 f.; and Streeter's *Four Gospels*, p. 191 (note).

[2] For similar confusions elsewhere in Mark, see *supra*, p. 113.

But it is likewise possible that Mark is here giving a purely Greek version of the saying, influenced, it may be, by the staff and sandals of the wandering Sophist. At any rate, what we have in Mark is not literal translation nor ignorant mistranslation, but probably considered interpretation, the work, not of a translator but of a Greek writer.

Mk. vii. *19*

'Because it entereth not into his heart, but into the belly, and goeth out into the draught, purging all meats (καθαρίζων πάντα τὰ βρώματα).'

The difficulties of the participle are well known. If the masculine form be read (it has the support of the better manuscript authorities), it is generally referred back to the subject of λέγει (Jesus) in verse 18; or the clause is explained as a gloss from the pen of a scribe thus recording his view of the implications of the saying: Jesus is rescinding the distinction between clean and unclean food. Neither explanation is very satisfactory.

The Sinaitic Syriac connects the words closely with the clause immediately preceding, incorporating them in the main sentence, and by reading a passive, making βρῶμα (in the singular) the subject of the clause, '. . . for it enters not his heart but his belly, *all the food being cast out and purged away*' (the clause is circumstantial).[1]

The Palestinian Aramaic for βρῶμα, namely *'ukhla*, is regularly used in the sense of *excrementum*.[2] The variant text assumed by the Old Syriac, so far as it has Greek attestation, goes back into an Aramaic, '(quod non intrat in cordem, sed in ventrem,) *dum omne excrementum* (*kulla 'ukhla*) *expellitur et purgatur*'

[1] Merx (*Die vier kanonischen Evangelien*, in loc.) thought the Syriac read a Greek text καὶ ἐκβάλλεται ἔξω καὶ καθαρίζεται πᾶν τὸ βρῶμα: no Greek MS. has ἔξω; the Syriac *l^ebhar*, extrinsecus, is probably an interpretation of εἰς τὸν ἀφεδρῶνα. But there is support for the other variants: ἐκβάλλεται occurs in א; καθαρίζει is read by D and has Latin support; one cursive of von Soden's I group, the Mt. Athos MS. 1354 (Gregory 1047) has καθαρίζεται.

[2] The word translating βρῶμα in the Old Syriac is not the usual one (cf. Burkitt, *Evangelion da-Mepharreshe*, ii, p. 281 f.); it is found in Targumic Aramaic in the above sense of *'ukhla* (Judges xiv. 14).

(מידכי). The passive of the last verb is generally not distinguished in form from the active,[1] and this may have given rise to *καθαρίζων*; or the translator may have preferred to read an active and connect with the subject of *λέγει*.

Mk. viii. 33

It has been pointed out more than once that the expression 'Get thee behind *thee*' at Mt. iv. 10 Sy^s^. is a Syriac idiom for 'Withdraw, retire'.[2] In a note in the *Expository Times*, lxi. 5, p. 159, F. Bussby has suggested that the idiom was an Aramaic one and lies behind Mk. viii. 33, where 'an underlying Aramaic statement has been misunderstood and therefore mistranslated into Greek'. The true reading is *ὀπίσω σοῦ*. Bussby compares Mt. iv. 10 D where the *ὀπίσω μοῦ* 'preserves an inaccurate recollection of the right reading' of Sy^s^. The argument is supported by the observation that *Σατανᾶς* is an Aramaic form and *ὕπαγε* an Aramaic locution.

The idiom in question is a Syriac one, *zel l^e^best^e^rakh* (the latter a Syriac adverb), and we would require to assume that the equivalent Aramaic *zel 'el 'aḥorakh* could be used in the same way. Moreover, the Bezan reading may be due to the influence of the Old Syriac.

We have also to take into account the parallel expression to the usual text of Mk. viii. *33* at 2 Kings ix. 19, where Jehu turns to the messenger of Ahab with the words 'What hast thou to do with peace? turn thee behind me' LXX, *ἐπιστρέφου εἰς τὰ ὀπίσω μοῦ*, i.e. 'away from me that I no longer see thee', the exact sense of Mk. viii. 33. This seems the more likely explanation. The locution, however, appears still to be a Semitic one.

Mk. ix. *33–7*

How to relate the Marcan 'interpretation' of the acted Parable of the Child in the Midst ('Whosoever shall receive one of such children in my name, receiveth me,' &c.) to the previous teaching on humility and service in connexion with which the Parable

[1] Examples in the Targum are 2 Chron. xxx. 17, Prov. xx. 9, Ezek. xxii. 24.

[2] Cf. Merx, *Die vier kanon. Evangelien*, i, pp. 54 ff.; Torrey, *The Four Gospels*, p. 294.

was enacted, is the *crux interpretum* of Mk. ix. 33–7. It is, however, one only of several puzzling features in the Marcan version of the Parable.[1] Indeed, for preaching purposes, one turns with relief to the simple clarity of the fuller version of St. Matthew (xviii. 1 ff.). Scholarship, however, has to deal with problems; and Marcan *stromata* (if the Clementine term may be applied to the occasional 'patchwork' on the Marcan tapestry) have yielded before to critical analysis.

In answer to the first question, the connexion of ix. 37 with ix. 35, it has been said that in verse 37 Jesus 'is affirming again, in his striking way, that humility and service are the marks of greatness in his kingdom. . . .'[2] Obviously that is what this commentator felt ought to be the meaning of the Parable: but to go on to claim that in verse 37 it actually is stated to be so, is paralogizing. The inability to recognize a *non sequitur* where one is manifestly present arises, in all such interpretations, from the assumption of the infallibility of the Marcan order and arrangement.

If Mark is right, then Jesus spoke verse 37 after verse 36: in that case, so far as a connexion between verse 37 and verse 35 is concerned, we stand before a *non liquet*. If, on the other hand, the Marcan arrangement of these Child-sayings is open to question, then it may be suggested that the only connexion between verse 37 and its present context is a purely formal one, namely, the word παιδίον.[3]

In x. 13 ff., the next group of Child-sayings in Mark, the story of Jesus' reception of children when His disciples would have driven them away, verse 14, 'Suffer the little children', &c., is followed at verse 15 by 'Verily I say unto you, Whosoever shall not receive the kingdom of God ὡς παιδίον, he shall not enter therein.' Again the connexion is imperfect. But we do have in x. 15 what the context so urgently requires and does not get at ix. 36, namely, the Child held up as an example of humility.

[1] This is, I believe, the correct term. See below.

[2] E. P. Gould, *Mark* (I.C.C.), in loc.

[3] Cf. A. H. McNeile, *The Gospel according to St. Matthew*, p. 260: '. . . this verse [37 = Mt. xviii. 5] must originally have been unconnected with the incident'.

A. W. F. Blunt, who noted this,[1] but without further comment, might easily have gone on to point out (their congruity is patent) that ix. 37 forms the logical conclusion and climax to the incident and Child-sayings group at x. 13 ff.

Are these two sayings then, ix. 37 and x. 15, simply in their wrong places? If they are, then it can only be due to faulty editing on the part of the author of Mark or an early editor of the Gospel, for both Matthew and Luke have Mark's erratic logion (Mt. xviii. 5, Lk. ix. 48). That the Marcan editor of the sayings has had some difficulty with his material may be further deduced from ix. 35a, where Jesus 'called' His disciples in the middle of a conversation with them. The position of ix. 35b too, the teaching on humility and service, which in Mark leads into the Parable, must also arouse suspicion, for in Luke, who is here following an independent tradition,[2] this is regarded as the whole point of the incident, and he places his ix. 48c appropriately at the end.

When we turn from questions of sequence to interpretation, a problem meets us in the presence in Mark alone of ideas of *service* as well as humility in connexion with the Parable of the Child in the Midst—'If any man desire to be first, the same shall be last of all, *and servant of all* (πάντων διάκονος)' ix. 35b). Both Matthew and Luke omit all mention of service or 'the servant of all': their parables teach humility and childlikeness only. In omitting Mark's 'servant of all', their reasoning may have been that, while a child may be held up as a fitting example of humility, it can scarcely be made an example of service. For whatever reason, the words are simply dropped in Matthew and Luke.

It may be that these words are another 'erratic word-block' in Mark, this time from the parallel sayings-group on greatness as service in x. 43 ff. But before acquiescing in this or in any other explanation, it is worth looking again at the Marcan text. The juxtaposition of διάκονος, and three words later, παιδίον (ix.

[1] *Mark* (Clarendon Bible), p. 210.

[2] Luke's 'moral' (ix. 48c) is not identical with ix. 35b in Mark, but points to some common source.

35, 36), while of no significance in Greek, arrests attention and becomes immediately illumining in the well-known ambiguity of Aramaic *talya*, 'child' or 'servant'. If in the Aramaic story it was this word which was first rendered by διάκονος in ix. 35b and then by παιδίον in ix. 36 (or vice versa, in the above sequence), then the Child in the Midst becomes a dramatized play on the Aramaic word for Child and Servant. Further, if x. 15, as has been suggested, is really part of the exposition of the Parable and belongs together with ix. 35b, then it ought to be understood as, 'Verily I say unto you, Whosoever shall not receive the kingdom of God *as a servant* (*talya*), he shall not enter therein.'[1]

The Parable would then be in the prophetic (and Semitic) tradition. Teaching based on animate or inanimate objects as texts, as it were, and also turning on a paronomasia or play on the same or similar sounding words are familiar from Jer. i. 11 and Amos viii. 2. Jeremiah is shown in a vision the 'branch of an almond tree'; the latter in Palestine is called 'the wakeful one' (*shaqedh*) because of its early blossoming (in February); and the interpretation of the vision is that God is the Divine Waker or Watcher (*shoqedh*) over His Word to perform it. In Amos, the prophet sees 'a basket of summer fruit' (*qayiṣ*); and the meaning of the vision is that 'the end (*qeṣ*) is come upon my people Israel'. So Jesus sets the Child (*talya*) in the midst of His disciples, and teaches them that true greatness consists in becoming the servant (*talya*) of all.

The 'incident' is thus a true *mashal*, an enigmatic comparison requiring interpretation; and it is at the same time gnomic, containing or leading up to the *sententia*.[2]

That this may well put the Ariadne's thread of the teaching of Jesus on the Child into our hands can be supported by other evidence.

[1] In Aramaic, *man d^{e}la m^{e}qabbel malkuth '^{e}laha hekh talya likka 'allel lah.*

[2] The Parable proper may have had its origin in the 'riddle' or *ḥidha*. Cf. *H.D.B.* iii, pp. 660 ff. The rabbis relate a number of parables 'concerning a king' and each is known as *mashal l^{e}melekh*, 'parable with reference to a king'. Jesus' Parable is a *mashal* (or *math^{e}la*) *l^{e}talya*, 'parable with reference to a child'.

So far as the equivalence of παιδίον and *talya* is concerned, the reader who knows no Aramaic may have no misgivings (*talitha*, κοράσιον [Mk. v. 51] is the fem.). But the real test of the worth of this theory of the incident as a dramatized pun comes when we ask: Can it be shown that Mark's διάκονος also in ix. 35b goes back to this same Aramaic word? If evidence can be given that it does, then the acted play on words, if not a virtual certainty (certainty it could never be till we possessed the Aramaic teaching), becomes, at any rate, free from reasonable doubts.

A comparison of the sayings-group on service as the true greatness in Mk. x. 43 ff. with Lk. xxii. 24 ff. reveals, not only that the Lucan version is fuller and shows traces of being independent of Mark, but also that Luke is incorporating into his Gospel a different Greek translation of the Aramaic teaching from that used by Mark.[1] Whereas Mt. xx. 25 ff. simply reproduces Mark, Luke contains a number of Synoptic variants which display all the characteristics of being different translations of the same underlying Aramaic. Thus we find Mark's μέγας = Luke's μείζων (*rabba*); πρῶτος = ἡγούμενος (*rish*); δοῦλος = διακονῶν (*'abhda*): and, more particularly to our present purpose, Mark's διάκονος = Luke's νεώτερος. These last two variants can be satisfactorily explained in the light of one common original only, namely, *talya*.[2] We need not hesitate, therefore, in assuming this word as the original behind the Marcan διάκονος at ix. 35.

It may be conceded that in the original Aramaic story and teaching this same word *talya* was used for both παιδίον and διάκονος, and yet at the same time be maintained that no importance is to be attached to the fact; it is simply coincidence

[1] For a discussion of some of Luke's additions with reference to Aramaic see *infra*, pp. 228 ff.

[2] The word means 'infant', 'child', or 'youth', 'servant' (cf. Gael. *gille*, *gillie*); the Pal. Syr. renders νεώτερος at Jn. xxi. 18 by this word: it similarly renders παῖς, 'servant' in the story of the Centurion's Servant, and in the Servant passages of Isaiah; cf. also Jer. xxx. 10. The ambiguity of *talya* is, of course, shared by παῖς, and παιδίον is found meaning 'a young slave lad' (Aristophanes, *Ran.* 32, *Nub.* 137). But there can be no question of such a meaning for it in Mk. ix. 35–37; Mark clearly means 'child'.

and no play on words was ever intended. The answer to such an objection is to ask: What did Jesus teach about greatness in the Kingdom of God? In what did it consist? Mark gives the answer in his words πάντων διάκονος (*talya*). The idea of service is central to the teaching, and if Jesus took a child (*talya*) in such a connexion and set him in the midst, then any suggestion of coincidence in the use of the common word can scarcely be entertained.[1]

Other interpretations of the Parable of the Child are not excluded by such a suggestion. Indeed, the sheer genius of the Parable lies in the singular appropriateness of a Child to convey, not only a primary lesson on true greatness as humblest service, but secondary and related teaching—that the 'first' should become 'last', the 'greatest' the 'least' (cf. Luke's μικρότερος). Matthew's 'Except ye be converted and become as little children' does, however, suggest a later reflective interpretation. His saying about 'humbling oneself' ὡς τὸ παιδίον τοῦτο, however, perhaps takes on an even profounder meaning if *talya*, 'servant', and not 'child' lies behind it. The difficulty would then be the deictic τοῦτο. If not original, is it Matthaean interpretation? It is always possible, too, that the 'child' in question was really a humble *famulus*, perhaps the humblest of all the 'boys' in the household at Capernaum, which some think was Peter's. Can it have been such a *servulus* whom Jesus 'summoned' (Mark's ἐφώνησε as an echo of the true tradition preserved in Matthew's προσκαλεσάμενος παιδίον)?

But the main emphasis in Jesus' teaching on Christian greatness does lie, on such a reading of the Parable of the Child in the Midst, upon the humblest service. Mark alone has preserved the primitive tradition and original point of the Parable.

Mk. xiv. *3* (cf. Jn. xii. *3*)

'And being in Bethany in the house of Simon the leper, as he sat at meat, there came a woman having an alabaster box of ointment of spikenard (ἀλάβαστρον μύρου νάρδου πιστικῆς) very precious; and she brake the box, and poured it on his head.'

[1] For Jesus' employment of the pun in teaching see *supra*, pp. 160 ff.

There are objections to taking the adjective πιστικός in the sense of 'genuine, real', as opposed to 'adulterated, artificial', of an ointment or perfume. The derivation from πίνειν, 'liquid', is also difficult. Various alternatives have been proposed: Wetstein noted that the Romans knew of a costly ointment called σπίκατον, used by wealthy Roman ladies, and he suggested that πιστικ in πιστικῆς had arisen by a scribal error from the first two syllables of σπίκατον.[1] Similarly, πιστικῆς has been explained as a corruption of σπειστικῆς.[2]

In his *Horae Hebraicae* Lightfoot cited Pliny for the composition of *nardinum*, the nard perfume, oil, or ointment of the ancients: along with five other ingredients it contained, or rather was probably contained in, *balaninum*, the fluid oil or liquid ointment extracted from the ben nut.[3] The latter is also called *myrobalanum*, balanine ointment, by Pliny, who says that it was to be found in southern Palestine.[4] The fluid extract of the *balanus, the* nut, i.e. the ben nut, was no doubt the most important ingredient, next to the precious nard itself, in *nardinum*; it is used as a liquid solvent for perfumes; it is itself odourless and is much prized by perfumers for its great powers of retaining the most fugitive odours.[5]

Lightfoot suggested that *myrobalanum* was a possible name for the nard ointment used by Mary, *nard* and *myrobalanum* being the chief ingredients. It is significant that it was a fluid ointment which Mary poured over the feet of Jesus. It may be that the less costlier kinds of nard were called *myrobalanum*, receiving their name from the chief ingredient; the price probably varied with the number of the other ingredients and the quantity of nard contained.

Myrobalanum is the oil or fluid ointment of the *balanus*, μύρον βαλάνου, the ben nut or pistachio nut, which, in Aramaic, is פיסתקא: Lightfoot cited the Babylonian Talmud, *Gittin*, 69.

[1] In his Commentary on Mark, in loc.

[2] *Z.N.T.W.* iii, p. 169 f.

[3] Vol. ii, p. 446; Pliny, Book 13. 1.

[4] Book 12. 21. For βαλάνου μύρον see Josephus, *Antiquities* (ed. Niese), ii, § 118.

[5] Watt, *Dictionary of the Economic Products of India.*

1, *Kethub.* 17. 2, but the word is also to be found in the Palestinian Talmud, *Demai*, ii, f. 22*b*, 8 lines from foot; *Kila'im*, i. 4, f. 27*a*, line 52; *Ma'asroth*, i. 2, f. 48*d*, 11 lines from foot. Myrobalanum would be in Aramaic 'ointment of pistachio', perhaps *mura pistaqa.*[1] For a translator who was not familiar with the Aramaic name, *pistaqa* would present difficulties. Was it simply transliterated, and then taken into the sentence as an adjective πιστικῆς?

Mk. xiv. *41*

'And he cometh the third time, and saith unto them, Sleep on now, and take your rest: it is enough (ἀπέχει), the hour is come; behold, the Son of man is betrayed into the hands of sinners.'

The *crux* of this verse is well-known: ἀπέχει is used with a very rare meaning and one which is not really adequate to the context. It has been suggested that an Aramaic *kaddu*, '*Already* the hour is come', was given the Syriac meaning *satis* by the translator.[2] But any translator who was capable of rendering *kaddu* here by *satis* can have had little knowledge of either Palestinian Aramaic or Syriac, for the word in both dialects means *iam*. For this mistranslation we are required to assume that in translating his Aramaic the translator passed over the usual meanings of the adverb and went out of his way to give it a less common and much less suitable meaning in the context. Moreover, even if this were credible, how are we to account for the selection of so rare a verb as ἀπέχειν for *satis est*?

The manuscript tradition of the sentence after ἀπέχει varies: D has ἀπέχει τὸ τέλος καὶ ἡ ὥρα, which means, 'far-off is the end and the hour', the very opposite of what the context requires. If, however, we render this unsuitable Greek sentence into Aramaic, a solution of the problem of ἀπέχει suggests itself. The sentence would read, 'procul abest (רחיק) finis et hora'. A quite different Aramaic verb is דחיק, written with initial Dalath; it means 'to press', 'to urge'; it renders, e.g., compounds of θλίβειν and synonyms in the Palestinian Syriac version of Mk. v. 24,

[1] The Bezan text of John omits νάρδου and reads πιστικῆς μύρου, occurring in the Old Latin in the order *unguentum pistici* (myrobalanum?).

[2] *Our Translated Gospels*, p. 56 f.

31; Lk. viii. 42, 45. It is a well-known Jewish Aramaic verb and, in addition to its literal meaning, has in several places a derived and metaphorical sense, e.g. in the Jerusalem Targum II of Exod. xxii. 24 of a creditor 'pressing' or 'dunning' his debtor, or in Exod. iii. 9, in the same Targum, of 'pressing' with arguments, 'urging', 'persuading'. A proverb from the Babylonian Talmud (*Berach.* 64*a*) gives an exact parallel to the sense required for Mk. xiv. 41: it is written in Mishnaic Hebrew and may be translated literally, 'He who tries to press the hour, him the hour presses (הדוחק את השעה השעה דוחקתו).' For the Hebrew phrase 'the time is pressing' (העת דחוק) see Jacob Mann, *The Jews in Egypt under the Fatimid Caliphs*, ii, p. 110. The general meaning is that on him who tries to command the hour to yield him what he wants from it, the hour (time, fate) itself comes to press hard; the noun *d*ᵉ*ḥoq* is 'oppression' and renders ἀνάγκη in the Palestinian Syriac of Lk. xiv. 18.

This verb and sense fit admirably the context of Mk. xiv. 41, 'The end and the hour *are pressing*'; we have the same metaphor when we speak of time 'pressing'. And the mistranslation assumes no more than the misreading by a translator of a Dalath as a Rish, giving the verb *r*ᵉ*ḥeq*, ἀπέχει.[1]

Luke

Lk. xx. 34

'And Jesus answering said unto them, The children of this world marry, and are given in marriage.'

(D) 'And Jesus answering said unto them, The children of this world *are born and beget children* (γεννῶνται καὶ γεννῶσι), marry and are given in marriage.'

A different form of the Western 'interpolation' appears in the Old Syriac:

The children of this world *bear and beget children* (*yaldin w*ᵉ*mauldin*), Marry and are given in marriage.

The order of the verbs in the first clause is reversed in Irenaeus

[1] Perhaps the original read, 'The end is pressing, (and) the hour has come.'

and Cyprian and in the Old Latin MSS. *a, c, e, l.*[1] Following this order, with the Old Syriac reading, we get an exact parallelism of clauses:

The children of this world beget and bear children,
Marry and are given in marriage.

The natural order of the lines would be:

The children of this world marry and are given in marriage,
Beget and bear children,

but that order has no manuscript attestation of much weight.[2]

F. C. Burkitt was inclined to regard the 'interpolation' of D as a genuine part of the saying of Jesus.[3] The reconstructed parallelism (restored on the basis of attested readings) may be urged in support of his view. Moreover, the peculiar form of the Bezan addition may be shown to have arisen in an attempt to translate Aramaic 'bear and beget children', *yal^edhin umol^edhin*: a translator of these words would have two alternatives: the first, to render the first participle by its natural equivalent in Greek leads to the (in Greek only) incongruous *οἱ υἱοὶ τοῦ αἰῶνος τούτου τίκτουσι καὶ γεννῶσι*; he could avert the difficulty by rendering the first verb by a passive *γεννῶνται* (ילדין read as יִלִידִין), thus retaining the same word in both cases as in the Aramaic.[4] But by such a translation both sense and parallelism are seriously impaired.

The words form an appropriate, if not integral, part of the saying. They may also have been in the original of the parallel verses 35, 36: the children of the resurrection neither marry nor are given in marriage, neither beget nor bear children, but are themselves the children of God.

[1] F. C. Burkitt (*Evangelion da-Mepharreshe*, ii, p. 299) tried to defend the Old Syriac as a rendering of D in the order of Irenaeus, Cyprian, and the Old Latin, *yaldin* = *γεννῶσι*, *mauldin* = *γεννῶνται*, the latter a passive participle Aphel. But this is against Semitic usage, where the simple form of the verb, *iledh* is reserved for the woman, 'to bear children', and the Aphel *'aulēdh*, for the man, 'to beget'. Cf. F. H. Chase, *Syro-Latin Text of the Gospels*, p. 55 f.

[2] One MS. only, Gregory 1093, but in the 'Ferrar' Group.

[3] l.c.

[4] It is less likely that ילידין, with the short vowel of the participle represented *plene* by *Yodh*, was mistranslated by a passive.

Lk. xxiii. 17

'For of necessity (ἀνάγκην δὲ εἶχεν) he must release one unto them at the feast.'

Modern editions omit this verse altogether, mainly on exegetical grounds; there was no one to compel Pilate; his word was law. Some prefer to place the verse after verse 19 where it is found in D, and Huck, in his synopsis, goes so far as to restore in Greek the variant 'was accustomed' (εἰώθει) of the Old Syriac, which has been harmonized here with Matthew.

Luke uses the phrase ἀνάγκην ἔχειν earlier at xiv. 18, where the Palestinian Syriac version renders it by *d^{e}ḥoq*, an Aramaic word already discussed.[1] Using this word, we may translate xxiii. 17, 'And there was necessity (דחוק) to him at the feast to release one unto them . . .' The Matthaean parallel reads, 'Now at that feast the governor was wont (εἰώθει) to release unto the people a prisoner . . .' The idea of a statutory custom, the 'law' of a feast, is expressed in Hebrew by *ḥoq*. The word is not used in Aramaic, but is common in all strata of Hebrew literature, as the regular legal term; it is employed in connexion with a 'feast' in Ps. lxxxi. 4. If we translate Matthew into Aramaic, using the Hebrew legal term, we get: 'Now it was statutory custom (חוק) at the feast that (ד) the governor should release unto the people a prisoner . . .'

Lk. xxii. 27 (D)

'For whether is greater, he that sitteth at meat, or he that serveth? is not he that sitteth at meat? but I am among you as he that serveth.'

The Bezan text omits the first question and has the second question in the form μᾶλλον ἢ ὁ ἀνακείμενος; the rest of the verse according to WH is contained in D within a sentence which reads:

> ἐγὼ γὰρ ἐν μέσῳ ὑμῶν ἦλθον οὐχ ὡς ὁ
> ἀνακείμενος, ἀλλ' ὡς ὁ διακονῶν καὶ ὑμεῖς ηὐξήθητε
> ἐν τῇ διακονίᾳ μου ὡς ὁ διακονῶν.

The words τίς γὰρ μείζων, ὁ ἀνακείμενος ἢ ὁ διακονῶν appear to have

[1] *Supra*, p. 225.

been omitted through a scribal error. The second question in D is unintelligible as it stands, but preceded by *ὁ διάκονος* (*διακονῶν*), perhaps omitted by haplography, it gives a parallel question:

Which is greater, the guest or the servant?
(*man* **rabba rabhᵉʿa** *'e ʿabhda*)
(D) Is the servant (greater) than the guest?
(*ma ʿabhda yattir min* **rabhᵉʿa**)

The words *μᾶλλον ἤ* reflect the Aramaism *yattir min* in comparison; cf. the Targum of Job vii. 6, 'My days are swifter than (*yattir min*) a weaver's shuttle.'[1] The paronomasia, *rabba*, *rabhᵉʿa*, will be noted.[2]

The sentence from *καὶ ὑμεῖς ηὐξήθητε* does not make sense in Greek, and that is probably why the words have been removed from other texts. But it makes admirable sense in Aramaic, once *ηὐξήθητε* (רביתון) has been recognized as the result of a misreading or misunderstanding of רבעתון; the two words would readily be confused in writing, and even more readily in oral transmission, with the falling away in pronunciation of the guttural. The paronomasia in the passage, *rabba* (*μείζων*) and *rabhᵉʿa* (*ὁ ἀνακείμενος*), may have contributed to the confusion, or a pun with *rᵉbhithon* (*ηὐξήθητε*) have been originally intended. With the reading *rᵉbhaʿton* we obtain two full lines in synonymous parallelism:

I came among you, not as guest, but as servant
(*'ᵃna 'ᵃtheth benathkhon la kᵉ***rabhᵉʿa** *'ella kᵉʿabhda*),
And *ye have been the guests at table*, while I served as servant
(*wᵉ' attun* **rᵉbhaʿton** *bᵉʿobhadhi kᵉʿabhda*).

A comparison of WH with D suggests that the former represents a rearranged abbreviation of the latter; the words *οὐχ* (*ὡς*) *ὁ ἀνακείμενος* have been taken from the sentence in which they make good sense in D to replace, as a question, the unintelligible *μᾶλλον ἢ ὁ ἀνακείμενος*.

Lk. xxii. *16*

'For I say unto you, I will not any more eat thereof, until it be

[1] *Einl.*², p. 21.

[2] *Supra*, p. 173.

fulfilled in the kingdom of God' (ἕως ὅτου πληρωθῇ ἐν τῇ βασιλείᾳ τοῦ θεοῦ).[1]

The most likely view of this verse is that it is to be understood in the light of verses 29, 30—'And I appoint unto you a kingdom . . . that ye may eat and drink at my table in my kingdom.' Luke's Passover is in some way to be regarded as 'prophetic' of the Messianic Feast in the heavenly Kingdom, in which it will find its perfect 'fulfilment'.

But Luke is dependent on sources, and we cannot be certain that the saying about the Messianic Feast in verse 30, which concludes the teaching about priority among the disciples, was actually spoken by our Lord on the same occasion as the Words of the Last Supper. The 'priority' incident in Mark (x. 35–45) occurs in a quite different connexion—before the Triumphal Entry. Luke's arrangement of the incident is editorial, and his introduction of ideas about a Messianic Feast in this chapter is probably due to Mark, where there is an explicit reference in the Words of Jesus Himself at the Last Supper to a coming Messianic Feast.

There is, therefore, justification for considering verse 16 without reference to verse 30 as a possibly genuine tradition of a Word of Jesus, incorporated by Luke from his special source in his Gospel, and interpreted by him in the connexion in which he has placed the words in his account of the Last Supper.

By itself, verse 16 may not contain any reference to a Messianic Feast: πληρωθῇ may perhaps be taken as reflecting a Semitic impersonal or 'internal' passive where the real subject, which is thus emphasized, is contained in the verb.[2] The latter may then be connected, not with the preceding Passover, but with its following predicate, 'in the kingdom of God'. The main subject of the clause, and indeed of the whole verse, would then be, not the Passover at all, but 'the fulfilment in the kingdom of God': 'I will not any more eat thereof, until there is a fulfilment

[1] 'Die so schwerwiegenden und bedeutungsvollen Abendmahlsworte müssen auf jedem Fall auch darauf hin angesehen werden, wie sie in der Ursprache gelautet haben mögen.' Meyer, *Jesu Muttersprache*, p. 90.

[2] For an example, see Burney on 1 *Kings* ii. 21, in *Notes on the Hebrew Text of the Book of Kings* (Oxford, 1903), p. 20; cf. *Ges.-Kautzsch*, § 121, 1, p. 387.

in the kingdom of God.' The verse then becomes parallel to the saying over the wine: 'I will not drink of the fruit of the vine, until the kingdom of God shall come.'

There is support for this view. The Sinaitic Syriac renders, 'until the kingdom of God *is fulfilled*'. If a variant ἡ βασιλεία τοῦ θεοῦ ever existed, no trace of it has survived outside of Syriac tradition.[1] But it is arguable that this is the true text of the passage, so far as the original saying of Jesus is concerned, Luke's ἐν τῇ βασιλείᾳ τοῦ θεοῦ coming from Mark.[2] In Greek tradition an echo of such an understanding of the verse is to be found in the Epiklesis of the Liturgy of St. Chrysostom: the Bread and the Wine, as the communion of the Body and the Blood of Christ, are to be, for the participants, '. . . unto the remission of sins (Mt. xxvi. 28), unto the fellowship of Thy Holy Spirit, *unto the Kingdom's fulfilment* (εἰς βασιλείας πλήρωμα).'[3]

If there was such an original meaning behind πληρωθῇ, what was the nature of 'the fulfilment' in the Kingdom of God? Was it a fulfilment of prophecy (cf. verse 37)? Or was it a realization of the Kingdom itself? The idea of a fulfilment or consummation of the Age by the coming of the Messianic Kingdom is a familiar one in contemporary Judaism: in the Syriac Apocalypse of Baruch (xxx. 3) it is made clear that the coming of the Messianic Age was expressly known and referred to as 'the fulfilment' or 'the consummation' of the times; it is there connected with the end of the reign of the Messiah upon earth and His return to Heaven. In 1 Enoch 'the consummation' (xvi. 1, τελείωσις) is in the Great Judgement.[4] In His last hours Jesus

[1] A relic of the reading is found in the Palestinian Syriac version (Cod. B and C).

[2] Lietzmann (*Messe und Herrenmahl*, p. 215) is convinced that Luke took these words from Mark, but he also believes that the whole saying is Lucan interpretation and not a genuine saying of Jesus.

[3] Swainson, *Greek Liturgies*, p. 92.

[4] There are many such passages referring to the Fulfilment: in the Assumption of Moses (i. 18), 'the consummation of the end of the days' is to be preceded by a general repentance (cf. Mk. i. 15); the Pirke R. Eliezer (xliii) preserves the contemporary belief that 'Israel will not fulfil the great repentance before Elijah comes'; for Jesus, Elijah had already come; the Fulfilment was imminent. Cf. Lk. xix. 11. Cf. also J. Jeremias, *Gleichnisreden Jesu*[6] (1962), p. 151, n. 5 (*das eschatologische Mass* (πλήρωμα)).

may have been looking for just such a consummation of the Age in a heavenly Kingdom, brought about by the Advent of Himself as Son of Man, coming in power and with judgement (cf. Mk. xiv. 61, 62).

But in the Apocalyptic and rabbinical literature, the Kingdom itself is never referred to as being or about to be 'fulfilled', as in the Old Syriac version of Luke; the Fulfilment is always of 'the Age' or 'the times'. The usual expression is that the Kingdom 'comes' or 'is revealed'.[1] This may account for the unusual 'until *it is fulfilled in* the kingdom of God', the meaning being 'until there is the Fulfilment of the Age in the kingdom of God'. But if this was what was intended, we should expect it to have been more clearly expressed and not left so indefinite that the words could be taken in a quite different meaning and connexion.

In Aramaic there are several expressions which would correspond to πληρωθῆναι in its different uses: *'ithqayyam*[2] is used of the 'fulfilment' of prophecy, and *'ishtᵉlam* is the verb employed by the Syriac versions to render Lk. xxii. 16. There is, however, a third verb, corresponding to πληροῦν in its less common meaning, 'to finish perfectly', 'to complete'[3]: it is the Semitic *k l l*, used in Aramaic in the causative Shaphel and its passive in the sense 'to make perfect' and so simply 'to complete' of any piece of work[4]: the word is used of the 'perfection of beauty' in both Hebrew and Targum of Ezek. xxvii. 3 and xxviii. 12; the causative Shaphel renders κατασκευάζειν in Isa. xliii. 7 in the Palestinian Syriac of God's 'fashioning' of His servant.

It is doubtful whether this word could ever have been employed of the 'perfecting finishing' of the Kingdom of God, in the sense of its perfect realization. It may not be altogether impossible; *k l l* has special associations in both Hebrew and Aramaic with the 'perfect finishing' of the work of Creation.[5] Similarly, in Lk. xxii. 16, the meaning may perhaps be 'until it is perfectly

[1] *Worte Jesu*, p. 82 f.

[2] *Jesus-Jeschua*, p. 119.

[3] See J. B. Lightfoot, *Colossians*, p. 225.

[4] The causative *shakhlel* renders ἐξαρτίζειν in the Palestinian Syriac version of Exod. xxviii. 7; cf. Ezra iv. 12, v. 11, vi. 14, and for the passive, iv. 13, 16, 'to be completed' (of walls).

[5] *Genesis Rabbah*, 10, and Targum, Gen. ii. 1.

finished in (ב, Beth Essentiae) the kingdom of God', i.e. 'until the kingdom of God is perfectly completed'.

In two other intensive forms, the Pael and its passive Ithpaal, the verb *k l l* is used in Aramaic in the sense of 'to crown', 'to be crowned'; *'ithkallal* renders στεφανοῦσθαι in the Palestinian Syriac version of 2 Tim. ii. 5. The Ethpaal in Syriac means 'to be crowned with martyrdom'; it is used in exactly the same way as τελειοῦσθαι of the 'perfection' attained by the saint or martyr in death.[1]

There is no passage hitherto adduced from Palestinian Aramaic for the use of *k l l* with this meaning, but Lk. xiii. 32, already discussed in another connexion, makes it very probable that the verb was so used in the Aramaic of first-century Palestine, and by Jesus Himself. Jesus says of Himself in this verse, 'Behold . . . I do (ἀποτελῶ) cures day by day, then one day soon *I am perfected* (τελειοῦμαι).' That the reference was to the 'perfection' of Himself by His death is probable from the context and becomes certain in the light of the parallel, πορεύεσθαι, 'I pass on', i.e. I die.[2] The word-play in the Greek may reflect a similar play on words in the Aramaic; for ἀποτελῶ we may set *shakhlel* and for τελειοῦμαι *'ithkallal*. The Aramaic paronomasia is introduced by the word for ἀλώπηξ, the abusive epithet applied to Herod, and the 'fox' or 'jackal' of Palestine; in Aramaic it is *ta'la*.

Go ye (**hallikhu**) and tell that fox (**ta'la**),
Behold I cast out (**shall^{e}ḥeth** ?) demons and I perform (**shakhl^{e}leth**) cures, day by day;
Then one day soon I am perfected (in death) (**'ithkall^{e}leth**).

If we set the Ithpaal of *k l l* for Luke's πληρωθῇ we get, 'I will not any more eat thereof till it is completed in the kingdom of God' (*la 'ekhol 'odh 'adh d^{e}'ithkall^{e}lath b^{e}malkuth '^{e}laha*). The third person singular feminine perfect אתכללת, πληρωθῇ, may be read as a first person, 'until *I am perfected* (by death) in the kingdom of God'; on this suggestion, the Aramaic should have been rendered, ἕως ὅτου τελειωθῶ ἐν τῇ βασιλείᾳ τοῦ θεοῦ. One Old Latin manuscript *e* reads the first person, *adimplear*. The

[1] *Supra*, p. 206, n. 4.

[2] *Infra*, p. 302.

conjecture gives a characteristic paronomasia, *'ekhol* (φάγω) and *'ithkall^eleth*. Moreover, an original *'ithkall^eleth* can account for the curious Bezan variant βρωθῇ; the latter has arisen through the confusion of the verb *'^akhal* and *k^elal*; an example of the confusion occurs in the LXX of 2 Chron. xxx. 22, ויאכלו, 'and they ate', LXX συνετέλεσαν. In the parallel in Mark, immediately after the Supper, Jesus declared (xiv. 27), 'All ye shall be offended (*kull^ekhon tittaqq^elun*) because of me this night . . .'; we have the same consonants as have been suggested in Lk. xxii. 16 continuing the word-play.

In view of the τελειοῦμαι in a Word of Jesus at Lk. xiii. 32, we do not require to commit ourselves to this conjectured original for πληρωθῇ to go on to ask the question: How may our Lord have conceived of His τελείωσις? Whether, at Lk. xxii. 16 (or at xiii. 32), we may detect the presence of the rabbinical idea of the Rule of God, is difficult to say, for Jesus does not appear to have made much, if any, use of the expression in this way. There is, however, one possible parallel, in addition to Lk. xvii. 21 sometimes claimed in this connexion. In Mk. xii. 28 f. one of the scribes (in Matthew and Luke it is 'a certain lawyer') asked Jesus which was the first commandment of all. Jesus replied by quoting the first part of the *Shema* (Deut. vi. 4–8), the central and primary obligation of the Torah, adding, as the sum of the rest of the commandments, the injunction about loving one's neighbour. The scribe fully approved, and Jesus thereupon declared 'Thou art not far from the kingdom of God'. The Kingdom of Heaven in the rabbinical sense of the Rule of Heaven or the Divine Rule was closely associated with the observance of the Torah and in particular with the *Shema*: the proselyte who receives the Law and the Israelite who obeys it are both said 'to take on themselves the Divine Rule (Kingdom of Heaven)'; 'to take on oneself the yoke of the Divine Rule' comes, in rabbinical language, to be synonymous with 'reciting the *Shema*'.[1] The scribe, in Jesus' view, was not far from the realization of the Divine Rule, but he had not yet attained it, for that depended, for Jesus, on the recognition of a higher Law

[1] *Worte Jesu*, p. 79 f.

than the Law of Moses; and He gives an indication of one aspect of such a Law in the following parable (in Luke) of the Good Samaritan.

The 'I say unto you' of Jesus fulfils the Law of Moses (Mt. v. 17), so that for Jesus Himself, no less than for His disciples, 'to be perfected' in the Divine Rule implied perfect obedience to the higher Law; Jesus' τελείωσις, in the sense of the word in the Epistle to the Hebrews, was the perfection of His obedience unto death; 'I shall not any more eat thereof, until I am perfected in the Rule of God'.

A much less conjectural solution, however, is to connect πληρωθῇ in this sense with 'the Passover' as subject: '. . . I will not any more eat thereof until it (the Passover) is perfected in the kingdom of God'. If we are justified in turning such a passive into an active (cf. J. Jeremias, *Die Abendmahlsworte Jesu*, 2nd edit., pp. 91, 120), we might render 'until God perfects it (or brings it to a perfect end) in the kingdom of God'. The reference in that case would be unmistakably to a Messianic Feast. Hebrew *kalah* is rendered more than once by πληροῦν in the LXX (e.g. 2 Chron. xxiv. 10). Such a meaning would not only suit the context admirably, but would be especially appropriate if we regard these words as a solemn vow, binding the speaker to abstinence until the 'consummation' of the Passover in the Messianic Banquet (cf. Jeremias, p. 118 f.).

The Marcan saying over the wine is even stranger and more difficult than Luke's πληρωθῇ. In verse 25 πίνω καινόν is impossible in Aramaic and can scarcely have been original. The 'new wine' may be explained as a new kind of wine in Greek, but for Semitic ideas it can only be 'new wine' as contrasted with 'old wine', and it is the latter, as a well-known passage in the Targum of the Song of Songs informs us (viii. 2), which is to be drunk at the Messianic Banquet. There is a decided failure in the Greek and no variants to suggest any alternatives.

One hesitates to make any conjecture. But there are several hints to guide us from the parallel saying over the bread. If the reference in Lk. xxii. 16 was to the final 'perfection' of the Passover, what we require in the parallel verse is a cognate idea or expression. That is not given by πίνω καινόν, which is parallel to D's καινὸν βρωθῇ, but not to πληρωθῇ. The word-play in the first saying may point to a similar play on words in the parallel; 'I will not any more drink' is *la 'eshte 'odh*; πίνω καινόν is *'eshte ḥadath*. What we require is a verb parallel to πληρωθῇ and with consonants the same as or similar to the Aramaic of πίνω καινόν.

The parallel is obtained by some form of the verb *ḥadath*, a word specially used of the Ἀνακαίνωσις or 'renewal of all things' in the Messianic Kingdom. That there is a reference to the 'renewed world' in πίνω καινόν has been suggested by Dr. Jeremias (op. cit., p. 122); it would be even more explicit if this verb was originally employed. The πίνω καινόν, moreover, may represent an attempt at translation, though the original word referred to the 'renewal' of the Passover, 'the drinking of the fruit of the vine', and not to a 'drinking of it new' in any bald literal sense. This Aramaic verb is regularly employed for the Ἀνακαίνωσις, 'the renewal' of all things in the Messianic Kingdom[1]; in the Jerusalem Targum of Deut. xxxii. 1 we find both *kalah* and *ḥadath* applied to the heavens and the earth which according to Isa. li. 6 are to be 'finished' (כליין) 'for the world to come', and 'renewed' (לאתחדתא) 'for the world to come'. The 'renewal' of the 'drinking of the fruit of the vine' may thus be similarly interpreted as πληρωθῇ of the coming Messianic Feast.

Note on the Passover and Jewish Messianic Expectations

In his *Abendmahlsworte Jesu*, Dr. J. Jeremias has drawn attention to some Jewish traditions which associate the night of Passover with Jewish Messianic expectations. 'In dieser Nacht kommt der Messias!' (p. 101; cf. Dalman, *Jesus-Jeschua, Ergänzungen und Verbesserungen*, p. 9 f.). 'In this night they were delivered and in it they will be delivered' is a saying attributed in the Mechilta on Exod. xii. 42 to R. Joshua b. Hananya (*fl. c.* A.D. 90). 'The Messiah who is called the First

[1] The Targum of Micah vii. 14 speaks of 'the world that is about to be renewed'; the idea is a commonplace of Messianic Judaism; cf. 2 Baruch xliv. 12, lvii. 2; 1 Enoch xlv. 4, lxxii. 1; in 2 Baruch xxxii. 1–4, the 'renewal of all things' follows the 'perfection' or 'consummation' of the present age. Cf. further, *Worte Jesu*, p. 145, and in the New Testament, Mt. xix. 28, 2 Cor. v. 17, Gal. vi. 15, 2 Peter iii. 13, Rev. xxi. 5.

(Isa. xli. 27; cf. Jn. viii. 25) will come in the first month (Nisan)' is from Exod. rabb. 15. 2. And St. Jerome tells us: 'Traditio Judaeorum est Christum media nocte venturum in similitudinem Aegyptii temporis, quando pascha celebratum est.' (Jeremias, l.c.)

In view of this it is of special interest to find in one Aramaic Passover *haggada* an allusion to Dan. vii. 13 in connexion with the Messiah. The poem is called 'The Four Nights', and is to be found at Exod. xii. 42 (F) (in some texts at Exod. xv. 18 (cf. Ginsburger, p. 36)). The 'Four Nights', said 'to be written in the Book of Memorials', are nights on which God (so Ginsburger's text) revealed Himself or will reveal Himself to Israel; and it is clear from Pseudo-Jonathan that they are all nights of 15th Nisan. The first was the Night of Creation, the second the Night of the Covenant with Abraham, the third is the Night of the deliverance from Egypt, and

The Fourth Night, when the world shall have consummated its end to be delivered:
The bands of iniquity will be destroyed and the bonds of iron will be broken;
Moses will come forth from the desert, and King Messiah will come forth from Rome (? מרומה)*;*
The one will lead forth on the summit of a cloud and the other will lead forth on the summit of a cloud(?)
And the Memra of Jahweh will lead between them; and they shall go together.

The 'leading forth' of the people by the Messiah and Moses and the 'cloud' motif are reminiscent of the deliverance from Egypt. Dalman is probably right, however, in detecting a further allusion to Dan. vii. 13 (*Worte Jesu*, p. 201).

It is exceedingly difficult to date these poetic pieces in the Palestinian Targum (cf. my note on 'The Aramaic Liturgical Poetry of the Jews', *infra*, p. 305). It seems to me unlikely, however, that the Jewish association of 15th Nisan with the inauguration of the Messianic Age can be later than Christianity; Christian associations with that historic date would certainly make it difficult for Jews of a later time to centre their Messianic hopes on a day and month which had become so prominent in the Christian calendar.

Dr. Kahle writes that he has consulted Dr. J. Weinberg (Montreux) who has replied: 'Der Gedanke von der Erscheinung des Messias in dieser Nacht befindet sich auch im Midrash Rabba zur Stelle, und auch in den andern Midraschim. Ich teile nicht Ihre Ansicht, daß dieser Gedanke vom Erscheinen des Messias am 15ten Nisan aus der Zeit vor der Zerstörung des Tempels stammen muß. Dagegen spricht, daß im Piut gesagt wird, daß Moses von der Wüste kommen wird und der Messias von Rom. Die Verbindung von Moschiach mit der Stadt Rom ist sicher auf die Zeit der völligen Vernichtung Judaeas durch Rom zurückzuführen (siehe Traktat Sanhedrin 98a, wo es heißt: R. Jehoschua ben Levi fragte den Propheten Elia wann kommt der Moschiach, und wo befindet er sich jetzt. Er antwortete ihm, Er befindet sich im Stadttor von Rom (die Zensur hat das Wort Rom gestrichen) unter den armkranken Leuten).'

The appearance of the Messiah 'from Rome' and 'on the summit of a cloud' are somewhat incongruous conceptions, so that we may well wonder if the original reading was not ממרומא 'from on high'. It may even be possible that מרומה ought to be so interpreted.

The Original Language of the Last Supper

In his *Jesus-Jeschua* Dalman expressed the view that the Words of Institution of the Lord's Supper may have been originally uttered in Hebrew rather than Aramaic; he was impressed by the fact that 'in der jüdischen Literatur, abgesehen von den Targumen, ein aramäischer Ersatz für *berit* nirgends auftritt. Nur hebräisch ist davon die Rede. Daraus könnte gefolgert werden, daß Jesus sein Deutewort zum Wein, somit auch das Deutewort zum Brote und die Benediction beider, hebräisch gesprochen hätte. Es wäre auch kühn, völlig auszuschließen, daß Jesus in solchen Fällen sich der heiligen Sprache bediente.'[1]

Several reasons from the texts themselves may be urged in support of a Hebrew original: they contain two 'Hebraisms', Lk. xxii. 15, ἐπιθυμίᾳ ἐπεθύμησα,[2] Mk. xiv. 25 οὐ μὴ προσθῶ πεῖν D *a d f* arm, οὐ μὴ προσθῶμεν πιεῖν, Θ.[3] Dr. Jeremias draws

[1] p. 148. [2] Ibid., p. 116.

[3] Cf. Jeremias, *Abendmahlsworte Jesu*², p. 93 (note 6).

attention to the inclusive sense of πολλοί; it is the equivalent of the rabbinical *rabbim*, going back to Isa. liii. 11, 12; 'many' is practically equivalent to 'all'. But does this apply if an Aramaic *sagi'in* lies behind πολλοί? No doubt, in view of the allusion to Isa. liii. 11, 12, the Aramaic word could take on the inclusive sense of *rabbim*. The allusion would have been much more impressive, however, in Hebrew, while the inclusive meaning of *rabbim* would then be in no doubt.

Dalman maintained that 'die Wahl der verwandten Sprache in diesem Fall (Word over the Wine) keinen sachlichen Unterschied bedeutet'. Is this also the case with the Word over the Bread? One of the reasons which induced Dr. Jeremias to reject the Pauline 'addition' τὸ ὑπὲρ ὑμῶν (1 Cor. xi. 24) was that, though perhaps possible in Hebrew (Schniewind), it was impossible in Aramaic.[1] Some may feel that even this brief (and somewhat abrupt) *Deutewort* is necessary, and that the parallelism with the words over the wine calls for an even fuller form of words.

Are any of the traditional 'expansions' capable of being rendered back into Hebrew (or Aramaic)? Dalman regarded the Lucan τὸ διδόμενον as a possible original, but thought that the readings at 1 Cor. xi. 24 D* θρυπτόμενον, F G K etc. it sy κλώμενον only added to our difficulties, since an Aramaic *mithqᵉse* (κλώμενον) could hardly be used in connexion with *guphi* (τὸ σῶμά μου). This is probably true,[2] nor in that case could this technical term for the breaking of the *maṣṣoth* be employed in connexion with *garmi* (Meyer) or *biṣri* (Jeremias). But there is no objection to taking another term for the breaking of the *maṣṣoth*, viz. *paraṣ*, with any of the Hebrew terms for 'body'. Indeed there is prophetic precedent at Mic. iii. 3. If the 'expansion' is to be rejected, it must be on textual grounds.[3]

[1] Ibid., p. 82 (note 4).

[2] But cf. Sy^{vg} 1 Cor. xi. 24.

[3] The commoner term is Heb. *baṣa'*, a word which is also used figuratively, e.g. Job vi. 9 of 'dissevering (from life)' (par. *widhak'eni*, 'and crush me'); cf. Isa. liii. 5. Heb. *paṣa'* means 'to wound', and has a pass. partc. *paṣuᵃ'*, Deut. xxiii. 2; cf. Joel ii. 8 and RVmarg. Aram. *bᵉza'* (another form of the same root) means 'to pierce' (= *mᵉḥolal*, Isa. liii. 5). Greek κλάω has also such wider uses, e.g. Plut. 2. 1138C ('broken limbs').

John

Jn. xi. 33. (38)

'When Jesus therefore saw her weeping, and the Jews also weeping which came with her, he groaned in his spirit, and was troubled' (ἐνεβριμήσατο τῷ πνεύματι καὶ ἐτάραξεν ἑαυτόν).

Torrey's suggestion that the unusual ἐμβριμᾶσθαι is to be explained in the light of Semitic *r g z* has been welcomed for its solution of the exegetical problem raised by John's Greek: the Semitic verb may be used of any deep emotional disturbance; when David heard the news of the death of his son Absalom, 'the king *was deeply moved* (*ragaz*), and went up to the chamber over the gate, weeping and lamenting as he went' (2 Sam. xix. 1 or xviii. 33).[1]

An objection, however, may be raised to the assumed equivalence of Aramaic *r^egaz* with the rare ἐμβριμᾶσθαι; the Greek verb is a very strong one, meaning literally 'to snort with rage', whereas, while the Aramaic verb is also used of strong anger, its usual equivalent in the LXX is ὀργίζεσθαι. If *r^egaz* was the original, why did a translator go out of his way to select so unusual an expression in Greek? Another strange feature of the Greek is the combination ἐνεβριμήσατο τῷ πνεύματι. The expression emphasizes the turmoil of emotion within Jesus, apparently a violent rage, and it is not to be overlooked.

This association of τῷ πνεύματι with this Greek verb raises a philological problem that takes priority to the exegetical. The phrase 'he fumed with rage in his spirit' is a most extraordinary one in Greek. A valuable study of the verb by Friedrich Gumlich makes it clear that the only meaning which ἐμβριμᾶσθαι can have is that of expressing 'einen starken oder stärksten Grad des Zorns . . . der eben wegen dieser Stärke umfähig sich im innern zu halten, nach aussen ausbricht, jedoch sich in unarticulirten Lauten mehr als Worten Luft macht'.[2] Yet the addition of τῷ πνεύματι makes the last part of this meaning impossible,

[1] *Our Translated Gospels*, pp. 39, 41–3, 80; *Harvard Theological Review*, xvi, p. 330 f.; cf. E. Littmann, in *Z.N.T.W.* xxxiii, p. 25.

[2] 'Die Räthsel der Erweckung Lazari', in *Studien und Kritiken*, i, p. 248 f.

for the violent rage is suppressed, not expressed, as in all other instances of the verb. We have to do with an apparently Johannine use of the Greek word; and this points to translation or to 'the hampering influence of a foreign idiom'.

The foreign idiom in question is a Syriac one: the combination of the Greek verb ἐμβριμᾶσθαι with τῷ πνεύματι is impossible, but the same expression is an idiomatic one in Syriac. The Syriac verb corresponding to ἐμβριμᾶσθαι is *'az* in the intensive Ethpaal form *'eth'azaz*; it is this Syriac verb which renders (προσ)εμβριμᾶσθαι in Sir. xiii. 3, Dan. xi. 30; the verb is the strongest one that Syriac has and is in common use, e.g., of paroxysmal rage, in *Acta Martyrum* (ed. Assemani, Rome, 1748), i. 112, 217; ii. 72, 76, 79, 85, 106, 117, &c.; *Ephrem Syrus* (ed. Rome), iii, xxxi (translated *vehementer stomachari*). In the combination with either *b^eruḥa* (in spirit) or *b^enaphsha* (in soul) a number of examples will be found in Payne-Smith's *Thesaurus Syriacus*; thus from Assemani's *Bibliotheca Orientalis*, ii. 233, 'he quivered with rage in his spirit'. The strange Johannine expression which causes so much difficulty in Greek is a 'Syriacism'.[1]

In Syriac *'eth'azaz b^eruḥa* has a much wider significance than its translation equivalent in Greek. In the Syriac *History of John of Ephesus* there is a passage where it means 'to take heart' (*sich ermannen*): 'The Lord roused the spirit of John . . . to raise up and to care for the Church of the Lord. And that Saint *took heart* and spoke up to his fellow-bishops, saying . . .'[2] In Mk. viii. 12 it renders ἀναστενάξας ἐν πνεύματι in the Old Syriac; Merx thought that there was a genuine variant, *er ergrimmte in seinem Geiste*, behind the Syriac,[3] but the Syriac verb is no more than a translation of the Greek, meaning 'he was deeply moved' and hence 'he groaned in spirit'; the emotion is one of bitter disillusionment. In Jn. xiii. 21 the same Syriac expression renders ἐταράχθη τῷ πνεύματι in the Peshiṭta. Here

[1] See further my note in the *Transactions of the Glasgow University Oriental Society*, xi (1946), pp. 50 ff.

[2] J. P. N. Land's *Anecdota Syriaca*, ii, p. 171, line 23.

[3] *Markus*, p. 79.

there is nothing in the Greek to suggest that Jesus was 'enraged' at the apostasy and betrayal of Judas, but *He was deeply moved and disturbed in spirit*; the Peshiṭta is a faithful reflection of the Greek. In Jn. xi. 33, in the Old Syriac, the curious thing is that it is not this expression which corresponds to the Johannine ἐνεβριμήσατο; for that the translation is 'he boiled or seethed (*r^{e}thaḥ*) in his soul'. The phrase *'eth'azaz b^{e}ruḥeh* does, however, occur in the verse, but it renders ἐτάραξεν ἑαυτόν. Later, however, at verse 38, *'eth'azaz* translates ἐμβριμώμενος. Obviously the translator of the Old Syriac was anxious in verse 33 to give a near equivalent of the Greek meaning of ἐμβριμᾶσθαι, rendering 'he seethed (with rage) in his soul'. But it is significant that the Syriac expression *'eth'azaz b^{e}ruḥa* means in the Old Syriac version of verse 33 not 'he was enraged in his spirit' but 'he was deeply moved in his spirit'.

This wider use of the Syriac expression makes it clear that the Syriacism ἐνεβριμήσατο τῷ πνεύματι in verse 33 need not refer to violent rage at all; it may have the meaning 'he was deeply moved in his spirit'; and similarly, in verse 38, ἐμβριμώμενος may have the sense 'being deeply moved'. But this meaning is already conveyed in verse 33 by ἐτάραξεν ἑαυτόν. With the recognition of the Syriacism, we are left with an intolerable tautology, 'he was deeply moved in his spirit and he was deeply moved in himself (lit. he disturbed himself)'.

The assumption of an Aramaic source of which the two expressions are 'translation-variants' can account for the Johannine Greek. The Aramaic equivalent of ἐτάραξεν ἑαυτόν is a reflexive form of the verb *za'*; in Esther iv. 4, when Esther heard of the decree of Haman against the Jews, '. . . then was the queen exceedingly grieved'; the verb here is a very strong one in Hebrew; it means literally 'she writhed with anxiety'; it is rendered in the Targum by the equally strong and expressive verb *za'*; the LXX renders ἐταράχθη. The latter was selected by a Greek translator of the Aramaic of John xi. 33, but he set alongside it the Syriac expression ἐνεβριμήσατο τῷ πνεύματι, an even more expressive equivalent of the Aramaic, and rendered the same verb *za'* in verse 38 by the Greek equivalent of the corresponding Syriac *'eth'azaz*. Clearly the translator of the Lazarus story came from a bilingual circle such as Syrian Antioch where Greek and Syriac were both well-known.

How the unusual *ἐνεβριμήσατο τῷ πνεύματι* arose must be a matter for conjecture. What is important for our understanding of the Johannine verse is the recognition of this expression as a *Syriacism*—on this point I do not entertain any doubt—and the consequent possibility of an exegesis *which rules out any ideas of paroxysmal rage, or indeed of anger of any kind.* It is arguable, of course, that rage here, even unmotivated rage, is an element of the Johannine Christology (cf. Mt. ix. 30). If so, however, there is no parallel elsewhere in John. It seems to me more probable that the Greek expression was a translation equivalent of the Syriac one, but with the original meaning 'he groaned deeply in spirit'; and, in that case, the Authorised Version has, in fact, preserved the original meaning: 'he groaned in the spirit'. It is possible that the expression was not a Syriacism only, but an Aramaism, and this provides the simplest explanation of the difficulty: the original Aramaic read אתעזז ברוחה, meaning 'he groaned deeply in spirit' and this has been *misrepresented* in Greek by a phrase meaning 'he raged in spirit'. Unfortunately for this explanation, this idiomatic Syriac expression has not yet been found in Jewish Palestinian Aramaic or Palestinian Syriac.

CHAPTER IX

ARAMAIC AS A CAUSE OF TEXTUAL VARIANTS

THE hypothesis of 'translation-variants' is assumed by Nestle.[1] It has been recently revived by A. J. Wensinck, who explained a number of variant readings in the Western text of Luke as due to 'different attempts of translation' of an original Aramaic.[2]

Not all the examples adduced by Wensinck possess equal value for his hypothesis of two 'strands' of translation of Aramaic in the Gospel of Luke. It is, for instance, doubtful if the variant τὸ γενόμενον for τὸ ἐσόμενον in Lk. xxii. 49 (D) is to be traced to Aramaic.[3] In Lk. xvii. 33 Wensinck explains the Bezan variant θελήσῃ for WH's ζητήσῃ as coming from an ambiguous Aramaic *beʿa*:[4] but θελήσῃ is here a variant due to harmonistic influence (cf. Mk. viii. 35 = Mt. xvi. 25; Lk. ix. 24); the real difference which is to be explained from an ambiguous Aramaic verb is that between Lk. xvii. 33 and its parallels; it is then a Synoptic variant and not a textual one which Aramaic explains. The meaning 'to seek (to do)' for *beʿa* is common; for that of 'wish', we may compare the Palestinian Talmud, *Taʿanith*, i. 4, f. 64*b*, line 61. There are no Synoptic parallels to Lk. xiii. 31, where for WH's θέλει D has ζητεῖ, and the hypothesis of a 'translation variant' may perhaps best account for the difference.

Greek Textual Variants due to Aramaic

From Greek texts there is not a great deal of evidence of 'translation-variants' which can be explained with any confidence as certainly the result of translation of an Aramaic original. There are so many alternative possibilities. In the Bezan text of Acts in particular there are many synonyms of words in the WH text which may well point to 'different attempts at translation'; thus in the speech of Peter in chapter

[1] Cf. his *Philologica Sacra*.

[2] *Semitisms*, p. 42.

[3] Ibid., p. 45; cf. *supra*, p. 142.

[4] Ibid., p. 43.

iii, D reads for οἶδα at verse 17 ἐπιστάμεθα. Both may be due to translation. On the other hand, such synonyms may have arisen in Greek texts in the process of διόρθωσις to which they were subjected in the earliest period of the formation of the text. Examples of different translations of the ambiguous particle *d*[e] have already been discussed and are among the most probable instances. The following Greek variants are probably best accounted for as 'translation-variants'; I have included one example from a patristic quotation which seems to me to admit of no doubt.[1]

Mt. x. *42*

'And whosoever shall give to drink . . . a cup of cold water . . . he shall in no wise lose (Bא ἀπολέσῃ) his reward.'

The text of D reads, 'his reward will not be lost (ἀπόληται)'.[2]

The variant was accounted for by Chase as due to the influence on D of a Syriac version.[3] The Bezan reading occurs in the Sinaitic Syriac, and the difference between the two readings is slight (ܢܘܒܕ, ἀπολέσῃ, and ܢܐܒܕ, ἀπόληται). In Aramaic there is occasionally no distinction at all in spelling between the Peal and Aphel imperfects of *'abhadh*; examples of a Peal imperfect in the usual Aphel form, ܢܘܒܕ, occur in the Palestinian Syriac Lectionary at Mt. v. 29 (ABC) and Lk. xxi. 18 (BC). The Waw may be an error for Yodh, but, even if it is, יובד (ἀπολέσῃ) and ייבד (ἀπόληται), the regular Peal and Aphel forms, would be readily confused.

Mt. xvi. 16 (direct speech)

'And Simon Peter answered and said, Thou art the Christ, the Son of the living God' (τοῦ Θεοῦ τοῦ ζῶντος).

D has τοῦ Θεοῦ τοῦ σώζοντος. Both verbs may go back to Aramaic חיי, 'to live'; perhaps דחיי, 'who liveth' was read as דמחי, 'who saveth', the Aphel participle.

[1] *Infra*, p. 246 f.
[2] Cf. Gen. xl. 12 (P-J) for the expression in Aramaic.
[3] *Syro-Latin Text of the Gospels*, p. 6.

Mk. xiv. *15*

'And he will shew you a large upper room (ἀνάγαιον μέγα), furnished and prepared . . .'

The Bezan text of Mark reads ἀνάγαιον οἶκον . . . μέγαν, a variant found in the same text at the Lucan parallel (xxii. 12), with, however, the omission of μέγαν. The Aramaic for ἀνάγαιον, 'an upper room', is *'alitha, 'ilitha*, and a 'large upper room' is *'alitha rabbetha*. Out of the adjective רבתא (רביתא), the variant οἶκος, ביתא, has probably arisen.

Lk. x. *21*

'In that hour, Jesus rejoiced in spirit, and said, I thank thee, O Father . . . even so (ναί), Father . . .'

There is no variant in any Greek text, but an important reading is preserved in the quotation of the passage by Irenaeus,[1] where there can be no doubt that we have the correct translation of the Aramaic, of which the Greek is a mistranslation. For ναί Irenaeus reads οὐά: in Aramaic וה (*wah*) is an exclamation of joy (cf. Luke's ἠγαλλιάσατο); it is explained in *Midrash Echa*, 1, 'וה is the expression of joy, וי of pain'. The Greek source of both Matthew and Luke has obviously read the word as if it were אי, אין, ναί.[2]

Old Latin Variants due to Aramaic

The case for the hypothesis of 'translation-variants' becomes much more impressive when we take into account the variants of the ancient versions, in particular the Old Latin and the Syriac. They give access to a text earlier than that of any existing Greek manuscript; and there can be no doubt about the value of the text they assume.

To the instances of variants from Aramaic *de* in Greek texts we can add those examples where the Latin Vulgate or the Old Latin reads a relative.[3] To those instances we ought perhaps to add Jn. i. 13, where all Greek texts read οἵ . . . ἐγεννήθησαν, but

[1] i. 13. 2.

[2] Cf. Merx, *Matthaeus*, p. 200.

[3] *Supra*, p. 70 f.

the Old Latin *b*, supported by Irenaeus and Tertullian, have *qui . . . natus est.*[1] The relative in the singular makes the verse refer to Christ. We require, however, to assume further that the verb read by the Old Latin was ἐγεννήθη ; a singular verb is read by the Curetonian Syriac. Dogmatic considerations may also have played some part in the genesis of the variant.

Lk. xxiv. 21 (direct speech)

'But we trusted (ἠλπίζομεν) that it had been he which should have redeemed Israel . . .'

The verse is quoted in Tertullian, *Contra Marc.* 4. 43, 'nos autem *putabamus* ipsum esse redemptorem Israel'. It is probable that the Old Syriac is also so to be understood, but its verb is ambiguous: a significant marginal note, however, is found in the Harclean Syriac; the translator comments on the verb, '(it comes) from *sabra* (hope), and not from *masb*^{e}*ranutha* (opinion)'.[2] The latter is the reading of the Arabic Tatian, 'But we *thought* that he was going to deliver Israel'. The variants are perhaps to be traced to a common and ambiguous Aramaic סבר, meaning either *sperare* or *putare*; in the Targum of Hos. xii. 7 and Lam. iii. 25, we find the verb used in the meaning 'hope' in the same connexion as in this verse of Luke of 'hoping' for the redemption of Israel; the passive participle *s*^{e}*bhir* is used in the sense *spe tentus* or *putans*; for the latter meaning, we may compare Onkelos Exod. x. 10, 'the evil which ye think (*d*^{e}*'attun s*^{e}*bhirin*) to do' (there is no verb in the Hebrew).

The Variants and Expansions of the Syriac Versions and Tradition[3]

A number of variants which can be accounted for in this way, as alternative renderings of Aramaic, are to be found in the Syriac, and in particular the Old Syriac, versions and tradition.[4]

[1] Cf. Burney, *Aramaic Origin*, p. 34, and Torrey, *Our Translated Gospels*, p. 151 f.; see also Harnack, *Studien zur Geschichte des Neuen Testaments und der alten Kirche*, i, pp. 115–27.

[2] Cf. Merx, *Lukas*, p. 526.

[3] For a recent discussion of the Syriac Versions and Tradition see Kahle, *The Cairo Geniza*, pp. 179 ff.

[4] This includes Syriac patristic quotations and the descendants of Tatian's Diatessaron, in particular the Arabic.

Several of these Syriac variants have a feature in common which has led to their being rejected as genuine *variae lectiones*; on a first impression they appear to be nothing more than inner Syriac corruptions, where, by a remarkable coincidence, the 'corruption' in the Syriac gives good sense. F. C. Burkitt drew attention to this 'series of readings, which taken together make up one of the most curious features of the Syriac version'.[1] In Lk. ii. 30, for instance, for *τὸ σωτήριόν σου*, the Old Syriac and the Peshiṭta have ܚܢܢܟ, 'Thy mercy', which looks like an inner Syriac corruption of ܚܝܝܟ, 'Thy salvation', but the mistake gives a suitable sense, and no Syriac version or manuscript makes the correction; the Palestinian and the Harclean Syriac both render *τὸ σωτήριόν σου*, but not by ܚܝܝܟ. If a Greek variant, *τὸ ἔλεός σου*, had existed, then it could have been suggested with some confidence that both readings derived from the Aramaic, the first assuming חייך, 'Thy salvation', the second חננך, 'Thy mercy'. But there is no such variant, and it is unlikely that Luke ever wrote anything other than *τὸ σωτήριόν σου*.

It is, however, highly probable that Luke is making use of Aramaic sources or of Greek translations of such sources in this chapter, and it is possible that an extra-canonical tradition of the Lucan hymns, in other Greek translations than those preserved in Luke, left some trace in later tradition; 'Thy mercy' may be a variant rendering of the Aramaic which has come into the Syriac tradition from a Greek translation of the Nunc Dimittis other than the one which has survived in Luke.[2]

Moreover, not all the Syriac variants of this kind are explicable as 'inner Syriac corruptions'. In Jn. iv. 25 the Sinaitic Syriac reads for *ἀναγγελεῖ*, 'he will give (ܢܬܠ)': the rendering of the Curetonian Syriac is 'he will expound (ܢܦܫܩ)' and of the Peshiṭta 'he will teach (ܢܠܦܢ)', both translations of the Johannine Greek. The Sinaitic variant cannot be explained as deriving by Syriac corruption from either of these renderings, but it can be successfully accounted for as coming from a common

[1] *Evangelion da-Mepharreshe*, ii, p. 287.

[2] Different Greek versions have survived of the Canticle of Hab. iii; see Bévenot, 'Cantique d'Habacuc', in *Revue Biblique*, Vol. xlii (4), p. 499 f.

Aramaic: ἀναγγελεῖ is יתני, and 'he will give', יתין. The Palestinian Syriac renders ἀναγγελεῖ by ܢܬܢܐ, but there is no possibility of an Edessene Syriac version having ever contained this verb, for in that dialect the word means 'to narrate', not 'to announce'; and even if this verb had been used in an Old Syriac version, it is practically impossible to get ܢܬܠ, 'he will give', out of it by way of corruption. The use of the Aramaic *tanni* in the sense 'to announce' appears to be confined to the Jerusalem Targums[1]; an example occurs in the Palestinian Pentateuch Targum of Gen. xxxviii. 24 (D and E), אתני (LXX ἀπηγγέλη).

In the Introduction to his edition of the Curetonian Syriac, Cureton traced such variants to an Aramaic origin. On the strength of their evidence he propounded the theory that the Syriac Gospel to which he gave his name was a lineal descendant, without the mediation of any Greek text, of the lost Aramaic original of St. Matthew; the Curetonian Syriac had retained 'the identical terms and expressions which the Apostle himself employed'.[2] The theory has come to be regarded as something of a curiosity in Biblical Criticism; and it is a sufficient refutation of it to point out, as Burkitt did, that Edessene Syriac, the language of the Curetonian version, is a quite different branch of Aramaic from the Palestinian Jewish dialect which the Apostles spoke and in which any writings of theirs would presumably have been composed.[3] Moreover, it is everywhere obvious to anyone who takes the least trouble to compare the Syriac with the Greek that the former, in any part of the Gospels, is a version of the latter.

But Cureton's theory cannot be dismissed as a mere curiosity of textual criticism without some account being given of the basis of fact on which it was raised. The original observation that certain Syriac variants can best be explained as deriving from Aramaic is of unaltered value as factual evidence for a less ambitious hypothesis. We certainly cannot infer from the

[1] Cf. Levy, *Chaldäisches Wörterbuch*, ii, p. 546.

[2] Op. cit., p. xciii.

[3] Op. cit., p. 16. Burkitt recalls that much the same claim had been made for the Peshiṭta by Widmanstadius in the Preface to his *Editio Princeps* of 1555.

presence of such variants in the Old Syriac that the Syriac anywhere reproduces an Aramaic Gospel verbatim and without Greek mediation. But it is possible that an extra-canonical Gospel tradition, presumably but not necessarily in Greek, has influenced the Syriac versions at their source, thus giving rise to such 'translation-variants'.

The following examples of Syriac variants are divided into three classes. The first class consists of variants which can be best accounted for as representing alternative translations of an original Aramaic from that which we find in our Greek texts; they are, I believe, taken together, sufficient to establish the hypothesis of 'translation-variants' for the Syriac versions. The second class is less impressive as evidence for this hypothesis, but no less important for the criticism and exegesis of the Gospels, in view of their possible origin in an Aramaic original. The third class consists of Syriac expansions, which, for the same reason, are not unimportant textually and exegetically.

Class I

Mt. xi. 5 = Lk. vii. 22

For '. . . the poor have the Gospel preached (εὐαγγελίζονται) to them', the Curetonian Syriac of Mt. xi. 5 (lacking in Lk. vii. 22, and there is a lacuna in the Sinaitic text of the verse) reads, '. . . the poor are *sustained*'. The difference between the two verbs is that of a Yodh, *mestabbᵉrin*, 'are evangelised', and *mestaibᵉrin*, 'are sustained'. There is no support for any such 'variant' in Greek or in any of the versions of Isa. lxi. 1, from which the words have been taken and adapted. It has all the outward appearance in the Syriac of being a scribal mistake. Burkitt writes, 'The reading of C . . . *sustained* must be a mere error for . . . *evangelised*, as the Greek is εὐαγγελίζονται, but like other scribal errors or conjectural emendations in Syriac Biblical texts it makes singularly good sense.'[1] But the variant is a genuine one and not a 'mere error' of a Syriac scribe. It did not escape Cureton's notice that the words occur in the apocryphal Matthew in the form 'et pauperes *fruantur bonis*'; the full

[1] Op. cit. ii, p. 271.

quotation reads, 'et videant caeci et claudi ambulent recte et pauperes fruantur bonis et reviviscant mortui'.[1]

Adalbert Merx took the view that 'the Latin apocryphal text goes back directly or indirectly to an Aramaic original'.[2] The best explanation of the variant is, in fact, that it represents an individual interpretation, no doubt a wrong one, of the original Aramaic verb; the passives of *s^ebhar* and *sobhar* have the same meaning as in Syriac. It is not impossible that a pun was intended; and if so, then it is not unexpected to find the punning allusion to the 'feeding' of the poor in the 'Hebrew' tradition. The interpretation in the Curetonian Syriac version is thus ultimately an inner-Aramaic one and has nothing to do with corruption or error in the Syriac; the translator knew what he was doing when he so rendered the verse. The source of the variant in the Syriac is an extra-canonical, in this case apocryphal, Gospel tradition.

Mt. xi. 20

'Then began he to upbraid the cities wherein most of his mighty works were done (*ἐγένοντο*) . . .'

The reading of the Old Syriac is 'wherein he *shewed* (ܚܘܝ) many mighty works . . .'; Cureton noted the variant and remarked: 'The variation must have arisen from the similarity of . . . חוי, ἔδειξε . . . and הוו, *ἐγένοντο*.'[3]

Mt. xx. 21 (dialogue)

'And he said unto her, What wilt thou? She saith unto him, Grant (*εἰπέ*) that these my two sons may sit, the one on thy right hand, and the other on thy left, in thy kingdom.'

Both the Sinaitic and Curetonian Syriac have, 'She saith to him, My Lord (ܡܪܝ), that these my two sons may sit . . .' Cureton's note is: 'Instead of *My Lord* the Greek reads εἰπέ. This has doubtless arisen from the similarity of מרי *My Lord* and אמר *bid* . . .'[4]

[1] *Remains of a very Antient Recension of the Four Gospels in Syriac*, Preface, p. xxi.

[2] *Lukas*, p. 236.

[3] *Remains, etc., Preface*, p. xxi.

[4] Ibid., p. xxxv.

Mt. xxiii. 16

'Woe unto you, ye blind guides, which say, Whosoever shall swear by the temple, it is nothing (*οὐδέν ἐστιν*) . . .'

The Sinaitic Syriac has preserved the curious variant, '. . . Whosoever shall swear by the temple, *doeth not harm* (لا محا) . . .' The variant is explicable from the Aramaic: for 'it is nothing' Aramaic uses a compound of *la 'ith* (לית), which, in an emphatic form, combined with the emphasizing enclitic כא, becomes ליכא; Dalman notices the combination and cites instances of its use from the Palestinian Talmud and the Targum;[1] in the II Targum of Esther i. 9, e.g. we read, '. . . *he is not* (לכא) eating, and *he is not* drinking, and *he is not* sleeping . . .' The Aramaic *verb* נכא in the Aphel means 'to harm'; it renders *βλάπτειν* in the Palestinian Syriac version of Mk. xvi. 18; cf. Lk. iv. 35, x. 19. The source of the Old Syriac variant has obviously read its Aramaic text as לא יכא, 'doeth not harm'. It is difficult to choose between the two variants.

The repetition of the consonants Lamadh and Kaph is noteworthy in the Aramaic of the verse: 'Woe unto you (*wel^echon*), ye blind guides, which say, Whosoever shall swear by the temple (*hekhla*), it is nothing (*likka*) . . .'

Lk. ii. 20

'And the shepherds returned, glorifying and praising (*αἰνοῦντες*) God for all the things that they had heard and seen, as it was told unto them.'

The Sinaitic Syriac reads: 'And those shepherds returned, glorifying God and *speaking* (*m^emall^elin*) about the things they had seen and heard, as it had been told them.'

Two points may be noted: (1) in the Syriac the words 'as it had been told them' follow naturally on the variant 'speaking'; as the words stand in Greek, they require to be taken with 'had heard', a much less natural connexion. (2) The words 'glorifying' and 'praising' are synonymous; one of them alone is sufficient to convey the meaning.

[1] *Gramm.*², p. 219.

The common Hebrew word *hillel*, 'to praise', is used in the Pael *hallel* in Palestinian Syriac, e.g. in Ps. xlvi. 2 as well as in this verse of Luke: מהללין (*αἰνοῦντες*) and ממללין (speaking) differ in one letter only.

Lk. xiii. *26*

'Then shall ye begin to say, We have eaten and drunk in thy presence, and thou hast taught (ἐδίδαξας) in our streets.'

The Curetonian Syriac reads, 'and thou hast *walked* in our streets'. The usual explanation of the variant is that ܐܠܦܬ, the Sinaitic Syriac translation of ἐδίδαξας, has been corrupted to ܗܠܟܬ (thou hast *walked*). But the 'corruption' is not only singularly appropriate; it gives a much more natural parallel to the first clause, 'we have eaten and drunk in thy presence'. Jesus did not wish to convey in his parable that the 'master of the house' was a Rabbi; the interpretation of the parable as referring to Christ, would, on the other hand, readily give rise to the reading, 'thou hast taught'. Both readings may be traced either to an original הלכת, 'thou hast walked' misread as אלפת, 'thou hast taught', or vice versa.

Lk. xviii. *13*

'And the publican, standing afar off, would not (*οὐκ ἤθελεν*) lift up so much as his eyes unto heaven . . .'

The Curetonian Syriac reads: 'Now that publican was standing from afar, and *was not daring* (*mamraḥ*) to lift up so much as his eyes unto heaven . . .' The equivalent of *'amraḥ*, *τολμᾶν*, in Palestinian Aramaic is the Aphel of *ḥᵃsaph*, *'aḥseph*; it is this verb which regularly renders *τολμᾶν* in the Palestinian Syriac (Mt. xxii. 46; Rom. v. 7); *θέλειν* is *ṣᵉbha*. An original 'he was not daring' (לא יחציף) has been read by the Lucan Greek source as 'he was not willing (לא יצבי)'. The non-pronunciation of the guttural would contribute to the confusion between the two verbs.

The Syriac variant reappears in the Dutch Harmony tradition, in the Gravenhage and Stuttgart MSS.: 'Mar die puplicaen stont van verren ende en *dorste* sine ogen niet up heffen te hemele.'[1]

[1] Edit. Bergsma, cap. 161, p. 160.

Lk. xxiv. 32 (reported speech)

'And they said one to another, did not our heart burn within us (οὐχὶ ἡ καρδία ἡμῶν καιομένη ἐν ἡμῖν), while he talked with us by the way . . .'

Torrey has suggested that Luke has mistranslated Aramaic יקיר, 'heavy', by καιομένη (יקיד) in this verse.[1] Certainly his description of the emotion of the disciples in their Lord's presence is, as Greek, unusual. It implies, moreover, that they did have some premonition of the identity of their interlocutor, and one, too, which caused a deep stirring of their emotions. Yet it is explicitly stated later that it was not till He broke bread with them that recognition first came. Howard points out that 'variants for καιομένη in D and the oldest versions. . . . testify to difficulty felt from the beginning'.[2]

The Old Syriac has the word for 'heavy' (*yaqqir*), an adjective which implies the very opposite of καιομένη; an exact equivalent is the Old Latin *optusum* (*l*) and D's κεκαλυμμένη conveys the same meaning; the Semitic word refers to the crassness of mind and the slowness to understand which the disciples showed, and to which Christ Himself refers in verse 25.

The variant κεκαλυμμένη of D is appropriate, and if it goes back to the Aramaic, as a free rendering of the general meaning, then what we have in καιομένη is a Greek translation-variant. But the word may have been suggested to an editor who found difficulty with καιομένη by 2 Cor. iii. 13. The Old Syriac may be a rendering of D, but if the latter is a later editorial emendation, we have to find an alternative explanation. The theory of inner Syriac alteration of ܝܩܕ to ܝܩܝܪ cannot adequately explain the variant. The only remaining alternative, unless we take the view that the Syriac translator is arbitrarily substituting the more appropriate adjective, is that the Old Syriac has preserved the true Aramaic tradition of what the disciples were reported to have said from an extra-canonical source.

One difficulty with this view is that, if Luke is translating Aramaic in this chapter, then he has correctly rendered the

[1] *Our Translated Gospels*, p. 106 f.

[2] Moulton, *Gramm.* ii, p. 472.

adjective in verse 25. But Luke may not be himself translating but editing translation Greek sources; in his source for verse 32 he may have inherited the mistranslated adjective.

Lk. xxiii. 5

'And they were the more fierce (ἐπίσχυον), saying, He stirreth up the people, teaching throughout all Jewry . . .'

The Old Syriac has, 'And they were yelling (C ܡܙܕܥܩܝܢ, S ܡܥܩܝܢ) . . .' In the LXX, ἰσχύειν is the regular translation of חזק; for זעיק in Palestinian Aramaic meaning 'to scream' we may compare Onkelos and the Pseudo-Jonathan Targum of Exod. ii. 23.

Jn. xx. 16

In the Resurrection encounter of Jesus and Mary Magdalene in the Garden we read, according to our Greek text, 'Jesus saith unto her, Mary. She turned herself (στραφεῖσα), and said unto him, Rabboni . . .' For 'she turned herself', the Sinaitic Syriac reads, 'and *she recognized him* (ܘܐܣܬܟܠܬܗ)'. Burkitt renders the Syriac verb, 'and she perceived him', but the sense 'recognize' is what is required by the context.[1] The variant adds a detail that is not only vivid but important and necessary to the narrative. The Greek reading, on the other hand, leads to serious exegetical difficulty; in verse 14 Mary has already turned herself to face the approaching Figure; 'to turn herself' again would amount to turning her back on Him.

For 'recognize' this same verb is used in Aramaic; it is a word which is well-known in Jewish Aramaic; we may compare the Pseudo-Jonathan Targum of Gen. iv. 15, where a mark is set on Cain 'in order that anyone who found him, in recognizing him (or it) (*b*ᵉ*'istakkalutheh beh*) would not kill him'. The earlier ἐστράφη in verse 14 is rendered in the Palestinian Syriac version by the Ithpeel of the verb *s*ᵉ*ḥar*, *'ist*ᵉ*ḥar*, 'to turn oneself'; the verb is fully attested for Jewish Aramaic. It is difficult not to believe that there is a connexion between these two Aramaic verbs in the Johannine variants, namely that אסתכל in verse 16 has been misread as אסתחר, the translator having been mis-

[1] Cf. the Old Syriac rendering of Lk. xxiv. 16 and Merx, *Johannes*, p. 443.

led by the use of the latter verb in verse 14. The Aramaic word *Rabboni* has been discussed above.[1]

Class II

Mt. xxiv. *51* = Lk. xii. *46*[2]

Explanations of διχοτομήσει usually refer to *dichotomy*, the 'sawing asunder' of the slave's body, a punishment that seems unnecessarily severe in the circumstances, but which was not unknown in Greek and Roman times.[3] The strongest argument against such a meaning as original here is that the slave apparently lives on, unless his portion with the hypocrites is conceived of as set in some after-life.[4] Whatever Jesus Himself meant, however, it is clear that the translator of Q intended dichotomy; other attempts to explain the Greek verb have proved less successful.[5]

The Sinaitic Syriac has a text which reads, 'And *he will divide him his portion*[6] and set him with the unbelievers'. Burkitt, who would render, 'And he will divide his portion and set it with the unbelievers', explains the translation as an attempt

[1] *Supra*, p. 23.

[2] Cf. Jeremias, *Die Gleichnisse Jesu*², p. 44, on Mt. xxiv. 51 par.

[3] Plummer, in his Commentary, cites Suetonius, *Calig.* xxvii.

[4] Cf. Merx's *reductio ad absurdum* (*Lukas*, p. 307): 'Das Zweiteilen paßt in keinem Falle, wenn danach die Hälften mit den Ungläubigen Strafe erleiden, wo Heulen und Zähneklappern ist.'

[5] Some interpret *flagellis discindere*, a meaning not attested for the Greek verb. Beza and Grotius understood the word of the slave's segregation and separation from his home (*Novum Testamentum*, in loc., and Grotius's *Annotationes* (London, 1727), p. 299). The interpretation finds some support in the use of the verb in an inscription apparently in the sense of 'separate' (Moulton–Milligan, *Vocabulary*, p. 165). It is as old as Tatian; Ephrem's Commentary has 'eum abscindet medium et *separabit*' where the two interpretations are placed side by side, and it is followed by the Arabic. The Dutch Harmonies understand the punishment to consist in the 'cutting off' of the slave from the society of the righteous.

[6] This use of the Pa'el of the Syriac verb with an accusative of the person for whom the division is made occurs again in the Peshiṭta of Isa. liii. 12, 'I will divide him (ܐܦܠܓܝܘܗܝ) (a portion) with the great'; the Hebrew has 'for him'.

The suffix after the verb is not the usual one, and Burkitt (*Evangelion da-Mepharreshe*, ii, p. 296) proposed to correct it to the feminine, giving a proleptic suffix anticipating 'portion', 'and he will divide it (ܢܦܠܓܝܗ for ܢܦܠܓܝܘܗܝ), namely his portion'. But there can be no question here of confusion with the

to overcome the difficulty of the barbarous punishment. Where we find the verb *palleg*, 'to divide', in Aramaic, in the sense of the Old Syriac, the person *for whom* the division is made is in the indirect object, e.g. in the Targum of Isa. liii. 12. Nevertheless, Torrey may be right in conjecturing an Aramaic, *y*^{e}*phallᵉginneh m*^{e}*natheh*, 'he will divide him his portion'.[1] If this was the original, how are we to account for the preservation of the Aramaic reading in the Old Syriac? It can only have come from some extra-canonical source, for there is no other verb or variant in Greek tradition.

Mt. xii. *19*, 'He shall not strive (ἐρίσει) nor cry . . .'

The LXX of this verse of Isa. xlii. 2 reads *οὐ κεκράξεται οὐδὲ ἀνήσει*. All the older Syriac versions (S, C, Peshiṭta) render, 'He shall not cry nor *rail* (*naribh*). The variant ἐρίσει in Matthew corresponds to nothing in a Greek or Hebrew source, but bears a curious resemblance to the Syriac *naribh* (*ribh* in *Hebrew* means 'to strive'). The Syriac *naribh* comes from a Syriac Old Testament version of Isa. xlii. 2 (cf. Sy^{vg}) and is an Aphel of *rubh* meaning 'to shout, rail', and has nothing to do with Hebrew *ribh*, 'to strive' (cf. Num. xiv. 1 in Sy^{vg}). If in the New Testament it is an alternative rendering of a common Aramaic (*'arebh*), then ἐρίσει may be the mistranslation. The difficulty is that *'arebh*, 'to rail', is not attested for Palestinian Aramaic. G. S. Margoliouth (*Expository Times*, xxxviii, p. 278) regarded the Syriac as the original of Matthew's ἐρίσει; the translator was more familiar with the meaning of the Hebrew *ribh* than with Syriac *rubh*, and has given the Hebrew meaning. In that case we must assume that Matthew's quotations go back at points to a Syriac Old Testament, a fact of importance for the question of the provenance of the Gospel.

feminine suffix; the same form of masculine suffix is repeated after both 'divide' and 'set'; the unusual masculine suffix form is well attested in the Sinaitic Syriac by Burkitt himself (op. cit. ii, p. 54 f.).

[1] *Studies in the History of Religions* (New York, 1912), p. 314 f.; *Our Translated Gospels*, pp. 155, 157.

Jn. xviii. 16, 17

'But Peter stood at the door without. Then went out that other disciple, which was known unto the high priest, and spake unto her that kept the door (τῇ θυρωρῷ), and brought in Peter. Then saith the damsel that kept the door (ἡ παιδίσκη ἡ θυρωρός) unto Peter, Art thou also one of this man's disciples?'

The Sinaitic Syriac has: 'Now Simon Peter was standing outside; then entered and came forth to him the disciple that was the acquaintance of the high priest, and he had spoken to the *Porter*, and he (the Porter) let Simon in. When *the female slave of the Porter* saw Simon, she said unto him, Art thou not also one of this man's disciples?'

The Syriac is not only much fuller than the Greek, giving a more coherent sense, but it is also a version of the incident that shows an acquaintance with Semitic, and particularly, Jewish ways and customs. It is a remarkable fact that, according to our Greek text, the Porter or Doorkeeper of the Palace of the High Priest was a girl, a mere serving-maid (παιδίσκη). One would imagine that the Porter of the High Priest's Court would have been a personage of some importance, perhaps even a Levite assigned to such duties; the Levites provided the 'keepers of the gates' of the Temple.[1] We should certainly expect a man, not a serving-maid, to be in charge of the door, especially on an occasion such as the present one.

The Sinaitic Syriac speaks unmistakably of a porter or door-keeper; he it was who let Peter in, on the request of the disciple who was an acquaintance of the High Priest; influence had had to be brought to bear on the porter to persuade him to allow a stranger to enter the court. The female slave of the porter is clearly distinguished from the porter himself, and it is to her, and not to a female porter, that Peter makes his first denial; so also in the Synoptics, it is with a simple serving-maid that Peter's first conversation on entering the court takes place. In an original Aramaic the 'porter' would be נטר (ת) תרעא,

[1] Cf. Neh. xiii. 22.

which, with a dittograph of the Tau as indicated, gives ἡ θυρωρός.[1]

Class III

Mt. xxiii. *13* = Lk. xi. *52*

'But woe unto you, scribes and Pharisees, hypocrites! for ye shut up (ὅτι κλείετε) the kingdom of heaven against men. . . .'

The Sinaitic Syriac has, in Mt. xxiii. 13, 'Woe unto you, scribes and Pharisees, hypocrites! *Ye hold the key* of the kingdom of heaven . . .', which Burkitt regards as a wrong interpretation of the correct Syriac translation of the Greek such as we find in the Peshiṭta; the verb *'eḥadh* in Syriac means either 'to shut' or 'to hold'.[2] Burkitt does not explain how the wrong interpretation arose, but presumably he means that the original and correct, 'ye *shut* the kingdom' has been interpreted 'ye *hold* the kingdom', and this has finally become, perhaps as the result of an attempted harmonization with Luke, 'ye *hold the key* of the kingdom'.

The variant is found in Aphraates in the form of a free citation, 'ye are the holders of the keys',[3] and Burkitt conjectures that it has come direct out of the *Evangelion da-Mepharreshe.*[4] But Justin Martyr quotes the verse with the same variant, ὅτι τὰς κλεῖς ἔχετε,[5] so that if it is an inner Syriac interpretation, we are bound to conclude that Justin's quotation too comes direct from a Syriac version. There is nothing, however, to show that Justin had any acquaintance with Syriac, and it is doubtful if the Gospels existed in any form in Syriac in Justin's lifetime; if they did, they would scarcely have been known in the West. The variant is a genuine extra-canonical one, and it has found its way into the Sinaitic Syriac from some such source; it may

[1] A similar error can account for the strange simile of Christ as the Door of the Sheep in Jn. x. 7: 'I am the Shepherd of the sheep' is אנא איתי (ת) רעיה דענא; with a dittographed Tau before the Rish, we get 'I am the door of the sheep'. The suggestion was first made by Torrey (*Our Translated Gospels*, p. 111 f.). The Aramaic here proposed is simpler, and, with the Tau read twice, is an exact equivalent of the Greek text.

[2] Op. cit. ii, p. 276.

[3] Edit. Wright, p. 287. [4] l.c. [5] *Dialog.* 17.

have been the reading of Tatian (Aphraates used the Syriac Diatessaron).

The variant is not easily accounted for as a harmonization with Luke, in spite of the common word 'key'; αἴρειν, 'to take away', could not be rendered by *'ᵉḥadh*. The Sinaitic variant may well be an original clause in the saying coming before the ὅτι in Matthew; its original form may have been simply, as in Aphraates, 'Ye are the holders of the key(s)' or 'Ye hold the key of knowledge'. In the verse in Matthew ὑποκριταί is *shaqqarin(e)* in Aramaic, and the following κλείειν *sakkar* or *sᵉgar*; an earlier example of the word-play has been noticed.[1] If, in the original Aramaic source of Q, Luke's ὅτι clause followed directly on Matthew's, then we get a continuation of the paronomasia in ἤρατε, *shᵉqalton*. Luke's clause gives a good parallel to Matthew's: the scribes and Pharisees, described in the Syriac as the 'holders of the keys', not only shut the kingdom of heaven against men, but they take away the key; the second part of the verse in Luke, 'ye entered not in yourselves, and those that were entering in ye hindered', follows much more appropriately on the ὅτι clause in Matthew than on Luke's clause; otherwise we have to explain that the scribes and Pharisees prevented men from 'entering into' knowledge, a most unusual connexion. The aorists in Luke may be accounted for as literal equivalents of the Semitic perfect of general truths;[2] Matthew has the correct present tense. That both Matthew and Luke go back to a common Aramaic in this verse is clear if only from the variants γραμματεῖς and νομικοί; the Semitic word is *sopher*. The original arrangement of the verse in Q may have been:

But woe unto you scribes and Pharisees, hypocrites (**shaqqarin**)!
Ye hold the key (of knowledge) *or* Ye are the holders of the key(s) (of knowledge)
(*'attun 'ᵃḥidhin 'aqlidha*[3] *dᵉdaʿta* or *'attun 'ᵃḥidhe 'aqlidha dᵉdaʿta*),
Who[4] shut (**sakkartun**) the kingdom of heaven against men,
And take away (**shᵉqaltun**) the key (of knowledge);

[1] *Supra*, p. 178.
[2] *Supra*, p. 128.
[3] The noun *'aḥᵃdha* for 'key' in the Targum of Prov. xviii. 19 appears to be a Syriac word.
[4] Hilary read a relative, *qui* (teste Tischendorf).

Ye enter (**'altun**) not in yourselves, and them that enter in ye hinder (**k^e^lethon**).

Mk. ii. *21* (= Mt. ix. *16*, Lk. v. *36*)

'No man also seweth a piece of new cloth on an old garment: else the new piece that filleth it up taketh away from the old, and the rent is made worse.'

The Sinaitic Syriac of Mk. ii. 21 and Mt. ix. 16 (the Old Syriac is lacking for Lk. v. 36) translates this verse as follows:

No man putteth a new patch on a worn-out garment:
Else the fullness (ܡܫܠܡܘܬܗ) of the new tears away (cf. Lk. v. 36 σχίσει)
the weakness (ܡܚܝܠܘܬܗ) of the old,
And the rent becomes worse *than it was before.*

The lines in the Syriac fall into a natural rhythmic structure: there is assonance (in recurring labials) and a paronomasia. The latter, however, is so far not attested for Palestinian Aramaic in which the word for 'weakness' is not found. The addition to the last clause occurs in the Palestinian Syriac and is found in the Dutch Harmonies.

It is unlikely that these additions ever appeared in any Greek text or tradition. They may be the Syriac translator's own poetic expansion of the saying. But they may also come from an extra-canonical form of the saying of Jesus.

Lk. xxi. *25*

'And there shall be signs in the sun . . . and upon the earth distress of nations, with perplexity; the sea and the waves roaring. . . .'

The Peshiṭta has the following rendering of the last part of the verse: '. . . and on the earth distress of peoples and irresolution (ἀπορία), *from the confusion of the sound of the sea*'; the Latin Vulgate has the same phrase, *prae confusione sonitus maris*. The Greek source of the reading might at first appear to lie to hand in D, the chief authority for the variant ἠχούσης θαλάσσης. If it is, then both Peshiṭta and Latin are free renderings, with, however, some connexion between them. An alternative suggestion would be that ἀπορία has been connected with ἤχους. Such an explanation of the variants, however, assumes a meaning for the Greek word which is without parallel; ἀπορία is used of confused mental states only, the bewilderment of fear or stupefaction. Moreover, in that case, the versions must have read ἀπορία twice, or else given side by side two different interpretations of it, the first connecting it with the previous words, the second with what follows. None of these considerations gives a very satisfactory explanation of the variants or common variant preserved by the Syriac and Latin Vulgate.

If we render the Peshiṭta and Latin variant into Aramaic an equivalent of *confusio* may be found in the word that corresponds to the Hebrew *tohu*, the 'confusion' or 'formlessness' of the world before the Creation; the verb *t^eha* renders the Hebrew word in the Pseudo-Jonathan Targum of Gen. i. 2 (cf. *Genesis Rabbah* 2) and occurs again in the Jerusalem Targum II of Exod. xii. 42. The substantive תהייא in the sense of a confused noise appears in the Babylonian Talmud, and is given in Aruch in the form תיוהא.[1] For the earlier ἀπορία a suitable equivalent is *tiw^eha*, from the verb *t^ewah*. These two words in an original Aramaic would give an effective contrast and paronomasia:

And on the earth distress of peoples and bewilderment (תיוהא),
From the roaring (תהייא) of the sound of the sea.

Some further attestation of the second noun is desirable; it was probably a rare word in Aramaic.

The Old Syriac has a word-play of its own, 'a sound like that of the sea' (*qala d^edhame lad^eyama*). The paronomasia may be original; the Washington Codex (W) reads ὡς ἠχούσης.

The Sources and Antiquity of the Old Syriac

The possibility that a Palestinian Aramaic Gospel or Gospel tradition may have directly influenced the Old Syriac version through an extra-canonical source is one which at first seems highly improbable; variants in the Syriac versions, which might be so accounted for, are more likely to have come from a Greek

[1] Levy, *Chaldäisches Wörterbuch*, ii, p. 530.

extra-canonical or apocryphal source. But we cannot be certain. For the most part the evidence of translation-variants may be interpreted as supporting either hypothesis. But occasionally an unusual Syriac equivalent may be held to support the view of direct Aramaic influence.

In Jn. x. 12, 'But he who is a hireling and not the shepherd' is rendered by the Sinaitic Syriac, 'But the hireling, the false one (ܫܩܪܐ). . . .' If *sakhir* was the original word used by Jesus for 'hireling',[1] then 'the hireling, the false one' (*sakhir shaqqar*) gives a characteristic paronomasia. In that case the Sinaitic Syriac preserves the 'Urwort'.

A similar example is Mt. v. 23, 'Therefore if thou bring thy gift to the altar, and there rememberest that thy brother hath ought against thee . . .'; both Peshiṭta and Old Syriac render '. . . and there rememberest that thy brother hath animosity (ܐܚܢܐ) against thee.' The Syriac noun is even stronger than the translation suggests; a nearer equivalent is the German *Groll*. The word appears in the Targum of Prov. xii. 28 where the Greek has *μνησικακοί*.[2] It is a most appropriate expression in this context in Matthew; and it gives a paronomasia with the previous *'ahukh*, 'thy brother'. There is nothing corresponding to the Syriac variant in Western textual tradition.

A further observation supports this hypothesis of the direct influence of an Aramaic tradition on the Syriac. F. C. Burkitt pointed out that there were a number of anomalous features in the language of the Old Syriac.[3] Many of these linguistic anomalies consist of Palestinian Aramaic words and forms. Thus, the usual Syriac for 'my Father' is ܐܒܝ, but in several places in both the Old Syriac and the Peshiṭta, all Words of Jesus, the anomalous form ܐܒܐ for 'my Father' is found; the form is Jewish Palestinian Aramaic.[4]

Another example is the use of the noun *karka* in the Old Syriac of large cities; e.g. in Jn. vii. 31 it is applied to Jerusalem. This is not a Syriac usage; the word in Syriac means a 'fortified place'. Merx believed that the scene in this verse had been

[1] Cf. *supra*, p. 177.
[2] See Levy, *Chaldäisches Wörterbuch*, i, p. 28.
[3] *Evangelion da-Mepharreshe*, ii, p. 39 f.
[4] See *infra*, Appendix A.

shifted from Jerusalem to Bethany, the reference being to the smaller town. He admits, however, that such an assumption disturbs the natural connexion and meaning of the verses; John, however, may have taken this verse, referring to a 'town' or 'fortified place', from a source and placed it in its wrong connexion. But the solution is not very satisfactory; '... meantime we stand before a Non liquet'.[1] The solution is that the use of *karka* in this context is Jewish Palestinian Aramaic; in the latter the word is regularly applied to large cities; an example has already been encountered of its application to Rome.[2]

Such evidence may be differently interpreted. Burkitt sees in such apparent anomalies 'the last trace of a vanishing idiom' in Syriac.[3] The difficulty with such a view is that the idiom has vanished elsewhere: there are no parallels to such forms and usage in Edessene Syriac. One parallel which could be cited is that of the Peshiṭta Pentateuch where Palestinian Aramaic forms appear. But the explanation there is that the ultimate basis of the Syriac Pentateuch was a Jewish Palestinian Pentateuch Targum, that is, a West Aramaic document.[4] Torrey, who greatly over-estimates the extent of Palestinian Aramaic in the Old Syriac,[5] thinks that this evidence indicated 'that the version was made early in the second century, by Christians who had emigrated from Palestine to the neighbourhood of Antioch'.[6] Perhaps the most we have any right to claim for such evidence is that it points to Jewish-Christian authorship of the translation. If, however, it was a version made by Jewish Christians as early as the second century, it is not unlikely that some recollection of the Aramaic sayings of Jesus influenced the first translators.

Considerations of the date and sources of the Syriac versions, especially the Old Syriac, give further support to this suggestion of direct Aramaic influence. The Old Syriac Gospels must have been at least as early as the second half of the second century, and they were probably earlier; and there is both external and

[1] *Johannes*, p. 167.
[2] *Supra*, p. 3.
[3] Op. cit. ii, p. 47.
[4] See *supra*, p. 23.
[5] *Our Translated Gospels*, p. 65.
[6] l.c.

internal evidence in the Old Syriac for the use of extra-canonical apocryphal sources.

One of the most difficult and complicated problems of Syriac Biblical scholarship is to decide the relation of the Old Syriac Gospels to the Syriac Diatessaron of Tatian. The question of priority has been much debated, but since so little is known directly of Tatian's work, the results are based less on evidence than on probabilities. The only thing that is certain and established is that a connexion did exist between the two forms of the Syriac Gospel.

The Syriac Diatessaron was probably introduced by Tatian himself to the Church of Edessa on his return to the East after the death of his master Justin, not earlier than A.D. 175. The Harmony enjoyed a wide popularity in the Syrian Church till as late as the fifth century: Bishop Rabbula found it still in use in his diocese when he became bishop in A.D. 411, and set out to destroy as many copies as he could find; a full century later, Theodoret of Cyrrhus found and destroyed two hundred copies of the Syriac Harmony.[1]

But the Gospels must have existed in Syriac before Tatian's arrival in Edessa and the introduction of his Harmony. The problem of the origins of the Syriac versions is bound up with that of the origin of the Christian Church itself in Syria and Mesopotamia. The Syriac prose romance called the 'Doctrine of Addai', which cannot be much later than the third century, relates how the Evangel was planted in Edessa by Addai, an apostle, shortly after the Resurrection; Addai was later identified with Thaddaeus, one of the Seventy sent out by Jesus (Lk. x). Two anachronisms in the legend betray its historical basis: the mission of Addai is said to have taken place in the reign of Abgar Ukama, who can be identified with Abgar IX of Edessa (A.D. 179–214), and the Gospels are said to have been read in the newly founded Church from the Diatessaron.[2] The latter statement has suggested to Burkitt that Addai, a genuine Syriac name, was really Tatian and that it was he who

[1] *Evangelion da-Mepharreshe*, ii, p. 3.

[2] Op. cit., p. 36.

founded the Syrian Christian community in Edessa.[1] Certainly there is no foundation in language or history for the identification of Addai with Thaddaeus. Tatian, however, was not a missionary and in giving the Church at Edessa a copy of the Gospels in Syriac to be read in public as a kind of Authorized Version, his work rather presupposes the establishment at an earlier period of an organized Church already in possession of some form of the Syriac Scriptures.

There is one scrap of evidence for the existence of a pre-Tatian Syriac Gospel. Eusebius informs us that Hegesippus, who died in A.D. 180, quoted 'from the Syriac', and it is clear that a Syriac Gospel was meant.[2] It is most unlikely that this was the Harmony of Tatian; it probably refers to one of the earliest attempts at translation of the Gospels into Syriac. It is certainly difficult to believe that there was no Christian mission to Syria and Mesopotamia earlier than the third quarter of the second century, or that in bilingual Antioch the Gospels were not translated in Syriac early in the second century. It would indeed be strange if the Gospel which reached Rome by the middle of the first century had not found its way from Antioch to farther Syria till more than a century later. Edessa was a vassal state of Rome and on the main caravan route to the East. Moreover, the first Christian century was characterized by a remarkable proselytizing activity in Judaism in Syria and Mesopotamia; there was constant intercourse between Palestine and the Tigris–Euphrates basin and centres of population.

The Old Syriac Gospels may well be the lineal descendants of this early Gospel tradition in Syriac, if much in them is the work of later translators and revisers; their composite character is well known; they contain different attempts at translation of the Greek. But this does not preclude the influence upon them of the Syriac Diatessaron, as it can imply the use of the Diatessaron by their editors and translators.

The *auto-da-fé* of all copies of the Diatessaron undertaken by Rabbula and Theodoret suggests that its institutors may have had motives not unconnected with the nature of the Syriac

[1] *J.T.S.* xxv, pp. 128–30.

[2] *H.E.* iv. 22. 8.

Harmony itself as well as a desire to give a more faithful rendering of the now standard Greek text. Their reasons may not have been dissimilar from those which prompted Serapion of Antioch at an earlier period to suppress the Gospel of Peter in the Church of Rhossus; the Syriac Diatessaron may have contained or been influenced by an apocryphal Gospel which had come to be associated with heresy. Epiphanius, writing in the second half of the fourth century, says that some people called the Diatessaron 'the Gospel according to the Hebrews'[1] and there may have been some grounds for such an identification. Victor of Capua (sixth century), who discovered and edited the sole surviving Latin descendant of Tatian's Harmony, the Codex Fuldensis, mentions in the Preface to his edition of the New Testament that Tatian called his Harmony *diapente*; *diapente* is usually explained as a scribal error for *diatessaron*, but it is a strange one. It may be the original name and testify to the use of a fifth source, perhaps an apocryphal Gospel, by Tatian.[2]

One well-known point of contact between Tatian and the apocryphal Gospel to the Hebrews is the famous *lumen magnum* which, according to Justin Martyr, the Ebionite Gospel (probably one form of the Gospel to the Hebrews), and two Old Latin manuscripts (*a*, lumen ingens, and *g*, lumen magnum), is reported to have shone round Jesus at His Baptism. Ephrem, in his Commentary on the Diatessaron, mentions simply 'lumen super aquam exortum'; the Ebionite Gospel apparently had καὶ εὐθὺς περιέλαμψε αὐτὸν φῶς μέγα. A much fuller version is given as Tatian's by Ishodadh of Merv and Barsalibi:[3]

And immediately,
(as the Gospel of the Diatessaron testifies)
. . . a mighty light flashed upon Jordan,

[1] *Haer.* xlvi. 1. 9; Migne, *Patrol. Graeca*, xli, col. 840.

[2] *Codex Fuldensis* (edit. E. Ranke, Marburg, 1858): 'Tatianus, vir eruditissimus et orator illius temporis clari, unum ex quattuor compaginaverit evangelium cui titulum *diapente* composuit.' Both *diapente* and *diatessaron* are musical terms, and it has been suggested that Tatian had this in mind when he named his work; *diapente*, the fifth, is the perfect harmony; cf. A. Baumstark, *Biblica*, xvi.

[3] Cf. *Evangelion da-Mepharreshe*, ii, p. 115; the translation is that of Burkitt.

And the river was girdled with white clouds,
And there appeared his many hosts that were uttering praise in the air;
And Jordan stood still from its flowing, though its waters were not troubled,
And a pleasant odour therefrom was wafted
(*w^e^reḥa basima men taman pa'eh h^a^wa*).

Burkitt, following Rendel Harris,[1] does not think that any more than the words,

And immediately a (mighty) light flashed upon Jordan
(*w^e^meḥda nuhra* (*'aziza*) *'azleg 'al yord^e^nan*)

came from the Diatessaron, in spite of the testimony of Barsalibi and Ishodadh that the whole quotation is Tatian's. He believed that the remainder of the apparent quotation must have been taken from some early hymn, perhaps one of Ephrem's own.

It is noteworthy that the quotation is poetry and not prose; there is a regular rhythm throughout, and the language and thought are those of exalted religious verse; the last line is a perfect Syriac line both in content and form. It is extremely unlikely that the hymn was Ephrem's; the lines cannot be fitted into any scheme of exact syllabication such as we find in Ephrem. Poetry of this kind, where it is impossible to measure the lines by the exact number of their syllables, belongs to the first and earliest stage in the development of Syriac verse, where it was the rise and fall of the rhythmic beat, together with parallelism, paronomasia, assonance, and alliteration, which alone provided the poetic 'form'. Exact syllabication is said to have been the invention of Bardaisan (fl. *c.* A.D. 150), the Father of Syriac poetry, but it was Ephrem who made of it a fine art. We have to go to two of the oldest known pieces of extant Syriac literature, the apocryphal Acts of Thomas and the Odes of Solomon, both belonging to the third century, to find examples of this freer verse style, untrammelled by rules about the number of syllables to each line.

The poetry in the quotation of Barsalibi may have been the work of Tatian himself, or he may have taken his account of

[1] *Fragments of the Commentary of Ephrem Syrus upon the Diatessaron*, p. 44.

the Baptism, incorporating the whole of the above quotation, from an apocryphal Syriac poem. A reminiscence of the line which is generally agreed to be Tatian's is found in one of Ephrem's hymns:[1]

The Holy One was baptized, and immediately came up (s^elaq);
And there flashed forth ('azleg) His light upon the world.

This same word-play must have been in the Syriac Diatessaron; the verb *'azleg* is employed in the quotations of Barsalibi and Ishodadh, and *s^{e}laq* corresponds to ἀνέβη of the Gospel text. If this one poetic feature comes from the Syriac Tatian, the rest of the quotation, in its poetic form and content, may have come from the same source. Certainly, if the whole quotation is from the Diatessaron and is at all typical, it testifies to a not inconsiderable apocryphal element.

Cureton made a point of noting all readings shared by his Syriac version of Matthew and the remains of the apocryphal Gospel to the Hebrews, including, in his Preface, in a convenient form, the patristic and other evidence for the connexion between that Gospel and the Hebrew 'Matthew'.[2] The evidence is not very extensive, but it is sufficient to establish the connexion.[3] The apocryphal 'Woe' which we find in Greek in the Gospel of Peter, 7, attested for the Diatessaron and occurring also in the Old Latin Codex Sangermanensis (*g*), appears in Lk. xxiii. 48 of the Old Syriac: 'And all they that happened to be there and saw what had happened were beating on their breasts and saying, 'Woe to us! What hath befallen us? Woe to us for our sins!'

There is therefore no doubt that the earliest Syriac Gospel translations drew on the apocryphal Gospels, so that the possible influence of a non-Greek tradition of the sayings of Jesus or the events of the Gospels cannot be ruled out of consideration in our explanation of the curious variants which have survived in the Syriac Gospels and Gospel tradition.

[1] *Sancti Ephremi Syri Hymni et Sermones* (edit. Lamy), tom. i, p. 127.

[2] p. lxiv f.

[3] Examples at pp. xv, xxi, lxxxiii of Cureton's Preface are the most important.

Distribution of Variants from Aramaic

Most of the above variants are to be found in the fairly exhaustive lists of Burkitt in his *Evangelion da-Mepharreshe* and in Merx's *Die vier kanonischen Evangelien.* Few Syriac variants of any note escaped either of these scholars, so that a survey of the distribution of this special group of variants over the four Gospels should prove of value. In the following table, M stands for Matthew's special material and L for Luke's.

	Words of Jesus	*Dialogue*	*Narrative*
1. Variants in Greek Texts	Mt. x. 42 (M) Mk. xiv. 15 Lk. x. 21 (Q)	Mt. xvi. 16 (M)	
2. Latin Variants		Lk. xxiv. 21 (L)	Jn. i. 13
3. Syriac Variants	Mt. xi. 5 = Lk. vii. 22 (Q)	Lk. xxiv. 32 (L)	Mt. xi. 20 (M)
	Mt. xxiii. 13 = Lk. xi. 52 (Q)	Jn. iv. 25	Lk. ii. 20
	Mt. xxiii. 16 (M)	Lk. ii. 30	
	Mt. xxiv. 51 = Lk. xii. 46 (Q)		Jn. xviii. 16, 17 Jn. xx. 16
	Mk. ii. 21 Lk. xiii. 26 (Q) Lk. xviii. 13 (L) Lk. xxi. 25 (L, supplementing Mark) Lk. xxiii. 5 (L) Mt. v. 23, xii. 19. Jn. x. 12		

Out of a total of 24 such variants no less than 14 come from sayings of Jesus; 5 are from dialogue or reported speech; of the remaining 5 instances, 1 is from the Johannine Prologue and 1 from the second chapter of Luke, the story of the Shepherds. This leaves *three* cases only from narrative and two of them are from the Fourth Gospel. This distribution of variants caused by the translation of Aramaic thus confirms the results obtained earlier by the observation of the distribution of Aramaisms in the Gospels. The five instances of Aramaic variants from the source Q above will not have escaped notice.

CHAPTER X
SURVEY OF RESULTS
Aramaic Source-Criticism

A SURVEY of the results of this study in this connexion yields one conclusion only which can be regarded as in any degree established, that an Aramaic sayings-source or tradition lies behind the Synoptic Gospels. Where any one Semitic or Aramaic construction could be observed recurring, its distribution showed that it tended to be found most frequently, and sometimes exclusively, in the Words of Jesus. The same conclusion emerged from a study of the translation and mistranslation of Aramaic in the Gospels. Not all the observations made there or the arguments advanced are of equal value or cogency: much is inevitably exploratory; but individual objections and difficulties do little to weaken the main impression that we have to do with a translation-tradition, sometimes literal, mostly, however, literary and interpretative, but generally bearing the stamp upon it, in one feature or another, of its Aramaic origin. Whether that source was written or oral, it is not possible from the evidence to decide.

The only other place where evidence could be adduced of Aramaic influence of any extent outside of the sayings of Jesus in the Synoptics was in the Marcan narrative or in non-dominical sayings and dialogue. Mark has a monopoly of asyndeton in narrative; in the other two Synoptics this construction was seen to be confined to the sayings of Jesus. Mark could also show more instances of the paratactic construction, while in Mark alone of the Synoptics the Aramaic proleptic pronoun occurs chiefly in narrative.[1] It is difficult, however, to decide whether such typical features of Mark's Semitic style allow of any inference as to his use of sources outside the sayings of Jesus. They may conceivably be construed as evidence of the kind of Greek which an Aramaic-speaking Jew would write. The sug-

[1] *Supra*, p. 100.

gested mistranslation in xiv. 3 is too conjectural to have any cogency as proof of source. The evidence of iv. 41 and ix. 38 is more convincing, and may be decisive, but both examples occur significantly enough in reported speech. Certainly what evidence we do possess makes the assumption of Aramaic sources for the Marcan narrative much less difficult than for the non-Marcan narrative portions of Matthew and Luke.

In the latter, apart from the sayings of Jesus, there are far fewer indications of Aramaic influence. The asyndeton openings, *λέγει, λέγουσι*, characteristic of the first Gospel, though Aramaic in origin, are more likely to be a feature of Matthew's Jewish Greek style than an indication of source. Similarly, Luke's temporal conjunction, *ἐν αὐτῇ τῇ ὥρᾳ*, need not imply the use of sources; it may be a Lucan Aramaism or Syriacism. The most likely places where Semitic sources were used by Luke, apart from the sayings of Jesus, are in the first two chapters of his Gospel and in the speeches of Peter and Stephen in the early chapters of Acts. The hymns embodied in the Infancy narrative are thoroughly Semitic, but not necessarily translations, though the observation of word-play when we render them in Aramaic strongly supports the translation hypothesis.[1] In the narrative peculiar to Luke of the Emmaus Appearance it is very probable that the Greek text of Luke in WH mistranslates an Aramaic adjective in xxiv. 32. Some slight evidence of an Aramaic source was found in the speeches of Peter and Stephen in Acts. But all this, though not unimportant, gives but poor foundation upon which any source-criticism of value could build.

What of the Fourth Gospel? Is it a translation of an Aramaic document, as Burney maintained? How far is the linguistic evidence adduced by Burney, which certainly proves a strong Aramaic element, capable of proving more than that St. John is written in 'Aramaized' Greek, the work perhaps of an Aramaic-speaking writer with Greek as his second language? The evidence by which translation can be most convincingly demonstrated is that of mistranslation. When all other explanations are considered and the evidence weighed, there remains a resi-

[1] *Supra*, p. 151 f.

duum of such evidence where, if the element of conjecture cannot be eliminated altogether, it may nevertheless be said that alternative suggestions are inferior as explanations. Thus the evidence for the mistranslation of the particle *d*[e] is not unimpressive. It is true, as was seen, that much of Burney's evidence loses its value in view of the loose use of ἵνα in Hellenistic Greek. But how otherwise than by the hypothesis of translation of Aramaic can we account for those cases where the conjunction ὅτι as well as the relative have survived in Greek textual tradition? The reading of the fragment of the extra-canonical 'Unknown Gospel' for Jn. v. 39, whether it preserves a genuine Johannine variant or not, seems to me to be of importance as proof of an Aramaic source for this Johannine saying of Jesus.[1] The observations made on Jn. iii. 31 and 33 suggest the use and translation of a fixed Aramaic tradition of the words of the Baptist, perhaps even a documentary one.

These observations yield perhaps the most cogent proof of an Aramaic source: they cannot be adequately explained otherwise than on the hypothesis of an Aramaic original. But is it necessary to seek that original in an Aramaic document covering the whole of St. John's Gospel?

It has been noted that the same distribution of Aramaisms, mainly in the Words of Jesus, occurred in John as in the Synoptics. Less importance could be attached to this observation in the Fourth Gospel, however, as there is less surrounding narrative there to offer a contrasting background. Nevertheless it is possible that an Aramaic sayings-tradition may have been utilized by John, most probably in early Greek translation sources. A not dissimilar conclusion was reached by G. R. Driver, who, while rejecting the theory of an Aramaic documentary source, thought that the evidence supported the hypothesis that John 'was mentally translating, as he wrote, logia handed down by tradition and current in Christian circles in Aramaic, from that language into the Greek in which he was actually composing his Gospel'.[2]

[1] *Supra*, p. 72 f.

[2] 'The Original Language of the Fourth Gospel' (*Jewish Guardian*, 1923).

John is thus doing much the same as the other Evangelists, incorporating into a Greek Gospel a logia source or logia sources, but with probably this difference, that not all his longer speeches of Jesus are derived from his Aramaic tradition. Such a sayings-source in the Fourth Gospel may have been no more than the nucleus around which the longer speeches of Jesus were composed. There is, of course, so far no confirmation of this, any more than it can be regarded as certain that all the sayings of Jesus in the Synoptics go back to Aramaic. But such a theory seems more probable than to believe that in all the speeches of Jesus St. John is translating an Aramaic original.

In addition to the existence of an Aramaic sayings-source behind the Fourth Gospel, the evidence points to a similar Aramaic tradition forming the basis of the Prologue and the sayings of the Baptist in the third chapter.

'Translation Greek'

What is the character of the Greek 'translation' in the Gospels where Aramaic sources can be shown to have been employed? In view of the results already obtained, we are bound to consider the Greek of the sayings of Jesus only; and in this connexion, it cannot, I think, be sufficiently emphasized that in the majority of the longer connected parables, for example in Q, the 'translation' is not literal but literary; in other words, it is doubtful if it can be justly described as translation at all in some cases, even where the evidence points to the existence and use of an Aramaic source. The Evangelists, that is to say, are for the most part writing Greek Gospels, even where they are dependent upon sources. There were, of course, exceptions to this, two important ones being in the parables themselves: the first was the parable of the Sower in Mark, where we have good reason to speak of 'translation Greek'; in the parable of the Well-behaved Guest, in the Bezan text of Matthew at xx. 28, there was found a good sample of 'translation Greek' in a passage long enough to be studied as Greek. The parable in Luke, on the other hand, is the literary version, the work of the Greek writer Luke, whereas D's parable probably comes from the hand of an unknown translator, it may be the Greek author of Q. Whatever its source, it is almost certainly to be regarded as a rough unliterary and literal Greek translation of the Aramaic of Jesus. If the claim which is made for this passage is recognized, then we have in it an even better example than the Marcan parable of the Sower in which to observe the difference between an early unliterary translation form of the Aramaic tradition of the Words of Jesus and the later literary form in our canonical Gospels.

What is thus claimed for the character of the Greek 'translations' of the Evangelists in the parables and longer connected passages is also largely true of the shorter sayings and apophthegms. They are not all literal translations of Aramaic, but translations which have passed through the minds of the Greek Evangelists and emerged as, for the most part, literary productions. Many examples of literal translation Greek where the literary hand of the Evangelists is less in evidence have been encountered, e.g. Mt. x. 11 f., xxiii. 9; Lk. iv. 43, ix. 16, xii. 49; Jn. xx. 10, &c.: but far more complicating factors than a translator's relatively simple purpose of giving a faithful rendering have been constantly at work. The key to the understanding of this was found in the word 'interpretation'. The Greek Evangelists or the first Greek translators of the Gospels have not simply transmitted a tradition unaltered: they have interpreted a tradition originally circulating in one language, Aramaic, and composed in more or less literary Greek the results of their interpretation. All translation involves interpretation, but the Gospels are not just the interpretation of translators; they are also the 'Targum' of Evangelists.[1]

The consequence is that, in the transmission of the Teaching of Jesus, the end-product in Greek is often less the mind of Jesus than the ideas and interpretation of the Greek Evangelists. To reach the original meaning the intervening thoughts of the Greek writer have to be discounted, and then often we can only conjecture the nature and sense of the original Word. No more instructive example of this can be found than Mk. iv. 12 f.

[1] For the same parallel, see M. Jousse, 'Le Formulisme Araméen des Récits Évangéliques' (*L'Ethnographie*, Nouvelle Série No. 30, Décembre, 1935).

Here it is certain that neither in Mark nor in Matthew or Luke do we have the mind of the Lord. Had we not the Aramaic Targum and the evidence that the Marcan text is drawing on it, we should have been much less fortunately placed than we are for conjecturing the nature of the original saying and quotation. Mark is not simply transmitting unaltered a saying of Jesus; he is himself interpreting or recording a later interpretation which probably reflects the attitude of the Christian community in which the writer lived. In the sayings recorded in the Gospels at the Last Supper all that we can be relatively sure of from a consideration of them in Aramaic is that what we have in Greek in at least two of the key expressions Luke's πληρωθῇ and Mark's *πίνω καινόν*, are interpretations, probably quite remote from the meaning of the original.

Such a view may be exaggerated. Many of the sayings of our Lord are so simple and concrete that they were bound to remain the same in meaning in Greek as in Aramaic. But while this is true, examples such as Mt. v. 13, vi. 7, vii. 6 show how even the simplest sayings have passed through this process of interpretation when assuming their Gospel form. Such a view must not be overstated or too much claimed for it: but neither can it be overlooked.

Semitic Poetic Form

That the sayings of Jesus were cast originally in poetic form has for long been well-known. In his *Poetry of our Lord* Burney drew attention to such features as parallelism, rhythmic structure, and even rhyme which could be detected in the underlying Aramaic of the Words of Jesus. But such characteristic features of Semitic poetry are also to be found in the hymns of Luke, in the sayings of the Baptist, and perhaps even in several non-dominical sayings in the Gospels.

The most striking and one of the most characteristic features of all Semitic poetry is paronomasia, together with its associated alliteration and assonance. When the sayings of Jesus and especially the longer connected passages are turned into simple Aramaic many examples of paronomasia, alliteration and assonance come to light. Paronomasia in particular appears to have been a regular feature of the style and teaching of our Lord in His native Aramaic. It has for the most part disappeared in the Greek Gospels.

The Textual Problem[1]

A definite conclusion is possible on the textual issue. The Bezan text in all the Synoptic Gospels, if less so in some respects in Mark, is more frequently stained with Aramaic constructions and idiom than the Bא text. For that reason, it has a better claim to be regarded, on the whole, and certainly where such Aramaisms are found, as representative of the more primitive type of text in earliest circulation. The differences between the texts of D and Bא in John are, in this respect, less marked than they are in the Synoptics and Acts.

In two cases, asyndeton in Mark and the survival of circumstantial clauses in Luke, the Bא text preserves the Aramaic idiom more faithfully than the text of D. But in almost all other cases where style and grammar are concerned, *casus pendens*, parataxis, proleptic pronoun, ethic dative, Aramaic relative, comparative and superlative, the distributive, the participial indicative, &c., as well as in translations of Aramaic, the Aramaic idiom or construction is found predominantly, sometimes exclusively, in D. The conclusion at which Wensinck arrived from his study of the Semitisms in Bezan Luke holds good for all the Synoptics: D represents the Aramaic background of the Synoptic tradition more faithfully than do non-Western manuscripts.

From much the same kind of observations Wellhausen stated this view of the Bezan text more than a generation ago in the first edition ot his *Einleitung*.[2] In an additional note to his first edition of the *Prolegomena* Moulton called attention to this approach of Wellhausen to the textual problem, remarking on 'the great importance of his (Wellhausen's) treatment of the Bezan text': 'He shows that D in a large number of places stands distinctly nearer the Aramaic which underlies the Synoptic records. If this is proved, we have manifestly taken a large step towards the solution of our great textual question.'[3]

[1] Cf. Wilcox, op. cit., p. 185. [2] Cf. p. 15 [3] p. 242.

No statement could be clearer in its implications: if the Bezan text 'stands distinctly nearer' the Aramaic underlying the Synoptic records than the Bℵ text, then it has a stronger claim than the latter to represent, on the whole, the primitive text of the Gospels.

How are we to account for the differences, often substantial as far as form and language goes, between the type of text we find in the Bezan Uncial, with its Semitisms and unliterary Greek, and the text of Bℵ? Wensinck has recourse to the earlier hypothesis by which Blass accounted for the wide divergence between the Bezan text of Acts and the non-Western text, that Luke himself had issued two editions of Acts, the second (represented in the text of Bℵ) a revision of the first (in D): similarly, Wensinck found in the non-Western text of Luke's Gospel a second edition of an earlier draft of that Gospel represented mainly by D.[1] The theory is more easily defended in Acts than in the Gospel, for in the former the difference between the two texts is unparalleled in the history of any Biblical or non-Biblical writing, with the exception perhaps of some of the plays of Shakespeare.

A comparison, however, of the Bezan and the Bℵ texts of Luke's Gospel shows that the divergence is not so far-reaching as to necessitate such a theory. Wensinck's hypothesis is largely based on the observation that in the Bezan text of Luke 'different translations' from an Aramaic source exist from those we find in Bℵ. We can infer two different strands in the translation of the Aramaic sources of Luke, one, an earlier, represented by the text of D, the second a later revised edition in Bℵ. A closer examination of this evidence showed, however, that 'translation-variants' are not very numerous in Greek texts. A few examples there are which can be so explained, but they are not sufficient to support Wensinck's hypothesis. Moreover, the same kind of variants are to be found in the Bezan text of Matthew and Mark, and the differences between the Bℵ text and the text of Codex Bezae in the first two Gospels are as great as and comparable with those between the two texts in the third

[1] *Semitisms*, p. 47 f.

Gospel. If the evidence is such as to support a two-edition theory of Luke's Gospel, the hypothesis ought also to be applied to Matthew and Mark.

There is no need, however, for such a theory. The differences between D and Bא do not point to the existence of two editions of the Gospels, but they do suggest two (or more) different redactions of what was substantially, if not verbally, the same original Gospel text. In what may be termed the 'Bezan redaction' more of the primitive 'Aramaized' Greek text has been left unrevised than in the redaction—a word which we may now use in this connexion—represented by the Vatican and Sinaitic Uncials.

Gospel variants which may be traced to an Aramaic source are most probably survivals from the earliest period of the Gospel text. They remind us that our canonical Greek Gospels are four only of a large number of early Greek forms of the Gospel tradition. All these Greek Gospels, in so far as they transmitted the sayings of Jesus, must have embodied translations of Aramaic which often differed from the translations used or made by the Four Evangelists. The most probable explanation of the few remaining Greek variants from Aramaic is that, in the earliest period of textual transmission, the writings of the Evangelists have been variously influenced by or assimilated to other well-known extra-canonical Greek versions of the Words of the Lord. Such variants, it was seen, could be multiplied from the ancient versions, the Old Latin and the Old Syriac, and from patristic quotations. And it seemed very probable that the Old Syriac had been influenced at its source by an extra-canonical and apocryphal Gospel tradition of the sayings of Jesus, which may even have been non-Hellenistic, transmitted directly in Syriac from an original Palestinian Aramaic source.

The difference between sacred writings in constant popular and ecclesiastical use and the work of a classical author has never been sufficiently emphasized in the textual criticism of the New Testament. Principles valid for the textual restoration of Plato or Aristotle cannot be applied to sacred texts such as the Gospels (or the Pauline Epistles). We cannot assume that it is possible by a sifting of 'scribal errors' to arrive at the prototype or autograph text of the Biblical writer. While we have no reason to doubt that the textual tradition of the Biblical writers derives from such single autographs, we also know that in the earliest period these writings in use in Church and Synagogue were subject to the most radical changes and alterations in both their subject-matter and text, with little regard for the author's original work. As far as the substance and contents of the Gospels are concerned, we have no reason to believe that they have suffered in any material way; the danger of a radical treatment of the Biblical authors such as that of Marcion was early realized and countered. But while the tradition in this respect remained constant, its form in text and language went through the same stages of historical development as the Hebrew and Greek Old Testaments, the Aramaic Targums, or the Qoran. An early period of a 'fluid text' with different 'editions' varying in form and language, if substantially the same in message and import, circulated in different localities. It was not till some degree of ecclesiastical unity was achieved over sufficiently wide areas that standard or Vulgate texts took the place of the local Gospels and finally superseded them.

The textual criticism of the Greek New Testament has not been accustomed to thinking in terms of a Greek Vulgate, parallel in its development with standard ecclesiastical texts such as the Latin or the Syriac Vulgate, the LXX or the Massoretic Hebrew Text. Nevertheless it is such a conception which must replace the classical idea and ideal of a reconstructed or restored autograph or 'true' text.

Such revised standard Greek texts are to be found in the Uncial Manuscripts B, א, and D, though whether they ever existed and circulated as ecclesiastical standards and Vulgate texts is a question that is open. But this issue does not affect the conclusion to which this investigation has led us that the redaction represented by the Bezan Codex has preserved more of the characteristics of the pre-Vulgate 'fluid' textual period, the primitive type of text in earliest circulation, than the Vatican-Sinaitic redaction.

APPENDIX A

THE WEST ARAMAIC ELEMENT IN THE OLD SYRIAC GOSPELS[1]

A NUMBER of linguistic anomalies in the Old Syriac Gospels cannot be explained in terms of Edessene Syriac. Many of these forms and uses are regular in West Aramaic. The following study of the West Aramaic element in the Old Syriac is based for the most part on the chapter on the Grammar and Syntax of the Old Syriac in the second volume of Burkitt's *Evangelion da-Mepharreshe.*

Passages cited in italics are sayings of Jesus.

Vocabulary

(i) The word *ṭura,* which in Syriac means 'a hill', is used in two places in the Old Syriac to render ἄγριος and ἀγρός respectively: in Mt. iii. 4 (Sy^s), μέλι ἄγριον is rendered *debhsha d^eṭure,* 'honey of the hills' or 'honey of the mountains'. But the expression here probably means 'honey of the open country'; in Lk. xii. *28,* the second example, the same word renders ἀγρός. This is not a classical Syriac use, but the word has this meaning regularly in Palestinian Syriac.[2]

(ii) The word for ἀνάστασις in the Old Syriac is the Jewish Palestinian Aramaic term, 'the coming to life of the dead', *ḥayath mithe* in its Syriac form. The word is found in Mt. xxii. 23 (dialogue), 28 (dialogue), *30* in Sy^sc, and partly also in the Peshiṭta. The usual Syriac for 'resurrection' is *q^eyamta* or *nuḥama,* e.g. in the Peshiṭta of Jn. xi. 24, 25.

(iii) In Lk. ii. 14 (direct speech), εὐδοκία is rendered in Sy^s by *'ar'utha,* which is the Jewish Aramaic *r^e'utha,* as in Ezra v. 17, vii. 18; the corresponding Syriac is *ṣebhyana* (as in both verses of Ezra in the Peshiṭta) or *ṣ^ebhutha.* The unusual and un-Syriac *'ar'utha* of Sy^s is replaced in the Peshiṭta by *sabhra ṭabha,* 'good hope', no doubt because the Jewish Aramaic expression gave difficulty to Syriac readers; it nowhere appears in Syriac.

(iv) In Lk. xi. *10,* xiii. *25* in Sy^s, we find the Aphel of *n^eqash* rendering κρούειν. These appear to be the only passages in Syriac where the Aphel of this verb is used; usually the word occurs in the Peal, as in Sy^c in both verses. The Aphel is regular in the Palestinian dialect.[3]

[1] Cf. G. C. C. Torrey, *Documents of the Primitive Church* (New York, 1942), pp. 249 ff.

[2] *Supra,* p. 133.

[3] Consult Schulthess, *Lexicon Syropalaestinum,* s.v.

(v) Side by side with the usual Syriac word for *νόμος*, *namosa*, the Greek word, we find in the Old Syriac the Jewish Palestinian Aramaic *'oraita* (in the Targum the word is read *'urayy*ᵉ*tha*). The word is a borrowing in Syriac from Jewish Aramaic; it is found elsewhere in Syriac literature.

(vi) In Jn. iii. 2 (dialogue) in Sy^s and iv. *48* in Sy^c, the Palestinian Aramaic word *nissa* renders *σημεῖον*. The noun occurs elsewhere in Syriac but is rare.

(vii) In Lk. xxiii. 2 (dialogue), *Χριστὸν βασιλέα* in Sy^sc is *malka m*ᵉ*shiḥa*, in the order of the Jewish Aramaic title (the same words).[1]

Morphology

1. *Nouns*

(i) The spelling ܚܪܘܩ in Mt. viii. *12* (Sy^s) (*βρυγμός*) Burkitt states 'must be a mere scribal error for ܚܘܪܩ.'[2] But the form is regular in Palestinian Aramaic; cf. Sy^pal. Mt. viii. 12, xiii. 50 (A), xxii. 13.

(ii) The forms ܒܪ̈ܢܫܐ and ܒܢܝܢܫܐ in Mt. xix. *6* (Sy^c) and Lk. ix. *26* (Sy^c) for the more usual ܒܪ̈ ܐܢܫܐ, ܒܢܝ̈ ܐܢܫܐ, in classical Syriac, are regular in the Western dialect.

(iii) In Lk. xxiii. 5 (dialogue), Sy^s has the Greek form *Galilaya* (*Γαλιλαία*) for the more usual Syriac *Galila*; it is the first form which is used in Palestinian Syriac.

(iv) For the usual Syriac ܬܠܡܝ̈ܕܘܗܝ, 'his disciples', Sy^c has twice the form of the suffix, ܬܠܡܝ̈ܕܘܝ, in Mt. xi. 2, Jn. iv. 8; the latter is the spelling of Jewish Palestinian Aramaic and of Palestinian Syriac.

(v) On the anomalous Syriac form ܣܥܘܪܢܝܟܝ, Lk. xix. *44* (Sy^s), Burkitt remarks (p. 46): 'ܣܥܘܪܢܝܟܝ . . . must be a scribal error for ܣܥܘܪ̈ܢܝܟܝ.' The regular form in the Targum is סעורנא.

(vi) In Lk. xxi. *14* (Sy^sc), *b*ᵉ*lebbaikon* renders *ἐν ταῖς καρδίαις ὑμῶν*; the Edessene Syriac plural of *lebba* is *lebbawatha*; the Palestinian Aramaic form is *libbayya* and 'in your hearts' is *b*ᵉ*libbekhon*.

(vii) The usual form of suffix for 'my father' in Syriac is *'abh*(*i*), and this form is regular in the Old Syriac except in Sy^c Mt. x. *32*, Sy^s Mt. xv. *13*, Sy^c Lk. ii. *49*, Sy^c Jn. vi. *32*, where we find the form *'abba*, though no Greek manuscript omits *μοῦ* after *πατήρ*.[3] The form is Jewish Palestinian; it is transcribed in Greek characters as *ἀββᾶ*

[1] Cf. Dalman, *Worte Jesu*, p. 240.

[2] Op. cit., p. 46.

[3] Burkitt found the form ܐܒܐ for 'my Father' in a number of Peshiṭta manuscripts for Jn. vi. 32, x. 17, xii. 27, xiv. 26, xvi. 17, xvii. 25 (p. 47). But an examination of the examples shows that the Peshiṭta here is rendering *ὁ πατήρ* not *ὁ πατήρ μου*. The form ܐܒܐ for 'my Father' belongs to the Old Syriac only.

in Mk. xiv. 36; Rom. viii. 15; Gal. iv. 6. All the above examples of the anomalous form in the Old Syriac occur in Words of Jesus.

Burkitt argues: 'It is, I venture to think, not unlikely that ܐܒܐ, i.e. *Abba,* was once used for "my father" in Edessene, as in most forms of Palestinian Aramaic, and that these variations are the last trace of a vanishing idiom' (p. 47). The difficulty with this explanation is that the idiom has completely vanished elsewhere in classical Syriac.

The familiar phrase '*the* Father' in the speeches of Jesus in the Fourth Gospel (e.g. xii. 50, xiv. 26, xvi. 17) renders ὁ πατήρ. This may be 'my Father' in Greek where the pronominal adjective is not emphasized. But it could not be 'my Father' in the Gospel passages where the pronoun is not without significance. In any case, the use of the definite article for the pronominal adjective is not Johannine nor, for that matter, New Testament Greek, which, as a rule, has the personal pronoun in the genitive; so ὁ πατήρ μου, e.g. Jn. vi. 32. It is possible that 'the Father' in the Johannine sayings and speeches of Jesus reflects the ambiguous Aramaic *'abba,* 'the Father' or 'my Father'. The latter was probably original.

(viii) The unusual form ܦܡܝ occurs in Mt. xiii. *35* (Sy[s]) for τὸ στόμα μου: the regular Syriac spelling is ܦܘܡܝ and the form in the Sinaitic Syriac is otherwise unknown in the classical language. The word פם is always written without Waw in the Aramaic portions of Daniel, and with a suffix we find בפמה in Dan. vii. 5. Burkitt drew attention to the form פמי in an old West Aramaic inscription from Nerab near Aleppo (p. 49).

(ix) A Palestinian Aramaic plural form in *ayya* occurs in the phrase 'to lay hands (*'idhayya*) on' in the Old Syriac of Mt. xxvi. 50; Lk. xxii. *53*.

(x) In Mk. vi. 9, Sy[s] has the unusual ܟܘܬܘܢܐ for the regular Syriac form of this Greek word, ܟܘܬܝܢܐ; Jewish Palestinian Aramaic is כתונא, χιτών.

Adjectives, Adverbs, Prepositions

(i) The adjective ܐܚܪܝܢ (ἄλλος) is consistently spelled ܐܚܪܢ in Sy[s]; the Palestinian Aramaic form is אוחרן; ܚܪܢ is found in Sy[pal.] in Jn. v. 7 (B). The spelling ܐܚܪܢ occurs also in Sy[c] in Jn. iv. *37*, v. *32*, vii. *33*.

(ii) The ancient form of the demonstrative adjective ܗܠܘܢ is found rarely in Edessene Syriac; it occurs a number of times in the Old Syriac, mainly in sayings of Jesus: Mt. xv. 22 (Sy[c]), xx. 9 (Sy[c]), xxi. *40* (Sy[c]), xxii. *7* (Sy[c]); Lk. viii. *13* (Sy[sc]), xii. *37* (Sy[c]); Jn. iv.

38 (Syᶜ), 43 (Syᶜ). The form occurs in Palestinian Syriac[1] and appears in Jewish Aramaic as the indeclinable הליך ; ܗܠܟܝܢ is found in Mt. xv. *24* (Syᶜ) as a feminine.

(iii) The anomalous *men ruḥaq* (ἀπὸ μακρόθεν) occurs in Mk. viii. *3*, Lk. xvi. *23* (both Syˢ) : the absolute of *ruḥqa* is otherwise unknown in Syriac. The adverbial phrase is not a Syriac one, but it occurs in Jewish Palestinian Aramaic, Targum Prov. xxxi. 14, *min roḥaq*; *min raḥiq* is the usual Targumic form.

(iv) For the adverb *meḥda*, 'immediately', invariably so spelled in Syriac, *men ḥᵃdha* appears in Mk. vi. 45 (Syˢ). This spelling is regular in Palestinian Syriac.

(v) On the preposition ܚܠܐܦ in Syˢ Lk. ix. *23*, Burkitt (p. 51) writes: 'I have not met with any other resolution of ܚܠܦ into its original elements.' This *scriptio plena* is common in Palestinian Syriac, e.g. Mt. viii. 10 (B), 19 (A, B), 22 (B); Mk. ii. 14 (C), viii. 34 (B).

Numerals and Interrogatives

(i) Occasionally numerals are found in West Aramaic forms: Mk. viii. 5, 6 in Syˢ (both verses in dialogue); Lk. xx. 29 Syˢ (dialogue), ܫܘܒܥܐ; Mk. xii. 23 Syˢ (dialogue) ܫܘܒܥܬܝܗܘܢ; Lk. xiii. 14 Syˢ, ܫܘܒܬܐ (Sabbath); Lk. x. 17 Syˢ ܫܘܒܥܝܢ. Burkitt's note reads: 'These variations of the ordinary ܫܒܥܐ, ܫܒܥܝܢ, ܫܒܬܐ, are all the more interesting because they are found in the Christian Palestinian Aramaic as well as in various forms of Jewish Aramaic' (p. 48).

(ii) In translating Lk. viii. *30*, τί σοι ὄνομά ἐστιν, by *man shᵉmakh*, 'Who is thy name?' both the Old Syriac and the Peshiṭta reproduce an ancient Hebrew and Aramaic idiom which appears to be unknown in Edessene Syriac; thus Judges xiii. 17 in Hebrew; in Gen. xxxii. 28, where the Hebrew has 'What is thy name', the Aramaic Targum has this idiom, 'Who is thy name?'

(iii) For the usual Syriac *man hi*, 'Who is (it)?' we find *mani* in Mt. xii. *48* Syˢ, Mk. iii. *33* Syˢ, Lk. vii. 39 Syˢ (dialogue). This spelling is unknown in Syriac but found in Jewish Aramaic (Burkitt, p. 42).

Verbs

(i) Suffix forms to verbs are frequently irregular. Occasionally they have *Nun Energicum* as in the Western dialect; ܚܘܢܢܝ for the more usual Syriac ܚܘܐܘܢܝ in Mt. ii. 8 (dialogue), xxii. *19*; Lk. xx. *24*. The form occurs in Syˢ; Syᶜ has the regular form in all three passages.

Lk. ii. 35 (dialogue) contains one of the curious variants of the Old Syriac: for καὶ σοῦ δὲ αὐτῆς τὴν ψυχὴν διελεύσεται ῥομφαία, Syˢ reads

[1] See Schulthess, *Grammatik des christlich-palästinischen Aramäisch*, p. 33.

ܘܠܢܦܫܟܝ ܕܝܠܟܝ ܬܥܒܪܝܢܗ ܪܘܡܚܐ, which Burkitt renders, '. . . and thine own soul thou shalt cause a spear to pass through'. The verbal form in Syriac can only be the second person singular feminine imperfect Aphel with the third singular feminine suffix. But if we take the form as West Aramaic with *Nun Energicum* the verb may be parsed as the third singular feminine imperfect Peal with the third singular feminine suffix; in that case the Syriac is a rendering of the Greek, ' . . . and thine own soul also will a spear pass through.'

(ii In three places in the Old Syriac Gospels we find ܝܗܒ written for the passive participle, ܝܗܝܒ; Mk. iv. *11* Sy[s], Lk. iv. *6*, *17* Sy[s]. The form appears to be found in Aphraates but in a quotation of Mt. xix. 11 (ed. Wright, p. 355). This defectively written passive participle is found in Biblical Aramaic, Dan. vii. 14, and frequently in Palestinian Syriac, Mt. xix. 11 (A, B, C); Lk. vii. 25 (B, C); Jn. vi. 66 (B), vii. 39 (B, C), xix. 11 (B, C).

(iii) In Mt. xxiii. *13* Sy[sc], the participle ܐܚܝܕܝܢ is passive in form but active in meaning; there are parallels in Edessene Syriac, and the passive form of this verb has an active meaning in Jewish Palestinian Aramaic; see Levy, *Chaldäisches Wörterbuch*, i, p. 19.

(iv) Lk. i. 63 Sy[s] has the Peʿil form ܬܡܝܗܘ (ἐθαύμασαν) for the more usual ܬܡܗܘ;[1] another Peʿil occurs in Lk. ix. 32, ܝܩܝܪܘ. The Peʿil is well-known from Biblical Aramaic; see H. L. Strack, *Abriss des Biblischen Aramäisch*, p. 29.

(v) The imperatives of *'etha* and *'ezal* are written, contrary to the usual Syriac orthography, with Alaph, in a number of passages in the Old Syriac, Mt. xi. *28*, xix. *21*, xxii. *4*; Lk. ix. *59*; Mt. ii. 20, v. *41*, viii. *4*, 9, ix. *6*, *13*, xvii. *27*; Mk. vii. *29*; Lk. vii. *22*, x. *3*, xiii. 31, xxii. *10*. All examples are from Sy[s]. Cases not in Words of Jesus occur in dialogue.

The Alaph in the imperative of *'ᵃtha* is common in Sy[pal.] and usual in Jewish Aramaic, e.g. in the Palestinian Talmud, *Demai*, vi, f. 25*b*, line 12. The imperative of *'ᵃzal* is regularly written with Alaph in Jewish Palestinian Aramaic and in Palestinian Syriac.

These linguistic peculiarities of the Old Syriac have been explained by Burkitt as Syriac archaisms. The weakness in this view is that there are scarcely any parallels in Syriac; we should expect some trace of such forms in other early Syriac writings, such as the Acts of Thomas or the Psalms and Odes of Solomon. Wellhausen wrote: '. . . man gewinnt den Eindruck dass solche Raritäten stehen geblie-

[1] Merx (*Markus und Lukas*, p. 187) wrote: 'Die Form . . . dürfte . . . einem alten westaramäischen Dokumente entlehnt sein.'

bene Reste sind. . . .'[1] But of what? An analysis of the above survey yields the following result: 79 instances in all of anomalous usage have been noted; of these no less than 50 cases (63–64 per cent.) occur in Words of Jesus; 16 (19–20 per cent.) appear in dialogue or direct speech, and the remaining 13 (16–17 per cent.) in narrative. Such evidence supports the hypothesis that these anomalous forms come from a West Aramaic source or tradition of the Gospels, in particular of the Words of Jesus, which has directly influenced the language of the Old Syriac.

[1] *Nachrichten der königlichen Gesellschaft der Wissenschaften zu Göttingen*, Phil.-hist. Klasse, 1895, i, p. 5.

ADDITIONAL NOTE

Recent studies have, if anything, tended to support the view here argued. P. Kahle (*The Cairo Geniza*, 2nd edition, p. 283) has suggested that the small Jewish kingdom of Adiabene rather than Edessa may well have been the cradle of Syrian Christianity; and his views are now supported by Arthur Vööbus' 'Studies in the History of the Gospel Text in Syriac' (C.S.C.O., 128, Subsid. 3, 1951, p. 20 f.), 'History of Asceticism in the Syrian Orient', I (C.S.C.O., 184, Subsid. 14, 1958, pp. 3–10). For the links between Essenism (ascetic Judaism) and Syrian Christianity, see *ibid.*, pp. 17–30, 97–103.

The discovery of a manuscript of the original Syriac of Ephraim's Commentary on the Diatessaron and of a Persian Diatessaron promises to contribute valuable new evidence for the question of the origins of the Syriac Gospel tradition, see L. Leloir, *Saint Éphrem: Commentaire de l'Évangile Concordant Texte Syriaque* (*Manuscrit Chester Beatty* 709), Dublin, 1963, and B. M. Metzger, *Chapters in the History of New Testament Textual Criticism*, Leiden, 1963, p. 97 f.

APPENDIX B

THE ARABIC AND MEDIEVAL GOSPEL HARMONIES[1]

ALTHOUGH so little is known of Tatian's original Harmony of the Gospels, we do know that it exercised an extensive influence on the text of the Greek Gospels as well as on later versions. That influence has been variously estimated, and, in some cases, much overrated; one of the tasks of a future textual criticism must be a truer valuation of its nature and extent. But Tatian's Harmony certainly enjoyed a wide popularity in both early and later centuries of the Church; translations were made from it into a number of languages, the best known and the earliest being the Arabic and the Old Latin.

The Arabic Diatessaron, in the different manuscripts which we possess, goes back ultimately to an Arabic translation of Tatian's Syriac work, but has been standardized to conform to the text of the Peshiṭta.[2] It is not, however, without textual value and certainly not so unimportant as the meagre account given of it in the text-books suggests. It does not, however, have the value which von Soden gave it in collating it consistently with the Greek text; in doing so he was simply noting again in the vast majority of cases the reading of the Peshiṭta. It is only where the Arabic departs from the Peshiṭta that it may contribute a genuine variant; in such divergences from the Peshiṭta it has been found to agree very often with other Tatian authorities, so that it may sometimes be possible to assume that other variants, which are otherwise unattested for the Tatian tradition, come from the same ancient source.[3]

[1] For an up-to-date account of work on the Arabic Diatessaron, see Kahle, *The Cairo Geniza*, pp. 211 ff., 2nd ed. pp. 297 ff.

[2] The first edition of the Arabic text of the Diatessaron was A. Ciasca's *Tatiani Evangeliorum harmoniae arabicae* (Rome, 1888). A critical study and translation of the Arabic text appeared in 1926, *Tatian: Diatessaron*, translated by E. Preuschen and edited by A. Pott (Heidelberg). Other MSS. have been collated in A. S. Marmardji's *Diatessaron de Tatien* (Beyrouth, 1935). An account of the history of the Arabic text will be found in S. Euringer's 'Überlieferung der arabischen Übersetzung des Diatessarons', in *Biblische Studien*, xvii. 2; I. Guidi's *Le Traduzioni degli Evangelii in Arabo e in Etiopico* (Rome, 1888) and O. Guildemeister's *De Evangeliis in arabicum e simplici syriaco translatis* (Bonn, 1865) are important studies.

[3] A further Eastern source for Diatessaron variants is to be found in the recently published Coptic Manichaean documents; Mani knew the Gospels in the form of the Syriac Diatessaron; cf. A. Baumstark, 'Ein Evangelium Zitat der Manichäischen Kephalaia', *Oriens Christianus*, IIIte Serie, xii, pp. 169–91. The texts are, Schmidt and Polotzky, 'Ein Mani-Fund in Ägypten' (*Sitzungsberichte*

The only extant representative of the Latin Diatessaron is the Gospel Harmony discovered by Victor of Capua (sixth century).[1] Its textual value, however, like that of the Arabic, is not great, for its text has been accommodated to the Latin Vulgate. The consequence of these well-intentioned efforts of the Church Fathers to produce a uniform ecclesiastical text has been the loss to us of almost everything in the Old Latin Harmony which was originally and distinctively Tatian.

But though no pre-Vulgate Latin Harmony, with the exception of the emasculated Codex Fuldensis of Victor, has come to light, there have survived descendants of these lost Latin harmonized Gospels in the form of unofficial people's Bibles written in the vulgar European languages of the Middle Ages, Dutch, Old French, Venetian and Tuscan Italian, Old High German, Low German, and Middle English. The discovery and valuation of these medieval Gospel Harmonies, and the recognition that they belong to the original Harmony tradition of Tatian, and that, in spite of the declared policy of the medieval Church, they have preserved material from Old Latin sources as early as the second century, are not the least interesting of the results of Biblical scholarship in recent years. From the point of view of originality and the ancient variant readings contained in them, the most notable have proved to be the Dutch Harmonies.[2] The Italian have been published recently in an excellent edition.[3] The Middle English Harmony is the so-called Pepysian Gospel Harmony, the prized possession of Mr. Samuel Pepys;[4] Wiclif's Harmony, which probably belongs to the same tradition, is still in manuscript in the British Museum.[5] The textual value of this Medieval Harmony tradition is being carefully estimated.[6]

None of the Dutch Harmonies, of which the most important is the Liége Diatessaron, is dated, and their authors are all anonymous. Apart from the fact that they are Flemish, we have no information

der preussischen Akademie der Wissenschaften, 1933, i, pp. 57–9); H. J. Polotzky, *Manichäische Homilien* (Stuttgart, 1934).

[1] *Supra*, p. 266.

[2] To the late Professor Plooij of Leyden belongs the credit for the textual valuation of the Dutch Harmonies; see his *A Primitive Text of the Diatessaron* (Leyden, 1923), and *A Further Study of the Liége Diatessaron* (Leyden, 1925).

[3] *Il Diatessaron in volgare Italiano* (Vatican, Studi e Testi, 1938), edited by Vattasso and Vaccari.

[4] Edition by M. Goates, English Texts Society, clvii (1922).

[5] Cf. *A Further Study*, p. 5.

[6] *The Liége Diatessaron*, edit. D. Plooij, C. A. Phillips, A. H. A. Bakker (Amsterdam, 1938, in progress).

about their place of origin. That they were intended for the laity and had neither the sanction nor the blessing of the medieval Church is certain. The Liége manuscript was clearly intended for private perusal; the harmonist tells us in his Preface that he undertook to compose 'a beautiful story' (*ene schone historie*) of the life of our Lord for and on the request of a friend. The manuscript has been assigned to the end of the thirteenth or the beginning of the fourteenth century, but the Dutch text may be earlier: at the beginning of the thirteenth century a Flemish poet, Jacob van Maerlant, sacristan of Maerlant on the island of Oost-Voorne, attempted in a *Rijmbijbel* to render the Gospels into Dutch verse, and the basis of his poem was a Dutch Harmony text, which Plooij suspected to be an ancestor of the Liége Diatessaron; a transcriptional error in Mt. xxvii. 10, where the 'potter' has become the 'porter' (citizen) is shared by the *Rijmbijbel* and the Liége Harmony.[1]

A century or so earlier we learn from a curious document, containing the *Apologia* of one Lambert le Begue (*c.* A.D. 1150), of a 'liber psalmorum . . . in vulgarem linguam a quodam magistro Flandrensi translatus';[2] the beginnings of the translation of the Gospels into the vulgar tongue may well have been as early. But it was not until the fifteenth century that the demand for such Scriptures became articulate: Gerard Groot, the founder of the Brethren of the Common Lot, and his assistant Florentius Radevynszoon publicly contended for the translation of the Gospels into the language of the people, proclaiming that 'the root of study and the mirror of life must, in the first place, be the Gospel of Christ'.[3] It may safely be said that these Dutch harmonized Gospels which we still possess were among the first signs of the great religious quickening of the later Middle Ages out of which the Reformation was born.

The evidence for the antiquity of some of the variant readings preserved in the Dutch Harmonies has been given by Professor Plooij. Whether the Old Latin texts which the Dutch harmonists are translating were themselves translations, as Plooij claims, of Syriac and not Greek originals of Tatian's work, is a question which is open. But several examples of the ancient material in these Harmony texts are striking. The usual text of the Gospels in Mt. i. 24 reads (in the A.V.), 'Then Joseph . . . did as the angel of the Lord had bidden him, *and took unto him his wife*'; the free paraphrase of Tatian, reflecting his encratite views on the sinfulness of marriage

[1] Cf. *A Further Study*, p. 5. [2] Ibid., l.c.

[3] Cf. T. M. Lindsay, *History of the Reformation*, ii, p. 228.

and the flesh, avoids the straightforward statement that Joseph took Mary his wife and substitutes for it, 'He (Joseph) was dwelling in holiness with her'; the same reading appears in the Curetonian Syriac, 'and purely was he dwelling with her'; Maerlant's *Rijmbijbel*, drawing on its Harmony source, reads, 'and he remained with her in purity' (*ende bleef met hare in suverhede*).[1] To appreciate fully the significance of this agreement of the Dutch text with Tatian, it must be borne in mind, not only that this rendering is Tatian's own peculiar paraphrase, but that it is found nowhere else outside Syriac tradition. In the previous verse of Matthew (i. 23) a fifteenth-century Cambridge manuscript of a Dutch Harmony has the words, 'and he (Joseph) kept her in protection'; Plooij has pointed out that the task of Joseph, according to the apocryphal Protevangelium Jacobi, was 'to take Mary into his custody'.[2] An example of a deliberate alteration which again reflects Tatian's encratite philosophy occurs in the Liége text of Mt. xix. 4: in the discourse on the lawfulness of divorce, the harmonist regards marriage in its spiritual aspect only as consecrated and ordained by God; it is Adam, not God, who says that they shall be one flesh. On this curious alteration Plooij remarks: 'Perhaps such a view was not altogether impossible in the medieval Church, but it is scarcely probable that after the second century any one would have ventured to alter a Gospel text so freely'.[3]

Genuine *variae lectiones* of importance have been preserved in the Dutch Harmonies. In Lk. xviii. 13, discussed above,[4] the Dutch follows the Old Syriac in its rendering, 'But the publican stood afar and *durst not* lift up his eyes to heaven'. The Dutch translator of the Liége text is also a stylist, and his imagination gives life and drama to a story or parable. How much in this respect he owed to his Old Latin source, and so ultimately to Tatian himself, it is difficult to decide, and perhaps Plooij errs on the side of attributing too many of the excellences of the Dutch text to Tatian. But there need be no doubt about the quality of the harmonist's Gospel in style and language as in arrangement and imagination. The translation of Mt. vi. 28 is in the style of the Aramaic poetry of our Lord Himself: *sich ane de lilien die wassen in den felde. noch sine pinen noch sine spinnen.* Many of the fresh details which the harmonist adds give verisimilitude to the narrative: in Mt. xii. 10, the story of the man with the withered hand, the Liége text reads 'There was a man there whose right hand was withered, so that he could not work any more

[1] *A Primitive Text*, p. 21.
[2] Ibid.
[3] Op. cit., p. 55.
[4] p. 253 f.

with it', an addition which is not unlike that of the apocryphal *Gospel to the Hebrews*, which, after describing the man as a 'mason', adds that *he could not earn his living because of his infirmity*. The importunate friend in the Gospel parable who came at night asking three loaves of bread (Lk. xi. 5), according to the Liége Harmony, 'continues knocking and shouting' till he finally gets his request. The woman of Samaria in Jn. iv. 4 f., who met Jesus by the well, 'set down her crock and ran into the city' after Jesus had spoken to her; in the A.V., verse 28 reads calmly, with the dignity of a scholarly version in both Greek as well as English, 'The woman then left her water-pot, and went her way into the city'; the Liége translation is all the more interesting as here again it agrees with the Old Syriac. It is a Golden Drachma which the housewife loses in Lk. xv. 8, and, in order to find it, instead of sweeping the house (A.V.), the Liége harmonist tells us that 'she turned the house upside down'. In the Parable of the Lost Sheep the harmonist says that the shepherd left his ninety and nine sheep on the mountain 'where they were grazing', and when he has found the sheep that was lost, 'places it upon his shoulder and brings it home'. Finally, for such details are numerous in the Harmony texts, the Prodigal Son complains in his misery that the hired servant has plenty of bread 'in my father's house', and when he returns, his father kisses him 'on the mouth' (*vor dem mond*), as Plooij, to whom I am indebted for these examples, recalls, 'the Semitic expression for the tenderest love'.[1]

The medieval Italian Harmonies are divided into two groups, according as they belong to the Venetian or Tuscan dialects. They have been dated to the thirteenth or fourteenth centuries; nothing is mentioned in the manuscripts as to authorship, provenance, or use. It has been thought, however, that they may have been designed for circulation within the Church. But it is more likely that they were originally intended, like the Dutch Harmonies, for popular use; the theological expositions, frequent in the Venetian Harmony and clearly ecclesiastical in origin, may be of later date than the Harmonies themselves. In addition to the many manuscripts which exist of these vulgar Italian Harmonies (for the Tuscan group alone the editors have collected and collated no less than twenty-four), there is also preserved, in medieval Tuscan Italian, a Diatessaron in verse like Maerlant's *Rijmbijbel*, the work of a certain Jacopo Gradonico who lived towards the end of the fourteenth century. As in the case of the *Rijmbijbel*, the basis of Gradonico's verse translation is a

[1] *A Primitive Text*, p. 79 f.

Gospel Harmony, in this case in Tuscan Italian. It is curious to find, as in the Dutch Harmonies and the *Rijmbijbel*, a scribal error in Gradonico's verse shared by the Tuscan Harmony, thus giving a *terminus ad quem* for the dating of the Tuscan manuscripts; Gradonico's work was completed at Padua, A.D. 1399. Mk. xvi. 20 is rendered in the Vulgate *et profecti praedicaverunt ubique*; the Tuscan text has 'and going forth *perfect* they preached everywhere'; obviously the Latin *profecti* has been read twice and the second time, by a scribal error, as *perfecti*. It is not surprising to find this error reproduced in Gradonico's Italian verse, but it is a curious coincidence that we should find the same mistake in the old Anglo-Saxon Gospels, which have 'then they perfect (*fulfelde*) preached everywhere'.[1] Another point of contact, however, between English and Italian Harmony tradition is not so easily explained as coincidence. In one of Wiclif's unpublished Harmony manuscripts, based on the work of Clement of Llanthony, the same interpretation of the first verse of St. John as we find in the Italian Harmonies occurs. Wiclif and the Italian Gospels avoid the literal rendering 'the Word' and popularize by interpreting 'the Son': thus Wiclif:[2] 'In the beginning or first of all things: was goddes sone: and goddes sone was at God: and God was goddes sone . . .'; the Tuscan text has, 'Nel principio era Figliuolo di Dio, e 'l Figliuolo di Dio era appo Dio, e era Iddio il Figliuolo di Dio.'

An example of a Tatian reading in the vulgar Italian occurs in the rendering of both Venetian and Tuscan families of Mt. xxvii. 5, where Judas 'went and hanged himself'; Tatian and the Italian and Dutch Harmonies add 'with a rope'. A unique form of the Lord's Prayer occurs in the Venetian manuscript though it is clearly not a genuine variant; the expansion is probably the work of the Italian or Latin translator, though it is surprising to find liberties of this kind taken: it reads, 'Suffer us not to enter into *danger* or temptation (*no ne lasare vegnire in pericolo ne in tentatione*)'. For 'our daily bread' the Tuscan Harmony has 'our super-substantial daily bread (*il pane nostre soprasustantiale cotidiano*)', thus combining the usual version with the ancient Latin interpretation of 'metaphysical or spiritual sustenance'.

There are no parallels to the extraordinary rendering of Mt. xii. 32, where the A.V. has: 'And whosoever speaketh a word against the

[1] *The Holy Gospels in Anglo Saxon, Northumbrian and Old Mercian Versions*, edit. W. Skeat (Cambridge, 1887), in loc.

[2] The first few verses of St. John from Wiclif's MS. are given in Plooij's *A Primitive Text*, p. 3.

son of Man, it shall be forgiven him: but whosoever speaketh against the Holy Ghost, it shall not be forgiven him'; the Tuscan Gospels have: 'Whosoever speaketh a word *against the Father* (parola contra 'l Padre), it shall be forgiven him: and whosoever speaketh a word against the Son, &c.' Probably the desire to include all the Persons of the Trinity led to the introduction of the *parola contra 'l Padre*. Another unusual rendering is the Tuscan version of Lk. xix. 38, '*Peace be on earth* (pace sia in terra) and glory in the highest'.

In the manner of all the medieval Harmonies the Italian Diatessaron seeks to simplify the many difficult foreign terms in the Gospels. The Herodians (Mt. xxii. 16) are described as 'i cavalieri d'Erode', a translation which is reproduced in Gradonico's verse. The Good Samaritan is described as 'un homo mondano'; Joseph of Arimathaea is a 'nobile conestabile di diece cavalieri ed era da Marimattia'. The Aramaic word *raca* in Mt. v. 22 is 'cosa non formata'.

Of the Gospel Harmonies in other medieval languages not the least interesting, if of less value critically, is the Middle English Harmony used by Samuel Pepys and called after him *The Pepysian Gospel Harmony*. This Middle English Gospel was part of the manuscript described as *Pepys 2498* in the Library of Magdalene College, Cambridge, and had been erroneously catalogued as a collection of Wiclif's sermons. The real contents of the manuscript were discovered in 1902, when it was found to contain, in addition to Pepys's Gospel, eight other works of a religious or moralizing nature, including the earliest of the nine known Middle English manuscripts of the *Gospel of Nicodemus*. On the front cover of the manuscript containing the Harmony is one of Pepys's own book-plates, imprinted in gold, and decorated with two anchors entwined with ropes: the inscription reads,

SAM. PEPYS
CAR. ET IAC.
ANGL. REGIB.
A SECRETIS
ADMIRALIAE

There does not appear to be any further information about Pepys's use of the Harmony, but, to judge from his elaborate and costly book-plate, the book was much treasured by him. The date is given in a note on p. 370 of the volume:

> The age of this book. by conferring with an other coppy, was wretten when k henry the. 4. had busines agayste the welshmen. Ano/1401/.

There appear therefore to have been other copies of the Harmony. Actually we can trace the existence and use of popular Scriptures in the vulgar tongue in this country to a much earlier date than on the Continent. In England the demand for popular Scriptures is said to have begun as early as King Alfred, who is said not to have overlooked the importance of vernacular Scriptures.[1] It is usually believed that the Anglo-Saxon Gospel tradition took its beginnings in the ninth or tenth centuries.[2]

The editor of the Pepysian Harmony text draws attention to the Harmony tradition begun in Tatian, but does not appear to find any connexion between the two. The Pepysian Gospels are very probably lineal descendants of the Tatian tradition, at the third remove, for the Middle English text is based on a French translation of an Old Latin version of the Diatessaron. One remarkable point of contact with Tatian is the presence in the English Harmony of the *lumen magnum* at the Baptism: 'And when he was baptised, . . . so com the brichtnesse of heuene & the Holy Gost & alichteth withinne hym'. Another well-known apocryphal element in the Harmony is the statement that the infant Jesus was laid in a manger, where 'an ox and an asse stoden'; the earliest mention of the ox and the ass at Bethlehem is in the pseudo-Matthew of the fifth century. The Harmony also contains the legendary tradition that Judas ' . . . went hym forth and henge hym self on a nelren tree (elder tree)'.

The aim of the English harmonist is to present the life of our Lord with simplicity, and in his effort to achieve it we find abundant evidence that the Harmony was written for simple, unlettered folk. The Pharisees are 'the folk of religioun in that tyme'. The publicans are 'the hethene baylives servaunts', and the Samaritans 'in one half weren Jews & in another half hij weren payens (pagans)'. Biblical words and phrases are replaced by homely parallels: in Mt. iii. 4 John the Baptist ate not 'locusts and wild honey' but 'garlic and bryony' or 'ramesones (broad-leaved garlic) and wilde-nepes'. In the miracle of the Water that was turned to Wine the 'gode man' (the 'ruler of the feast' in the A.V.) summoned, not the bridegroom (Jn. ii. 9), 'he cleped the botiler (butler)'. When Mary Magdalene recognized Jesus in the Garden on Easter Sunday, 'she fel adoun to his feete and seide, Ha! Swete Sir.'

Whether the credit is to go to the English harmonist or his sources, certainly the joint product of the tradition has claims to real literary merit. The blind man whom Jesus restored to sight on the Sabbath,

[1] See Skeat, op. cit., Preface to Mark, p. ii.

[2] Ibid.

when the Pharisees questioned him, 'answered so swetelich and so dignelich for Jesus sake that for pure jre hij dryven him away.' In Lk. ix. 55, for the A.V. 'ye know not what manner of spirit ye are of', the harmonist paraphrases, 'ne witen ye how ye scholden bere you swetelich and soft.' Before His Ascension our Lord blessed His disciples, 'and he kyssed hem all by and by'. After the cock had crowed the third time, Peter went forth and wept, not only 'wel sore' but 'tenderlich', a detail which appears to have been in the Gospel tradition.[1] The gorgeous robe of Lk. xxiii. 11 is in the Vulgate *vestis alba*, which the English harmonist thus interprets: '. . . and (Heroude) cladde hym in a white cloth as he hadde ben a foole'. The harmonist's picture of Jesus comes out clearly in the story of the woman taken in adultery, to whom the Lord turned 'wel suetelich', a favourite expression.

We can well realize why Pepys treasured this 'litel tretis of diuinitie'. No doubt he was a busy man who preferred an abridged form of his Bible; but its greater appeal, as may indeed be said of all the Harmonies of the Middle Ages, lay in its straightforward and intelligible treatment of Holy Writ, and in its simple beauty and unfailing charm.

An Old Hebrew Gospel of St. Matthew (not a Harmony text) belonging to the sixteenth century has been shown to contain several unexpected variants found elsewhere in Syriac sources only. It is Mercier's 1555 Hebrew Matthew, acquired by a certain Jean du Tillet while travelling in Italy in 1553. The publisher of the Hebrew text firmly believed that it was a descendant of the lost 'Hebrew' original of St. Matthew's Gospel; he claims on the title-page: 'The Gospel of Matthew, until this day laid up among the Jews and concealed in their recesses, and now at last, from out of their apartments and from darkness, brought forth into the light.' This claim has been recently revived by H. J. Schonfield in an introduction to his translation of the Hebrew;[2] Schonfield makes much of the agreement with the Old Syriac tradition, but this is satisfactorily accounted for by the assumption of an Old Latin original for the Hebrew text, which, like the Old Latin tradition elsewhere, had points of contact with the Syriac versions. The author of the Hebrew Matthew was probably a certain Shem-Tob ben Shaprut, a famous Jewish polemical writer who flourished in Spain in the fourteenth century.[3]

[1] Cf. *Mandeville's Travels* (edit. G. F. Warner, English Texts Society, cliii, 1923), p. 61, line 64: 'Et la est le lieu ou seint Piere ploroit mult tendrement'.

[2] *An Old Hebrew Text of Matthew's Gospel* (T. & T. Clark, 1927).

[3] Cf. A. Herbst, *Des Schemtob ben Schaphrut hebraeische Übersetzung des Evangeliums Matthaei* (Göttingen, 1879).

APPENDIX C

THE UNPUBLISHED WORK OF THE LATE A. J. WENSINCK OF LEIDEN

THE name of A. J. Wensinck of Leiden is well known to orientalists and only less so to Biblical scholars. His untimely death in 1939 was perhaps an even greater loss to those Aramaic and New Testament studies to which, in his later years, he had come increasingly to devote himself, than to the Islamic scholarship in which he made his name. His published work in the former field is not large; his most important study was a brief monograph on the Aramaic strand in the Western text of St. Luke's Gospel.[1] Its scope, however, was much wider than his occasional articles attest, and his actual achievement has only become fully known with the examination of his unpublished notes and studies on the Palestinian Targum and Talmud.[2]

The Aramaic literature cited by Wensinck in illustration of Bezan Semitisms makes it clear that he no longer shared current assumptions about our principal sources for first-century Jewish Palestinian Aramaic; Targum Onkelos, the primary source employed by Gustaf Dalman, hitherto the recognized authority on the subject,[3] is tacitly replaced by the evidence of the old Palestinian Pentateuch Targum found in the Cairo Geniza, together with its related *haggadic* portions preserved in the so-called Pseudo-Jonathan and Fragment Targums. This choice of literary sources for first-century Palestinian Aramaic is fully confirmed (and no less amply justified) by Wensinck's unpublished notes: together with the Aramaic of the Palestinian Talmud (and excluding the older Imperial 'West Aramaic' of Daniel, Ezra, and the Elephantine Papyri) the Palestinian Targum constitutes an authority of the first magnitude for the West Aramaic actually spoken and written in Palestine from the first century down to the time of the Arab Conquest.[4]

[1] 'The Semitisms of Codex Bezae and their Relation to the non-Western Text of the Gospel of Saint Luke', in the *Bulletin of the Bezan Club*, vol. xii (Leiden, 1937).

[2] By the courtesy of Mrs. Wensinck and Professor P. A. H. de Boer part of this material, until recently in Leiden University, has been sent to this country and placed in the custody of a fellow-orientalist and personal friend of its author, Emeritus Professor Paul Kahle, formerly of Bonn University. Dr. Kahle has very kindly given me access to the collection.

[3] The *Worte Jesu* was first published some fifty years ago.

[4] See further Kahle, *The Cairo Geniza*, p. 129, and *supra*, p. 19 and pp. 35 ff.

Wensinck had also come to realize the importance of Palestinian Syriac and of Samaritan Aramaic, and recognized that his work would require to be extended to include their evidence in order to complete the study of West Aramaic as a whole.[1] The former is already represented by the Grammar and Lexicon of Friedrich Schulthess:[2] only one extensive piece of the literature known to exist remains unedited; it is a Christian Palestinian Syriac Horologion of some 200 folios, on which I am at present engaged, and contains a number of valuable additions to the vocabulary of the language.[3] My former colleague in Leeds, Dr. John Bowman, has been working for some time on an edition of the *Memar*, a kind of Midrash, of the Samaritan fourth-century author Marka; here too the editor must precede the lexicographer.

The unpublished material comprises a completed collection of the Aramaic vocabulary of the Palestinian Pentateuch Targum from the Geniza; a lexicon of the Aramaic portions of the Palestinian Talmud, incomplete; a completed grammar of this Targumic and Talmudic Aramaic; a vocabulary of Greek words and expressions in the New Testament with Semitic equivalents and cross-references to both lexica; and a collection of philological notes and jottings on the Gospels and the first half of Acts. Words are arranged alphabetically on cards, or, in the grammar, grouped in cards according to subject; the notes on the Gospels and Acts are also on cards, ordered according to chapter and verse. The purpose of both grammar and two-part lexicon is to furnish an adequate basis for the study of the Aramaic spoken and written in Palestine in the time of Christ, and in so doing to provide an instrument for the further elucidation of the New Testament.

In his Greek vocabulary and philological notes Wensinck refers to the Palestinian Targum material as a whole, distinguishing individual sources by the contractions *pal.* (Geniza fragments), *fragm.* (Fragment Targum), *ion.* (Pseudo-Jonathan). The abbreviations are slightly misleading, for the Fragment Targum and the older material in Pseudo-Jonathan both derive from the same Palestinian tradition as *pal.*; in this Appendix and my Supplementary Notes I refer to them simply as G (Geniza source), F (Fragment Targum), and P-J (Pseudo-Jonathan).

[1] I owe this information to Dr. Kahle.

[2] *Gramm. des christlich-palästinischen Aramäisch* (Tübingen, 1924); *Lexicon Syropalaestinum* (Berlin, 1903).

[3] See 'A Christian Palestinian Syriac Horologion', in *Studia Semitica et Orientalia*, ii (Glasgow, 1945), Cambridge *Texts and Studies*, Second Series, Cambridge, 1954.

The main object of the notes and vocabulary is to determine the Semitic equivalents of suspected Greek expressions, or to illustrate abnormal Greek from Semitic usage, mainly Aramaic, but with reference also to Hebrew and Old Testament Greek; Wensinck does not appear to have been impressed by theories of Syriac influence. References to Aramaic literature are frequent but not complete, and the notes themselves are not all of equal value, and could hardly be published in their still inchoate form. But they contain much relevant material and a number of acute observations.

The most valuable illustrations come from the Palestinian Pentateuch Targum; and one need not, in fact, read far there to be convinced that its language, down to its actual pronunciation,[1] belongs to the New Testament period. Some of its most characteristic modes of expression come from the religious vocabulary of Aramaic poetry, preserved in the poetic *haggada* of the old Targum. An example is the expression found in Q, *γεννητοὶ γυναικῶν* (Mt. xi. 11 = Lk. vii. 28): the Semitic phrase ילוד אתתא occurs twice in the dialogue between Moses and the Red Sea, at Exod. xiv. 29 (F).[2] The metaphor of 'tasting' death, as is well known, does not occur in the Old Testament; for it we have to go to rabbinical sources: the same holds good for the metaphor of the cup in the Gospels (Mk. xiv. 36 *et par.*); the following parallel occurs at Gen. xl. 32 (F): 'Now Joseph forsook the mercy from above and the mercy from beneath . . . he trusted . . . in the flesh that passeth away, and in the flesh *that tasteth the cup of death* (דטעים כסא דמותא).'[3] Some indication of the extent to which the old Targum of Palestine employs the same religious language as the Gospels may be gathered from some of the parallels which Wensinck gives to expressions in the Lord's Prayer[4] and in the Johannine Prologue.[5] For the latter, the accumulated evidence creates a strong

[1] See *The Cairo Geniza*, p. 129; *supra*, p. 23.

[2] I have noted the Hebrew expression ילוד אשה Job xiv. 1, xv. 14, xxv. 4, and in 3 Enoch (ed. Hugo Odeberg, Cambridge, 1928) vi. 2 (Trans., p. 20, Text, יב).

[3] See further my note on 'The Cup Metaphor in Mk. 14[36]' in *Expository Times*, lix, p. 195.

[4] Exod. xvii. 11 (F), 'And it came to pass, when Moses had lifted up his hands in prayer to his Father in Heaven (אבוי דבשמיא) . . .'. Cf. Exod. i. 19, 21 (F), Num. xxi. 9 (F); Gen. xxxviii. 25 (P-J) cf. (*Shebi'ith* iv. 2, *Berach.* iv. 2); Exod. xiv. 29 (F); Gen. xliv. 18 (G), xxxvii. 33 (F), xlix. 10 (F); Exod. xv. 3 (F), xx. 1 (G), xx. 3 (F), &c.

[5] Exod. xv. 8 (F), 'By a Memar from thy presence, O God, the waters became

presumption that in this early Targum source we have a Jewish doctrine only a little less developed than that which we find in the *haggada* of Philo. Perhaps we need not look beyond Palestine for the inspiration of the Logos doctrine of John.

The language and idiom of simple narrative and everyday speech is also fully represented. In the free paraphrase of Gen. xxxii. 25 (P-J), xlix. 2 (F), עני ואמר occurs.[1] The 'Hebraism' *καὶ ἐγένετο* is found also in the free Aramaic, Gen. iv. 16 (F). Gen. xlix. 1 (F) has the form אפתח (cf. the imperative *ἐφφαθά*, Mk. vii. 34). The Semitism *ἄρχομαι ἀπό* (Lk. xxiii. 5, xxiv. 27, 47; Acts viii. 35; Jn. viii. 9) appears in Aramaic at Gen. xliv. 18 (F), מינך אנא מתחיל. The locution at Lk. xviii. 11, *σταθεὶς ‹ταῦτα› πρὸς ἑαυτὸν προσηύχετο* is fully elucidated by Exod. xx. 15 (G, F) (cf. Exod. xiv. 15 (P-J)), וקמין להון מצלין (מן רחיק), 'and *they took their stand, praying*, at a distance': that this was the regular expression is clear from two further examples (also with the ethic dative) from *Shabb.* i. 2, *Rosh. Hash.* ii. 5.[2] Among proper names we meet the familiar טור מישחא, *ὄρος τῶν ἐλαιῶν*, at Gen. viii. 11 (P-J), and מלפי אוריתא (*νομοδιδάσκαλοι*) occurs at Gen. xlix. 7, 10 (F). Wensinck had also detected the Aramaic idiom in Luke's *σήμερον καὶ αὔριον* (xiii. 33), comparing Gen. xxxix. 10 (F).[3]

In the material from the Palestinian Talmud, the following parallels are not without interest. In *Nedar.* vi. 3, a semi-proverbial saying occurs:

> 'It is not the way of a man to say to his friend,
> Buy me a fish—and he buy him a כלכיד.'

The last word is the Greek *χαλκίς* (*χαλκιδική*), a small edible fish,

an heap' (cf. Wisdom ix. 1). Cf. Gen. xi. 2 (F); Exod. iii. 14 (F); Exod. vi. 7 (G); Lev. xxii. 26 (G); Exod. xx. 1–2 (G); Exod. xiii. 21 (F), xv. 18 (F); Gen. xxi. 33 (F), xl. 32 (F); Exod. xiv. 31 (F); Gen. xxx. 22 (F); Exod. xiv. 4 (F), xx. 21 (F); Exod. xxii. 22 (G).

[1] Cf. Dalman, *Worte Jesu*, p. 19.

[2] Cf. Torrey, *Our Translated Gospels*, p. 76, and *supra*, p. 78. These examples convince me that Torrey is right, but cf. Wensinck, op. cit., p. 43 (note). The *dativus ethicus* makes it clear that the *σταθείς* is not just an auxiliary (Dalman, op. cit., p. 18, *völlig bedeutungslos*).

[3] My application of this idiom to the elucidation of *ἐπιούσιος* in the Lord's Prayer has been criticized recently by Professor A. Debrunner (*Theologische Zeitschrift*, Oct. 1947), who refers me to his own derivation (Blass–Debrunner, *Grammatik*, §§ 123, 124, and p. 296; cf. Moulton, *Gramm.*, p. 313). The identification with *diurnia*, however, assumed by Debrunner, is anything but certain for the Preisigke papyrus (cf. *J.T.S.* xxxv, p. 376 f.); and the derivation from *ἐπὶ τὴν οὖσαν* (*ἡμέραν*), 'for the current day', on the analogy of *ἐφημέριος*, *ἐπιμήνιος*, seems to me to be as precarious. I am also referred to Debrunner's account of

perhaps to be identified with a sardine;[1] the point of the saying is obviously humorous. The term כלכיד was also used for a species of ὄφις, but it is doubtful if we can find here any connexion other than a general one with Lk. xi. 11. From *Ma'aser Sheni* v. 4, שלמכון יסגא, 'May your well-being increase', it is worthy of note that the greeting which we find in a Christian formula at 1 Peter i. 2 (χάρις ὑμῖν καὶ) εἰρήνη πληθυνθείη, was also in epistolary use among the rabbis: if the tradition is genuine, it occurs in a letter of Rabbi Gamaliel;[2] the only other place where the greeting has been found is in the letter of Nebuchadrezzar (also in Aramaic) in Dan. iii. 31. An Aramaic form of greeting in the Greek Epistle may well be taken as confirmation of its Petrine inspiration; similar Semitic greetings accommodated to Greek forms are familiar elsewhere in the Epistles.[3] For compounds of εἰρήνη in its literal meaning with ποιεῖν (Mt. v. 9 εἰρηνοποιός; Col. i. 20 εἰρηνοποιεῖν; Jas. iii. 18 ποιεῖν εἰρήνην), Wensinck compares *Berach.* ix. 1 מיעבד שלמא, 'to reconcile'.

A rabbinical use of ἀκούειν, especially when followed by παρά or ἐκ, claims a number of cards and references in the Greek vocabulary; the Gospel examples are Jn. iii. 29, v. 30, vi. 45, viii. 26, 38, 40, 47, xii. 34; Mt. v. 21, 27, 33; Lk. viii. 18. The usage reflects the corresponding Talmudic שמע, 'to receive a שמעתא, opinion, tradition, from', and hence 'to receive (traditional) teaching from', especially on a point of *halacha*; and so simply 'to be taught', 'to learn from'; *Shabb.* vii. 1 *et pass.* So Lk. viii. 18, 'Take heed, therefore, how ye are instructed'; Jn. xii. 34, 'We have been taught from the Law', &c. Other less usual uses of ἀκούειν which Wensinck suspects are Mk. ii. 1, ἠκούσθη, 'it was reported' (cf. Acts xi. 22, 1 Cor. v. 1); cf. Gen. xliv. 18 (G), הלא אשתמע לך, 'Has it not been reported to you?' The meaning 'to hear and understand', 'to grasp', is found in Greek authors, but it may perhaps be doubted if it is as common in Greek as it is regular in Semitic languages; thus Mk. iv. 33, καθὼς ἠδύναντο ἀκούειν (cf. iv. 20).

With several uses of ἄνθρωπος, standing alone and with little more force than *quidam*, Wensinck compares the use of the corresponding

ἐν αὐτῇ τῇ ὥρᾳ (op. cit., § 288). But no explanation of this Lucan peculiarity can afford to ignore (as Debrunner's does) its use in the LXX of Daniel as a rendering of the Aramaic. For both points see *supra*, p. 205 and pp. 108 ff.

[1] See Liddell and Scott, s.v.

[2] The letter has been published by Dalman in his *Aramäische Dialektproben*, p. 3 (in *Ma'aser Sheni* v. 4 it is one letter, not three). Was Aramaic the recognized medium of communication with the Diaspora in the first century?

[3] Consult *I.C.C.*, 1 Cor. i. 3.

Aramaic ברנש, *τις*, with negative לית, *οὐδείς*; e.g. *Nedar*. v. 4 *et pass.* Examples are Mk. vii. 11, *ἐὰν εἴπῃ ἄνθρωπος*, 'if anyone says', viii. 36; Jn. iii. 27, v. 7, *ἄνθρωπον οὐκ ἔχω ἵνα* . . ., 'I have no one to . . .'.[1] Aramaic בר אנשא, (*ὁ*) *υἱὸς τοῦ ἀνθρώπου* = (*ὁ*) *ἄνθρωπος*, is fully attested for first-century Palestinian Aramaic; Dalman's view that אנשא is the regular expression follows on his assumption that Onkelos alone can be our authoritative source;[2] an example is Gen. ix. 6 (G).[3]

An Aramaism is found in the expression *ἐργάζομαι ἐν* (*ἐμοί*) at Mk. xiv. 6, and Wensinck compares Gen. xxxi. 43 (G), '. . . and what shall I do to them (ומה אעבד באלין)'. Cf. also Gen. xxxi. 50, 52 (P-J), where the expression is עבד ל לות, as in the parallel in Mt. xxvi. 10, *εἰς ἐμέ* (Syriac Vss. ܠܘܬܝ). With Mk. xiv. 8, *Hagiga* ii. 2, 'Thou, what is in thy power, do (את מה אית בך עבד)', is compared.

The Semitism at Lk. xiv. 20 (D), *γυναῖκα ἔλαβον* (Bא *γυναῖκα ἔγημα*) might be set down to the influence of the LXX; cf. Gen. xxiv. 4. The example is noted by Wensinck in his vocabulary under *λαμβάνειν γυναῖκα* = *γαμεῖν*, and illustrated from *Kethub*. x. 5, '. . . and they took for themselves wives (ונסבין להון נשין)'. Its source in the Bezan text of Luke is not improbably Palestinian Aramaic (it occurs in a parable). The appearance of the Aramaism in D is significant.

In view of the attestation in Classical and later Greek of *λέγειν* in the meaning 'to enjoin', 'to command', it might seem a work of supererogation on Wensinck's part to trace this usage in the New Testament to Semitic influence. The broad distinction, however, between the two languages appears to be that, whereas in Greek the meaning is (comparatively) rare, in the Semitic group (so in Arabic) it is regular. Thus where Luke substitutes *παρήγγελλεν γὰρ τῷ πνεύματι* . . . (viii. 29) for Mark's *ἔλεγεν γὰρ αὐτῷ, ἔξελθε* (v. 8), it is reasonable to suppose that he felt that *λέγειν*, in the context, was, from a literary point of view, inadequate; and that Mark reflects the regular Semitic use of the word. Similarly, where in Lk. xvii. 10 (D) we find the clumsy *ὅταν ποιήσητε ὅσα λέγω, λέγετε* . . . (a saying of Jesus from *L*), it is a likely inference that we have here the primitive translation text, and that Bא's *ὅταν ποιήσητε πάντα τὰ διαταχθέντα ὑμῖν, λέγετε*, is a literary *diorthosis*. Other examples in the New Testament which I have noted are Lk. vi. 46,[4] xii. 13, xix. 15, Jn. ii. 5; cf. Rom. ii. 22.

[1] See further p. 107.

[2] *Worte Jesu*, p. 193.

[3] See pp. 316 ff.

[4] Cf. the Egerton Papyrus parallel, *μὴ ἀκούοντες ὃ λέγω*, 'not hearkening to what I enjoin'; Bell and Skeat, *Fragments of an Unknown Gospel*, p. 26.

Lk. xviii. 4, Bℵ εἶπεν ἐν ἑαυτῷ contains a well-known Semitism, 'to speak in the mind', 'to think' (the full Semitism at Rev. xviii. 7, ἐν τῇ καρδίᾳ αὐτῆς λέγει; cf. Isa. xlvii. 8, LXX). The reading of D is ἦλθεν εἰς ἑαυτὸν καὶ λέγει, where λέγει by itself, like its Semitic equivalent, means 'thinks'; with this passage Wensinck compares, *inter alia*, Gen. xliv. 18 (F), 'Judah reflected in his mind, thinking . . . (חשב יהודא בליביה ואמר)'.

Both in the notes and the vocabulary, a number of cards are devoted to some less familiar uses of ποιεῖν. In some cases Greek and Semitic usage again overlap, which need not mean, however, that the latter may be overlooked. Thus ποιήσατε at Mt. xii. 33 in the sense 'regard (the tree) as', 'ponite' is found in both Greek and Aramaic; the use is common, however, in rabbinical Aramaic to an extent which makes it not unlikely that the latter has been the main influence in Matthew's form here of the Synoptic saying.[1] A parallel is cited from *Bikkurim* i. 6 (*bis*), עבד את־האילן כקשין, '. . . he regarded the tree as (the equivalent of) stubble'; cf. also *Erub*. viii. 2, *Shabb*. xix. 5 *et pass*. Wensinck would include under this use Jn. viii. 53, 'Whom do you make yourself out (ποιεῖς) to be?'; xix. 7, '. . . because he regarded himself, made himself out to be a son of God'; xix. 12, 'Everyone who takes himself to be, makes himself out to be, a king'. Other uses of ποιεῖν are less familiar, and some quite unattested, in Greek, such as ποιεῖν καρπούς, with which Wensinck compares Gen. xlix. 15, 21 (Onk.); he connects with this meaning the sense of 'produce' at Mk. iv. 32, ποιεῖ κλάδους μεγάλους, and Lk. xix. 18, ἡ μνᾶ σου . . . ἐποίησεν πέντε μνᾶς, '. . . thy mina *made* five minas'. For the expression ποιεῖν ἄριστον ἢ δεῖπνον, Lk. xiv. 12, Gen. xxix. 22 (F), ועבד שירו, is cited, and *Baba Mes*. ii. 5, עבד אריסטון, compared (cf. also Dan. v. 1, Theod.). Mt. xx. 12, ἐποίησαν, 'worked', is noted, but no references to the literature are given; we may perhaps compare Exod. xxxvi. 1 (P-J) and Prov. xxxi. 13.

With reference to πορεύεσθαι in Lk. xxii. 22 (cf. xxii. 33), *Yoma* iii. 7 (אזל, *discedere a vita, mori*) is quoted. One undoubted Greek instance of πορευθῆναι in this sense[2] and the usage of Hebrew and the LXX must also, however, be borne in mind. But there do not appear to be any Greek or LXX parallels to ὑπάγειν so used as in the parallel passage at Mk. xiv. 21, or to the frequent use of this verb in the

[1] Cf. *supra*, p. 202. In view of the above usage, it could now be added that the Matthaean form at xii. 33 is a rabbinical misinterpretation of the Aramaic phrase καρπὸν ποιεῖν, or else a rabbinical alternative interpretation to that in Q.

[2] Julian, *Epistolae*, 4 ed. Loeb; 384 D. The translation of the Loeb edition is almost certainly wrong; cf. Liddell and Scott, s.v.

Fourth Gospel, especially of the final *discessio Domini*. It is extremely doubtful if we are justified in interpreting and rendering the Johannine usage as meaning 'to go home' on the basis of a few instances only of such a use in the Greek Tobit.[1] The usage both in Mark and John is, moreover, sufficiently unusual to suggest alien influence; the frequency of the word in John, in this and in other senses,[2] as compared with its comparative infrequency in Greek authors, is a sufficient indication of the hampering influence of a foreign idiom. It seems probable, in view of the Aramaic colouring in the Fourth Gospel and the presence of the expression in a saying of Jesus in Mark, that the influence in question is Aramaic. In addition to the example given by Wensinck, a typical instance occurs at *Hagiga* ii. 2, 'One committed a sin and died by it (ואזל בה); and the one that did this good work, died by it.'[3] Cf. also *Kethub.* xii. 3, 'As a man departeth this life so he will return (כמא דברנש אזל הוא אתי).'

Two Semitic idioms are reported in the same verses at Acts viii. 39, 40; ἐπορεύετο τὴν ὁδὸν αὐτοῦ is claimed as Aramaic both in the notes and vocabulary; Gen. iv. 7 (F), אזל חבל לאורחיה, 'Abel went his way' is quoted in support and *Mo'ed Qaton* iii. 7 also cited; for other New Testament examples, cf. Lk. ix. 57, Acts viii. 36. For the second idiom, Φίλιππος δὲ εὑρέθη εἰς Ἄζωτον, Wensinck compares *Ma'aser Sheni* v. 2, and Gen. xxviii. 10 (F, Paris MS., Ginsburger, p. 15), '. . . the land was shortened before him, and *he arrived in* Haran (ואשתכח בחרן).'[4]

A number of the examples of Semitisms discussed above are found exclusively in the Bezan Uncial. In directing attention to this Semitic element in D in Luke, Wensinck made a valuable contribution to the textual criticism of the New Testament. The following are additional instances where the primitive text can be recognized by its Semitic character. They come from both notes and vocabulary.

Lk. viii. 41 (D) reads, πεσὼν ὑπὸ (Bא παρὰ) τοὺς πόδας Ἰησοῦ: 'to fall at (lit. under) the feet of' contains an idiomatic Semitic use of

[1] Cf. Abbott, *Johannine Vocabulary*, p. 123 f.

[2] For an auxiliary use, *supra*, p. 126; Torrey, *Our Translated Gospels*, p. 39 f. For inchoative or auxiliary verbs cf. Wensinck, op. cit., p. 21 f. I am doubtful if διαβλέψεις (Lk. vi. 42 *et par.*) could reflect an auxiliary חמא, 'endeavour', as Wensinck thinks. But other uses of that verb besides 'to see' deserve consideration for this passage; it means 'to be fit to', 'worthy to', e.g. Gen. xlix. 22 (F); the use of אהמי (Targum אחמי) with an infinitive, *renoncer à* (cf. Syriac ܐܬܚܡܝ), is also worth noticing. Cf. Prov. xxviii. 17, Job. vi. 17.

[3] Given by Dalman in his *Aramäische Dialektproben*, p. 34.

[4] Cf. Wilcox, op. cit., pp. 100, 137 ff.

the preposition (Hebrew תחת, Aramaic תחות, 'under'). Wensinck illustrates from Exod. xix. 17 (Hebrew and Aramaic), Gen. xxxv. 8 (G), and Gen. xxxviii. 25 (F), '. . . and she cast them at the feet (תחות ריגלוי) of the judges'.

In Mt. xv. 24, *εἰς τὰ πρόβατα <ταῦτα> τὰ ἀπολωλότα*, the addition is that of D (= Sy^{vet}). As Greek, the demonstrative adjective is meaningless; as an Aramaism it may be accounted for as an instance of relative with preceding demonstrative antecedent, 'the sheep, the ones (these) that are lost'; the particle ד employed thus correlatively with a previous demonstrative need only be rendered by the Greek article. Wensinck rejects the explanation that the intrusive *ταῦτα* is a Syriacism; D is here the source of the Syr^{vet}.

But it is not always D which preserves the Aramaism. An unobtrusive example is detected by Wensinck in B at Lk. vii. 32 (= Mt. xi. 17). The text of Matthew introduces the words of the children's game with an asyndeton *λέγουσι*; in Luke, the manuscripts offer the choice of several readings:

1. *λέγοντες* אD (*λέγοντα* 157).
2. *καὶ λέγουσι* T. R.
3. *οἳ λέγουσι* Λ, 262.
4. *ἃ λέγει* B.

The last variant is the most difficult as Greek; Wensinck equates it with the Aramaic דאמר, *comme on dit*, and cites more than a dozen instances of the idiom from the Palestinian Talmud; it occurs, in fact, there, as John Lightfoot remarked of the rabbinical 'flesh and blood', 'infinite times': *Erub.* v. 1, *Kil'aim* ix. 7, *Shebi'ith* ii. 10, &c.; the formula varies with דאת אמר (= *ἃ λέγεις*), e.g. *Bikkurim* iii. 5, דאת אמר פטירין עם מרורין, 'As one says, the vases with the spices' (a proverbial saying). The source of the variations in Greek manuscripts is probably the *difficilior lectio* of B.

While much in this material is new (the references to the literature are particularly welcome), such a survey necessarily covers familiar ground. But it would be an advantage to have the Semitisms of the New Testament conveniently put together in a single dictionary; and the Wensinck collection contains the raw material for such and for the indispensable Aramaic Grammar and Lexicon, which must be the foundation of any work on the Aramaic element.

APPENDIX D

THE ARAMAIC LITURGICAL POETRY OF THE JEWS

IN no field of Jewish studies has the Cairo Geniza contributed more positively than in that of post-Biblical Hebrew poetry. Until the examination of the 10,000 or so photographs of Geniza fragments in the Research Institute for Hebrew poetry in Jerusalem, our knowledge of the history of the *Piut* or Hebrew liturgical poem was of the sketchiest; even the most celebrated of the *Peitanim*, Elasar b. Kalir, of whose work some 200 piuts have survived in the Mahzors or liturgies, was nothing more than a name, unillumined by its halo. Now, we know that Kalir (a Hebrew form of the Greek Cyril) was neither innovator nor legislator in this type of poetry; he was, in fact, a late eighth-century imitator of earlier poets of the sixth and seventh centuries, of whom one of the most famous was a certain Yannai, some 800 of whose poems have been recovered.[1]

Not even Yannai nor his sixth-century contemporaries, however, were the creators of the piut, the origins of which Dr. Paul Kahle, in his chapter on the Liturgical Poetry of the Jews in *The Cairo Geniza*, has traced into the fifth century A.D. He there writes:

> 'Very little is known to us of Jewish liturgical poetry of that older time. . . . But a great amount of liturgical poetry composed in the fourth and fifth centuries in Palestine is preserved in the Samaritan Liturgy. Especially the so-called 'Defter', a kind of Common Prayer, which is the oldest part of this Liturgy, contains a number of interesting liturgical poems of the fourth century poet Marka and his followers. They were composed in the Aramaic language which was spoken in Palestine by Jews and by Samaritans, and it may be that the Jews too used the Aramaic language for their liturgical poetry of that time.'[2]

It is the purpose of this note to point out, not only that the Jews did employ the Aramaic language for their liturgical poetry of this early time, but also that Aramaic liturgical poems from this period have actually survived in some of the poetic haggadoth of the Palestinian Pentateuch Targum, important Geniza fragments of

[1] Cf. Kahle, *The Cairo Geniza*, p. 20 f., and *Piyyute Yannai.* Liturgical Poems of Yannai, collected from Geniza Manuscripts and other sources and published by Menachem Zulay, Berlin, 1938. See also M. Wallenstein, 'The Piyyut, with special reference to the textual study of the Old Testament', in *Bulletin of the John Rylands Library*, vol. xxxiv, No. 2, March 1952, pp. 469 ff.

[2] p. 32.

which have been published by Dr. Kahle, supplementing the printed editions.[1]

A notable feature of a number of the Aramaic piuts in this Palestinian Targum material is their connexion with the Jewish festival year; thus in MS. G from the Geniza (probably eleventh century) there are several pieces, including a setting of the Song of Moses at Exod. xv, designed for recitation at Passover or the Feast of Weeks. We do not know when the practice of composing such Aramaic piuts for the festivals began; it certainly survived to a late date, for it was still customary in the Middle Ages to compose Aramaic poetic 'Introductions' to the lections for feast days. In two separate studies of Hebrew and Aramaic piuts for the seventh day of Passover, M. Ginsburger has collected more than fifty such pieces, including several of the poetic *haggadoth* of Jerusalem II.[2]

It is doubtful, however, if all the poetic additions in the Targum owe their origin and inspiration to the feasts. In his *Literaturgeschichte der synagogalen Poesie*, Leopold Zunz has suggested that some of the earliest Aramaic poetry of the Synagogue took its rise in the public exposition of Scripture in Aramaic.[3] It may be that such poetic targumizing began with the rendering of Hebrew poetry, such as the Song of Moses. Some sixteen Aramaic piuts were suspected by Zunz to belong to this type, and he regarded them as *prekalirisch*.[3] Eight of these passages come from the Targum, four from the Second Targum of Esther, and four from Jerusalem II, including a Prayer with attached poetic homily at Gen. xxxv. 1 and a long poem called the Four Nights at Exod. xii. 42 (occasionally placed at Exod. xv. 18).

Apart from the general impression of early origin given by their primitive poetic form or formlessness, none of these poems has so far been exactly dated, and it is on the dating of one of them, the Aramaic haggadic Prayer at Gen. xxxv. 9, found both in the Geniza fragments and in the Targum text published by Ginsburger, Jerusalem II, that I rest my main case for the origin of this and comparable poetic pieces in the Palestinian Pentateuch Targum in the earliest period of *piut* composition, i.e. at least prior to the sixth century A.D.

It is with the assistance of the recently published *Piyyute Yannai*

[1] In *Masoreten des Westens*, ii. For editions of the Targum, consult *The Cairo Geniza*, pp. 117 ff.

[2] 'Aramäische Introduktionen zum Thargumvortrag an Festtagen', in *Z.D.M.G.* liv (1900), p. 113 f.; 'Les Introductions Araméennes à la Lecture du Targoum', in *Revue des Études Juives*, lxxiii–lxxiv (1921–2), pp. 14 f., 186 f.

[3] Berlin, 1865, p. 21.

that we are in a position to establish the date of this poem. The editor of this recent volume, Dr. Menachem Zulay, began his work on Yannai in the early thirties on the instigation and under the supervision of Dr. Kahle in Bonn, with a doctoral thesis entitled *Zur Liturgie der babylonischen Juden*, subsequently published in the *Bonner Orientalistische Studien*, Heft 2 (1933). In the course of this study, Zulay brought conclusive evidence for the Palestinian origin, not only of the poet Yannai himself, but of much in his work. In an appendix to his thesis he pointed out that 'Yannai derives the material for his *piuts* to a large extent from the Palestinian Targum'.[1] He then calls attention to a remarkable identity in content between a Keroba of Yannai on Gen. xxxv. 9 and the corresponding paraphrase in the Geniza Targum. It is quite clear that Yannai is basing his Hebrew poem on the Aramaic paraphrase of the Targum.[2]

What is not clearly recognized or indeed mentioned is the character of these twenty-four lines of Targum text which form the basis of Yannai's Keroba. Zulay was mainly concerned with Yannai, not with the Targum, except as a means of proving Yannai's Palestinian origin. These twenty-four lines of Aramaic are, however, not a translation of the Hebrew, but a long poetic *haggada*, beginning as a Prayer. And it was recognized as such and regarded as a very old Aramaic poem by Leopold Zunz who was acquainted only with the text in printed rabbinical Bibles and had neither the advantage of the Ginsburger text nor the Geniza fragments; the discovery of Yannai's dependence on this poem is a remarkable confirmation of that great scholar's critical judgement.[3]

Dr. Kahle has fixed the date of Yannai's poetic activity within relatively narrow limits, between the middle of the sixth century and the beginning of the seventh;[4] and this provides a *terminus ad quem* for the Aramaic translation he has utilized. A liturgical text of this kind, in circulation in the sixth century, is quite certainly much older; it may even be centuries older. It clearly belongs to the public expositions of Scripture called in the Talmud 'Blessings and Consolations', used at weddings and funerals and similar solemn occasions; it springs, in fact, direct from the life of the people of Palestine.[5]

These haggadic poems are composed in a literary Aramaic, with

[1] Op. cit., *Anhang*, p. 64. [2] Cf. *The Cairo Geniza*, p. 23.

[3] *Literaturgeschichte*, p. 22. Archaisms in the form of the Geniza text further corroborate the impression of antiquity derived from its poetic form; *min yomath 'alma* (Yannai, *miyyimuth 'olam*) is given in the *Lexica* for Ezra iv. 15, 19 only (Ginsburger, *min dugmath* (δεῖγμα) *'alma*). [4] Op. cit., p. 27.

[5] Cf. Zunz, *Die gottesdienstlichen Vorträge der Juden* (1892), p. 348.

all the familiar embellishments of Semitic verse, assonance, paronomasia, &c. A striking example is Deut. xxxii. 10 (F):

He found (ארע) *them wandering in a desert land* (ארעא),
In a wilderness of night and desolation;
He cast over them the clouds of his glorious Shekhina (שכינתיה) , . .
He watched (עיין) *over them and protected them,*
As the eyelid (שכינא) *protecteth the eye* (עין).

Several other typical examples will be found at Exod. xix. 4 (F), xx. 1–2 (G); in Jacob's last words at Gen. xlix. 18 (F), there is a poem of Messianic expectation:

Not for the redemption of Gideon doth my soul wait,
Which is the redemption of an hour;
Nor yet for the redemption of Samson awaiteth my soul,
For a redemption that passeth is his:
But for the redemption which thou hast promised to bring to thy people Israel,
For it doth my soul wait, for thy redemption is an eternal one (דפורקנך פורקן עלמין).[1]

The classic passage for the doctrine of the Messiah is Gen. xlix. 11 (F). Two quite different pictures are given, the first that of the Avenging Warrior (cf. Isa. lxiii), the second a figure more closely resembling the Servant of peace and gentle will in Isa. xlii: a comparison of the language and contents of both passages suggests that the second is a deliberate repudiation of the first.

The Avenging Warrior

How fair is the King Messiah, to arise from the House of Judah!
Setting forth, with girded loins, to war against his foes:
Kings will be slain with rulers; his hills will he redden with the blood of their slain,
And his vales will be white with the flesh of their warriors.
His garments are dipped in blood, like the juice of the wine-press.

The Peaceful Servant

How beautiful the eyes of the King Messiah!
Fairer are they to behold than the wine that sparkles:
They will not look on naked shame nor the shedding of innocent blood;
His teeth are purer than milk, innocent of rapine and violence.
His hills will be red with vines, and his presses with wine;
And his vales will be white with harvest and the flocks of (his) sheep.

References to the Last Judgement are frequent; it is generally referred to as 'the Day of the Great Judgement', e.g. Num. xxxi.

[1] This significant variant is not given by Ginsburger, but it will be found in rabbinical Bibles.

50 (F), Deut. xxxii. (F). For a further example, see *supra*, p. 236 f. In Abraham's vision in Gen. xv. 12 (F), the whole setting of the Judgement scene and even the language are taken from Dan. vii:

And behold! Abraham looked, till the seats were arrayed and the thrones were set (וכורסין רמין),
And Gehenna prepared for the wicked in the world to come.

In another poetic fragment at Deut. xxxii. 24 (F), the divine vengeance on Israel is to be executed by 'the teeth of the four Kingdoms, which are like the beasts of the wild (דמתילן לחיות ברא)'.[1]

We can actually trace some of the poetic pieces preserved in the Targum still further back, with the help of the New Testament. I have already referred to the couplet, 'As our Father is merciful in heaven, so be ye merciful on earth.'[2] Even more striking is a poetic fragment found in Jerusalem I as part of the Aramaic version of the Blessing of Jacob at Gen. xlix; this couplet appears to have been a 'floating midrash', for it appears again, in a variant Aramaic text, at *Bereshith Rabba*, 98, a further indication of its antiquity. It might be Lk. xi. 27 itself which is being quoted, if such an explanation were not quite unhistorical.[3] The lines are:

'Blessed are the breasts from which thou hast sucked,
And the womb which bore thee.'

Both these quotations are short fragments, but their antiquity is beyond doubt, and they give grounds for confidence in the equal antiquity of some of the longer piuts. The number of these will only be known when the whole material has been investigated, and a critical text established. A beginning, however, can be made with the piuts in the Geniza material: Gen. xxxv. 9 (MS. C); xxxviii. 26 (C, E), containing the proverbial saying at Mk. iv. 24 *par.* in Aramaic;[4] Lev. xxii. 27 (F= Ox. e 43); Exod. xv and xx (G); Exod. xx. 2 (F). The last passage contains a poetical setting of the Ten Commandments in a very old piece of text.

If the claim here made is justified, a selection of these poems might be read by students interested in Aramaic poetry comparable with that which is found in Greek translation in the Synoptic Gospels.

[1] The Messiah is not associated with the Judgement in any of the fragments, but he is invested with the office of Judge in a fragment of the Palestinian Targum on Isa. xi. 1; see Lagarde, *Prophetae Chaldaice*, p. xxvii.

[2] *Supra*, p. 181.

[3] Cf. Strack-Billerbeck, *Kommentar zum Neuen Testament aus Talmud und Midrash*, on Lk. xi. 27.

[4] Cf. Dalman, *Jesus-Jeschua*, p. 202 (Hebrew).

APPENDIX E

THE USE OF בר נשא/בר נש IN JEWISH ARAMAIC

By GEZA VERMES, *Reader in Jewish Studies, University of Oxford*

'THE Son of Man problem in the Gospels is one of the most perplexing and challenging in the whole field of Biblical theology. . . . If I may so put it without irreverence (and without begging the question) the fundamental problem is this: What did the man mean when he called himself "son of man", or simply "man". . . .?'[1]

These words of Matthew Black point to the real issue confronting the unbiased student. Ignoring the elaborate theological and exegetical superstructures built on the 'son of man' passages during the last hundred years or so, he has to apply himself to the task of examining their foundations, to discovering, if he can, the real significance of *ὁ υἱὸς τοῦ ἀνθρώπου*.

The basic facts upon which there is general agreement are as follows. (*a*) It is accepted that the expression used in the Gospels is not a genuine Greek idiom but the literal translation, or mistranslation, of a Semitic original, the Aramaic בר נש or בר נשא. (*b*) The phrase is never applied to Jesus by his interlocutors as a title of address, but is always placed by the Evangelists on his own lips. (*c*) No question is ever raised in the Synoptic Gospels as to its meaning nor any objection to its use.

In short, strange though this may appear to modern scholars, there was in the beginning no 'problem' at all. To the contemporaries of Jesus, friend and foe, the expression 'son of man' presented no difficulties of communication and aroused no religious hostility—as would have been the case had the phrase been, so to speak, 'loaded'. 'Er gebraucht ihn', writes Wellhausen, 'durchaus nicht esoterisch, nicht bloß den Jüngern gegenüber, aber niemand wird dadurch befremdet und verlangt Aufklärung, alle lassen ihn unverwundert passieren, auch die streitsüchtigen Pharisäer . . . die doch nicht geneigt waren unverständliches zu acceptieren.'[2]

Disagreements, of course, cover the whole field and are too complex and numerous to examine here. But at the root of them all lies

[1] 'The Son of Man Problem in recent Research and Debate' in *Bulletin of the John Rylands Library*, xlv (1962/63), p. 305.

[2] *Skizzen und Vorarbeiten*, vi (Berlin, 1899), p. 197.

an insufficiency of research into the Jewish–Aramaic idiom. It might seem from the vast mass of 'son of man' literature that the linguistic aspect has been explored in such depth that nothing new can possibly emerge; but this is not so. There is still room for fresh philological discovery, as I hope to demonstrate.

What has been done so far in the philological field?

The appearance in 1896 of Arnold Meyer's *Jesu Muttersprache* (*Das galiläische Aramäisch in seiner Bedeutung für die Erklärung der Reden Jesu und der Evangelien überhaupt*), and of Hans Lietzmann's thesis, *Der Menschensohn* (*Ein Beitrag zur neutestamentlichen Theologie*), marks the beginning of a first wave of systematic inquiry into our subject.

Meyer, considering in his monograph only a small number of Gospel sayings, finds that in a first group of these, *ὁ υἱὸς τοῦ ἀνθρώπου*, like the Aramaic בר נש, refers not to any particular individual but to man in general (Mk. ii. 28; Mt. xii. 32; Mk. ii. 10),[1] whilst in another group of logia, בר נש stands for 'I', particularly when 'I' (a man) is contrasted with God, other beings, or animals (Mt. viii. 20;[2] Mt. xi. 19[3]). He bases the latter interpretation on a presumed parallel use in Galilaean Aramaic of ההוא גברא (that man = I) and ההוא בר נשא (pp. 91–97).

Lietzmann's survey is by contrast massive, but his source-material is restricted to five tractates of the Palestinian Talmud only: Pea, Demai, Kila'im, Yoma, and Ta'anith. Tackling his subject with youthful enthusiasm—he was then only twenty-one years old—he gives it as his opinion that any further extension of the inquiry would be a waste of time and profitless (p. 34). His main findings are that the term is a common one, and that it is used as a kind of indefinite pronoun (בר נש = *jemand*; לית בר נש = *niemand*; בני נש = *Leute*). It is, he writes, 'die farbloseste und unbestimmteste Bezeichnung des menschlichen Individuums' (p. 38). He then goes on to postulate what seems to him to be the only logical corollary: as a designation, בר נש is by nature inapplicable to any particular man, let alone to Jesus, the greatest of all men (p. 40). He protests emphatically against the unjustified replacement of ההוא גברא (a circumlocution for 'I' and an Aramaic mannerism) by בר נש (p. 84) and urges his point still further by drawing attention to the fact that although ancient Jewish exegesis interprets Dan. vii. 13

[1] Mt. ix. 6; Lk. v. 24. [2] Lk. ix. 58. [3] Lk. vii. 34.

messianically, it was not בר אנש but בר ענני which became for the Rabbis a messianic name (p. 40).

Thus Lietzmann is obliged finally to infer that since no Aramaic-speaking person could ever have used 'son of man' as a title, the formula ὁ υἱὸς τοῦ ἀνθρώπου must be a *terminus technicus* of Hellenistic theology (p. 95).

This thesis soon attracted considerable opposition. In 1898, Gustaf Dalman, the then authority on Palestinian Aramaic, presented an altogether different theory in the first edition of his *Die Worte Jesu mit Berücksichtigung des nachkanonischen jüdischen Schrifttums und der aramäischen Sprache erörtert.*[1] After undertaking a thorough analysis of the phrase in various groups of Aramaic writings, he finds that in biblical Aramaic אנש is the ordinary word for 'man' and that the expression בר אנש in Dan. vii. 13 is uncommon and poetic (p. 235). The same use occurs in Jewish Palestinian Aramaic of the earlier period—by which Dalman means the Targums of Onkelos and Jonathan: בר אנש is not to be found in Onkelos at all, and only rarely, in poetry, in the Jonathan Targum (p. 236 f.). It is not until the later appearance of Jewish–Galilean and Christian–Palestinian Aramaic documents that בר אנש signifies 'man' (p. 237). The definite form, בר אנשא, like בן האדם in Hebrew, is unheard of in the older Jewish Aramaic literature (p. 238). Consequently, Dalman asserts, in complete contradiction to Lietzmann, בר אנשא is wholly suitable for employment as the special name of a definite personality (p. 240).

Paul Fiebig was the next to criticize some of Lietzmann's overstatements, in particular his contention that בר נש is merely an indefinite pronoun. The title of his monograph, *Der Menschensohn: Jesu Selbstbezeichnung mit besonderer Berücksichtigung des aramäischen Sprachgebrauches für 'Mensch'*, published in 1901, reveals his thesis, viz., that בר נש was chosen by Jesus as his peculiar 'Selbstbezeichnung'. He stresses the fact that in no Jewish (or Samaritan) Aramaic dialect is בר אנש or בר נש the only expression for 'man'; אנש or אינש is just as common (pp. 20, 25, 44). He firmly maintains, therefore, that there is no linguistic reason why בר נשא should not refer to a definite person and be employed as a self-appellation. Fiebig further argues and proves that neither the addition of בר to אנש, nor the substitution of the definite form אנשא or בר נשא for the indefinite, affects the meaning of the phrase: each may signify either 'the

[1] The page references follow the English edition. (*The Words of Jesus*, Edinburgh, 1909.)

man', 'a man', or 'someone' (pp. 20, 25, 29, 44). On the other hand, he agrees with Lietzmann's refusal, if not with his motives for it, to accept any parallelism between ההוא גברא and ההוא אנשא or ההוא בר נשא. If the New Testament phrase had been derived from the latter, ὁ υἱὸς τοῦ ἀνθρώπου would have been preceded by οὗτος (p. 74 f.).

Thus ended the first period of philological inquiry into the Aramaic background and original meaning of the phrase 'son of man'. For the next nearly fifty years no significant linguistic contribution came to light. But there was a considerable change in the general approach to Aramaic studies themselves. The Dalmanian dogma concerning the chronological priority of the language preserved in the Targums of Onkelos and Jonathan was challenged and overthrown as a result of the publication by Paul Kahle of the Geniza fragments of the Palestinian Targum.

The second period opened in 1947 with the publication in the *Journal of Theological Studies* of a provocative article by J. Y. Campbell. From the linguistic point of view, 'The Origin and Meaning of the Term Son of Man' contains nothing particularly new, but its powerful claim, both unorthodox and unsubstantiated, awoke new interest in the matter. Denying that Jesus borrowed the phrase either from Daniel, or from the 'stupid' Book of Enoch, Campbell whole-heartedly throws himself into the defence of the self-reference theory. If St. Paul could write, he asserts, 'I knew *a man* in Christ fourteen years ago', and mean himself, then Jesus could also allude to himself as *bar nāsh*. Misunderstanding would have been avoided if Jesus, instead of simply calling himself *bar nāsh*(*ā*), had added a demonstrative adjective. An unusual construction such as ההוא בר נשא or בר נשא ההוא, instead of the normal ההוא גברא, would have been noticed and remembered. But by the time of its translation into Greek, בר נש was already thought to be a title and the demonstrative was therefore omitted (p. 152 f.). Campbell wastes no time in inquiring into the Aramaic usage of these phrases. 'The available instances of ההוא גברא and the like . . . are too few to throw much light upon the use of the idiom', he writes (p. 153 f.)—a patent inaccuracy. He is content to elaborate a series of hypotheses and lend them vigour by means of forceful insistence. But he appears to have started the ball rolling again.

In fact, two 'son of man' studies appeared in the following year in the *Expository Times*. One of the authors, John Bowman,[1] although

[1] 'The Background of the Term "Son of Man"' in *Expository Times*, lix (1947/48), pp. 283–8.

defending the view that in some circles the expression represented a messianic title, is the first to introduce new evidence from the Geniza fragments of the Palestinian Pentateuch Targum showing 'that בר נש could be used for 'anyone' or 'a man' in early Palestinian Aramaic' and quotes Gen. iv. 14 and ix. 5–6 to this effect (p. 286).

The other article, 'The "Son of Man" in the Teaching of Jesus'[1] by Matthew Black, raises three points worthy of mention in this context. Firstly, he states authoritatively, against Campbell's hypothesis, that the phrase ההרא בר נשא is found nowhere in Aramaic sources. Secondly, he shows that he is in sympathy with the theory sustained by, among others, T. W. Manson, that in passages such as Mt. xi. 19 or Lk. vii. 34 'son of man' may possess 'the regular sense which *bar-nāsh* had come to have in Palestinian Aramaic of "one", "a man" with reference to the speaker himself'. Thirdly, he is the first to suggest an actual Aramaic parallel to this type of locution by referring to *Genesis Rabba* vii, a passage to be discussed later (pp. 34–35).[2]

The one detailed philological study to have appeared in recent years is that of Erik Sjöberg. After the publication of *Der Menschensohn im äthiopischen Henochbuch* (1946), but preceding *Der verborgene Menschensohn in den Evangelien* (1955), he wrote two articles in *Acta Orientalia* (1950–51) under the title 'בן אדם und בר אנש im Hebräischen und Aramäischen'.[3] His findings are mixed. On the one hand he asserts, against Dalman, that far from being poetic, בר נש is a common everyday expression in Aramaic, both in the individual and in the pronominal sense of 'a man' and 'someone' (p. 97). On the other hand, he wonders whether it acquired solemnity in the Volksprache through its association with Dan. vii. 13 (p. 107). He agrees with Fiebig in not differentiating between the meaning of the definite and indefinite forms; even בר נש, without the emphatic ending, can be a 'Bezeichnung eines individuellen Menschen' (p. 99). In another publication, Sjöberg pronounces firmly against the self-reference theory: 'The attempt to understand בר נשא, like ההוא גברא, as a circumlocution for "I" . . . is doomed because such a use of בר נשא is nowhere to be found in Aramaic sources'.[4]

The intention of this preliminary survey has been to establish the points of agreement among philologists and discover problems

[1] Ibid. lx (1948/49), pp. 32–36.
[2] Cf. also *An Aramaic Approach* . . ., 2nd ed., p. 250, n. 2.
[3] Vol. xxi, pp. 57–65; 91–107.
[4] *Der verborgene Menschensohn in den Evangelien*, p. 239, n. 3.

requiring further investigation. In regard to the former, it seems that it may safely be accepted that בר נש(א) was in common use, both as a noun and as a substitute for the indefinite pronoun, in the early as well as in the later stages of the development of the Galilean dialect, and that the employment of the definite or indefinite forms does not substantially affect the meaning. The two problems which remain outstanding and on which no agreement has so far been reached concern the use of the phrase, firstly as a circumlocution for 'I', and secondly as a title of possibly messianic character, connected in some way with Dan. vii. 13.

Clearly, these questions cannot be answered with any reasonable degree of probability without extending the field of research. Even Lietzmann, whose study was the most comprehensive of all, used—as I have mentioned—only five tractates of the Palestinian Talmud. I have therefore brought within my scope the whole of Talmud Yerushalmi, the Aramaic portions of *Genesis Rabba*, the Qumrân *Genesis Apocryphon*, and a great deal of Palestinian Targum material, including the Geniza fragments and the Neofiti Codex.[1]

But the mere augmentation of the sample, necessary though this is, will still lead nowhere unless at the same time more attention is paid to the various types of Aramaic writings (in particular to the difference between the translation Aramaic of the Targums and the spontaneous style of midrashic and talmudic passages), and to the variety of speech-forms (descriptive halakhic arguments, anecdotes, and especially monologues and dialogues, the real parallel to the New Testament style).

In the following pages, I propose to outline methodically the various usages of *bar nāsh*(*ā*) in post-biblical Aramaic.

The Targums

In the translation passages of the Palestinian Pentateuch Targums, *bar-nāsh* normally represents *'ādām*, and *bar nāshā*, *hā-'ādām* (Gen. i. 26, i. 27, ii. 18, viii. 21 [N], ix. 5–6 [TY, N]), although the latter is also not infrequently rendered—despite the definite article—as בר נש (Gen. ix. 6 [TY, N]; Dt. v. 21 (24), xx. 19 [1J], &c.). But

[1] Sources and abbreviations. Codex Neofiti [N], unpublished. *Pseudo-Jonathan or first Jerusalem Targum* [1J], ed. Ginsburger. *Fragmentary or second Jerusalem Targum* [2J], ed. Ginsburger. *Geniza fragments of Targum Yerushalmi* [TY], ed. Kahle. *Jonathan or Targum to the Prophets*, ed. Sperber. *Palestinian Talmud*, ed. Krotoschin. *Babylonian Talmud*, ed. Wilna. *Genesis Rabba*, ed. Theodor–Albeck. Qumrân *Genesis Apocryphon*, ed. Avigad–Yadin.

when אדם is understood collectively, the Targumist may use the Aramaic plural בני אנשא (Gen. vi. 1–5, 7, vii. 21, 23, viii. 21, xi. 5, xvi. 12 [N]; Gen. vii. 21, 23 [TY]) or בני נשא (Gen. vi. 1, xi. 5 [1J]). In addition, בר נש is sometimes substituted for איש (Ex. xix. 13 [TY]; Num. xxiii. 19 [1J]; Dt. xxxiv. 6 [TY, 1J]; &c.) and נפש (Lev. ii. 1, iv. 2, v. 1–2, 4, 15 [1J]).

A similar usage is encountered in the midrashic sections. In Gen. i. 2, תהו ובהו, waste and void, is paraphrased as 'empty of בר נש [N] or בני נש' [1J]. In Gen. ii. 23, 'This is now bone of my bones and flesh of my flesh' becomes, 'This time, but not again, woman shall be created out of בר נשה, as this one has been created out of me' [N]. The concept of men in general is expressed either by the definite plural—'Are the thoughts of בני אנשא[1] not revealed before the Lord?' (Gen. l. 19 [N])—or by the definite singular—'For the seeing of the eyes and the cogitation of the heart destroy בר נשא' (Gen. xlix. 22 [N, 2J]).

As might be expected, the Hebrew *ben 'ādām* is rendered in the Targums to the Prophets and Writings as *bar nāsh(ā)* (cf. Ps. viii. 5, lxxx. 18, cxlvi. 4, &c.).

To sum up, it would appear that with the exception of Gen. iv. 14 [TY], which will be examined later, the Targums attest only the most straightforward usage of the phrase under discussion.

Other Sources

The bulk of the examples assembled from the Talmuds, *Genesis Rabba*, and 1Q *Genesis Apocryphon*, offer a much wider variety of shade and nuance within a similar general pattern. The texts are classified under two headings, according to whether *bar nāsh(ā)* describes, with more or less emphasis, a member of the human race, or whether it is employed as an indefinite pronoun.[2]

1. *bar nāsh(ā)* = *a human being*

A. The sources, both Galilean and Babylonian, provide only a few instances of the non-emphatic use.

Y. Ter. 45d (line 7): All sweat proceeding from בר נש[3] is a deadly poison.

Y. San. 26b (line 15): Whoever says, Here are five (pieces of money), give me something worth three, is a fool. But he who speaks thus—

[1] 1J has בני נשא.

[2] Where no problem arises, I will limit the illustrations to a strict minimum to avoid tediousness.

[3] בר נשא in *Y. Ab. Z.* 41a, line 2 from bottom.

Here are three (pieces of money), give me something worth five—is בר נש.

The phrase, אורחיה דבר נשא (this is a human custom), may also be listed here.[1]

In the Babylonian Talmud the expression is בר אינש.

B. Ned. 54b: Entrails are no meat and he who eats them is no בר אינש.[2]

B. When used with emphasis בר נש may indicate a relative distinction between man and man.

Y. Baba B. 13c (line 28 from bottom): If he does not judge himself as he judges all others, לית הוא בר נש (he is no man).

B. Shab. 152a: (A Sadducee), seeing that R. Joshua b. Karkah was barefooted, remarked, He who rides on a horse is a king; on a donkey, a nobleman. He who has shoes on his feet is בר אינש. But the dead and buried is better off than one who has none of these.

Normally however, adjectives provide the necessary qualification. Thus we often read of someone being בר נש רב, or בר נשא רבא, a great, important man, whereas another is described as בר נש זעיר, an insignificant, unimportant person.

Gen. R. lviii. 7: בר נש רב should not buy anything from בר נש זעיר.[3]

Finally, there are the instances in which בר נש emphasizes the distinction between man, animals, angels, and God.

Y. Dem. 21d (lines 9–10 from bottom): If the ancient (teachers) were angels (בני מלאכין), we are בני נש. If they were men, we are asses.[4]

Y. San. 26a (line 14 from bottom): It is a dog that eats meat raw. He who eats it boiled בר נש הוא.

Y. Yoma 41a (line 1): A certain physician (חד אסי, an Essene?) in Sephoris said to R. Pinhas bar Hama, I will hand down to you (the divine Name). You must not, he replied. Why? Because I eat of the tithe; but whosoever is familiar with the Name must eat nothing which comes from בר נש.

Y. Yoma 42c (line 33): I do not tell you it was בר נש. I say that it was the Holy One, blessed be He.

An anecdote containing a pun on בר נש may aptly conclude this section.

[1] Cf. *Y. Ned.* 40a (line 2 from bottom); 40c (line 35); 40d (lines 21 and 27). Compare this with the Hebrew דרך בני אדם: *Y. Ab. Z.* 43c (line 13).

[2] Cf. *B. Meil.* 20b.

[3] See also ibid. lviii. 8; *Y. Pea* 21b (line 14 from bottom) = *Y. Sheq.* 49b (line 29); &c. *Y. Kil.* 32b (line 11 from bottom) = *Y. Ket.* 35a (line 12 from bottom).

[4] See also *Y. Shek.* 48c (last line), 48d (line 1); *B. Shab.* 112b; *Gen. R.* lx. 8.

Y. Pea 17d (lines 23–24): There were in Ashkelon two brothers who had Gentile neighbours. These said, When these Jews go up to Jerusalem, we will take all their property. But when they had gone, God set in their place angels who, coming and going, resembled them. On their return, the brothers sent presents to their neighbours. Where have you been? they asked. In Jerusalem. Whom did you leave in the house? They said, **לא בר נש**.

This can, of course, mean either 'nobody' or 'no man'.

2. *Bar nāsh*(*ā*)—*b*^e^*nē nāsh = an indefinite pronoun*

Although, as has been said, it is generally accepted that *bar nāsh* is used as an indefinite pronoun ('someone', **בר נשא** or **בר נש**, 'no-one', **לית בר נש**, 'some', **אית בני נש**, and 'everyone', **כל בר נש ובר נש**),[1] careful analysis uncovers a wider range of meaning than suggested hitherto. I intend to illustrate as many of these usages as possible, whether already postulated or not.

To begin with there is **כל בר נש ובר נש**, signifying 'everyone', 'each man'. R. Mena quotes a proverb used among millers:

The worth of **כל בר נש ובר נש** is in his basket.[2]

Then in a great number of cases a simple **בר נש** conveys the meaning 'anyone', especially, but not necessarily, in questions introduced by **אית**.

Y. Dem. 25b (line 36): Is there **בר נש** who speaks thus?
Y. Shek. 47b (line 29): Is there **בר נש** who says to his master . . . ?
Y. Meg. 74a (line 11 from bottom): If **בר נש** comes to you. . . .
Y. Kil. 32b (line 36): Rabbi was very humble and used to say, I am prepared to do whatever **בר נשא** tells me.[3]

In negative sentences we find **לית בר נש**[4] or **לא בר נש**[5] for 'nobody'. The same sense is obtained when the negative is placed before the verb, as is manifest already in the Qumrân *Genesis Apocryphon* xxi. 13: **די לא ישכח כול בר אנוש לממניה** (which nobody can count). It also appears frequently in the Galilean sources.

[1] G. Dalman, *Grammatik des jüdisch-palestinischen Aramäisch*, 2nd ed., pp. 122–3.—H. Odeberg, *The Aramaic Portions of Bereshit Rabba with Grammar of Galilean Aramaic*, ii (Lund–Leipzig, 1939), p. 8.

[2] *Y. Pea* 15c (lines 29–30 from bottom) = *Y. Qid.* 61b (line 31); see also *Y. Dem.* 23b (line 5 from bottom) = *Y. Hal.* 60b (line 27 from bottom); &c.

[3] See also *Y. Ket.* 35a (line 35 from bottom). But in *Gen. R.* xxxiii. 3 the reading is **בר נש**.

[4] *Y. Ter.* 46a (line 13 from bottom); *Y. Yeb.* 5d (line 5 from bottom); 9a (line 26).

[5] *Y. Pea* 17d (lines 23–24).

Y. Dem. 24a (line 16 from bottom): It occurs to nobody (לא סלק על בר נש).
Gen. R. xcii. 6: Nobody answered (לא הוה בר נש עני).

In many other instances בר נש refers to 'someone' in the sense of some definite individual.

Y. Yeb. 13a (line 23): I am sending you בר נש like myself.
Y. Baba M. 10c (line 8 from bottom): Kahana gave בר נש forty dinars.

The use of the plural בני נש as an indefinite pronoun can also refer to 'some people' in the sense of certain individuals.[1]

Y. Pea 21b (line 7 from bottom): There are בני נש who study the Law.[2]
Y. Yoma 45c (line 26): He who has sinned against his neighbour must go to him and say, I have offended you. If he accepts this, all is well. But if not, he shall bring along בני נש and try to appease him in their presence.
Y. Yeb. 3a (line 10 from bottom): How is it that you have sent me בני נש in need of learning and have told me that they are wise men of Israel?
Y. Ta'an. 65b (line 1): R. Yoshiah interpreted *Zeph.* ii. 1, *Gather yourselves together, gather,* thus: Let us correct ourselves before we correct others. For there are here בני נש who slander me before R. Yohanan. . . . Thereupon, R. Hiyya, R. Issi and R. Imi, who were present, rose and left.

Lastly, mention must be made of the familiar expression, חד בר נש, which opens many an Aramaic story. Here the addition of חד (one) makes it plain that the indefinite pronoun refers to a single subject: a certain man.

Y. Ter. 46a (line 37): חד בר נש invited a certain Rabbi (חד רבן).
Y. Baba M. 8c (line 3 from bottom): It happened to a certain man (עובדא הוה בחד בר נש).[3]

When the subject of the anecdote is feminine, we find the corresponding חדא איתתא.

Y. Hal. 57d (line 4 from bottom): חדא איתתא asked R. Mena. . . .

[1] It may be of interest to note that apart from the Targums, I have found no example of the definite plural בני נשא.

[2] Cf. *Y. Shek.* 49b (lines 36 and 38). See also *Y. Git.* 45b (line 25); *Y. Baba B.* 15c (line 18).

[3] This expression is more common in Hebrew in the form of מעשה באחד (*Y. Pea* 17d, lines 15, 16) or even מעשה באדם אחד (*Y. Bik.* 65d, line 5 from bottom).

3. *Bar nāsh(ā) = a circumlocution for 'I'*

It has often been postulated in the past that *bar nāsh* is sometimes used by a speaker as an indirect reference to himself; as, that is to say, a substitute for the personal pronoun **אנא**. This theory is based on the analogous employment of **ההוא גברא** (that man) or **ההיא איתתא** (that woman). But the matter is not quite so simple; **ההוא גברא** can allude as a circumlocution not only to 'I' but also to 'thou'. Therefore one has first to decide whether it is in fact a circumlocution, and then establish its exact meaning from the immediate context within which it occurs.

It is important to note that in order to act as a circumlocution, **ההוא גברא** must appear in dialogue of a certain type, viz., either when (*a*) a speaker wishes to avoid undue or immodest emphasis on himself, or (*b*) when he is prompted by fear or by a dislike of asserting openly something disagreeable in relation to himself, or (*c*) when he utters a curse, or (*d*) a protestation. In the first two contexts, 'that man' refers to 'I', and in the third and fourth to 'thou'.[1]

(*a*) *Gen. R.* lxviii. 12: A certain man came to R. Jose bar Halafta and said to him, It was revealed to **ההוא גברא** in a dream. . . .

(*b*) *Gen. R.* xiv. 7(8): The son of a notable of Sephoris died. It is said that the father was a *mīn* (a heretic rejecting faith in the world to come). . . . When R. Jose bar Halafta went to pay him a visit, the father saw that the Rabbi sat down and laughed. Why are you laughing? he asked. Because we trust in the Lord of heaven that you will see the face of the dead man in the world to come. Has not **ההוא גברא** enough trouble, said the father, that you too should come to bother him?

Gen. R. c. 5: Jacob asked Esau, What do you desire? Money or a burial place? Does **ההוא גברא** desire a burial place? Give me the money and take the burial place for yourself!

(*c*) *Y. Maʿaser Sh.* 55c: May the spirit of **ההוא גברא** perish!

(*d*) *Y. Moʿed K.* 81d: Were it not for the fact that I never anathematized anyone, I would do so to **ההוא גברא**!

Y. Sheb. 39a: (A woman speaking to her husband exclaims): **ההוא גברא** is suspect in regard to the *Shemitta* (laws relating to the Sabbatical year) and you dare to tell me, Set aside the *Hallah* (the priest's share)!

These introductory remarks are necessary to show that an inquiry into the possible use of *bar nāsh(ā)* as a substitute for 'I' is bound to fail unless particular attention is paid to the literary form in which it occurs and to its precise context. For despite Erik Sjöberg's denial

[1] See G. Dalman, *Grammatik* . . . p. 108, supplemented by *Worte Jesu*, p. 204 f.; cf. also H. Odeberg, op. cit. ii, p. 3, § 5.

of the circumlocutional usage of *bar nāsh(ā)*, I shall attempt to prove that it does indeed exist.

In the first place, there is a passage from *Genesis Rabba* to which Matthew Black has drawn attention.[1]

Gen. R. vii. 2 (ed. Theodor, p. 51): Jacob of Kefar Nibburayya gave a ruling in Tyre that fish should be ritually slaughtered. Hearing this, R. Haggai sent him this order: Come and be scourged! He replied, Should בר נש be scourged who proclaims the word of Scripture?

The question is repeated in the same paragraph in the framework of another argument about whether the son of a Gentile woman should be circumcised on the Sabbath day.

Theoretically, of course, *bar nāsh* may be rendered here as 'one', but the context hardly suggests that at this particular juncture Jacob intends to voice a general principle. Hurt by his opponent's harsh words, he clearly seems to be referring to himself and the indirect idiom is no doubt due to the implied humiliation.

This interpretation is further confirmed in the parallel text preserved in *Num. R.* xix. 3:

Should בר נש be scourged who proclaims the word of Scripture? R. Haggai said, Yes, because *you* did not give the right ruling (לא הורית טב).[2]

Another almost identical usage may be found in an anecdote inserted into the Palestinian Talmud. Here again, although it is possible to understand the question as a general one, the audience recognizes without a shadow of doubt that the speaker is referring to himself.

Y. Ber. 5c (lines 24 ff. from bottom): R. Ze'ira . . . wished to buy a pound of meat from a butcher. How much is this? he asked. Fifty minas and a lash, was the answer. (The Rabbi offered sixty, seventy, eighty, and finally a hundred minas to escape the lash, but to no avail. In the end he said), Do as is your custom! In the evening, he went to the school-house and said, Rabbis, how wicked is the custom of this place that בר נש cannot eat a pound of meat until he has been given a lash!

A slightly different language was used by Kahana, a Babylonian Rabbi who had come to Palestine but found life there disappointing. He approached his teacher, R. Yohanan, and asked him the following question:

[1] Cf. *supra*, p. 314.

[2] The same sentence appears also in *Genesis Rabba* (l.c.), but does not follow Jacob's question immediately.

Y. Ber. 5c (lines 29 ff.): If בר נש is despised by his mother but honoured by another of his father's wives, where should he go? He should go where he is honoured, replied Yohanan. Thereupon, Kahana departed. R. Yohanan was then told: Kahana has gone to Babylon. What! exclaimed Yohanan. Has he gone without asking my permission? The story he told you, they replied, was his way of asking permission.

The significance of Kahana's parable escaped none except the old Yohanan. The mother is Palestine, the step-mother Babylon, and *bar nāsh* the speaker. The concealed language was occasioned by the embarrassing implications in the message, namely, that the Palestinians despised him.

The next example comes from the Geniza fragments of the Palestinian Targum on Gen. iv. 14.[1] According to the biblical text, the words Cain addresses to God run as follows (R.V.):

(*a*) Behold, Thou hast driven me out this day from the face of the ground
(*b*) and from Thy face shall I be hid
(*c*) and I shall be a fugitive and a wanderer in the earth
(*d*) and it shall come to pass that whosoever findeth me shall slay me.

It should be noted that in Genesis both the statement of fact in respect to his expulsion, as well as the presentiment of Cain's future destiny, are given in the first person.

If this is compared with the Neofiti version of the Palestinian Targum, it appears that verse 14ab maintains the direct speech in the first person, but in verse 14cd it changes to the third person.

(*a*) Behold Thou hast banished *me* from the face of the earth this day
(*b*) but *I* am unable to hide from Thee
(*c*) *Cain* shall be an exile and a wanderer upon the earth
(*d*) and whoever meets *him* shall kill *him*.

In the Geniza fragment, the indirect speech is introduced already in 14b:

(*a*) Behold, Thou has banished *me* from the face of the earth this day
(*b*) but בר נש is unable, O Lord, to hide from Thee.
(*c*) *Cain* shall be an exile and a wanderer upon the earth
(*d*) and whoever finds *him* shall kill *him*.

Considered from the synoptic view-point, there is no doubt that בר נש, far from signifying 'anyone' or 'a man', as suggested by

[1] P. Kahle. *Masoreten des Westens*, ii, p. 7.

J. Bowman[1] and his followers,[2] means 'I'. The insertion of a general statement into such a context is more than unlikely.

In all the examples so far examined, reference to the speaker is effected by means of the indefinite form בר נש. It will be shown now that בר נשא, also, can be used in the same way.

> *Y. Ber.* 5b (lines 5 ff. from bottom): When R. Hiyya bar Adda died, son of the sister of Bar Kappara, R. Levi received his valuables. This was because his teacher used to say, The disciple of בר נשא is as dear to him as his son.

The fact that Levi actually became the heir of R. Hiyya indicates that the Rabbi's repeated saying was understood to express his will. In such a context, of course, the indirect reference to the self follows an already well-established pattern.

Another logion, connected this time with the speaker's burial, appears in several collections.

> *Y. Ket.* 35a (lines 9 ff.): It is said that Rabbi was buried wrapped in a single sheet because, he said, It is not as בר נשא goes that he will come again. But the Rabbis say, As בר נש goes, so will he come again.[3]

Rabbi's words express his desire for a simple burial and concern himself alone. The splendour of his resurrection, he thought, would not depend on the garments in which his body lay. He appears to be rephrasing a general principle according to which man's final state corresponds to his moral quality at the time of death. The use of the circumlocution is explicable, not only by the mention of death, but also by the speaker's humility before the prospect of his glorious resurrection.

Next, in a midrash presenting an argument between Nimrod and Abraham, the circumlocution theory appears to provide the key to a passage otherwise difficult to interpret.

> *Gen. R.* xxxviii. 13 (ed. Theodor, pp. 363–4): (Nimrod said) Let us worship the fire! (Abraham said) Let us rather worship the water (למייא) which extinguishes (דמטפין) the fire! (Nimrod said) Let us worship the water! (Abraham said) Let us rather worship clouds (לענני) which carry (דטעני) the water! (Nimrod said) Let us worship clouds! (Abraham said) Let us rather worship the wind(s)

[1] See *supra*, p. 313 f.

[2] E.g., J. Jeremias, 'Die aramäische Vorgeschichte unserer Evangelien', *Th.L.Z.*, 74, 1949, cols. 528 f.; S. Schulz, 'Die Bedeutung der neuen Targumforschung für die synoptische Tradition', in *Abraham unser Vater* (Festschrift für Otto Michel) (Leiden–Köln, 1963), pp. 425 ff.

[3] See also *Y. Kil.* 32b (lines 3 ff.) and *Gen. R.* c. 2, the former giving בר איניש, the latter בר נש instead of בר נשא.

(לרוחא) which disperse (דמובלי) the cloud(s) (עננא)! (Nimrod said) Let us worship the wind! (Abraham said) Let us rather worship לבר נשא דסביל רוחא! (Nimrod said) You are merely playing with words. We shall worship nothing but the fire. I will cast you into it and let your God . . . deliver you from thence!

It is Abraham's last remark, left partly untranslated, which is of interest. M. Jastrow interprets the expression: 'Let us worship man that carries the wind (whose body is filled with air)';[1] but this does not seem to make much sense. H. Freedman's rendering is not very satisfactory either: 'Let us rather worship human beings, who withstand the wind'.[2]

Considered closely, the text of Abraham's final suggestion exhibits a peculiar stylistic feature. Whereas in his earlier ones, the participles are always in the plural, whether the nouns to which they refer are in the plural (עננִי, מייא) or not (רוחא), in נסגוד לבר נשא דסביל רוחא both the noun and the participles are in the singular. When this is taken into account, Freedman's translation appears quite unjustified. The rendering should rather be: 'Let us worship the man who bears רוחא'. There is quite possibly a pun here on רוחא,[3] in that it first signifies 'wind' and is then meant to convey the sense of 'spirit', of רוחא קודשא, 'holy spirit'. Thus, 'Let us rather worship the man who bears the Spirit (i.e., on whom the Spirit rests). In plain words, I suggest that Abraham is speaking of himself, and with his tongue in his cheek, and that this does not escape Nimrod. 'You are merely playing with words', he says. 'Well, we will worship the fire into which I will throw you'.

If this interpretation is correct, the indirect reference to himself is prompted by Abraham's desire to express himself equivocally, and also by his humility in face of his real belief that God's Spirit rested on him.

My last two illustrations have two things in common: they are both contained in several versions, and they both convey the words of the same man, the Tannaite Rabbi Simeon ben Yohai.

Y. Ber. 3b (lines 15 ff.): R. Simeon ben Yohai said, If I had stood on Mount Sinai when the Torah was given to Israel, I would have asked the Merciful One to create two mouths for בר נשא—one to study the Torah, and one to provide him with all his needs.
He said again, If the world is scarcely able to subsist because of the

[1] *A Dictionary of the Targumim* . . . ii, p. 1458 *sub voce* רוחא.
[2] *Midrash Rabbah* (Soncino Press, 1951), i, p. 311.
[3] This was already suggested by P. Fiebig in *Der Menschensohn*, p. 43.

slanders uttered by one mouth, how much worse would it be if there were two!

In *Y. Shab.* 3a (lines 4 ff. from bottom) there is a second recension of the same saying with one notable variant. In place of לבר נשא it reads להדין בר נשא (to this man), or according to the *editio princeps*, להדין לבר נשא (to this, to the man).

Such a sentence can mean only one thing. If he had been privileged to attend the revelation of the Torah on Sinai, Simeon would have asked for two mouths for himself so that one of them could have been permanently occupied with the recitation of the Law. Any doubt concerning the significance of בר נשא in the *Berakhoth* account must, one imagines, be dispelled by the addition of the demonstrative pronoun in the parallel version in *Shabbath.*[1] And yet Erik Sjöberg (art. cit., p. 94, n. 66), although noticing the real implications of the substitution of להדין בר נשא for לבר נשא, rejects the simplest interpretation. He argues that unless Simeon is using בר נשא in the generic sense, he declares his own mouth responsible for a multitude of slanders, which is not very probable.

In fact, Sjöberg does not appear to realize that the second half of the passage is not an immediate continuation of the first. It is an afterthought expressed, very likely, on another occasion. It would be a blessing for Simeon himself to possess two mouths, but undesirable for mankind as a whole.

Moreover, I should add that a generic *bar nāshā* would not fit into the context. As the Torah was given to Israel alone, it is conceivable that Simeon should ask for a second mouth for the Jews, but surely not for the whole human race. The only satisfactory exegesis, therefore, leads one to understand that when uttering a humble prayer for a unique privilege, Simeon ben Yohai instinctively spoke of himself in the third person.

The other anecdote relating to the same Rabbi has survived in four recensions, *Y. Sheb.* 38d, *Gen. R.* lxxix. 6, *Koh. R.* x. 11, and *Esth. R.* iii. 113a. I will begin with the talmudic version which is in Aramaic from beginning to end.

> *Y. Sheb.* 38d (lines 24 ff.): Rabbi Simeon ben Yohai hid in a cave for thirteen years (during the reign of Hadrian). . . . At the end of those

[1] The Krotoschin edition of *Y. Shabbat* contains yet another variant. Instead of כל צורכיה (literally, all his need) it gives כל צורכיי (all my needs). If this is deliberate, and not a misprint, then the speaker is reverting to the use of the first person. The *editio princeps*, however, reads כל צורכוי (all his needs).

thirteen years he said, I will go forth to see what is happening in the world (literally, what is the voice of the world). He then went forth and sat at the entrance to the cave. There he saw a hunter trying to catch birds by spreading his net. He heard a heavenly voice saying, *Dimissio* (release), and the bird escaped. He then said, Not even a bird perishes without the will of Heaven. How much less בר נשא.

It should be pointed out that in this recension Simeon is the only *dramatis persona*. In the crucial last phrase, although a differentiation is no doubt intended between ציפור and בר נשא, it is noteworthy that whereas the former is indefinite, *bar nāshā* is not. Hence, it is justifiable to assume that the speaker has in mind not some random member of the human race, but one particular person, and that that person cannot but be himself.

In the longer version of the Midrash Rabba, the opening sentence is in Hebrew, the rest is in Aramaic, and R. Eleazar, Simeon's son, is said to share his father's exile.

Gen. R. lxxix. 6 (ed. Theodor, pp. 941–2): Rabbi Simeon ben Yohai and his son hid in a cave for thirteen years. . . . At the end, he went forth and sat at the entrance to the cave. There he saw a hunter trying to catch birds. When he heard a heavenly voice saying *Dimissio*, the bird escaped, (and when he heard it say) *Specula* (execution), it was caught. He then said, Not even a bird is caught without the will of Heaven. How much less the soul of *bar nāshā* (נפש דבר נשא). So he went forth and found that affairs had quietened down.

In this version, the *bar nāshā* saying is immediately followed by Simeon's departure from his hiding place, so we may once more conclude that *bar nāshā* whose soul will not perish must be the speaker himself. But here the interpreter's deduction is supported not by logical reasoning alone, but also by direct manuscript evidence. Among the variants listed in Theodor's critical apparatus there figures the reading of an Oxford codex in which נפש דבר נשא (the soul of the man) is replaced by נפשי (my soul).[1] In other words, *bar nāshā* is definitely a circumlocution for 'I' in this instance at least.[2]

Here the argument may rest. The evidence concerning *bar nāsh(ā)* as a circumlocution appears to be conclusive. The relatively small

[1] Ms. Opp. Add. 3, fol. 142 verso, in the Bodleian Library.

[2] Another, though less direct, confirmation is provided by *Esth. R.* iii. Here, נפשנא (our soul) or נפשתנא (our souls) is substituted for נפש דבר נשא, implying that Simeon was thinking of both himself and his son. For an exact parallel in the New Testament, compare Mt. xvi. 13 with Mk. viii. 27.

number of examples which I have so far been able to collect does not necessarily signify that the idiom is uncommon. It is more likely due to the rarity in the extant Aramaic sources of the sort of idiomatic setting in which such a grammatical phenomenon might normally occur.

From the philological point of view, the circumlocutional use of *bar nāsh(ā)* largely follows the pattern outlined in respect to *hāhū gabrā*. In most instances the sentence contains an allusion to humiliation, danger, or death, but there are also examples where reference to the self in the third person is dictated by humility or modesty. The only essential difference between the two pronominal substitutes is that whilst *hāhū gabrā* may describe either 'I' or 'thou', *bar nāshā* always refers to the first person.

Geographically, the idiom is Palestinian–Galilean. It is altogether absent from the dialect represented by the Babylonian Talmud and has no counterpart in post-classical Hebrew either. If the reading *ben hā-'ādām* introduced by a second copyist into 1*Q Serekh* xi. 20 (which, incidentally, is the first time that the Hebrew phrase is found with the definite article) is to be understood as an Aramaism of the *bar nāshā* type, we may infer that it existed also in the Judaean dialect.

In regard to chronology, the term is well attested in the earliest strata of Galilean–Aramaic, viz., the Palestinian Pentateuch Targum,[1] the Palestinian Talmud and *Genesis Rabba*. Although such attributions must always be taken cautiously, it is still worth remarking that the two most important logia are ascribed unanimously, by a variety of sources, to Simeon ben Yohai, a Galilean pupil of Akiba, who flourished in the first half of the second century A.D.

A comprehensive inquiry into the use and significance of *bar nāsh* cannot end without mention of its presumed messianic content, and in this respect I would put it on record that not one among the hundreds of examples scrutinized by me suggests that *bar nāsh(ā)* was ever employed as a messianic designation. This study, in fact, vindicates Lietzmann's thesis in so far as it was he who realized long ago[2] that although Daniel vii. 13 had been recognized in Judaism

[1] A. Díez Macho dates the final recension of Neofiti from the second century A.D. (*The recently discovered Palestinian Targum, Congress Volume*, Oxford 1959; *Supplements to Vetus Testamentum*, vii (Leiden, 1960), p. 229). The version found in the Cairo Geniza is certainly not later.

[2] Cf. *supra*, p. 311 f.

as a messianic text, and had served to create a new messianic name, this was ענני (Cloud-Man), possibly also בר ניפלי (νεφέλη = Son of the Cloud), but not בר נשא, Son of Man.[1] On the contrary, all the available Aramaic evidence appears to point to the unsuitability of *bar nāshā* as a name or title. Thus, whereas the Hebrew בן אדם appears no less than eighty-seven times in Ezekiel as a form of divine address (e.g. 'Son of man, stand upon thy feet and I will speak with thee', ii. 1), the Targum always translates it as בר אדם, son of Adam, not as בר (א)נש(א).

Finally, is it not revealing that when the Gospel phrase ὁ υἱὸς τοῦ ἀνθρώπου, which in the terminology of the early Church had certainly become a title, was translated into Syriac and Christian-Palestinian Aramaic, the expression chosen was not a simple בר נשא, but ברה דאנשא, ברה דברנשא, or ברה דגברה?

So the New Testament scholar is faced with the following dilemma:

Either the Greek phrase derives from the Aramaic, in which case research into its original meaning reveals that 'son of man' must be something other than a title.

Or it is not a translation but an original creation, in which case it must be explained why a Hellenist should have invented so alien an idiom, why this idiom was so promptly accepted by the writers of the Greek Gospels, and why it was nevertheless subsequently neglected by the Greek-speaking Church.

The Theological Implications of Dr. Vermes' Observations

The important evidence so clearly and convincingly set out by Dr. Vermes for the usage of *barnash* as a surrogate for the first person pronoun fully confirms the view for which I argued (on a much slenderer basis) in my study on 'The Son of Man in the Teaching of Jesus' in the *Expository Times*, vol. lx, no. 2, p. 32 f., namely, that this idiomatic substitute for the first person does in fact receive eschatological overtones in Jesus' employment of it in reference to himself as '*eschatologische Persönlichkeit*'. In this respect I find myself disagreeing with the view of Vermes that Aramaic *barnash* is not suitable for messianic use.

[1] This is not the place to discuss the use of 'son of man' in the *Similitudes of Enoch* and of 'man' in IV *Esdras*, or their connexion with Daniel vii. In my view, which I hope to expound in the near future, the phrase in question is not employed as a title in either of these works.

'No term was more fitted both to conceal, yet at the same time to reveal to those who had ears to hear, the Son of Man's real identity.

In Mt. xi. 19 = Lk. vii. 34 (Q):

"For John came neither eating nor drinking,
And they say, He hath a devil,
The Son of Man came eating and drinking,
And they say, Behold a man gluttonous, and a wine-bibber, a friend of publicans and sinners."

the contrast is unmistakably between John and Jesus Himself; to attempt to read a communal meaning into the expression does violence to the whole context. Moreover, the context is not evidently an apocalyptic one; it refers to an actual coming of the Son of Man in Jesus Himself, a man among men. Any affinities the expression has here with the old Biblical literature are with Ezekiel or the Psalter.

Would the saying be intelligible to those for whom it was intended without the expression being a Messianic title? The passage is one of several where "Son of Man" has been claimed as simply a synonym for the personal pronoun, and the use of Aramaic *hahu' gabra*, "that man", for the first person compared or cited in support. But the latter is not quite the same as the phrase "the son of man", and *hahu' barnasha* is nowhere found. Even if it were (like the Latin *hic homo*), the absence of the demonstrative in the Greek must be explained away, and to try to do so leads into pure guesswork. If however, *barnash* alone, the exact phrase in Daniel, was the original term, it could equally well be construed *either* as Son of Man Messianic title, *or* in the regular sense which *barnash* had come to have in Palestinian Aramaic of "one", "a man", with a reference to the speaker himself. In Aramaic the saying is skilfully ambiguous.

Although the saying in Aramaic is ambiguous, there is no doubt that the Evangelists were right in interpreting it as Messianic: Jesus intended the veiled allusion to His own identity as Son of Man. But the context (and the ambiguity of the phrase) are instructive: the whole elaborate scheme of apocalyptic Son of Man eschatology has been finally brought down to earth. The final revelation of the Son of Man may still be awaited, but none the less, the Son of Man has come, in one who is man indeed; the synthesis between prophetic Scripture and Jewish apocalyptic eschatology, begun in the Similitudes, is realized in Jesus.'[1]

[1] *Expository Times*, loc. cit.

In sum: in the Gospels there is a core of genuine 'Son of Man' sayings, stemming from the mind of Jesus Himself, both relating to His earthly ministry and to his future 'Coming' (e.g., Mt. viii 20 par., xii. 41 par.; Mk. xiv. 62 par.; Lk. xvii. 24 par., 30). The second group referring to the 'Coming' of the Son of Man have been certainly inspired by Daniel, but possibly also by Enoch; some have been shaped under the influence of Isaianic prophecy; and in view of the above idiom any or all of them might refer indirectly to the speaker, revealing, for those with ears to hear, the identity of the Son of Man in the Person of the speaker Himself.[1]

[1] Reference may be made to my further studies: 'The Son of Man Problem in Recent Research and Debate' in *Bulletin of the John Rylands Library*, vol. xlv., no. 2, pp. 305 ff. and 'The "Son of Man" Passion Sayings in the Gospel Tradition' in *Festschrift* for Ethelbert Stauffer, Friedrich Wittig Verlag, Hamburg, 1967.

INDEXES

GENERAL INDEX

INDEX OF AUTHORS

(The names of frequently quoted workers in the field and the authors of Lexica and standard grammatical works, quoted *passim*, are not included.)

BIBLICAL REFERENCES

OLD TESTAMENT

Genesis

NEW TESTAMENT

MARK

ROMANS

1 CORINTHIANS

2 CORINTHIANS

GALATIANS

EPHESIANS

COLOSSIANS

1 THESSALONIANS

2 TIMOTHY

HEBREWS

JAMES

1 PETER

NEW TESTAMENT APOCRYPHA, PATRISTIC AND GREEK REFERENCES

OLD TESTAMENT APOCRYPHA AND PSEUDEPIGRAPHA

INDEX OF GREEK WORDS

PALESTINIAN TALMUD

* References from Appendix E in Arabic notation.

MIDRASHIM